ARIS AND PHILLIPS CLASSICAL TEXTS

Minor Greek Tragedians

Fragments from the Tragedies with Selected Testimonia

Edited with Introductions, Translations and Notes

by

M. J. Cropp

VOLUME 1

The Fifth Century

LIVERPOOL UNIVERSITY PRESS

First published 2019 by
Liverpool University Press
4 Cambridge Street
Liverpool
L69 7ZU

Reprinted with corrections 2022

www.liverpooluniversitypress.co.uk

British Library Cataloguing-in-Publication data
A British Library CIP record is available

ISBN 978-1-786942-02-9 cased
ISBN 978-1-786942-03-6 paperback

Typeset by Tara Evans

Cover image: Würzburg H4781, Female Chorus, fragment of Attic krater. © Martin von Wagner Museum der Universität Würzburg, Foto: P. Neckermann.

For Christopher Collard

CONTENTS OF VOLUME 1

PREFACE

'Minor' is of course an unsatisfactory term: some of these poets were far from minor in their own time, and some were read and studied later for five or six hundred years. But the term is conventional and I have yet to find a better alternative.

My original plan was to offer a selection of both fragments (another problematic term) and testimonia. It has however proved convenient to treat all the remnants of actual tragic texts that can be identified with the 'minor' poets of the fifth to third centuries BC, along with the more essential testimonia (for the poets of the fifth century the text-fragments include fewer than three hundred complete verses, even including the doubtful cases of Neophron and Critias). The resulting content is explained more fully in my Introduction, pp. xxii–xxiii. In consequence, what was planned as one volume has become two, with the kind agreement of the Liverpool University Press and of Alan Sommerstein, now General Editor of the Aris and Phillips Classical Texts series.

I was persuaded to embark on this work by Christopher Collard near the end of his term as General Editor. It was also he who invited my first contribution to the series more than thirty years ago, and we later worked harmoniously together on several projects. His meticulous scholarship and generous encouragement have been invaluable to me, as I am sure they have been to many others. I gladly take the opportunity to dedicate this volume to him as a token of my esteem and friendship.

Martin Cropp
February 2018

INTRODUCTION

1. Tragedy in the fifth century: a sketch.

The history of tragedy begins, for practical purposes, in Athens at the end of the sixth century BC.[1] Ancient tradition credited it with an earlier development which is sketched in chapter 4 of Aristotle's *Poetics*. In this account, poetic composition in general is motivated by the basic human capacity for representation (*mimêsis*), exercised first through improvisation and later in various art-forms. The epic poet Homer anticipated drama insofar as he combined narrative with speeches delivered by his characters, and tragedy went a step further by adding actors (*hypokritai*, 'responders') to choral sung narratives (later known as 'dithyrambs'), thus generating fully enacted dramas (the Greek word *drâma* means 'enactment'). From such beginnings,

> [tragedy] was gradually augmented as they developed each of the capacities it revealed; and after going through many mutations it ceased to develop, once it had attained its own nature. Thus Aeschylus first brought the number of actors from one to two, and reduced the choral element and arranged for dialogue to take the lead . . . and also as to amplitude, starting from small plots and absurd diction, due to its mutating from a satyric character, it became dignified at a late stage . . . (*Poetics* 1449a13–21).

Aristotle sketches an analogous development for comedy, noting that details such as the introduction of masks, prologues and additional actors are in his time 'remembered' for tragedy but not for comedy which was taken less seriously in its early stages and was added to the festival programme later.

Aristotle's remarks were designed as a brief introduction to an analysis of tragedy in its developed form, not as a complete account of its history (he probably provided more details in his earlier and more

[1] Select bibliography for early tragedy: Pickard-Cambridge 1962, 60–131; Lesky 1972, 17–48 (= 1983, 1–24); Seaford 1984, 10–14 and 2007; Herington 1985, 103–50, 213–16; West 1989; Connor 1989; Csapo–Slater 1995, 89–101; Scullion 2002a, 2002b, 2005; Csapo–Miller 2007b; Depew 2007; Kowalzig 2007; Csapo 2015; Csapo–Wilson 2015.

discursive dialogue *On Poets*, but these are now difficult to identify precisely).[2] He presumably drew both on oral traditions and on earlier writers on poets, poetry and music such as Theagenes and Glaucus, both from Rhegium in southern Italy.[3] The key role of Aeschylus in the development of tragedy was already established in the late fifth century and is a commonplace of later criticism.[4] Members of Aristotle's school elaborated his work, notably Aristoxenus of Tarentum (c. 370–310), who wrote extensively on music history and theory but also *On Tragic Poets*, *On Tragic Dance* and much else, and Chamaeleon from Heraclea in Pontus (c. 350–280), whose writings included *On Thespis* (see Thespis **T 18** with note) and *On Aeschylus*. Traditions about early tragedy which we see in Hellenistic and later sources, notably the ideas of tragedy originating in primitive rustic festivals of Dionysus and of Thespis inventing tragic drama in the 530s, probably derive from this fourth-century work (see below on Thespis, pp. 3–17).

The Aristotelian account of the beginnings of tragedy became the basis of an orthodoxy which persisted throughout antiquity, and indeed until recent times. It fits a model of organic development that typifies much of Aristotle's theorizing on other subjects,[5] and it probably relied mainly on oral traditions and inferences from later tragedy and its cultic context. It is however unsupported by material evidence. As the authors of a recent survey put it,

> There is no good evidence of a theater or of dramatic competitions [in Athens or Attica] until the beginning of the Athenian democracy . . . At ca. 508 the plausible literary, epigraphic, iconographic, and architectural evidence converge . . . There is no reliable evidence for tragedy or any other contest for Dionysus anywhere in the Greek world before 508.[6]

---

[2] See F 33–35, 37–41 in Janko's edition of the fragments of *On Poets* (2011, 363–71, 385–89, 424–37, with commentary pp. 490–94, 498–504). Janko's fragments are not *verbatim* quotations from Aristotle's work but references inferred from later sources, and some of his attributions of the data to Aristotle are debated: see below on Thespis **T 6**, **T 7**, **T 9**, **T 18**.

[3] Such writings are conveniently listed by Janko 2011, 385.

[4] Pherecrates F 100 *PCG*; Aristophanes, *Frogs* 1004; cf. Nervegna 2014, 168ff.

[5] See especially Depew 2007.

[6] Csapo–Wilson 2015, 319–22. There is no iconographic evidence for 'proto-tragedy' in the 6th century as there is for 'proto-comedy' (Csapo 2015).

The material evidence referred to here, dating from the last years of the sixth century and the first years of the fifth, includes the earliest traces of archival records from contests at the City Dionysia (including the choral or 'dithyrambic' contests in which the Cleisthenic tribes competed with each other), the first representations in vase-paintings of tragic performers and of a 'choregic' monument commemorating success in a contest, and the first traces of a temple and theatre in the sanctuary of Dionysus Eleuthereus in Athens. This evidence suggests that tragic drama as we know it was developed in a particular historical context, as a striking addition to the Athenian democracy's newly elaborated spring festival of Dionysus.[7] This does not invalidate Aristotle's basic point that tragic drama was the result of adding a fully mimetic element to lyric narratives performed with some degree of mimesis by circular choruses (these may well underlie the traditions of 'tragic choruses' at Sicyon and Thespis's performances at Icarion: see on Thespis **T 1**). But it does suggest that the Aristotelian picture of tragedy 'growing' from primitive improvisational beginnings and 'gradually' approaching its mature form is misleading, and that most of our testimonia for the supposed invention of tragedy and some of those for the earliest documented tragic poets are unreliable.

If the prehistory of tragic drama is obscure, its development over the first three decades of the fifth century is scarcely less so. The information we have is all for the City Dionysia at Athens, although archaeological evidence suggests that tragic performances could have been instituted at a few festivals of Dionysus in outlying towns of Attica during this period.[8] Records for the contests at the City festival probably began with the year 501,[9] but how much information they provided for the early years is uncertain; it seems possible that until the 470s only the victor's name was recorded, or that if fuller records existed they were

[7] Csapo (2015, 106f.) suggests that the building of the Theatre of Dionysus led successively to the introduction of men's cyclic choruses, then tragedy, then boys' choruses, and, 'after a decade or so', comedy.

[8] See below, pp. xvi–xvii. Tragic contests were introduced at the Lenaea, the winter festival of Dionysus in the city, only about 440 or a little later (Pickard-Cambridge 1988, 108, 125).

[9] Capps 1943, 10f.; West 1989, 251; Scullion 2002a, 81; cf. Millis 2014, 429 n. 17.

lost in the sack of Athens in 480.[10] The competition formula of three productions of three tragedies plus one satyr-play may have existed from the beginning but is not actually attested before the year 472, when Aeschylus produced the tetralogy that included *Persians*;[11] the question is complicated by uncertainty about the first inclusion of satyr-plays in the programme.[12] As for competitors, the lost beginning of the Victors Lists inscription (DID A 3a: see pp. xviiif. below) may have included as few as four poets who won their first victories at the Dionysia before Aeschylus's first success in 484,[13] while only three more appear between 484 and Sophocles' first victory in 468.[14] Thus the total number of winning poets in this period can hardly have been more than ten.[15] Others may have competed without winning, but the field would appear to have been largely occupied by a few poets who possessed or had access to the necessary expertise in poetry, music, choreography, directing, staging and acting. Several passed on their skills to their sons (Phrynichus, Pratinas, Aeschylus, and a little later Sophocles) and/or nephews (Aeschylus, Euripides I), who probably assisted their productions from an early age.[16]

Almost nothing survives from the tragedies produced in this earliest period: for Choerilus, one title and two phrases amounting to six words; for Phrynichus, nine titles (plus one satyric), nine isolated words or

---

[10] Scullion 2002a, 82.

[11] Cf. Pickard-Cambridge 1988, 79–80.

[12] *GrSat* 6–9, Scullion 2005, 27f., O'Sullivan–Collard 2013, 22–25.

[13] The first 10 lines of the inscription are lost. Scullion (2002a, 83f.) argues that its heading probably occupied lines 1–6 rather than 1–2 as Wilhelm supposed, thus leaving room for four poets rather than eight before Aeschylus in 484. He suggests Euripides I (*TrGF* 16) as a possible fourth in addition to Choerilus, Phrynichus and Pratinas.

[14] Euetes, Phrynichus's son Polyphrasmon, and …]ippus (*TrGF* nos 6–8).

[15] If the Suda's number for Choerilus's victories (13) is right and relates to the period beginning in 501, we can identify the winners in twenty-one of the first thirty-two recorded years (501–468, excluding the years of the Persian invasions, 479 and 478), though mostly without the dates: Choerilus 13 (**T 1**); Phrynichus 1 (**T 4**); Pratinas 1 (**T 1**); Aeschylus 2 (484, 472); and from the Victors Lists Euetes, Polyphrasmon, …]ippus and Sophocles (468). Phrynichus and Aeschylus presumably won some of the other eleven (Aeschylus is credited with thirteen victories in all and can hardly have won all but two of these after 472).

[16] Cf. Csapo 2010, 88 on this early concentration of theatrical practice.

phrases, and ten excerpts of one to four verses each; for Aeschylus, a few fragments from *Women of Aetna* (produced in Sicily in 476/5) and presumably more from other plays of this period which cannot however be identified. Something can be said about the contents of Choerilus's *Alope* (pp. 20f. below), Phrynichus's *Alcestis, Capture of Miletus* and *Phoenician Women* (pp. 30f., 34f., 38f.), and Aeschylus's *Women of Aetna*, but none of this throws light on the earliest developments in dramatic design.[17] For these we have only the Aristotelian account, in which tragedy was originally lightweight and largely choral but later attained grandeur, with actors and dialogue scenes increasingly prominent, much of this being due to Aeschylus.[18] The extant plays of Aeschylus (all from the last seventeen years of his forty-year career) bear this out to some extent, with a profusion of grand poetic language and dynamic (often ritual) choral activity, one-actor scenes (actor interacting with chorus) interspersed with stylized two-actor scenes (only the *Oresteia* of 458 makes very limited use of a third actor), and a simple dramatic structure.[19] But the details of what went before are missing, and just how and why tragedy acquired its typically tragic character, focusing on disaster, death and the dead, remains unclear.

For the middle decades of the fifth century our information is more abundant. Didascalic records for the 460s mention, besides Aeschylus and Sophocles, Phrynichus's son Polyphrasmon (*TrGF* 7), Pratinas's son Aristias (*TrGF* 9), and Mesatus (*TrGF* 11). Aeschylus's sons Euphorion and Euaeon (*TrGF* 12, 13) and Aristarchus of Tegea (*TrGF* 14) were probably close contemporaries of Sophocles with careers beginning in the 460s, while Ion, Achaeus, Carcinus I and Philocles I (*TrGF* 19–21, 24) were close to Euripides and probably began like him in the 450s. Of Euripides I and II (*TrGF* 16, 17) we know only that the first was older than the famous Euripides III and that the second was a nephew of the first. Sophocles' son Iophon had a success at the Dionysia in 435 and must have made his début not many years before that. The same might be true of some of the *komoidoumenoi* of the 420s and later (see below on these), while several of the poets just named, including Ion, Carcinus,

---

[17] *Women of Aetna* with its multiple scene-changes was produced on commission for a special occasion in Sicily (»» Sommerstein 2008, 6f.) and was probably untypical.

[18] See above, p. ix and Thespis **T 6**, **7**, **8(b)**, **14**, **19**, Phrynichus **T 7**, **10(c)**.

[19] Suspense–crisis–reaction: »» West 1990, 3–25; Cropp 2005, 273f.

Philocles and Iophon, continued to produce alongside Sophocles and Euripides into the 420s or beyond.

All of these mid-century poets except the sparsely documented Polyphrasmon, Mesatus and Carcinus are treated individually in this volume.[20] Of 120 productions at the City Dionysia in the period 469–430 (three each year for forty years),[21] Aeschylus, Sophocles and Euripides must have supplied about thirty-five,[22] Aristarchus, Ion, Achaeus and Philocles (if the numbers of their plays given in the Suda are anywhere near the truth) about another thirty-five.[23] The rest supplied at least ten and perhaps twice that number.[24] Thus we can name the poets of something like three-quarters of all these productions. Text-fragments (not all from before 430) number about 150, mostly from Ion and Achaeus, a few from Aristarchus, Philocles and Iophon. Nearly half are isolated words or phrases, a quarter are single verses, and only eight run to four or five verses. We have titles of about sixty tragedies and satyr-plays by seven of these poets,[25] and of two tetralogies (Polyphrasmon's *Lycurgeia* of 467 and Philocles' *Pandionis*), but what can be said about their plots comes almost entirely from our knowledge of the relevant myths and comparisons with the plays of the canonical tragedians.

---

[20] For Polyphrasmon see notes 14–15 above, for Carcinus p. 134–35 below with his son Xenocles. Mesatus is known only from the Victors Lists inscription (2, 3 or 4 victories) and the well-known papyrus fragment (P. Oxy. 2256 fr. 3 = DID C 6) recording his third place behind Aeschylus and Sophocles in the later 460s. Neophron (*TrGF* 15) was probably not a 5th-century poet (pp. 66–68), and Melanthius I (*TrGF* 23) belongs a little later (p. 132 n. 8).

[21] Lenaea contests are relevant only towards the end of this period (see n. 8 above).

[22] Aeschylus about 6 after his production of 472, Sophocles about 18 from a career total of 30 beginning around 470, Euripides about 11 from a total of 22 beginning in 455.

[23] Aristarchus 70 plays, Ion 40, Achaeus 44, Philocles 100.

[24] The known ones are: Polyphrasmon 3rd place, 467; Aristias 2nd place, 467 and 1st place, late 460s; Mesatus at least three productions (above, n. 20); Euphorion 1st place, 431 (and see below, p. 55–57), Euripides II at least one production (Suda = **T 1**), Carcinus 1st place, 446, Iophon 1st place, 435. Some or all of Euripides I's three productions (the Suda's 12 plays, **T 1**) might have been after 470.

[25] Aristias 5 titles, Aristarchus 3, Euripides II 3, Ion 11, Achaeus 20, Iophon 8 or 12, Philocles 8. Some will be later than 430. For details see Index (b), pp. 261f.

The picture changes again in the last three decades of the fifth century, when we hear a lot about tragedy and tragic poets from the extant comedies of Aristophanes (whose first production was in 427) and from derivatives such as the scholia on Aristophanes and the remnants of reference works focused on the comic poets of this period and their language. The information these offer is however quite limited. Around twenty tragic poets are first attested in these years,[26] but only Agathon, Critias (questionably: pp. 180–84) and Diogenes (one fragment) are represented by substantial text-fragments. Four are known only from minimal didascalic information,[27] one from the famous Pronomos Vase,[28] and the rest exclusively or almost exclusively from the comic and related sources just mentioned.[29] The Aristophanes scholia are a prolific source, but what they say about these poets is nearly always an amalgam of

[26] *TrGF* has twenty-six (nos. 23 and 25–49), but at least three of these can be discarded. Spintharus of Heraclea (no. 40) belongs in the late 4th century and is not the Spintharus of Aristophanes' *Birds* 762. The sophist Hippias (no. 42) is identified as a tragedian only by Plato's casual allegation that he once went to Olympia equipped entirely with products of his own making including epics, tragedies and dithyrambs (*Hippias Minor* 368b–d). The story that Plato himself (no. 46) wrote tragedies and other poems in his youth but burned them all after meeting Socrates is very probably apocryphal. For other doubtful cases see n. 29.

[27] *TrGF* 35–38 Menecrates, Nicomachus I, Hera[clides?, Callistratus.

[28] The seated figure holding a papyrus roll and named Demetrius was presumably the poet for this production (*TrGF* 49).

[29] *TrGF* 23 Melanthius I, 25 Acestor, 26 Nothippus, 27 Gnesippus (probably active in the 430s), 28 Theognis, 29 Morsimus, 30 Morychus(?), 31 Hieronymus, 32 Sthenelus, 33 Xenocles I, 34 Datis(?), 41 Dorillus, 44 Pythangelus, 47 Meletus I, 48 Meletus II(?). Nothippus can hardly be the ...]ippus who won his only victory before 468 (*TrGF* 8). There is a little further information for Sthenelus (below on Agathon **F 29**) and Xenocles I (below, pp. 134–40). Morychus is probably misidentified as a tragedian in schol. *Acharnians* 885 (Morychus T 1: cf. Halliwell 1984, 85). The evidence for Datis as a third brother of Xenocles is also very slight. Meletus II, one of Socrates accusers, is described in Plato's *Apology* (23e) as 'aggrieved on behalf of the poets' and is confused with Meletus I in the scholia on *Apology* 18b (= Meletus I T 1); Snell identifies him as the author of the *Oedipodea* mentioned there, and as Meletus I's son, but it may be that Meletus I composed the *Oedipodea* and Meletus II was not a tragic poet at all (»» Nails 2002, 201f.). For brief discussions of these poets see Wright 2016 in a chapter aptly named 'The Very Lost'; also Wright 48f. on Theognis, 100f. on Morsimus, 106f. on Xenocles I.

didascalic and biographic information, other comic references, and ill-informed attempts to interpret the comic playwrights' jokes; nothing suggests any direct knowledge of their plays or their personalities.[30] The comic evidence, if cautiously interpreted, is a valuable source of evidence for contemporary attitudes to tragedy and tragedians, and for the importance of tragedy in late fifth-century Athenian culture, but it tells us very little about the substance of the plays or, except in the case of Agathon, about the character of tragedy in this period beyond what we already know from the plays of Sophocles and Euripides.

Tragic drama seems to have originated at Athens and to have remained primarily an Athenian property throughout the fifth century.[31] Nearly all of our evidence for this period is for plays composed by Athenian poets for the two major Athenian festivals. Only Pratinas and Aristias of Phlious, Aristarchus of Tegea, Ion of Chios and Achaeus of Eretria are reliably identified as non-Athenians, again in connection with the Athenian festivals; at least two of them (Ion and Achaeus) had close connections with the city.[32] The beginnings of tragedy's development into a panhellenic phenomenon can however be seen in the fifth century, especially its last three or four decades. If tragedies were originally composed for single performances at the Dionysia or the Lenaea, this

---

[30] Compare for example the scholia on Aristophanes' *Frogs* 71ff. (Iophon **T 5** with p. 119 below), or on *Birds* 279ff. (Philocles **T 6** with pp. 130f. below), and in general Halliwell 1980, 29–76 and 1984.

[31] For tragedy outside Athens see especially Vahtikari 2014, Csapo–Wilson 2015, Lamari 2017, Stewart 2017. Csapo–Wilson forthcoming will provide full documentary evidence down to 300 BC. Stewart argues that tragedy would have been transmitted rapidly and widely through the Hellenic world's pre-existing song-culture network (see summary of his argument, Stewart p. 18), but there is little evidence of this in the first half of the fifth century.

[32] For Ion see pp. 76f. below. Eretria was a day or two's journey from Athens and under Athenian control for most of Achaeus's lifetime. Stewart (2017, 83 with details in Appendix 2) lists five other possibilities, but Spintharus of Heraclea was not a 5th-century poet (above, n. 26), Neophron of Sicyon probably was not (below, pp. 66–68), Theognis should not be confused with the elegiac poet Theognis of Megara, Acestor may well have been resident in Athens despite being comically described as 'Thracian', and Aristophanes fr. 156 *PCG* (Meletus I T 2 *TrGF*) does not describe Meletus as having Thracian connections. The *komoidoumenoi* listed in n. 29 above were probably all Athenian or resident in Athens. The only non-Athenian tragic actor identified by Stewart in this period (Mynniscus) came from Chalcis, again very close to Athens.

soon ceased to be the case, at least for the more successful ones. Tragedies may have been performed or reperformed in deme theatres in Attica soon after 500; such performances are attested in inscriptions as early as the 440s,[33] and may also have occurred in strongly Athenian-influenced islands such as Salamis, Samos, Thasos and Lemnos.[34] The earliest known production outside Attica was Aeschylus's *Women of Aetna*, commissioned by the tyrant Hieron of Syracuse to celebrate the new city of Aetna which he founded on the depopulated site of Catana in 476. Aeschylus also produced his *Persians* in Syracuse soon after its production at Athens in 472 (and perhaps together with the first performance of *Women of Aetna*),[35] and was living at Gela in 456 when he died and was buried there. But while Syracuse certainly had theatres and a well-established comic tradition at the time (represented most notably by Aeschylus's contemporary Epicharmus), there is no evidence for regular tragic productions there or elsewhere in Sicily in the first half of the fifth century, or even somewhat later.[36] In southern Italy, discoveries of vases decorated with tragedy-related scenes make it likely that tragedies were being performed at coastal cities in the Gulf of Taranto which had economic ties with Athens (Tarentum, Metapontium, Heraclea [modern

---

33 See Csapo–Wilson 2015, 319–28, esp. for Thorikos and Icarion (early 5th C.), Euonymon and Piraeus (late 5th C.), and inscriptions probably recording productions at Anagyrous in the 430s (*IG* I^3 969 = *TrGF* DID B 2) and a little later at Halai Aixonides (*IG* II^2 3091 = DID B 5) and Eleusis (*IG* I^3 970 = DID B 3).

34 Csapo–Wilson 2015, 351–57.

35 Bosher 2012 revives the suggestion that *Persians* was composed for performance at Syracuse and only later in a revised version (the extant one) at Athens, but the arguments for this are largely circumstantial. No Athenians are named in the play, but this is because it is set in Persia and its characters portrayed as knowing nothing about the faraway land their forces have hubristically invaded. Aristophanes' *Frogs* 1028f. does not imply an alternative version as some ancient commentators supposed. »» Garvie 2009, liii–lvii, Broggiato 2014b.

36 Csapo–Wilson 2015, 328–39. There is little to support Stewart's inference (2017, 103–5) that Aeschylus travelled repeatedly to Sicily as a competitor in dramatic festivals. Wilson 2007 suggested that an inscribed lead tablet, perhaps from Gela, in which the dedicator Apellis curses the choregoi competing with his favourite Eunikos, might refer to a tragic contest related to the cult of Aeschylus at Gela, and that the cult and contest might have developed soon after the poet's death. I think it much more likely that it referred to a traditional choral contest (cf. Eidinow 2007, 162). On Phrynichus's possible death in Sicily see note on Phrynichus **T 6**.

Policoro], Thurii) as early as the 420s.[37] Euripides' *Andromache* may have been composed for the Molossian court in Epirus in the mid-420s, and Archelaus of Macedonia certainly brought Athenian tragic poets (Euripides, Agathon) to his court after his seizure of power in 413. Our information is of course very limited, but so far as it goes it suggests that in the fifth century tragedy was adopted for specific reasons in certain parts of the Hellenic world, and that it began to be spread more widely in the early fourth century as Athens recovered its economic and political prominence.

2. Sources

Much of our evidence for tragic productions in the fifth century is derived from the annual competition records of the Athenian festivals. Record-keeping probably began with the beginning of the tragic competition at the City Dionysia in 502/1, although it is not clear how detailed these records were before the 470s (above, pp. xi–xii). Aristotle must have relied mainly on them when he compiled his books *Victories at the Dionysia* (of which we have only the title) and *Didascaliae* (frs 618–630 Rose). The information which Aristotle used and compiled is reflected in three inscriptions now surviving in scattered fragments.[38] The so-called **Fasti inscription** (*IG* II^2 2318), inscribed probably in the 320s or about 306, listed the winning tribe and choregos in the competitions for boys' and men's cyclic choruses, the winning choregos and poet in the comedy and tragedy competitions, and (from the mid-fifth and late fourth centuries respectively) the winners of the tragic and comic actors' prizes at the City Dionysia. The **Didascaliae inscription** (*IG* II^2 2319–2323a, first inscribed about 279 BC) listed all the competing poets, the titles of their plays and (when relevant) the winning actors in comic and tragic competitions at both Dionysia and Lenaea.[39] The **Victors Lists**

[37] Taplin 2012, Csapo–Wilson 2015, 339–44.

[38] The extant parts of the inscriptions concerning tragedy are DID A 1–3 in *TrGF* 1^2.22–30, with addenda in 1^2.342f. and 5.1115. Millis–Olson 2012 is a full edition of these and related inscriptions, Millis 2014 a detailed description of the three main ones. See also Pickard-Cambridge 1988, 72–74, 101–25, 359–62, Sickinger 1999, 41–47, Tracy 2015 (esp. 555–59 on the date of the Fasti inscription).

[39] Some 4th century modifications of the festival programmes are reflected in the Fasti and Didascaliae inscriptions.

inscription (*IG* II² 2325, also first inscribed about 279) listed prize-winning comic and tragic actors and poets, in chronological order of their first victories (but without precise dates), with the numbers of their winning productions, at both Dionysia and Lenaea. This information was also incorporated in the relevant part of Callimachus's *Pinakes*,[40] the great annotated catalogue of all Greek literature compiled at the Alexandrian library in the second quarter of the third century, and in his more specialized *Pinax* of dramatic poets.[41] Remnants of these inscriptions are few,[42] and references to the *Didascaliae* and the *Pinakes* are rare in ancient sources,[43] but the data are reflected, sometimes inaccurately, in hypotheses and scholia on the plays of the canonical tragedians and other references to the competition results,[44] in chronographic works such as the Parian Marble, Apollodorus's *Chronika* (2nd C. BC) and the Chronicle of Eusebius (4th C. AD) with its derivatives,[45] and in the relevant biographical entries in the Suda.[46]

---

[40] Πίνακες τῶν ἐν πάσῃ παιδείᾳ διαλαμψάντων καὶ ὧν συνέγραψαν ἐν βιβλίοις κʹ καὶ ρʹ, *Tables of those distinguished in every form of learning, and of their writings, in 120 books*: frs 429–453 Pfeiffer.

[41] Πίναξ καὶ ἀναγραφὴ τῶν κατὰ χρόνους καὶ ἀπ' ἀρχῆς γενομένων διδασκάλων, *Table and register of dramatic poets, in chronological order from the beginning*: frs 454–56 Pfeiffer.

[42] For the 5th century, fragments from the Fasti inscription give the tragic prize-winners at the Dionysia in 472 and 458 (both Aeschylus), 447 (probably Sophocles), 446 (probably Carcinus I), 435 (Iophon), 422 (Menecrates); from the Didascaliae inscription, the second-prize winners at the Lenaea in 419 (Hera[clides?) and 418 (Callistratus); from the Victors Lists inscription, the first Dionysia victories of Aeschylus (484), Euetes, Polyphrasmon,]ippus, Sophocles (468), Mesatus and Aristias, with numbers of victories for Euetes (1),]ippus (1), Sophocles (18) and Mesatus (2, 3 or 4).

[43] Aristotle's *Didascaliae*: Philocles I **T 6(c)**, Sthenelus T 2, Meletus II F 1. Callimachus's *Pinakes*: Ion **T 1** (Harpocration).

[44] This information is collected as DID C 1–24 in *TrGF* 1² (pp. 43–49). The only item not focused on one of the three canonical tragedians is no. 24, a mention of Meletus's *Oedipodea* in the scholia on Plato's *Apology*. Other tragedians are also mentioned in nos 4 (Pratinas **T 2**), 6 (Mesatus T 2), 12 (Euphorion **T 2**), 13 (Ion **T 5** = Iophon **T 2b**), 14 (Xenocles **T 3**); see also Philocles **T 3**, and Nicomachus in n. 46 below.

[45] See DID D 1–3 in *TrGF* 1², and for the Parian Marble Thespis **T 2** with note.

[46] These are abbreviated from the lost *Onomatologos* (a literary-biographical dictionary) of Hesychius of Miletus (6th C. AD), itself based on earlier sources.

There is almost no other documentary evidence for productions by non-canonical tragedians in the fifth century,[47] nor is anything from their plays seen, or at any rate recognized, in Hellenistic and later papyrus fragments; the sole exceptions are Critias(?) **F 4a etc.** (*Pirithous*), **F 15** and **F 20** (the *Rhadamanthys* and *Tennes* hypotheses), which occur because the plays were transmitted as part of the Euripidean corpus. For the rest we depend on a great variety of other ancient and Byzantine writings which happen to have survived into modern times. A handful of these supply more than two-thirds of the quotations or 'book-fragments' in this volume and a similar proportion of the testimonia (see the Index of Sources, pp. 263–65). They include the comedies of **Aristophanes** (our only direct source of contemporary reactions to fifth-century tragedians and their works); **Aristotle** (important for Agathon and some fourth-century tragedians, as well as for his contributions to the study of tragedy); the moralist **Plutarch** (1st–2nd C. AD); the *Deipnosophists* (*Sophists at Dinner*), a literary miscellany compiled by **Athenaeus** in the 190s AD; the anthology of **Stobaeus** (Ioannes of Stobi in Macedonia, 5th C. AD); the lexica of **Hesychius of Alexandria** (5th/6th C., abridged and supplemented later) and the patriarch **Photius** (9th C.); the **scholia** to Aristophanes, Euripides and other classic authors (compiled in the 10th century from the ancient commentary tradition); and the massive Byzantine encyclopedia known as the **Suda** (10th C.).[48]

The nature of these sources determines, and limits, the kind of information they provide. Most of them quote the fragments without contexts, and in most cases without knowledge of their contexts, either for their moral content (as in Plutarch's essays or Stobaeus's anthology), or in reference works (dictionaries, grammars, handbooks, commentar-

---

See the testimonia for Thespis, Choerilus, Phrynichus, Pratinas, Euphorion, Aristarchus, Neophron, Euripides I and II, Ion, Achaeus, Iophon, Philocles I, Diogenes of Athens; also Nicomachus I (*TrGF* 36 T 1: 'Nicomachus, Athenian, tragedian, who unexpectedly defeated Euripides and Theognis. His plays include *Oedipus*').

[47] An inscription celebrating Themistocles' choregia with Phrynichus's production in 476 (Phrynichus **T 4**); possibly a production by an otherwise unknown Timotheus (*IG* II^{2} 3091 = DID B 5, *TrGF* 56 F 1); the Pronomos Vase commemorating a production by an otherwise unknown playwright named Demetrius (*TrGF* 49).

[48] The later sources mentioned here (Stobaeus, Hesychius etc.) and many others of this kind are helpfully described and explained by Dickey 2007.

ies), or for a variety of other purposes (rhetorical, historical, antiquarian, mythographic etc.). They rarely provide insight into the content or character of the plays from which the fragments were drawn. They do however help in tracing which dramatic texts continued to be read, and for how long. For most of our more than forty fifth-century poets, there is no evidence that any texts were current after their own time (if indeed they ever had a significant circulation): these include Euetes, Polyphrasmon, Mesatus, Euphorion, Euripides I and II, Carcinus I, and nearly all the late fifth-century poets listed above in notes 26–29.[49] This leaves at most a dozen whose texts, or rather some of them, survived through the fourth century and were still available in the Hellenistic period: these are Phrynichus, Pratinas, Aristias, Aristarchus, Ion, Achaeus, Iophon, Agathon, and perhaps (on very limited evidence) Choerilus, Philocles, Xenocles and Diogenes.[50] Significantly, all of these except Aristias, Xenocles and (surprisingly) Agathon have biographical entries in the Suda, and only poets from this group are represented in the excerpts found in Athenaeus and Stobaeus. Most if not all of Athenaeus's excerpts, and all of Stobaeus's, were however derived from earlier sources; it seems unlikely that any of these poets' texts, except perhaps some of Ion and Achaeus, were still available when Athenaeus compiled his miscellany towards the end of the second century AD.[51]

---

[49] Aristotle seems to have been acquainted with at least one play of Sthenelus since he comments on his 'low' style (*Poetics* 1458a18ff. = Sthenelus T 3); this is his only mention of a fifth-century tragic poet other than the canonical three and Agathon. Theognis F 1 (a metaphor cited by Aristotle without attribution and by Demetrius, *On Style* with attribution to Theognis) may or may not be from a tragedy, and F 2 (= Philocles I **F 2**) seems to refer to one of his plots. Fourth-century comic poets seem to have been just as unconcerned with non-canonical fifth-century tragedies as Aristotle was (for their interactions with tragedy in general see Wright 2013b, 612, 619; Farmer 2017, 41–63, 77f., 111).

[50] Neophron's *Medea* and the plays in the Euripidean corpus ascribed by some to Critias are special cases.

[51] On Athenaeus's tragic and satyric excerpts and his possible knowledge of the original texts see especially Collard 2007, 69–92 (orig. 1969), Cipolla 2006.

3. This edition

Editions of the Greek tragic fragments were until recently designed for specialists and remained almost inaccessible to others. The two editions which have dominated study since the middle of the nineteenth century (Nauck 1856, 1889, replaced by the five volumes of *TrGF* 1971–2004) include all the essential information available at the time of their composition but present it with references and apparatus in Latin, often heavily abbreviated, and are difficult for inexperienced readers to understand, especially now that familiarity with Greek and Latin and with the arcana of classical scholarship is increasingly rare. For the lost plays of the three canonical tragedians bilingual Greek–English volumes are now available in the Loeb Classical Library and the Aris & Phillips Classical Texts series (the latter for selected tragedies of Sophocles and Euripides, and with extensive introductions and notes), while a recent Aris & Phillips volume (O'Sullivan–Collard 2013) includes the major satyric fragments of the canonical three and seven others along with the extant *Cyclops* of Euripides and four papyrus *adespota* (texts of unidentified poets). A notable German edition includes the more substantial testimonia and fragments, both tragic and satyric, of thirty of the minor tragedians with seven papyrus *adespota*.[52] The present edition is intended to fill a remaining gap in the Aris & Phillips series by presenting in a relatively accessible form virtually all of the text-fragments of tragedies composed by non-canonical poets between approximately 500 and 200 BC, along with a selection of essential testimonia. This first volume covers the fifth century and includes eighteen of the more than forty tragic poets known from this period. Several of these are not in fact represented by any text-fragments but are included for their historical interest.

The material in this volume is based on the first volume of *TrGF*, which was published by Bruno Snell in 1971 and revised by Richard Kannicht in 1986 (*TrGF* 1^2), with further additions and corrections by

[52] B. Gauly *et al.*, *Musa Tragica* (Göttingen, 1991: abbreviated here as *MusTr*). This was a spin-off from the *TrGF* project, prepared under the supervision of Richard Kannicht. All of the satyric fragments, attested or probable, are treated very fully, with German translations, in R. Krumeich *et al.*, *Das griechische Satyrspiel* (Darmstadt, 1999: abbreviated here as *GrSat*).

Kannicht in *TrGF* 5 (Euripides), pp. 1102–17.[53] For obvious reasons I use the same identifications, numbering and (with a few exceptions) order of testimonia and fragments, although Snell's definitions of the latter can be confusing, with testimonia (**T**) limited to general evidence (the poet's life, dramatic production, style, reputation etc.) while fragments (**F**) include testimonia for individual plays (titles, plot-summaries, paraphrases, iconography etc.) as well as actual text-fragments.[54] My presentation of this material is however different in some respects. For each poet I provide (1) a general introduction with essential (mostly recent) bibliography; (2) selected testimonia (**T**) with translations;[55] (3) fragments (**F**) with translations and, where useful, introductory comments on individual plays (plus special bibliographies in a few cases); (4) detailed notes on both testimonia and fragments (some briefer notes are printed as footnotes to the texts and translations). Text-fragments consisting of isolated words or phrases are collected under the heading 'Brief fragments' at the end of each relevant section and are not treated in any detail. Sources and contexts for the other fragments are printed together with the fragments themselves (rather than at the foot of the page as in *TrGF*) since the fragments are often barely understandable without them. For the same reason I often quote source-contexts more fully than *TrGF* does. On the other hand, I list only essential sources (omitting or summarizing repetitive and derivative references), and my text-critical apparatus is limited to significant corrections of the transmitted texts and continuing uncertainties. All of this is intended to make this often obscure material more accessible than it has been in the past.

---

53 Relevant indexes appeared partly in *TrGF* 1^2.333–37 but more extensively in the combined indexes for *TrGF* 1^2 and 2 (Adespota) in *TrGF* 2.331–453. The latter are supplemented in *TrGF* 1^2.361–63 and 5.2.1150–58.

54 The later volumes of *TrGF* (3. Aeschylus, 4. Sophocles by Stefan Radt; 5. Euripides by Richard Kannicht) collect play-testimonia systematically before the text-fragments of each play. Kannicht refined this further by numbering them ('test. i' etc.).

55 I omit those that list didascalic information (this is summarized in the introductions for each poet) or that add nothing substantial to our knowledge of the poets and their works.

Some editorial markers are explained here. **In Greek texts**:

- [ ] enclose editorial supplements or other indications of text missing in papyri or inscriptions;
- ⟨ ⟩ enclose editorial additions or indications of text judged to be missing in book-texts;
- { } enclose word(s) present in a text but judged inauthentic;
- α̣ etc. subscript dots mark letters which are incomplete or uncertainly read in papyri or inscriptions; under a blank space, a missing letter;
- † † enclose words judged corrupt but not corrected;
- | vertical lines mark line-ends in papyrus texts and inscriptions;
- — in dramatic dialogue, indicates an unidentified speaker;
- ( ) enclose a speaker's name (or — as above) if the change of speaker and/or speaker's name are editorial supplements.

In English translations, corrupt words († †) and changes of speaker are marked as in the Greek text. All text-supplements are printed in *italics*, those that are likely but not certain within round brackets, the more tentative with a question-mark added. The basis for a supplement will usually be found in the critical apparatus below the Greek text.

Other:

- ~ in source-citations means 'similarly or with minor differences';
- »» directs readers to further information and bibliography;
- [ ] square brackets enclose the names of Greek authors wrongly or doubtfully identified with a given work;
- **[ ]** in the Notes, bold-faced square brackets enclose technical discussions of text and language;

Bold-faced **T 1, F 1** etc. indicate testimonia or fragments included in this volume.

MINOR GREEK TRAGEDIANS I

THESPIS
(*TrGF* 1)

Texts etc. *TrGF* 1^2.61–66 with *addenda* 1^2.344–45, 5.1104; *MusTr* 32–37, 269f.; Del Rincón Sánchez 2007, 101–49.

Discussions. Pickard-Cambridge 1962, 69–89; Lloyd-Jones 1966, 12–13; Lesky 1972, 49–56 (= 1983, 25–30); Connor 1989; West 1989; Scullion 2002a, 2002b; Csapo 2015, 90–92.

Thespis was the central figure in the Athenian tradition of tragedy's origins, but little can be said about him with confidence. His name recalls the epic θέσπιν ἀοιδόν/ἀοιδήν 'divinely inspired singer/song' (e.g. Odyssey *17.385, 1.328, 8.498) but this does not in itself make him a mythical figure; it would have been appropriate in a family of musicians.*[1] *The audience of Aristophanes'* Wasps *(422 BC) presumably thought of him as an early dancer and* tragoidos *(**T 5**, cf. **T 11**). Aristotle does not mention him in the* Poetics, *and may or may not have done so in* On Poets *(see on **T 6**, **T 7**, **T 9**, **T 18**), but Aristoxenus's* On Tragic Poets *probably included him (cf. **T 24**). Chamaeleon's* On Thespis *offered an extensive but probably largely speculative account.*[2] *There is enough, then, to suggest that Thespis was a real person, but the story that he invented tragic drama by adding an actor's role to rustic performances for Dionysus at some time in the 530s is unverifiable (see above, pp. x–xi and notes on **T 1** and **T 2**). The testimonia are best seen as evidence for traditions about the history of tragedy rather than its actual history.*

*There is no evidence that anyone in later times had information about performances by Thespis. The four play-titles listed in the Suda (**T 1**) and four quotations cited by later writers (**F [1c]–[4]**) are now commonly ascribed to Heraclides of Pontus, a senior figure in Plato's Academy in the mid-fourth century, who according to Aristoxenus composed tragedies under the name of Thespis (**T 24**).*[3] ***F [4]** is a learned joke (see note below) and is unlikely to have been part of a serious forgery.*

---

[1] Several other instances of the name are attested in *LGPN*.

[2] On Chamaeleon's treatment of early tragedy see recently Mirhady 2012.

[3] Ascription to Heraclides was first argued by Bentley (1699, 238–45). Lloyd-Jones (1966, 12f.) thought the titles and the first two fragments might possibly be genuine.

Testimonia

See also Phrynichus ***T 1***

T 1 Suda *θ* 282

Θέσπις, Ἰκαρίου, πόλεως Ἀττικῆς, τραγικὸς ις΄ ἀπὸ τοῦ πρώτου γενομένου τραγῳδιοποιοῦ Ἐπιγένους τοῦ Σικυωνίου τιθέμενος, ὡς δέ τινες δεύτερος μετὰ Ἐπιγένην· ἄλλοι δὲ αὐτὸν πρῶτον τραγικὸν γενέσθαι φασί. καὶ πρῶτον μὲν χρίσας τὸ πρόσωπον ψιμυθίῳ ἐτραγῴδησεν, εἶτα ἀνδράχνῃ ἐσκέπασεν ἐν τῷ ἐπιδείκνυσθαι, καὶ μετὰ ταῦτα εἰσήνεγκε καὶ τὴν τῶν προσωπείων χρῆσιν ἐν μόνῃ ὀθόνῃ κατασκευάσας. ἐδίδαξε δὲ ἐπὶ τῆς πρώτης καὶ ξ΄ ὀλυμπιάδος. μνημονεύεται δὲ τῶν δραμάτων αὐτοῦ Ἆθλα Πελίου ἢ Φόρβας, Ἱερεῖς, Ἠΐθεοι, Πενθεύς.

T 2 *Marmor Parium* (*IG* XII.5, 444 = *FGrH* no. 239 = *TrGF* I DID D 1), A 43 (lines 58–59)

ἀφ᾽ οὗ Θέσπις ὁ ποιητὴς [*c. 9–12 letters*] πρῶτος ὃς ἐδίδαξεν [*c. 8 letters?* ἆθλον ἐ]τέθη ὁ [τ]ράγος ἔτη ΗΗΓ[*3–5 numerals*] ἄρχοντος ᾿Αθ[ήνη|σι *3–4*]ναιου τοῦ προτέρου.

ποιητὴς [ὑπεκρίνα]το Keil (]το uncertainly Munro) ΕΔΙΔΑΞΕΝΑΛ…ΣΤΙΝ….. ΤΕΘΗ.. ΡΑΓΟΣ Selden 1629) [δρ]ᾶ[μα ἐν ἄ]στ[ει καὶ ἐ]τέθη ὁ [τ]ράγος [ἆθλον] Boeckh (1843: ἐ]τέθη ὁ [τ]ράγος [ἆθλον] wrongly Prideaux 1676; ἆθλον ἐ]τέθη ὁ [τ]ράγος Chandler 1763) [δρ]ᾶ[μα ἐν ἄ]στ[ει καὶ ἆθλον ἐ]τέθη ὁ [τ]ράγος Jacoby (1904). See Notes below.

T 5 Aristophanes, *Wasps* 1476–81

(Ξα.) ὁ γὰρ γέρων, ὡς ἔπιε διὰ πολλοῦ χρόνου
ἤκουσέ τ᾽ αὐλοῦ, περιχαρὴς τῷ πράγματι
ὀρχούμενος τῆς νυκτὸς οὐδὲν παύεται
τἀρχαῖ᾽ ἐκεῖν᾽ οἷς Θέσπις ἠγωνίζετο·
καὶ τοὺς τραγῳδούς φησιν ἀποδείξειν Κρόνους
τοὺς νῦν διορχησάμενος ὀλίγον ὕστερον.

T 6

(a) Themistius, *Or.* 26 (*ὑπὲρ τοῦ λέγειν*), 316d

ἀλλὰ καὶ ἡ σεμνὴ τραγῳδία μετὰ πάσης ὁμοῦ τῆς σκευῆς καὶ τοῦ χοροῦ καὶ τῶν ὑποκριτῶν παρελήλυθεν εἰς τὸ θέατρον; καὶ οὐ προσέχομεν Ἀριστοτέλει ὅτι τὸ μὲν πρῶτον ὁ χορὸς εἰσιὼν ᾖδεν εἰς τὸν θεόν, Θέσπις δὲ πρόλογόν τε καὶ ῥῆσιν ἐξεῦρεν, Αἰσχύλος δὲ {τρίτον} ὑποκριτὰς καὶ ὀκρίβαντας, τὰ δὲ πλείω τούτων Σοφοκλέους ἀπηλαύσαμεν καὶ Εὐριπίδου;

τὸν θεόν Themistius mss. ΣΨ τοὺς θεούς mss. ΑΛ {τρίτον} ὑποκριτὰς ms. Λ τρίτον ὑποκριτὰς ms. Α τρίτον ὑποκριτὴν ms. ΣΨ (cf. Garzya 1988, 75 n. 19)

Testimonia

See also Phrynichus ***T 1***

T 1 Suda, 'Thespis'
Thespis, from Icarion in Attica, tragic poet, placed 16th in order from the first composer of tragedies Epigenes of Sicyon, but according to some second after Epigenes; others say he was the first tragic poet. At first he performed his tragedies after smearing his face with white lead, then he covered it with purslane during his performances, and after that he introduced the use of masks, making them just with linen. He produced in the 61st Olympiad (536/5–533/2 BC). Plays by him on record are *Games for Pelias or Phorbas, Priests, Youths, Pentheus.*

T 2 The Parian Marble (inscription from Paros, c. 263 BC)
From when the poet Thespis first *(performed as an actor?)*, who produced *(. . . . . .)* the goat was assigned *(as a prize)*: 250+*(??)*[4] years, the earlier *(. . .)*naios being archon at Athens.

T 5 Aristophanes, *Wasps*
Xanthias. The old man had gone a long time without a drink, so when he heard the aulos he was overjoyed at the business and won't stop dancing in the night those famous dances that Thespis used to compete with. He says he'll hold a dance-off pretty soon and show today's tragic performers are yesterday's men.

T 6
(a) Themistius, *In defence of philosophers speaking in public*
And did solemn Tragedy arrive in the theatre with all its equipment and its chorus and its actors? Do we not hold with Aristotle that first the chorus entered and sang for the god, and then Thespis invented prologue and speech, and Aeschylus {thirdly} actors and raised boots, and that we owe the further refinements to Sophocles and Euripides?

---

[4] See note on **T 2** below.

T 7 Diogenes Laertius 3.56

ὥσπερ δὲ τὸ παλαιὸν ἐν τῇ τραγῳδίᾳ πρότερον μὲν μόνος ὁ χορὸς διεδραμάτιζεν, ὕστερον δὲ Θέσπις ἕνα ὑποκριτὴν ἐξεῦρεν ὑπὲρ τοῦ διαναπαύεσθαι τὸν χορὸν καὶ δεύτερον Αἰσχύλος, τὸν δὲ τρίτον Σοφοκλῆς καὶ συνεπλήρωσεν τὴν τραγῳδίαν …

T 8

(a) Dioscorides, *Anth. Pal.* 7.410

Θέσπις ὅδε, τραγικὴν ὃς ἀνέπλασα πρῶτος ἀοιδὴν
  κωμήταις νεαρὰς καινοτομῶν χάριτας,
†Βάκχος ὅτε τριθῦν κατάγοι χορόν ᾧ τράγος ἄθλων
  χὠττικὸς ἦν σύκων ἄρριχος ἆθλος ἔτι.†
εἰ δὲ μεταπλάσσουσι νέοι τάδε, μυρίος αἰὼν
  πολλὰ προσευρήσει χἄτερα· τἀμὰ δ' ἐμά.

3 ἆθλον Heinsius

(b) Dioscorides, *Anth. Pal.* 7.411

Θέσπιδος εὕρεμα τοῦτο, τὰ δ' ἀγροιῶτιν ἀν' ὕλαν
  παίγνια καὶ κώμους τούσδε τελειοτέρους
Αἰσχύλος ἐξύψωσεν, ὁ μὴ σμιλευτὰ χαράξας
  γράμματα, χειμάρρῳ δ' οἷα καταρδόμενα,
καὶ τὰ κατὰ σκηνὴν μετεκαίνισεν. ὦ στόμα πάντων
  δεξιὸν, ἀρχαίων ἦσθά τις ἡμιθέων.

5 πάντῃ Wilamowitz –ως Dilthey

T 9 Ioannes Diaconus et Logothetes, Commentary on [Hermogenes], *Περὶ μεθόδου δεινότητος* 33 (ed. H. Rabe, *RhM* 63 [1908], 150)

ἄμφω δὲ παρ' Ἀθηναίοις ἐφεύρηνται, καθάπερ Ἀριστοτέλης φησίν…τῆς δὲ τραγῳδίας πρῶτον δρᾶμα Ἀρίων ὁ Μηθυμναῖος εἰσήγαγεν, ὥσπερ Σόλων ἐν ταῖς ἐπιγραφομέναις ἐλεγείαις ἐδίδαξε. Στράτων δὲ ὁ Λαμψακηνὸς δρᾶμά φησι πρῶτον Ἀθήνησι διδαχθῆναι ποιήσαντος Θέσπιδος.

Στράτων Patzer Δράκων ms. V Χάρων Wilamowitz

T 11 Athenaeus 1.22a

φασὶ δὲ καὶ ὅτι οἱ ἀρχαῖοι ποιηταί, Θέσπις, Πρατίνας, Φρύνιχος, ὀρχησταὶ ἐκαλοῦντο διὰ τὸ μὴ μόνον τὰ ἑαυτῶν δράματα ἀναφέρειν εἰς ὄρχησιν τοῦ χοροῦ, ἀλλὰ καὶ ἔξω τῶν ἰδίων ποιημάτων διδάσκειν τοὺς βουλομένους ὀρχεῖσθαι.

T 7 Diogenes Laertius, *Lives of the Philosophers*
Just as in early tragedy first of all the chorus performed the whole play, and later Thespis introduced a single actor to allow the chorus to rest from time to time, and Aeschylus a second, and Sophocles the third, thus completing tragedy . . .

T 8 Dioscorides, epigrams from *The Palatine Anthology*

(a) I am Thespis, who first shaped tragic song, fashioning novel pleasures for the villagers †when Bacchus would lead down a *(meaningless word)* chorus for which a goat *was the prize(?)* and the Attic basket of figs *was also the prize*(?)†. Younger men may reshape these things, and infinite time will discover many others; but what is mine is mine.

(b) This was Thespis's invention, but Aeschylus raised up those rustic woodland diversions and these revels to higher perfection, he who carved letters not chiselled but washed as it were by a torrent, and recreated stagecraft. O voice skilled above all, you were truly one of the demigods of old!

T 9 John, Deacon and Logothete, Commentary on [Hermogenes], *Method for Forcefulness*
Both (i.e. comedy and tragedy) were invented amongst the Athenians, as Aristotle says . . . The first tragic drama was introduced by Arion of Methymna, as Solon indicated in his poems entitled *Elegies*. But Straton(?) of Lampsacus says that drama was first produced at Athens and composed by Thespis.

T 11 Athenaeus, *Sophists at Dinner*
They say also that the earliest poets, Thespis, Pratinas, Phrynichus, were called 'dancers' because they not only enacted their own dramas to the dancing of a chorus but also aside from their own compositions taught dancing to those who wanted it.

T 13 [Plato], *Minos* 321a

Σωκράτης. ἡ δὲ τραγῳδία ἐστὶν παλαιὸν ἐνθάδε, οὐχ ὡς οἴονται ἀπὸ Θέσπιδος ἀρξαμένη οὐδ᾽ ἀπὸ Φρυνίχου, ἀλλ᾽ εἰ θέλεις ἐννοῆσαι, πάνυ παλαιὸν αὐτὸ εὑρήσεις ὂν τῆσδε τῆς πόλεως εὕρημα. ἔστιν δὲ τῆς ποιήσεως δημοτερπέστατόν τε καὶ ψυχαγωγικώτατον ἡ τραγῳδία· ἐν ᾗ δὴ καὶ ἐντείνοντες ἡμεῖς τὸν Μίνων τιμωρούμεθα ἀνθ᾽ ὧν ἡμᾶς ἠνάγκασε τοὺς δασμοὺς τελεῖν ἐκείνους.

T 14 Horace, *Ars Poetica* 275–280

ignotum tragicae genus invenisse Camenae
dicitur et plaustris vexisse poemata Thespis,
quae canerent agerentque peruncti faecibus ora.
post hunc personae pallaeque repertor honestae
Aeschylus et modicis instrauit pulpita tignis
et docuit magnumque loqui nitique coturno.

T 18 Pausanias Att. ο 32 Erbse (~ Suda ο 806, Photius ο 618 Theodoridis; variants in Zenobius 5.40 and elsewhere; cf. Phrynichus **T 7**)

Οὐδὲν πρὸς τὸν Διόνυσον· Ἐπιγένους τοῦ Σικυωνίου τραγῳδίαν εἰς τὸν Διόνυσον ⟨οὐκ ἀνήκουσαν⟩ ποιήσαντος ἐπεφώνησάν τινες τοῦτο· ὅθεν ἡ παροιμία. βέλτιον δὲ οὕτως· τὸ πρόσθεν εἰς τὸν Διόνυσον γράφοντες τούτοις ἠγωνίζοντο, ἅπερ καὶ σατυρικὰ ἐλέγετο· ὕστερον δὲ μεταβάντες εἰς τὸ τραγῳδίας γράφειν κατὰ μικρὸν εἰς μύθους καὶ ἱστορίας ἐτράπησαν, μηκέτι τοῦ Διονύσου μνημονεύοντες· ὅθεν τοῦτο καὶ ἐπεφώνησαν. καὶ Χαμαιλέων ἐν τῷ Περὶ Θέσπιδος (fr. 38 Wehrli, 41 Martano) τὰ παραπλήσια ἱστορεῖ.

T 19 *Life of Aeschylus* 16 (*TrGF* 3, p. 36)

(a) *See Phrynichus **T 1** (*Φρύνιχος . . . μαθητὴς Θέσπιδος . . .*)*

(b) τὸ δὲ ἁπλοῦν τῆς δραματοποιίας (*sc.* τοῦ Αἰσχύλου) εἰ μέν τις πρὸς τοὺς μετ᾽ αὐτὸν λογίζοιτο, φαῦλον ἂν ἐκλαμβάνοι καὶ ἀπραγμάτευτον· εἰ δὲ πρὸς τοὺς ἀνωτέρω, θαυμάσειε τῆς ἐπινοίας τὸν ποιητὴν καὶ τῆς εὑρέσεως. ὅτῳ δὲ δοκεῖ τελεώτερος τραγῳδίας ποιητὴς Σοφοκλῆς γεγονέναι, ὀρθῶς μὲν δοκεῖ, λογιζέσθω δὲ ὅτι πολλῷ χαλεπώτερον ἦν ἐπὶ Θέσπιδι Φρυνίχῳ τε καὶ Χοιρίλῳ εἰς τοσόνδε μεγέθους τὴν τραγωιδίαν προαγαγεῖν ἢ ἐπὶ Αἰσχύλῳ εἰσιόντα εἰς τὴν Σοφοκλέους ἐλθεῖν τελειότητα.

T 24 Diogenes Laertius 5.92 (= Aristoxenus fr. 114 Wehrli)

Φησὶ δ᾽ Ἀριστόξενος ὁ μουσικὸς καὶ τραγῳδίας αὐτὸν (*sc.* Ἡρακλείδην) ποιεῖν καὶ Θέσπιδος αὐτὰς ἐπιγράφειν.

T 13 [Plato], *Minos*
Socrates. And tragedy is an ancient institution here (in Attica), not originated by Thespis as people think, nor by Phrynichus, but if you care to look into it you'll find it is a very ancient invention of this city. Tragedy is the most crowd-pleasing and most beguiling kind of poetry, and as we practice it intensively we get our own back on Minos for his compelling us to pay those tributes.

T 14 Horace, *Art of Poetry*
Thespis is said to have discovered the tragic Muse's unknown genre and conveyed his compositions on wagons; they'd sing and act them with faces smeared with wine-lees. After him Aeschylus invented mask and noble robe, spread modest boards on scaffold, and taught actors to speak big and rest on a platform boot.

T 18 Pausanias, *Attic Greek Wordlist*
Nothing to do with Dionysus. People called this out when Epigenes of Sicyon composed a tragedy *(that was not connected)* with Dionysus; hence the proverb. But better (explained) thus: previously they wrote in honour of Dionysus and competed with those compositions that were called 'satyric'; but later they switched to writing tragedies and gradually turned towards legends and histories, no longer mentioning Dionysus; hence people called out this complaint. Chamaeleon relates something like this in his work *On Thespis*.

T 19 *Life of Aeschylus*
(a) *See Phrynichus* ***T 1*** *('Phrynichus . . . pupil of Thespis . . .')*

(b) As for the simplicity of his (Aeschylus's) dramaturgy, if one compared it with those who came after him one would find it limited and unrefined; but if with his predecessors, one would admire the poet for his intelligence and inventiveness. Someone who thinks Sophocles was a more perfect tragic poet is certainly correct, but he should consider that it was much more difficult to enter after Thespis, Phrynichus and Choerilus and bring tragedy to such a level of grandeur than to enter after Aeschylus and achieve the perfection of Sophocles.

T 24 Diogenes Laertius, *Lives of the Philosophers* 5.92
Aristoxenus the writer on music says that he (Heraclides of Pontus) composed tragedies and ascribed them to Thespis.

FRAGMENTA SPURIA

ΠΕΝΘΕΥΣ

F [1c] Pollux 7.45

ἐπεὶ δὲ καὶ ὁ ἐπενδύτης ἔστιν ἐν τῇ τῶν πολλῶν χρήσει, ὅστις βούλοιτο καὶ τούτῳ τῷ ὀνόματι βοηθεῖν φαύλῳ ὄντι, ληπτέον αὐτὸ ἐκ τῶν Σοφοκλέους Πλυντριῶν . . . *(Soph. F 439)* . . . καὶ Θέσπις δέ πού φησιν ἐν τῷ Πενθεῖ·

ἔργῳ νόμιζε νεβρίδ' ἔχειν ἐπενδύτην.

Incertae Fabulae

F [2] Chrysippus(?) fr. 180, §12 von Arnim

Θέσπις ὁ ποιητὴς . . . ·

οὐκ ἐξαθρήσας οἶδ', ἰδὼν δέ σοι λέγω.

F [3] Plutarch, *Moralia* 36b

τὰ δὲ τοῦ Θέσπιδος ταυτί·

ὁρᾷς ὅτι Ζεὺς τῷδε πρωτεύει θεῶν,
οὐ ψεῦδος οὐδὲ κόμπον οὐ μῶρον γέλων
ἀσκῶν· τὸ δ' ἡδὺ μοῦνος οὐκ ἐπίσταται.

τί διαφέρει τοῦ *πόρρω γὰρ ἡδονῆς καὶ λύπης ἵδρυται τὸ θεῖον*, ὡς Πλάτων ἔλεγε;

F [4] Clement of Alexandria, *Stromata* 5.8.48.7

Θέσπις μέντοι ὁ τραγικὸς διὰ τούτων ἄλλο τι σημαίνεσθαί φησιν ὧδέ πως γράφων·

ἴδε σοὶ σπένδω κναξζβι λευκόν,
ἀπὸ θηλαμόνων θλίψας κνακῶν·
ἴδε σοὶ χθυπτην τυρὸν μίξας
ἐρυθρῷ μελιτῷ, κατὰ τῶν σῶν, Πὰν
δικέρως, τίθεμαι βωμῶν ἁγίων.
ἴδε σοὶ Βρομίου αἴθοπα φλεγμὸν
λείβω . . .

Text: Merkelbach 1985 (see note below)

Spurious Fragments

PENTHEUS

F [1c] Pollux, *Dictionary*

And since *ependytês* (a word for an outer garment) is in popular usage, someone who wanted to defend this word as well, common as it is, should take it from Sophocles' *Plyntriai (Clothes-washers*, also known as *Nausicaa)* . . . *(Sophocles F 439 quoted)* . . . And Thespis says somewhere in *Pentheus*:

> Be accustomed to wear a fawnskin for your garment.

Unidentified Plays

F [2] Chrysippus(?)

The poet Thespis . . . :

> I did not observe it thoroughly, but I saw it and tell you.

F [3] Plutarch, *How a young man should listen to poetry*

And this from Thespis:

> You see that Zeus surpasses all gods in this, not practising falsehood, nor boasting, nor foolish laughter; and only he has no acquaintance with pleasure.

How does this differ from 'The divine is situated far from pleasure and pain', as Plato used to say?

F [4] Clement of Alexandria, *Stromata*

But the tragic poet Thespis says that something else is meant by these words (i.e. κναξζβι, χθυπτης etc.), writing something like this:

> See, I make you a libation of white *knaxzbi* that I have pressed from tawny nanny-goats. See, I have mixed for you *chthuptês*-cheese with red-brown honey and set it down, two-horned Pan, on your holy altar. See, I pour for you Bromios's fiery *phlegmos* . . .

Notes on Thespis

T 1

An amalgam of ancient traditions about Thespis. **Icarion** (modern Dionysos, between Athens and Marathon) had a cult of Dionysus from around 530 BC and a theatre probably dating from the early 5th century (»» Csapo–Wilson 2015, 320f., 323). The myths of Icarius and his daughter Erigone linked Icarion with the introduction to Attica of the vine and the cult of Dionysus. The Parian Marble (**T 2**) A 39 similarly records that the comic chorus was invented by Susarion and performed by men from Icarion for the prize of a basket of figs, thirty or more years before Thespis's first tragic performance for the prize of a goat (cf. also **T 8**). Both accounts seem to have been designed to promote the Athenian claim that both comic and tragic drama originated in Dionysiac celebrations in rural Attica (»» Scullion 2002b, 108; Broggiato 2014a, 892f.; Csapo 2015, 90–93).

16th in order etc.: the options reflect the competing claims of **Sicyon** (a substantial *polis* in the NE Peloponnese) and Athens to be the original home of tragic drama. There is no substantial evidence for Sicyon's claim, but Herodotus 5.67 mentions 'tragic choruses' there in the early 6th century: the tyrant Cleisthenes (maternal grandfather of the Cleisthenes associated with the beginnings of democracy at Athens) transferred the sanctuary and cult of the Argive hero Adrastus to his Theban enemy Melanippus and 'restored' to Dionysus the choruses that had previously commemorated Adrastus and his 'sufferings' (a suggestive similarity with tragic drama). Sicyon's claim was probably made later in a public inscription (*FGrH* 550, from [Plutarch], *On Music* 1132a, 1134b) listing priestesses of Argos and famous poets and musicians; this was known to Heraclides of Pontus (fr. 157 Wehrli = 109 Schütrumpf), who may himself have compiled the list of fifteen tragic poets before Thespis (»» West 1989, 252). **Epigenes** and his role are mentioned only here and in **T 18**.

smearing his face with white lead etc.: masking is common in ritual performances in many societies, including archaic Greece. The idea that Thespis 'invented' it, first using rustic face-coverings and later the linen masks actually used in classical tragedy, is again due to the theorizing of later cultural historians who liked to give details of the discoveries of the arts and their development from primitive beginnings: thus the Suda on Choerilus (**T 1**), Phrynichus (**T 1**) and Aeschylus (*αι* 357, 'he first discovered the wearing of awesome masks smeared with colours, and the use of the shoes called *embatai*, by tragic actors': cf. **T 6** and **T 14** with notes).

in the 61st Olympiad: the date (535–532 BC) may coincide with the one given in the Parian inscription (**T 2** n.). West (1989, 253f.) noted that the Suda's dates for Thespis, Choerilus (64th Olympiad) and Phrynichus (67th Olympiad) place them at convenient 12-year intervals before Pratinas and Aeschylus (70th

Olympiad) and were probably educated guesses by Eratosthenes (late 3rd C. BC) or a later writer using his Olympiad dating system: cf. Scullion 2002a, 81.

Plays...on record: see above, p. 3.

T 2

The public inscription known as the Parian Marble listed important historical events and cultural innovations dated by numbers of years before 264/3 BC and by Athenian archon-years. The surviving, much damaged parts of the stone are now in the Ashmolean Museum, Oxford and the Paros Archaeological Museum. For the whole available text see now Rotstein 2016. The text of the entry for Thespis printed here is more cautious than Jacoby's (1904 and *FGrH*, reproduced approximately in *TrGF*), which incorporated an arbitrary conjecture of Boeckh (see below). The conjecture created a reference to a production 'in the city', i.e. at the City Dionysia, but there is no evidence for tragic performances at the City Dionysia before the first years of the democracy at the end of the sixth century (above, pp. x–xi), and Thespis is otherwise connected with Icarion (**T 1**) and rustic festivals (**T 8**, **T 14**).

***(performed as an actor?)*:** Keil's [ὑπεκρίνα]το fits the tradition about Thespis which was well established by the mid-3rd century when this text was inscribed.

who produced...: the first editor of the inscription (Selden 1629) restored ἐδίδαξεν Ἄλ[κη]στιν ('produced *Alcestis*'), but his reading ΑΛ...ΣΤΙΝ is unverifiable and the naming of a play is unlikely in this context (cf. Bentley 1699, 240). Boeckh's conjecture gave 'produced *(a drama in the city and)* the goat was assigned *(as a prize)*'. This has been widely accepted, but the conjecture itself was arbitrary and Jacoby's adjustment of it, placing ἆθλον correctly, puts twenty letters between ἐδίδαξε and ἐ]τέθη where Selden seems to indicate (perhaps inexactly) fourteen. For criticisms of the Boeckh–Jacoby text see Connor 1989, 26–32, West 1989, 253 n. 12, Scullion 2002a, 81 n. 4; cf. Rotstein 2016 (text and translation in ch. 2, comments in ch. 6.2.III).

the goat was assigned *(as a prize)*: the earliest attestation of the view generally held in antiquity that 'tragedy' (*trag-oidia*, 'goat-song') was performed for the prize of a goat, presumably to be sacrificed to Dionysus: »» Scullion 2005, 28–33.

250+*(??)* years: the number is damaged. West (1989, 253 n. 13) calculated that most of the numbers between 14 (ΔIIII) and 25 (ΔΔΠ) might have filled the missing part, thus indicating with some exceptions a complete number between 264 and 275; possible dates would then be in the range 538–533 and 531–526. Thus the date may well have agreed with the Suda's 535–532 (**T 1**). The incompletely named **archon *(...naios)*** cannot be identified but cannot be the archon of 533/2 (Therikles), 528/7 (Philoneos) or 527/6 (Onetorides or Onetor).

T 5

From the final scene of *Wasps* (422 BC): the old-timer Philocleon runs amok after his son has taken him to a sophisticated drinking-party. This is the earliest known reference to Thespis and suggests that he was remembered in Aristophanes' time as a dancer (cf. **T 11**) and *tragoidos* ('goat-singer'), though not necessarily as a performer of tragic *drama*. The scholia here (repeated in Suda θ 283) allege that the reference is to a citharode named Thespis but this is clearly mistaken (»» Bentley 1699, 264–66). Cf. on Phrynichus **T 10(g)**.

T 6

The philosopher-orator Themistius (4th C. AD) argues that all the arts have been developed through innovation, and have spread from their original homes to other places. **Do we not hold etc.** is a rhetorical question though sometimes misinterpreted as a statement, 'We do not hold etc.' (e.g. *MusTr* 33, Lesky 1972, 52 = 1983, 28; the sentence is confusingly printed without punctuation in *TrGF* and in Pickard-Cambridge 1988, 130). Themistius is obviously appealing to Aristotle's authority.

Thespis invented prologue and speech: Thespis is not mentioned in the *Poetics*. Aristotle may perhaps have said this in the lost *On Poets*, but that is uncertain.[5]

for the god: i.e. for Dionysus, a likelier reading than 'for the gods' as in some Themistius mss. (»» Garzya 1988, 67).

and Aeschylus actors: i.e. in addition to Thespis's speaker, who was presumably the poet himself. Aeschylus was generally credited with introducing a second actor (deuteragonist), while the third (tritagonist) was credited either to him (as in the *Life of Aeschylus* §14) or more commonly to Sophocles (e.g. *Poetics* 1449a18; **T 7** below). [The mss. have either 'and Aeschylus thirdly actors', with 'thirdly' marked for deletion in ms. Λ, or 'and Aeschylus a third actor', ignoring the introduction of a second actor.: »» Garzya 1988, 69–72; Janko 2011, 370 with n. 5, 434 (app. on F 38), 503.]

and raised boots: Aeschylus was credited in later antiquity with most of the innovations that gave tragedy its grandeur, including its elaborate costumes and boots (cf. above on **T 1**; *Life of Aeschylus* §14 in *TrGF* 3, 35f.). ὀκρίβαντες were the platform boots that gave tragic actors extra height, but they were not used before the Hellenistic period, so Aristotle could not have mentioned them as Themistius claims. He might have mentioned the fancy leather boots (κόθορνοι) worn by earlier tragic actors; according to the *Life of Aeschylus* (§14) it was these that Aeschylus developed, 'raising up the actors with enlarged κόθορνοι'. For the

[5] Janko includes Themistius 316d–319a as *On Poets* F 38 and F 43 (Janko 2011, 432–35, 439–43 with pp. 363, 369–71, 501–3, 505–8). The inference is disputed by Heath 2013, 5f., cf. 24f.

confusion cf. Philostratus, *Lives of the Sophists* 1.9.2f. (Aeschylus 'equipped tragedy with costuming and the high platform-boot [ὀκρίβαντι ὑψηλῶι] etc.'), Photius *ο* 184 (ὀκρίβαντας· ἐμβάτας). The plural **ὀκρίβαντας** here can hardly mean 'platform', i.e. 'stage', as argued by Garzya 1988, 70f., Janko 2011, 371, 503.

T 7

Diogenes (3rd C. AD) compares the development of philosophy with that of tragedy in much the same way as Themistius (**T 6**).[6]

T 8

Disocorides' epigrams (late 3rd C. BC) present Thespis as the creator of a rustic form of tragedy developed from the songs performed at village festivals of Dionysus (reflecting the false connection of κωμῳδία 'comedy' with κῶμαι 'villages') and later converted to a grand tragic form by Aeschylus: cf. pp. ix–xi and on **T 1** above. Fantuzzi 2007, 487–95 discusses these and Dioscorides' other 'pseudo-epitaphs' for dramatists. **a goat…and the Attic basket of figs:** see on **T 1** and **T 2** above. **not chiselled etc.:** 'not sharply cut but blurred as though water-worn or seen through water flowing over them' (Gow–Page 1965 *ad loc.*).

T 9

From a late Byzantine rhetorical commentary (cf. below on Critias(?) **F 1**) which here reflects the sub-Aristotelian tradition. **Straton** was head of the Peripatos after Aristotle's successor Theophrastus; for his name here rather than an unknown 'Dracon of Lampsacus' see Janko 2011, 496f. The semi-legendary **Arion** is elsewhere said to have invented the circular chorus (*kyklios choros*) or formal dithyramb,[7] from which tragedy was supposed to have developed. According to the Suda (*α* 3886) he also invented 'the tragic mode' (τοῦ τραγικοῦ τρόπου). What, if anything, Solon actually said about Arion is unclear, certainly not that he invented 'tragic drama' as such. »» (dithyramb and tragedy) Scullion 2005, 26f., Csapo–Miller 2007, 10f., Battezzato 2013, 94–96; (**T 9** and related testimonia) Janko 2011, 367f., 428f., 494–98; Heath 2013, 2–4.

Janko takes all of Ioannes' statement except the last sentence as reflecting Aristotle's *On Poets* (F 35, 36c), but see the objections of Heath who also (2 n. 9)

---

[6] The excerpt is part of Janko's *On Poets* F 42, again disputed by Heath 2013, 5f. A similar statement has been detected in the fragments of an introduction to Plato preserved in a 2nd-C. AD papyrus (P. Oxy. 45.3219 frs 3 + 4 = *On Poets* F 41 Janko, cf. Heath 24).

[7] On this tradition and the applications of the terms 'dithyramb' and 'circular chorus' see D'Alessio 2013, 113–18, Ceccarelli 2013.

justifies the phrase **τραγῳδίας δρᾶμα** ('drama of tragedy') against Janko's conjecture τραγῳδίας σχῆμα ('form of tragedy').

T 11

'dancers': cf. **T 5** with note above.

T 13

'Socrates' claims that tragedy was already being performed at Athens in the time of the legendary Cretan king Minos, more than a thousand years before his own time. This is sometimes taken seriously as evidence of a 4th-century debate about the antiquity of tragedy. It is really just a joke enabling 'Socrates', who in this dialogue portrays Minos as a great champion of justice, to blame irresponsible tragic poets for Minos's bad reputation as a persecutor of Athens.

T 14

Horace's picture of tragedy's rustic origins resembles that of Dioscorides (**T 8**) with some picturesque additions: wagons as a primitive kind of stage, wine-lees for face-coverings (suitable for vintage festivals), Aeschylus now inventing masks (cf. **T 1**, **T 6** with notes). The wagons may be connected with the use of wagons and shouting of ritual abuse from them in phallic processions during Dionysiac festivals (»» Csapo 2012).[8]

T 18

***Nothing to do with Dionysus*:** a saying used or mentioned by a number of ancient writers (e.g. Plutarch in Phrynichus **T 7**). Several accounts of its origin are reproduced, elaborated, or abbreviated in proverb collections; those connecting it with tragedy's alleged neglect of Dionysus are the commonest. Pausanias offers two such accounts, the first naming Epigenes of Sicyon as the offending innovator, the second naming 'they' (presumably Thespis and his successors)[9] and ascribed to Chamaeleon in his *On Thespis* (the only record of that work);[10] the alternatives

---

[8] Csapo 2015, 89f. suggests accepting Bentley's ἐν ἀπήναις ('on wagons') rather than ἐν Ἀθήναις ('at Athens') in the Parian Marble's account of the institution of comic choruses, but the phrasing is strongly in favour of ἐν Ἀθήναις (cf. A 17, A 19, A 38, A 57); and how could a chorus of *kômoidoi* be established 'on wagons'? Bentley was proposing to read differently, and implausibly, ἀφ' οὗ ἐν ἀπήναις κωμῳδίαι ἐφορήθησαν ὑπὸ τῶν Ἰκαριέων, 'Since comedies were carried on carts by the Icarians' (Bentley 1699, 207).

[9] Plutarch names Phrynichus and Aeschylus as the innovators who provoked the complaint (Phrynichus **T 7**), but his remark need not be strictly accurate.

[10] Some versions include the Aristotelian detail that tragedy was adapted from dithyrambs, notably Zenobius 5.40 (where ms. C. names Epigenes, others 'the

reflect the competing claims of Sicyon and Athens to have invented tragedy (cf. **T 1** with note). »»» Pickard-Cambridge 1927, 166–68 (1962, 124–26); Janko 2011, 430–33, 498–501; Mirhady 2012, 397–404.

Chamaeleon often inferred historical and biographical 'facts' from poetry, and his explanation of the proverb is not likely to reflect any real event. οὐδὲν πρὸς τὸν Διόνυσον is metrically a paroemiac ('proverb-length') or the second half of an anapaestic tetrameter, a typically comic metre. The phrase may well have originated in comedy and become proverbial later.

T 19(b)

This comment from an unidentified critic is included in the *Life of Aeschylus* which is transmitted in a number of medieval manuscripts of his extant plays. It sums up the common doctrine that it was Aeschylus who gave tragedy its proper grandeur in contrast with the simple, lightweight productions of Thespis and other early dramatists (cf. **T 1**, **T 6**, **T 8** n., **T 14**).

T 24

See above, p. 3.

F [4]

Metre: anapaests. A chorus (of satyrs?) makes an offering of milk, cheese mixed with honey, and wine to the goat-god Pan. The verses include three of the four words in the nonsense-verse κναξζβι χθυπτης φλεγμο δρωψ, which includes all twenty-four letters of the Ionic Greek alphabet once each and was probably used as a teaching device in Greek schools (δρωψ probably appeared soon after v. 6). Evidently the fragment is a whimsical literary invention attaching meanings to these words, rather than a serious piece of archaic poetry. The words attracted serious explanations and interpretations in antiquity which are exemplified in Clement's discussion of this and two similar nonsense-verses as examples of symbolic expression. He also reports that the verses κναξζβι etc. and βεδυ ζαψ χθωμ πληκτρον σφιγξ were said to have been composed by the legendary seer Branchus as a spell against a plague afflicting the people of Miletus, a story twice mentioned by Callimachus (frs 194.28–31 and 229.2–4 Pfeiffer) and perhaps earlier by Hipponax (fr. 105.6 *IEG*). »»» Merkelbach 1985 (cf. Bentley 1691, 47–49).

---

poets') and the writer on dithyramb in Berlin papyrus 9571 whom Janko tentatively identifies as Didymus. Janko includes the excerpts from Pausanias, Zenobius and the Berlin papyrus as *On Poets* *F 37a–d, on rather slender grounds. Aristotle certainly wrote about proverbs, but if he discussed this one Pausanias would probably have said so.

CHOERILUS
(*TrGF* 2)

Texts etc. *TrGF* 1^2.66–68; *MusTr* 37–39, 270; Del Rincón Sánchez 2007, 151–70.

Discussions. Lloyd-Jones 1966, 13; Lesky 1972, 57f. (= 1983, 31f.); West 1989; Scullion 2002a, 81f.

*Choerilus was remembered as one of the early tragedians whose plays fell short of the complexity and elevation attained by Aeschylus. The Suda gives a tragic production career starting in the late 520s (**T 1**), but there was probably no substantial evidence for this (cf. Thespis **T 1** n. at end). The statements that he competed with Aeschylus and Pratinas in the 70th Olympiad (Suda, **T 2**), that he 'flourished' in the same year as*

Testimonia

T 1 Suda *χ* 594
Χοιρίλος, Ἀθηναῖος, τραγικός, ξδ΄ ὀλυμπιάδι καθεὶς εἰς ἀγῶνας· καὶ ἐδίδαξε μὲν δράματα ἑξήκοντα καὶ ἑκατόν, ἐνίκησε δὲ ιγ΄. οὗτος κατά τινας τοῖς προσωπείοις καὶ τῇ σκευῇ τῶν στολῶν ἐπεχείρησεν.

σκευῇ Küster σκηνῇ Sud.

T 2 Suda *π* 2230 (cf. Pratinas **T 1**)
ἀντηγωνίζετο δὲ (*sc.* Πρατίνας) Αἰσχύλῳ τε καὶ Χοιρίλῳ ἐπὶ τῆς ο΄ Ὀλυμπιάδος . . .

T 5 *Life of Sophocles* 19 (*TrGF* vol. 4, p. 38)
Συνηγωνίσατο δὲ (*sc.* ὁ Σοφοκλῆς) καὶ Αἰσχύλῳ καὶ Εὐριπίδῃ καὶ Χοιρίλῳ καὶ Ἀριστίᾳ καὶ ἄλλοις πολλοῖς καὶ Ἰοφῶντι τῷ υἱῷ.

T 6 Marius Plotius Sacerdos, *Artes grammaticae* 3.3 (*GL* VI.507f. Keil)
choerilium metrum . . . constat penthemimerica caesura et syllaba et altera penthemimerica . . . huius metri est Graecum exemplum ἡνίκα μὲν βασιλεὺς ἦν Χοιρίλος ἐν σατύροις . . .

Phrynichus, i.e. 482 (Eusebius, T 3), and that Sophocles competed with him (i.e. in the late 470s or early 460s: ***T 5****),*[1] *are perhaps only approximations (»» Scullion 2002a, 81f.), and the Suda's total of 160 dramas may have been inflated to suit a career supposedly beginning in the 520s. The Suda's thirteen victories could derive from the Victors Lists inscription (though the number happens to match Aeschylus's thirteen), and a career spanning the first three decades of competition at the Dionysia is likely enough. The vague reference to innovations with masks and dress-style looks like another schematic invention placing him in the line of development from Thespis to Aeschylus.*

Testimonia

T 1 Suda, 'Choerilus'
Choerilus of Athens, tragic poet; entered the contests in the 64th Olympiad (524/3–521/0 BC). He produced a hundred and sixty dramas and won 13 victories. Some say he innovated with masks and dress-style.

T 2 Suda, 'Pratinas'
He (i.e. Pratinas) competed with Aeschylus and Choerilus in the 70th Olympiad (500/499–497/6 BC) . . .

T 5 *Life of Sophocles*
He (Sophocles) competed with Aeschylus, Euripides, Choerilus, Aristias and many others, and with his son Iophon.

T 6 Marius Plotius Sacerdos, *Grammar*
The choerilean measure . . . consists of a (dactylic) half-line plus one syllable and another half-line . . . A Greek example of this measure is *ἡνίκα μὲν βασιλεὺς ἦν Χοιρίλος ἐν σατύροις* ('When Choerilus was king among satyrs') . . .

[1] Plutarch, *Cimon* 8.7–8 puts Sophocles' first victory at the Dionysia in 468 and adds that this was his first production, but the second point is debatable (Scullion 2002a, 88).

T 10 *see Thespis* ***T 19***

ΑΛΟΠΗ

Discussion. Karamanou 2003, 27–29.

The play is known only from ***F 1****, in which Pausanias discusses various accounts of the parentage of the culture-hero Triptolemus, who was supposed to have received the knowledge of cereal-growing from Demeter at Eleusis. Cercyon is best known as the fierce wrestler who challenged and killed travellers on the road between Megara and Eleusis until Theseus overcame him, but he was also important in Athenian myth as the father of Alope, whose son Hippothoon was associated with Eleusis and gave his name to one of the ten Cleisthenic tribes; hence the definition of Cercyon as brother of Triptolemus, and of their grandfather Amphictyon (usually a son of the flood-survivor Deucalion) as one of the earliest kings of Attica.*[2] *Pausanias will not have known Choerilus's play and probably got his information from a work on Attic/Eleusinian myths. The play presumably told the story of Hippothoon's birth, exposure, survival, and recognition as Alope's son by the*

F 1 Pausanias 1.14.3
Χοιρίλῳ δὲ Ἀθηναίῳ δρᾶμα ποιήσαντι Ἀλόπην ἔστ⟨ιν⟩ εἰρημένα Κερκυόνα εἶναι καὶ Τριπτόλεμον ἀδελφούς, τεκεῖν δὲ σφᾶς θυγατέρα Ἀμφικτύονος, εἶναι δὲ πατέρα Τριπτολέμῳ μὲν Ῥᾶρον, Κερκυόνι δὲ Ποσειδῶνα.

Incertae Fabulae

Brief fragments. **F 2** γῆς ὀστοῖσιν ἐγχριμφθεὶς πόδα, **F 3** γῆς φλέβες

[2] »» Fowler 2013, 484f., and for the myth and cult of Hippothoon in general, Kron 1976, 177–87, Kearns 1989, 82f., 173.

T 10 *see Thespis* ***T 19***

ALOPE

god Poseidon. This was later the subject of Euripides' Alope, *of which seven fragments survive (*TrGF *5 F 105–111: »»» Collard–Cropp 2008a, 115–23), and of an* Alope *by the younger Carcinus (see Vol. 2). The summary in Hyginus (*Fab. *187) from which Euripides' plot is usually inferred has the baby twice exposed, suckled by a mare and discovered by herdsmen, the first exposure ordered by Alope herself and the second by Cercyon after the herdsmen have brought him the baby with his recognition tokens and thus caused Alope to be recognized as his mother. Choerilus's plot was probably simpler, perhaps without the first exposure and the discovery which facilitated Euripides' famous arbitration scene. It may have included Alope's death and transformation by Poseidon into a spring as mentioned by Hyginus (this is likely also for Euripides'* Alope: *»»» Karamanou 25f., 32, Collard–Cropp 2008a, 116).*[3] *The subject, the birth of an Athenian tribal hero, suggests a date later than Cleisthenes' reform of the Athenian tribal system in 508/7 (cf. Karamanou 27).*

F 1 Pausanias, *Description of Greece*
Choerilus of Athens, who composed a drama *Alope*, states that Cercyon and Triptolemus were brothers, that their mother was a daughter of Amphictyon, and that Triptolemus's father was Raros while Cercyon's was Poseidon.

Unidentified Plays

Brief fragments (examples of riddling metaphors or 'kennings'). **F 2** grazing his foot on earth-bones (i.e. stones), **F 3** earth-veins (i.e. rivers)

[3] Carl Robert thought that Theseus was originally Hippothoon's father and might have been so in Choerilus's play. Del Rincón Sánchez 2007, 163–65 suggests that Choerilus himself might have invented Theseus's paternity. It is however unattested before the 3rd century BC (Istros F 10 *FGrH*, whence Plutarch, *Theseus* 29). See also on Carcinus's *Alope* in Vol. 2.

Notes on Choerilus

T 1, T 2, T 5

See Introduction above and on Thespis **T 1**.

T 6

The 'choerilean' colon, (– ⏑ ⏑ – ⏑ ⏑ – x – ⏑ ⏑ – ⏑ ⏑ – , or D x D) appears occasionally in early poetry in dactylo-epitrite contexts, e.g. Stesichorus frs 209.3, 210.1, 212.1 *PMGF* (= 170.3, 172.1, 173.1 Finglass), Pind. *Ol.* 6.20 etc., *Pyth.* 3.21 etc; for drama see Dale 1968, 175f., 179. The term appears only in Latin grammarians (Plotius as cited; Marius Victorinus, VI.110 Keil; Servius, IV.461 Keil), and in Greek in schol. Ar. *Clouds* 467ff. referring to *Clouds* 475. It was probably coined by a Hellenistic grammarian and presumably alludes to the tragedian although our sources do not say so (other such terms allude to famous early poets, e.g. 'archilochean', 'telesillean'). Plotius's Greek example looks like a grammarian's mnemonic invention and tells us nothing useful about the poet; some have thought it refers to a different Choerilus (e.g. Pickard-Cambridge 1927, 97 = 1962, 68f.).

F 1

See introduction to *Alope* above.

PHRYNICHUS
(*TrGF* 3)

Texts etc. *TrGF* 1^2.69–79 with *addenda* 1^2.345, 5.1104; *MusTr* 40–49, 270f.; Del Rincón Sánchez 2007, 171–266.

Discussions. Lloyd-Jones 1966, 19–33; Lesky 1972, 58–62 (= 1983, 32–35); West 1989; Scullion 2002a. See also below for *Alcestis* and *The Capture of Miletus.*

Our information about Phrynichus is limited and a little confused. The Suda's article is not wholly reliable and should perhaps be supplemented from a separate article (φ 765) which is ostensibly about a different Phrynichus (see ***T 1*** *with note). Other sources sometimes confuse or do not clearly specify the early tragedian, the comic playwright, the late-fifth-century oligarchic politician, and other real or imagined bearers of the same name. The basic facts are however clear. Phrynichus was an older contemporary of Aeschylus with a successful career spanning the last years of the sixth century and the first three decades of the fifth. His son Polyphrasmon won a first victory at the Dionysia in or before 471 (below, p. 53). That Phrynichus himself died in Sicily is doubtful (****T 6*** *n.).*

Information from the later fifth century comes in Herodotus's anecdote about the reception of The Capture of Miletus *(****T 2****) and in several comedies of Aristophanes. In* Women at the Thesmophoria *Agathon admires the elegance of Phrynichus's compositions (****T 10a****). In* Frogs *'Euripides' alleges that Aeschylus found his audience 'daft from a diet of Phrynichus' (****T 10b****), and 'Aeschylus' claims to have improved on the older poet's fine lyrics (****T 10c****). In* Wasps *his old-fashioned songs are treasured by Philocleon and his friends (****T 10d–e****), while in* Birds *he is said to have drawn them from the songs of the birds themselves (see* ***F 19****). In the final scene of* Wasps *a drunken Philocleon performs wild dance-moves in imitation of a Phrynichus who is very probably the tragedian (****T 10(f)*** *with note); later writers also mention his virtuosity as a choreographer (T 13, 15, 16; Thespis* ***T 11****). None of this means that Phrynichus's plays were all undramatic song and dance, but if Aristotle and his school could credit Aeschylus with introducing the second actor while reducing the choral component of tragedy and promoting dialogue (*Poetics *1449a, 15ff.: above, p. ix) it seems likely that at least the earlier* *plays of Phrynichus were strongly chorus-oriented. According to Plutarch (**T 7**) it was Phrynichus and Aeschylus together who 'took tragedy into narratives and calamities'.*

The Suda mentions a total of nine plays but lists only seven, two of them with alternative titles;[1] *the last six, with Greek titles beginning with A or D, look like a truncated alphabetic list. Three more titles are known from other sources (*The Capture of Miletus, Tantalus, Phoenician Women*), and there must have been more of which we know nothing.* Aigyptioi (Egyptians*) and* Danaides *(*Daughters of Danaus*), represented by a single word each (**F 1a, F 4**), probably treated the same myth as Aeschylus's later trilogy (*Supplices, Aigyptioi, Danaides*).*[2] Actaeon *and*

Testimonia

See also Thespis ***T 13, T 19***

T 1 Suda *φ* 762
Φρύνιχος, Πολυφράδμονος ἢ Μινύρου, οἱ δὲ Χοροκλέους, Ἀθηναῖος, τραγικός, μαθητὴς Θέσπιδος τοῦ πρώτου τὴν τραγικὴν εἰσενέγκαντος. ἐνίκα τοίνυν ἐπὶ τῆς ξζ´ ὀλυμπιάδος. οὗτος δὲ πρῶτος ὁ Φρύνιχος γυναικεῖον πρόσωπον εἰσήγαγεν ἐν τῇ σκηνῇ, καὶ εὑρετὴς τοῦ τετραμέτρου ἐγένετο. καὶ παῖδα ἔσχε τραγικὸν Πολυφράσμονα. τραγῳδίαι δὲ αὐτοῦ εἰσιν ἐννέα αὗται· Πλευρώνια⟨ι⟩, Αἰγύπτιοι, Ἀκταίων, Ἄλκηστις, Ἀνταῖος ἢ Λίβυες, Δίκαιοι ἢ Πέρσαι ἢ Σύνθωκοι, Δαναΐδες.

T 2 *See below under* The Capture of Miletus

[1] The separate Suda article mentioned above (*φ* 765) might possibly supply the missing two: see note on **T 1**.

[2] A scholiast on Euripides' *Orestes* 872 (= Phrynichus F 1) says that in Phrynichus's *Aigyptioi* Aegyptus accompanied his sons to Argos. See also **F 14** n., and Theodectas's *Lynceus* in Volume 2.

Antaeus or Libyans *are known by their titles only,*[3] *and* Tantalus *by another isolated word (**F 7**); they probably treated the well-known myths about these figures.*[4] *The triple title* Dikaioi (Just Men) or Persians or Counsellors *is unusual; there are no fragments or other information, but the titles all presumably denote the play's chorus. Mazzarino (1957) plausibly suggested that* Dikaioi *reflects the Persian word* arta, *'justice' or 'truth', a component of Persian names such as Artaxerxes and Artabazos. It is not likely that this play was identical with* Phoenician Women *or was the source of the fragments ascribed to that play, nor that it was identical with* The Capture of Miletus *(cf. below, p. 35), but the titles do suggest that it too had a historical rather than a mythical subject.*

The other four plays are introduced below.

Testimonia

*See also Thespis **T 13, T 19***

T 1 Suda, 'Phrynichus'
Phrynichus, son of Polyphradmon or of Minuras, or some say of Chorocles, Athenian, tragic poet, pupil of Thespis who first introduced the tragic art. He was victorious in the 67th Olympiad (512/1–509/8 BC). This Phrynichus was the first to introduce a female character on the stage, and was the inventor of the tetrameter. He had a son who was a tragedian, Polyphrasmon. There are nine tragedies of his, as follows: *Women of Pleuron, Egyptians, Actaeon, Alcestis, Antaeus or Libyans, Just Men or Persians or Counsellors, Daughters of Danaus.*

T 2 *See below under* The Capture of Miletus

[3] Aristophanes, *Frogs* 689, 'If someone erred through being thrown by one of Phrynichus's wrestling-holds', refers to the late 5th-century oligarchic politician. A scholiast's comment there, 'The tragedian Phrynichus went into a lot of detail about wrestling-holds in his play *Antaeus*', is F 3a in *TrGF* but need not reflect any real knowledge of the play. Its likely subject (Heracles defeating the villainous wrestler Antaeus, son of Poseidon) suggests a satyr-play.

[4] Actaeon's fate was the subject of Aeschylus's *Toxotides (Archeresses*: F 241–244). Nothing substantial is known about Iophon's *Actaeon* (title only), Archestratus's *Antaeus* (*TrGF* 75: title only), Pratinas's *Tantalus* (title only), Sophocles' *Tantalus* (F 572–573), or Aristarchus's *Tantalus* (**F 1b**).

T 4 Plutarch, *Themistocles* 5.5
ἐνίκησε δὲ καὶ χορηγῶν τραγῳδοῖς . . . καὶ πίνακα τῆς νίκης ἀνέθηκε τοιαύτην ἐπιγραφὴν ἔχοντα· *Θεμιστοκλῆς Φρεάρριος ἐχορήγει· Φρύνιχος ἐδίδασκεν· Ἀδείμαντος ἦρχεν.*

T 5 = **F 8** *below*

T 6(?) Anon. *Περὶ Κωμῳδίας* (Koster 1975, p. 9 = Phrynichus test. 2 *PCG*)
Φρύνιχος Φράδμονος ἔθανεν ἐν Σικελίᾳ.

Φρύνιχος †† ⟨Πολυ⟩φράδμονος Koster (cf. Kaibel 1899, 8: see note below)

T 7 Plutarch, *Moralia* 614f–615a
οὕτω τοίνυν, ὅταν οἱ φιλόσοφοι παρὰ πότον εἰς λεπτὰ καὶ διαλεκτικὰ προβλήματα καταδύντες ἐνοχλῶσι τοῖς πολλοῖς ἕπεσθαι μὴ δυναμένοις, ἐκεῖνοι δὲ πάλιν ἐπ' ᾠδάς τινας καὶ διηγήματα φλυαρώδη καὶ λόγους βαναύσους καὶ ἀγοραίους ἐμβάλλωσιν ἑαυτούς, οἴχεται τῆς συμποτικῆς κοινωνίας τὸ τέλος καὶ καθύβρισται ὁ Διόνυσος. ὥσπερ οὖν, Φρυνίχου καὶ Αἰσχύλου τὴν τραγῳδίαν εἰς μύθους καὶ πάθη προαγόντων, ἐλέχθη τὸ 'τί ταῦτα πρὸς τὸν Διόνυσον;' οὕτως ἔμοιγε πολλάκις εἰπεῖν παρέστη πρὸς τοὺς ἕλκοντας εἰς τὰ συμπόσια τὸν Κυριεύοντα 'ὦ ἄνθρωπε, τί ταῦτα πρὸς τὸν Διόνυσον;'

T 10 Aristophanes:
(a) *Thesmophoriazusae* 164–67

(Αγ.) καὶ Φρύνιχος — τοῦτον γὰρ οὖν ἀκήκοας —
αὐτός τε καλὸς ἦν καὶ καλῶς ἠμπίσχετο·
διὰ τοῦτ' ἄρ' αὐτοῦ καὶ κάλ' ἦν τὰ δράματα.
ὅμοια γὰρ ποιεῖν ἀνάγκη τῇ φύσει.

(b), **(c)** *Frogs* 908–10, 1298–1300

(Ευ.) τοῦτον δὲ πρῶτ' ἐλέγξω,
ὡς ἦν ἀλαζὼν καὶ φέναξ, οἵοις τε τοὺς θεατὰς
ἐξηπάτα, μώρους λαβὼν παρὰ Φρυνίχῳ τραφέντας.

* * *

Αι. ἀλλ' οὖν ἐγὼ μὲν εἰς τὸ καλὸν ἐκ τοῦ καλοῦ
ἤνεγκον αὔθ', ἵνα μὴ τὸν αὐτὸν Φρυνίχῳ
λειμῶνα Μουσῶν ἱερὸν ὀφθείην δρέπων.

T 4 Plutarch, *Life of Themistocles*

He (i.e. Themistocles) also won a victory when acting as choregos for a tragic production . . . and he set up a plaque commemorating the victory with the following inscription: *Themistocles of Phrearrioi was choregos (producer), Phrynichus was didaskalos (director), Adeimantos was archon (chief magistrate).*

T 5 = **F 8** *below*

T 6(?) Anonymous Byzantine treatise *On Comedy*

Phrynichus son of Phradmon died in Sicily.

T 7 Plutarch, *Sympotic Questions*

Similarly, when philosophical men during the drinking plunge into subtle dialectical problems, annoying the majority who are unable to follow them, and they in turn launch into certain kinds of songs and silly stories and crude and common talk, the purpose of sympotic fellowship is lost and Dionysus is insulted. Just then as, when Phrynichus and Aeschylus took tragedy into narratives and calamities, people said 'What has this to do with Dionysus?', so it has often occurred to me to say to those who drag the Master Argument into symposia, 'My dear fellow, what has this to do with Dionysus?'

T 10

Allusions to Phrynichus in plays of Aristophanes:

(a) *Women at the Thesmophoria*

(Agathon). And Phrynichus — you've surely heard of *him* — was elegant himself and elegantly dressed;[165] that's why his plays were elegant. Our poetry must always match our nature.

(b), (c) *Frogs*

(Euripides). But first I'll show *him* up (i.e. Aeschylus) — how he was an impostor and a cheat, and the kind of tricks he used to fool his audience, finding them daft on a diet of Phrynichus.

* * *

Aeschylus. No, I took them (my choral lyrics) from a noble source to noble effect, so I shouldn't be seen reaping the same sacred meadow of the Muses as Phrynichus.

(d), (e) *Wasps* 218–21, 266–70

(Βδ.) ὡς ἀπὸ μέσων νυκτῶν γε παρακαλοῦσ' ἀεί,
λύχνους ἔχοντες καὶ μινυρίζοντες μέλη
ἀρχαιομελισιδωνοφρυνιχήρατα,
οἷς ἐκκαλοῦνται τοῦτον.

* * *

(Χο.) τί χρῆμ' ἄρ' οὐκ τῆς οἰκίας τῆσδε συνδικαστὴς
πέπονθεν, ὡς οὐ φαίνεται δεῦρο πρὸς τὸ πλῆθος;
οὐ μὴν πρὸ τοῦ γ' ἐφολκὸς ἦν, ἀλλὰ πρῶτος ἡμῶν
ἡγεῖτ' ἂν ᾄδων Φρυνίχου· καὶ γάρ ἐστιν ἀνὴρ
φιλῳδός.

(f) *Wasps* 1490–91, 1523–27

Φι. πτήσσει Φρύνιχος ὥς τις ἀλέκτωρ . . .
. . . σκέλος οὐρανίαν ἐκλακτίζων.

* * *

(Χο.) ταχὺν πόδα κυκλοσοβεῖτε, καὶ τὸ Φρυνίχειον
ἐκλακτισάτω τις, ὅπως
ἰδόντες ἄνω σκέλος ὤζωσιν οἱ θεαταί.

(g) *Birds* 747–50 (= F 19 in *TrGF*) with Scholia

(Χο.) ἔνθεν ὡσπερεὶ μέλιττα
Φρύνιχος ἀμβροσίων μελέων ἀπεβόσκετο καρπὸν ἀεὶ
φέρων γλυκεῖαν ᾠδάν.

(Schol.) Φρύνιχος τραγῳδίας ποιητὴς, ὃς ἐπὶ μελοποιίαις ἐθαυμάζετο. τέσσαρες δὲ ἐγένοντο Φρύνιχοι. ὁ μὲν εἷς οὗ νῦν μνημονεύει, Πολυφράδμονος παῖς, ποιητὴς ἡδὺς ἐν τοῖς μέλεσιν. ὁ ἕτερος, Χοροκλέους παῖς, ὑποκριτής. τρίτος, Φρύνιχος ὁ κωμικὸς . . . τέταρτος δέ ἐστιν Ἀθηναῖος τὸ γένος ὁ στρατηγήσας τὰ περὶ Σάμον . . .

T 12 Psellus, *Περὶ τραγῳδίας* 8

Περὶ δὲ μέτρου τραγικοῦ ἁπλοῦς πάντως ἐστὶν ὁ λόγος· σχεδὸν γὰρ δύο μέτροις οἵ γε δὴ πολλοὶ ἐν τραγῳδίᾳ κέχρηνται, τῷ ἰαμβικῷ καὶ τῷ τροχαικῷ τετραμέτρῳ. τὸ δὲ ἀναπαιστικὸν τετράμετρον παρὰ Φρυνίχῳ μόνον τῷ παλαιῷ τετύχηκε χρήσεως.

T 17 *see Thespis* ***T 11***

(d), (e) *Wasps*
(Bdelycleon). They regularly summon him soon after midnight, holding lanterns and warbling lovely-old-Phrynicho-honey-of-Sidon songs, with which they call him out.

* * *

(Chorus, of waspish jurors). What can have happened to our fellow-juror living here, that he hasn't come out to join the gang? He's never been a straggler before, but would take the lead in front of us singing Phrynichus's songs; for he surely loves to sing!

(f) *Wasps*
Philocleon. Phrynichus crouches like a cock . . . and kicks out a leg sky-high!

* * *

(Chorus-leader) Whirl your foot quickly all around, and someone kick out the Phrynichus-kick, so the audience will give a whoop!

(g) *Birds* with Scholia
(Chorus of birds) . . . whence Phrynichus, bee-like, gleaned his yield of ambrosial melody, ever bearing a sweet song.

(Schol.) Phrynichus, tragic poet, admired for his song-making. There were four Phrynichuses: the one he (i.e. Aristophanes) recalls here, son of Polyphradmon, a poet pleasing in his songs; the second, son of Chorocles, an actor. Third, Phrynichus the comic playwright . . . And the fourth Athenian by birth, the one who commanded the Samos campaign (412–411 BC) . . .

T 12 Psellus, *On Tragedy*
Tragic metre can be summarized quite simply. The great majority (of poets) use just two metres in tragedy, the iambic (trimeter) and the trochaic tetrameter. The anapaestic tetrameter was used only by the early (tragic poet) Phrynichus.

T 17 *see Thespis* ***T 11***

ΑΛΚΗΣΤΙΣ

Discussions. Lesky 1925, 63–65; Dale 1954, vii–xiv; Stephanopoulos 1980, 46–49; Conacher 1988, 30–35; Wildberg 2002, 26, 173–76; Parker 2007, xi–xix; Iakov 2012, 34–38; Markantonatos 2013, 88–93. Myth: Lesky 1925; *LIMC* I, 'Alkestis'.

The story must have been broadly similar to that of Euripides' Alcestis *(438 BC). In that play Apollo has tricked the Fates into allowing his protégé Admetus, lord of Pherae in Thessaly, to provide a substitute for his own appointed death, and Admetus's wife Alcestis has nobly agreed to die in his place after his parents and others have refused to do so, but when Death comes to take her Heracles outwrestles him and restores Alcestis to her husband (in other accounts Persephone releases Alcestis from the underworld because of her virtue, or Heracles goes there to retrieve her). Apollo and Heracles are both motivated by the noble hospitality of Admetus, who had treated Apollo kindly when Zeus enslaved him to Admetus as penance for killing the Cyclopes, and during the play conceals his wife's death in order to welcome Heracles as a guest. The fragments of Phrynichus's play, so far as they go, match Euripides' plot.* ***F 3*** *shows that he anticipated Euripides in bringing Death onto the stage to claim Alcestis, and* ***F 2*** *probably describes Heracles wrestling with Death (though this and a role for Heracles in Phrynichus's play are debated: see note there). Aeschylus's and Euripides' references to Apollo's tricking the Fates to save Admetus's life (****F **1c****, Aeschylus adding that he did so by making them drunk) are therefore likely to be reminiscences of Phrynichus's play.*

The story reflects a common folktale pattern in which a wife saves her husband from death on their wedding day by offering to die in his place, but some elements are peculiar to the plays, in particular Apollo's role in saving Admetus's life (his enslavement to Admetus was already known to Hesiod: Schol. Eur. Alc. *1 = Hes. fr. 54 M–W, cf. fr. 58) and Heracles' role in saving Alcestis's life (in some comparable folktales the bridegroom himself wrestles with Death, and loses). These elements could have been introduced by Phrynichus, and he might even have been*

ALCESTIS

*the first to attach the folktale pattern to the legendary figures of Admetus and Alcestis, but none of this is certain. What we know of the earlier poetic tradition concerning the couple is limited to the bare facts of their marriage and offspring (*Iliad *2.711–15, Hesiod fr. 37.20). Also uncertain is the character of Phrynichus's play. Some elements suggest a satyr-play: the ghoulish figure of Death, Heracles in his typical satyr-play role combating monsters and ogres, and perhaps the inebriation of the Fates if this was at all prominent. There is however no obvious role for satyrs in the story, and as the date of the play is unknown it could have been produced before satyr-plays became part of the programme of the City Dionysia. Euripides'* Alcestis *was produced instead of a satyr-play, and Phrynichus's play may likewise have fallen somewhere between the poles of the satyric and the tragic. Parker (2007, xvi) suggests that Euripides' play may have been an 'improved' version of Phrynichus's: 'more subtle, more morally sensitive, above all, more tragic'.*

TrGF *adesp. F 405 could be from Phrynichus's* Alcestis.[5] *A comic* Alcestis *by Antiphanes (4th C.) is represented by two uninformative fragments, and a tragedy by the Roman poet Accius by a single one. Other known or possible dramatic treatments of the story are comic.*[6]

[5] οὐ γάρ με Νὺξ ἔτικτε δεσπότην λύρας, | οὐ μάντιν οὐδ' ἰατρόν, ἀλλὰ †θνητὸν ἅμα† (ἡγήτορα Valckenaer) | ψυχαῖς: 'Night bore me not as master of the lyre, nor seer, nor healer, but as *guide?* for souls'. The speaker must be Death, probably confronting Apollo as in the prologue of Eur. *Alcestis* (»» Stephanopoulos 1988, 230)

[6] See Parker 2007, xvi–xix. Welcker imagined an *Alcestis* by Sophocles including his F 770, 851, 911 and 953, but the second hypothesis to Euripides' *Alcestis* states that neither Aeschylus nor Sophocles used the story. F 851 probably comes from a satyr-play about Apollo's servitude to Admetus: »» Radt on F 851, Parker xvii.

F **1c

(a) Aeschylus, *Eumenides* 723–28

Χο. τοιαῦτ' ἔδρασας καὶ Φέρητος ἐν δόμοις·
Μοίρας ἔπεισας ἀφθίτους θεῖναι βροτούς.
Απ. οὔκουν δίκαιον τὸν σέβοντ' εὐεργετεῖν,
ἄλλως τε πάντως χὤτε δεόμενος τύχοι;
Χο. σύ τοι παλαιὰς διανομὰς καταφθίσας
οἴνῳ παρηπάτησας ἀρχαίας θεάς.

(b) Euripides, *Alcestis* 10–14

(Απ.) ὁσίου γὰρ ἀνδρὸς ὅσιος ὢν ἐτύγχανον
παιδὸς Φέρητος, ὃν θανεῖν ἐρρυσάμην,
Μοίρας δολώσας· ᾔνεσαν δέ μοι θεαὶ
Ἄδμητον Ἅιδην τὸν παραυτίκ' ἐκφυγεῖν,
ἄλλον διαλλάξαντα τοῖς κάτω νεκρόν.

(c) *ibid.* 32–34

(Θα.) οὐκ ἤρκεσέ σοι μόρον Ἀδμήτου
διακωλῦσαι, Μοίρας δολίῳ
σφήλαντι τέχνῃ;

F 2 Hesychius *α* 1529 *(ἀθαμβές)*

Φρύνιχος Ἀλκήστιδι·

σῶμα δ' ἀθαμβὲς γυιοδόνητον
τείρει

γυιοδόνητον Toup γυοδονιστον Hesychius

F 3 Servius on Vergil, *Aeneid* 4.694

Alii dicunt Euripidem Orcum in scaenam inducere gladium ferentem quo crinem Alcesti abscidat, et Euripidem hoc a Phrynicho antiquo tragico mutuatum.

F **1c

Probable allusions to Phrynichus's Alcestis *in later tragedies:*

(a) Aeschylus, *Eumenides*
Chorus. You did this kind of thing in Pheres' house as well; you persuaded the Moirai to free mortals from death!
Apollo. And was it not right to benefit the man who respected me, especially when he was in need of it?
Chorus. You annulled the long-established order of things, and fooled those ancient goddesses with wine!

(b), (c) Euripides, *Alcestis*
Apollo. I, a holy god, encountered a pious man, the son of Pheres, and I saved him from dying by tricking the Moirai. The goddesses granted me that Admetus should escape the death that was at hand by giving those below another body in his place.

* * *

Death. Was it not enough for you to prevent Admetus's death by tripping the Moirai with a crafty trick?

F 2 Hesychius, *Lexicon*
Phrynichus in *Alcestis*:

> He wears down his dauntless, limb-wracked body.

F 3 Servius, Commentary on Vergil's *Aeneid*
Others say that Euripides brought Orcus onto the stage carrying a sword with which to cut a lock from Alcestis's head, and that Euripides borrowed this from the early tragic poet Phrynichus.

ΜΙΛΗΤΟΥ ΑΛΩΣΙΣ

Discussion. Rosenbloom 1993 (cf. 2006, 20–22).

*The play is known only from Herodotus's anecdote (**T 2**). The context makes it clear enough that Herodotus describes reactions that occurred fairly soon after the event (so the play was probably produced in spring 492), and that **their own misfortunes (οἰκήια κακά)** means simply that the Athenians, unlike the Sybarites, lamented the Milesians' misfortunes as if they were their own (Athens was supposedly the Ionians' mother-city). Rosenbloom (1993, 168–76) rightly rejects two other interpretations: 'misfortunes for which they were responsible' (having aided the Ionian revolt and then abandoned it),*[7] *or 'misfortunes that they themselves had suffered' (i.e. the Persian sack of Athens, assuming the play was produced after 480).*[8] *Rosenbloom himself argues that the Athenians' grief must have been compounded by their fear of Persian reprisals for their own contribution to the beginning of the Ionian revolt, including the sack of Sardis in 498 ('The Athenians watched a* Capture of Miletus, *yet they imagined a* Capture of Athens*': Rosenbloom 1993, 168). This and Rosenbloom's further speculations on the likely content*

T 2 Herodotus 6.21.2
παθοῦσι δὲ ταῦτα Μιλησίοισι πρὸς Περσέων οὐκ ἀπέδοσαν τὴν ὁμοίην Συβαρῖται, οἳ Λᾶόν τε καὶ Σκίδρον οἴκεον τῆς πόλιος ἀπεστερημένοι· Συβάριος γὰρ ἁλούσης ὑπὸ Κροτωνιητέων Μιλήσιοι πάντες ἡβηδὸν ἀπεκείραντο τὰς κεφαλὰς καὶ πένθος μέγα προσεθήκαντο· πόλιες γὰρ αὗται μάλιστα δὴ τῶν ἡμεῖς ἴδμεν ἀλλήλῃσι ἐξεινώθησαν. οὐδὲν ὁμοίως καὶ Ἀθηναῖοι· Ἀθηναῖοι μὲν γὰρ δῆλον ἐποίησαν ὑπεραχθεσθέντες τῇ Μιλήτου ἁλώσι τῇ τε ἄλλῃ πολλαχῇ καὶ δὴ καὶ ποιήσαντι Φρυνίχῳ δρᾶμα Μιλήτου ἅλωσιν καὶ διδάξαντι ἐς δάκρυά τε ἔπεσε τὸ θέητρον καὶ ἐζημίωσάν μιν ὡς ἀναμνήσαντα οἰκήια κακὰ χιλίῃσι δραχμῇσι, καὶ ἐπέταξαν μηκέτι μηδένα χρᾶσθαι τούτῳ τῷ δράματι.

---

[7] This interpretation is linked with a widely held view that the play rebuked the Athenians for abandoning Miletus and thus supported the policy of resistance to Persia promoted by Themistocles (who as archon in 493/2 was in charge of the City Dionysia of 492).

[8] For the latter interpretation and dating see Roisman 1988, Badian 1996.

THE CAPTURE OF MILETUS

and tone of the play might be true but go well beyond what Herodotus says or implies.

According to Herodotus, Phrynichus was fined one thousand drachmas for his offence, i.e. one-sixth of a talent or a few thousand dollars in terms of modern purchasing power, so not a huge sum.[9] *More significant from our point of view is the ban imposed by the Athenians on any future use of the play. Its terms may have been as vague as Herodotus's summary, and in practice it may have extended beyond revivals of the play itself to (for example) re-use of its subject-matter for other plays etc., use of its text in symposia or schools, or circulation in book form.*[10] *What is clear is that no trace of the text is known to have survived, and that the recent sufferings of a Greek community were never again used as a subject for tragedy.*

Snell's comment on the play-title (F 4b in TrGF*) suggests that it may have been not a title but a description of the content of the play otherwise known as* Dikaioi (Just Men) or Persians or Counsellors *(above, p. 25); but a grief-inducing play about the sack of Miletus is not likely to have had a chorus of Persian elders.*

T 2 Herodotus, *History*
When the Milesians suffered these things (i.e. the Persian capture and sack of Miletus in 494 BC) the Sybarites, who were now living in Laos and Skidros, bereft of their own city, failed to return them like for like; for when Sybaris was taken by Croton all the men of Miletus from the youth up had shaved their heads and gone into heavy mourning, as these two cities were more closely tied to each other than any that we know of. Not so the Athenians: they made it clear in many ways that they were extremely upset by the capture of Miletus; and in particular, when Phrynichus composed and produced a drama, *The Capture of Miletus*, the audience burst into tears and fined him one thousand drachmas for bringing to mind their own misfortunes, and ordered that no one should ever again use this drama.

---

[9] Pindar's near-contemporary dithyramb for the Athenians was rewarded with a gift of 10,000 dr.: Isocrates 15.166, cf. Pindar fr. 76 Snell–Maehler.

[10] The topic is much discussed. See recently Mülke 2000, Caroli 2012, Mastromarco 2012.

ΠΛΕΥΡΩΝΙΑΙ

The city of Pleuron (near the modern town of Mesolongi) was in legend the home of the Curetes and one of the chief cities of Aetolia, along with its neighbour Calydon. There was a long, complex and variable legendary history starting with the foundation of the two cities by Aitolos's sons Pleuron and Calydon and including many well-known names and stories: Pleuron's great-grandsons Oeneus, Thestius and Euenus; Oeneus's children Meleager, Deianeira and Tydeus (with Tydeus's son Diomedes); Thestius's daughters Althaea, Leda and Hypermestra; and

F 5 Tzetzes on Lycophron 433

μέμνηται δὲ τοῦ ἔθνους τούτου (*sc.* τῶν Ὑάντων) καὶ Φρύνιχος ὁ τραγικὸς ἐν δράματι Πλευρωνίαις λέγων·

στρατός ποτ' εἰς γῆν τήνδ' ἐπεστρώφα ποδί,
Ὕαντος ὃς γῆν ναῖεν, ἀρχαῖος λεώς,
πεδία δὲ πάντα καὶ παράκτιον πλάκα
ὠκεῖα μάργοις φλὸξ ἐδαίνυτο γνάθοις.

2 Ὕαντος ἣν ἔναιεν Unger

F 6 Pausanias 10.31.4

τοῦτον τὸν λόγον Φρύνιχος ὁ Πολυφράδμονος πρῶτος ἐν δράματι ἔδειξε Πλευρωνίαις·

κρυερὸν γὰρ οὐκ
ἄλυξεν μόρον, ὠκεῖα δέ νιν φλὸξ κατεδαίσατο
δαλοῦ περθομένου ματρὸς ὑπ' αἰνᾶς κακομαχάνου.

οὐ μὴν φαίνεταί γε ὁ Φρύνιχος προαγαγὼν τὸν λόγον ἐς πλέον ὡς εὕρημα ἄν τις οἰκεῖον, προσαψάμενος δὲ αὐτοῦ μόνον ἅτε ἐς ἅπαν ἤδη διαβεβοημένου τὸ Ἑλληνικόν.

WOMEN OF PLEURON

Euenus's daughter Marpessa. Thestius and Euenus are usually associated with Pleuron, Oeneus and Meleager more often with Calydon. (»» Gantz 1993, 168, 196f., 317–35, 807; Fowler 2013, 130–40.) The title presumably refers to the play's chorus and suggests a setting either in Pleuron or in a place where the women now reside. ***F 5*** *seems to refer to a remote past, while* ***F 6*** *suggests an event later than those which led to Althaea's killing her son Meleager. What event this might have been, amongst the many legends associated with Pleuron, remains uncertain (see further below on* ***F 6****).*

F 5 Tzetzes, Scholia on Lycophron's *Alexandra*

This people (i.e. the Hyantes) is also mentioned by Phrynichus the tragedian in his play *Women of Pleuron,* saying:

> There once came roaming over this land a host which inhabited
> the land of Hyas, an ancient people, and swift flame consumed
> in its furious jaws all of the plains and the lands along the coast.

F 6 Pausanias, *Description of Greece* 10.31.4

This story (i.e. Althaea burning away her son Meleager's life) was first mentioned by Phrynichus son of Polyphradmon in his play *Women of Pleuron*:

> He did not avoid cold death; swift fire consumed him as the
> brand was destroyed by his grim, ill-contriving mother.

But it seems that Phrynichus did not prolong his account as he would if it were his own invention, but rather just touches on it as a story already widely repeated throughout the Greek world.

ΦΟΙΝΙΣΣΑΙ

*The commemorative inscription quoted by Plutarch (**T 4**) refers to a production by Phrynichus financed by Themistocles, hero of the Battle of Salamis, in the archonship of Adeimantus, i.e. in the spring of 476. This probably included* Phoenician Women, *which Glaucus's comment (**T 5**) indicates was produced before Aeschylus's* Persians *of 472. That comment also suggests that Phrynichus's play was set, like Aeschylus's, at the Persian court in Susa and featured a meeting of Persian counsellors who received the news of the defeat at Salamis. The Phoenician women must have been the play's chorus, perhaps slaves or hostages held at Susa while their men served in the Persians' largely Phoenician fleet. The news of the defeat was announced by a eunuch in an iambic prologue-speech (this largely precludes the scenes of fearful anticipation that make the first quarter of Aeschylus's play). A fuller report of the battle by an eye-witness, as in Aeschylus, is likely and is probably represented by **F 10a**. Nothing is known of any other action or characters, and it is impossible to say to what extent Phrynichus's play might have matched the invention and dynamism of Aeschylus's drama (the Queen Mother and her dream, the summoning and appearance of the spectral King Darius, his prophecy of further defeat at Plataea, and the return and lamentations of the broken Xerxes).*[11]

F 8 Hypoth. Aeschylus, *Persae*
Γλαῦκος ἐν τοῖς περὶ Αἰσχύλου μύθων ἐκ τῶν Φοινισσῶν φησὶ Φρυνίχου τοὺς Πέρσας παραπεποιῆσθαι. ἐκτίθησι δὲ καὶ τὴν ἀρχὴν τοῦ δράματος ταύτην,

τάδ' ἐστὶ Περσῶν τῶν πάλαι βεβηκότων

πλὴν ἐκεῖ εὐνοῦχός ἐστιν ἀγγέλλων ἐν ἀρχῇ τὴν τοῦ Ξέρξου ἧτταν στορνύς τε θρόνους τινὰς τοῖς τῆς ἀρχῆς παρέδροις, ἐνταῦθα δὲ προλογίζει χορὸς πρεσβυτῶν.

---

[11] 'It has been contended that the announcement of the defeat right at the start [of the play] . . . shows that Phrynichus's treatment of the subject must have been markedly less dramatic than that of Aeschylus. Even that inference is obviously most unsafe': Lloyd-Jones 1966, 18 = 1990, 230.

PHOENICIAN WOMEN

*The title and **F 9** indicate a chorus of Phoenician women, though Glaucus's comment might suggest a chorus of Persian elders as in Aeschylus's play. The discrepancy has led to suggestions that* Phoenician Women *was yet another title for the play named in the Suda as* Just Men or Persians or Counsellors *(see e.g. Lesky 1972, 60 = 1983, 33), but it is unlikely that one play should have been named after two separate groups. Lloyd-Jones (1966, 23f. = 1990, 234) suggested that* Phoenician Women *and* Just Men etc. *were two plays from a single trilogy, and that Glaucus mistakenly named the former instead of the latter; but this would mean that Glaucus (or a successor) named a play called* Phoenician Women *with a chorus of Phoenician women, rather than a play sometimes called* Persians *with a chorus of Persian elders, as the model for a play called* Persians *with a chorus of Persian elders.*[12] *A better guess is that the elders were a secondary chorus or silent group in* Phoenician Women *and the main chorus in* Just Men etc. *The two plays may nevertheless have belonged to one trilogy.*

The famous 'Persians' vase, a huge Apulian volute-krater decorated by the 'Darius Painter' around the 330s BC and featuring king Darius enthroned amongst counsellors and tribute-bearers, with deities and allegorical figures looking on, is unlikely to be connected with Phrynichus's play, or indeed with any tragedy (»» Taplin 2007, 235–37).

F 8 Hypothesis to Aeschylus' *Persians*
Glaucus in his work *On Aeschylus's Plots* says that *Persians* was modelled on the *Phoenissae* of Phrynichus. He also sets out the beginning of that play as follows:

These are the *(counsellors?)* of those who went long ago…

but there it is a eunuch reporting Xerxes' defeat at the beginning of the play and furnishing some seats for the empire's counsellors, whereas here (i.e. in Aeschylus's *Persians*) a chorus of elders speaks the prologue.

---

[12] Scullion 2002a, 97f. suggests that the information attributed to Glaucus in the *Persians* hypothesis is entirely unreliable. His arguments do not seem to me to be compelling.

F 9 Schol.[VAld] Ar. *Wasps* 220, with Hesychius γ 668 (‘*γλυκερῷ Σιδωνίῳ*’)

Χο. Σιδώνιον ἄστυ λιποῦσαι καὶ δροσερὰν Ἄραδον

λιποῦσαι Schol.[V] -οῦσα Schol.[Ald] -όντες Hesych.

— Schol. *Wasps*: δι' ὀνόματος ἦν καθόλου μὲν ὁ Φρύνιχος ἐπὶ μελοποιίᾳ, μάλιστα δὲ τὸ ἐκ τῶν Φοινισσῶν αὐτοῦ τὸ *καὶ Σιδῶνος προλιπόντα ναόν* (**F 10**) ἢ ***Σιδώνιον ἄστυ λιποῦσα(ι)*** (**F 9**).

— Hesychius: δρᾶμα δέ ἐστιν, ἐν ᾧ †τῆς θεμέλης† ἄρχεται οὕτως· ***Σιδώνιον ἄστυ λιπόντες καὶ δροσερὰν Ἄραδον***. διεβεβόητο δὲ τὸ μέλος τοῦτο.

F 10 Schol.[VAld] Ar. *Wasps* 220 (see under **F 9**)

(Χο.) καὶ Σιδῶνος προλιποῦσα ναόν

προλιποῦσα τὸν ναόν Schol.[Ald] προλιπόντα ναόν Schol.[V]

F 10a Ammonius on *Iliad* 21.111 (P. Oxy. 2.221 [2nd C. AD], col. 3.4ff.)
Φρύ[νιχος δ' ὁ τραγ]ικὸς ἐν Φοινίσσαις δ̣ε̣⟨ε⟩ί̣λ̣η [. . .

. . . ὑ]π̣ὸ̣ τὴν δεείλην ἔ̣π̣λ̣ε̣τ̣ο [. . .
. . . ἄνδρες ἐκτείνοντο [*c. 11 letters*]ην ἐς δ⟨ε⟩ιέλην.

2 ἐσχάτ]ην Björck, Erbse

F 11 Athenaeus 14.635c
καὶ Φρύνιχος δ' ἐν Φοινίσσαις εἴρηκε·

ψαλμοῖσιν ἀντίσπαστ' ἀείδοντες μέλη

Incertae Fabulae

F 13 Athenaeus 13.604a (= Ion of Chios F 6 *FGrH* = F 108 Leurini)
ἔτι πολὺ μᾶλλον ἐρυθριάσαντος τοῦ παιδὸς εἶπε (*sc.* ὁ Σοφοκλῆς) πρὸς τὸν συγκατακείμενον· ὡς καλῶς Φρύνιχος ἐποίησεν εἴπας·

λάμπει δ' ἐπὶ πορφυρέαις παρῇσι φῶς ἔρωτος.

cf. Ath. 13.564f: Φρύνιχός τε ἐπὶ τοῦ Τρωΐλου ἔφη λάμπειν ἐπὶ πορφυραῖς παρῇσι φῶς ἔρωτος.

F 9 Scholia on Aristophanes, *Wasps*, with Hesychius's *Lexicon*

Chorus. Leaving Sidon's town and watery Arados . . .

— Schol. *Wasps*: 'Phrynichus was noted for his lyric compositions in general, and especially the one from *Phoenician Women* (that begins) *And forsaking Sidon's temple* (**F 10**) or *Leaving Sidon's town* (**F 9**).
— Hesychius: 'There is a play in which †*the song from the altar?*† begins thus: *Leaving Sidon's town and watery Arados*. This song was very celebrated.

F 10 Scholia on Aristophanes' *Wasps*

(Chorus.) . . . and forsaking Sidon's temple . . .

F 10a Ammonius, Commentary on *The Iliad*
Phry*(nichus the trag)*ic poet in *Phoenician Women* has (the form) δεείλη:

. . . *in* the afternoon there happened . . .

(. . . and also δ⟨ε⟩ιέλη:)

. . . men were being killed till *(latest?)* afternoon.

F 11 Athenaeus, *Sophists at Dinner*
And Phrynichus in *Phoenician Women* has said:

singing songs in response to pluckings (of the lyre)

Unidentified Plays

F 13 Athenaeus, *Sophists at Dinner*
When the boy blushed much more still, he (i.e. Sophocles) said to the guest lying beside him, How finely Phrynichus put it when he said,

The light of love glows on crimson cheeks.

— also from Athenaeus: 'Phrynichus said of Troilus that the light of love glowed on crimson cheeks.'

F 14 Hephaestion, *Enchiridion* 12.3

τῶν δὲ ἐν τῷ μέτρῳ μεγεθῶν τὸ μὲν ἐπισημότατόν ἐστι τὸ τετράμετρον καταληκτικόν, οἷόν ἐστι τὸ Φρυνίχου τοῦ τραγικοῦ τουτί·

τό γε μὴν ξείνια δούσας, λόγος ὥσπερ λέγεται,
ὀλέσαι κἀποτεμεῖν ὀξέϊ χαλκῷ κεφαλάν.

F 16a Photius *α* 2204 ('ἀπαγγελτῆρα')

ἐσθλῶν ἀπαγγελτῆρα μᾶλλον ἢ κακῶν

F 19 *See **T 10(g)** above*

Brief fragments. [13] **F 1a** (*Aigyptioi*) ἰαίνεται, **F 4** (*Danaides*) ἔγκαρπα, **F 7** (*Tantalus*) ἐφέδρανα, **F 12** (*Phoenissae*) σφηκῶσαι, **F 16** ταῦρος ἀργιμήτης, **F 16b** ἄξιος θέας, **F 16c** ἁμαρτωλή

Notes on Phrynichus

T 1

As for Thespis (**T 1**), the Suda reproduces data formulated in the 4th century BC and later, some of it speculative. **Minuras** is a fictitious comic name ('Warbler', cf. μινυρίζοντες 'warbling' in Ar. *Wasps* 219f. = **T 10(d)**). **Chorocles** ('Dance-famed') is probably similar (see below on **T 10(g)**). The **67th Olympiad** is an unlikely date for Phrynichus's first victory (see above, pp. 12f. on Thespis **T 1**). That he was **first to introduce a female character** is either a fiction or an inference from a limited selection of early tragic texts. Phrynichus was not **the inventor of the** (trochaic) **tetrameter:** it was used by much earlier poets such as Archilochus and Solon, and Aristotle says it was normal in early tragedy (*Poetics* 1449a, 21ff.); it was also common in the comedies of Epicharmus.

Some further information may perhaps be gathered from a separate entry in the Suda, *φ* 765: 'Phrynichus, son of Melanthas, Athenian, tragedian. These too are amongst his plays: *Andromeda, Erigone*. He also composed pyrrhics. (It is said) that the Athenians fined Phrynichus a thousand drachmas when he made a

---

[13] Photius attributes **F 16b–c** simply to 'Phrynichus', possibly the comic poet rather than the tragedian. F 20–24 (omitted here) are more likely the comic poet.

F 14 Hephaestion, *Handbook on Metres*
Of the lengths in this (ionic) metre the most noted is the catalectic tetrameter, such as this from Phrynichus the tragedian:

But to give hospitality, as the tale is told, and then to kill him
and cut off his head with sharp bronze!

F 16a Photius, *Lexicon*

a herald of good news rather than bad

F 19 *See **T 10(g)** above*

Brief fragments. **F 1a** (*Egyptians*) it festers, **F 4** (*Daughters of Danaus*) reaped corn, **F 7** (*Tantalus*) stools (for lyre-players), **F 12** (*Phoenician Women*) to bind, **F 16** a quick-witted (*or* white?) bull,[14] **F 16b** worth seeing, **F 16c** a misdeed

tragedy of the capture of Miletus'.[15] Snell assigns all of this except the last sentence to a second Phrynichus of later, perhaps 3rd-century date (*TrGF* 212), but it is possible that some or all of it originally belonged with the material of *φ* 762. Ceccarelli 1997 reviews the history of the question and argues for this possibility. *Andromeda* and *Erigone* would then be the two titles missing from φ 762's 'nine tragedies', Melanthas would be another invented patronymic, and Phrynichus would be documented as a composer of pyrrhic dances as well as tragedies.

T 4
See above under *Phoenician Women* (p. 38).

[14] i.e. the bull whose form Zeus took to carry Europa from Phoenicia to Crete. Lexicographers were uncertain about the sense of the epithet.

[15] Φρύνιχος, Μελανθᾶ, Ἀθηναῖος, τραγικός. ἔστι δὲ τῶν δραμάτων αὐτοῦ καὶ τάδε· Ἀνδρομέδα, Ἠριγόνη. ἐποίησε καὶ πυρρίχας. ὅτι Φρύνιχον Ἀθηναῖοι χιλίαις ἐζημίωσαν, ἅλωσιν Μιλησίων τραγῳδήσαντα. Adler prints Πυρρίχας as if this was the title of a composition, but a reference to pyrrhic dances is more likely (cf. Ceccarelli 1997, 83).

T 6(?)

The statement appears in a brief survey of famous comic poets found in two 14th-century manuscripts of Aristophanes, and ostensibly refers to the late 5th-century comic poet Phrynichus. It is clearly truncated, lacking biographical details of the kind given for other poets in the survey. **son of Phradmon** must be a corruption of 'son of Polyphradmon'. This may simply misidentify the comic poet's father (actually Eunomides); if so, the entire statement was really about the comic poet. Or it might have ended with a mention of the tragic poet's death (*...whereas Phrynichus son of Poly*phradmon died in Sicily'). Kaibel and Koster slightly favoured the second option (as does Stewart 2017, 223–25), but the first seems preferable. There was no need to mention the tragic poet at all in a brief note of this kind (cf. Harvey 2000, 114f.). Several other entries in this survey start with the poet's name plus patronymic (Aristophanes, Antiphanes, Philemon, Menander), and several say where they died (Antiphanes, Menander, Diphilus).

T 7

Phrynichus and Aeschylus...narratives and calamities: see above, pp. 23f. For brief explanation of **the Master Argument** (κυριεύων λόγος) see under 'Logic' in Baltzly 2014. **what has this to do with Dionysus:** see on Thespis **T 18.**

T 10 (a)–(e)

See above, p. 23, and under Agathon **T 4** for the scene in *Women at the Thesmophoria* which includes **T 10(a).**

T 10(f)

From the final scene of *Wasps*: a drunken Philocleon performs wild dance-moves imitating Phrynichus, and his fellow-jurors (the chorus) join in. This Phrynichus is probably the tragedian, whose songs delight Philocleon and his friends (**T 10d–e**) and who was noted as a dancer and choreographer (T 13, 15–17; Thespis **T 11**): »» MacDowell 1971 on *Wasps* 1490 (doubting the reality of the actor), Sommerstein 1983 and Biles–Olson 2015 on the same passage, Ceccarelli 1997, 90–92, Wright 2013a, 222, Farmer 2017, 147–53. Roos's argument (1951, 121–40) for 'Phrynichus son of Chorocles', named as an actor in Schol. *Birds* 750 (see **T 10(g)**) was accepted by Snell in *TrGF* and e.g. Rau 1967, 153–55.

Aelian (*Var. Hist.* 13.17, repeated in the scholia on *Wasps* 1490: see *TrGF* here and T 14) identifies **Phrynichus crouches like a cock** as a proverb and explains it as originating in Phrynichus's reaction to the audience's hostile reception of *The Capture of Miletus*. This has been recognized as a fiction at least since Bentley 1699, 266.

Nauck optimistically inferred his frs 17–18 from these two passages of *Wasps* but they are rightly rejected in *TrGF*. Fr. 17 (ἔπτηξ' ἀλέκτωρ δοῦλον ὣς κλίνας πτέρον, 'He cowered like a cock drooping a slavish wing', quoted by Plutarch three times without attribution) is now *TrGF* adesp. F 408a but is not necessarily tragic at all.

T 10(g)
The chorus of birds tells Aristophanes' audience that Phrynichus's songs imitated their own. This combines the common association of poetic or prophetic speech with honey (»» West on Hesiod, *Theogony* 83) with the idea that humans learned song from birds (e.g. Alcman frs 39–40 *PMG*; formulated as a theory in Democritus B 154 DK, Chamaeleon fr. 24 Wehrli, 26 Martano). In **T 10(c)** Phrynichus 'reaps' a sacred meadow of the Muses, and in **T 10(d)** his songs are 'honey-sweet'. *TrGF* makes these verses a fragment (F 19) rather than a testimonium as they may include reminiscences of Phrynichus's own verses (»» Dunbar 1995, 462, 465–67).

The scholion here names a **Phrynichus son of Chorocles, actor**, whereas the Suda (**T 1**) makes Chorocles a nickname for the tragedian's father. It is unlikely that both are correct. If the scholion is right, the actor's patronymic was mistakenly ascribed to the tragedian, but it seems more likely that the Suda is right and 'Phrynichus, son of Chorocles, actor' an illusion. See references in the previous note, especially MacDowell and Ceccarelli.

T 12
A paragraph on spoken metres in tragedy from the treatise *On Tragedy* now ascribed to the 11th-century Byzantine scholar Michael Psellus but recycling ancient grammatical doctrine (cf. Agathon **T 20c** and **F 3a** note). Anapaestic tetrameters were typically used in comedy, including the core of the parabasis in which the chorus-leader addressed the audience directly ('the anapaests', e.g. Ar. *Acharnians* 626ff., *Knights* 507ff.). Only two other examples are known, neither from tragedy: *TrGF* adesp. F *646a (»» *TrGF* 5.1135–37, *GrSat* 635–38, O'Sullivan–Collard 2013, 468–71, Cipolla 2011) and Alexander Aetolus fr. 7 Powell.

F **1c
See above, p. 30.

F 2
Hesychius gives no details, but the wrestling can hardly be other than that between Heracles and Death (cf. Eur. *Alc.* 846–49, 1139–42). Probably Heracles **wears down** Death (who would hardly have released Heracles if he had gained a firm hold on him). The metre (anapaests) suggests a description by the chorus visualizing an offstage event. Some scholars have thought that Heracles had no part in Phrynichus's play and was introduced to the story by Euripides: recently

Conacher 1988, 34f., Wildberg 2002, 26, 173–76. Wildberg ascribes **F 2** to an early scene in which Death has entered the house to claim Alcestis (as in Euripides) and the Chorus describes him wearing down 'her dauntless body, shaken by him in all its limbs' (176). But ἀθαμβὲς and γυιοδόνητον need not be quite so restricted in sense as Wildberg suggests, and Death's 'wearing down' Alcestis's 'dauntless etc. body' seems unlikely; she is in fact a willing victim (cf. Eur. *Alc.* 385–91).]

F 3

See above, p. 30.

F 5

Perhaps from a prologue speech giving the genealogical background to the plot of the play. The Hyantes were a pre-Greek people associated with Boeotia and Phocis (Strabo 7.7.2, 9.2.3 citing Hecataeus and Ephorus; Pausanias 9.5.1, 10.35.5), and also with Aetolia. Strabo 10.3.4 cites the Athenian scholar Apollodorus as saying that they migrated from Boeotia to settle amongst the Aetolians, while another tradition had them inhabiting the area before the Aetolians themselves settled there (Herodian, *General Prosody* p. 286 Lentz = Stephanus of Byzantium *α* 146, 'Αἰτωλία'). Lines 1–2 of the fragment as given by Tzetzes are consistent with Apollodorus (the Hyantes invade Aetolia from the land they previously occupied), while Unger's emendation makes them agree with Herodian ('Once a host roamed over this land which the ancient people of Hyas inhabited'). Both accounts suggest a peaceful settlement by the newcomers rather than the warfare and destruction described in lines 3–4. Huxley (1986) favouring Unger's emendation suggested that the fragment refers to an attack on the Hyantes, after their settlement in Aetolia, by a neighbouring people such as the Phlegyes who were known for having sacked the Delphic sanctuary and whose name suggests the **flame (φλόξ)** of v. 4.

[**came roaming etc.:** cf. Eur. *Telephus* F 696.15f., πρίν γ' Ἀχαϊκὸς μολὼν στρατὸς τὰ Μυσῶν πεδί' ἐπιστρωφῶν πατεῖ, 'until the Achaean host came roaming and trampling over the Mysians' plain'. **ναῖεν, inhabited**: unaugmented (epic) forms are not found elsewhere in tragic dialogue outside messenger speeches (Page 1938, 155 on *Medea* 1141). In this genealogical context it might be an intentional epicism.]

F 6

Probably from a choral lyric (metre aeolic, greater asclepiad: – – ¦ – ∪ ∪ –¦ – ∪ ∪ – ¦ – ∪ ∪ – ¦ ∪ –). Pausanias describes the murals painted by Polygnotus to decorate the *Leschê* or Meeting Hall at Delphi, a few decades after Phrynichus's production. For this account of Meleager's death see especially Bacchylides, *Odes* 5, and for others Gantz 1993, 328–35, Davies–Finglass 2014,

515–22 on Stesichorus's *Boar-Hunters*. Pausanias probably did not know the whole play, but his comment seems reliable: the chorus summarizes an event in the past, as in Aesch. *Cho.* 603–12 where the chorus uses the same event as an example of female criminality. So it is unlikely, though often asserted, that Phrynichus's play dramatized Meleager's death (recently Gantz 856 n. 25, Grossardt 2002, 76–79, the latter setting the play in Pleuron with a chorus of women reacting to reports of events outside the city culminating in the hero's death). The narrative is also notably unsympathetic to Althaea, so it is again unlikely that the play concerned her remorseful suicide or that it was the same as the *Althaea* named in the Suda's otherwise alphabetic list of Phrynichus's titles.

F 8

Aeschylus's opening (in anapaests) is τάδε μὲν Περσῶν τῶν οἰχομένων | Ἑλλάδ' ἐς αἶαν πιστὰ καλεῖται | καὶ τῶν ἀφνεῶν καὶ πολυχρύσων | ἑδράνων φύλακες... ('We are the trusty counsellors of the Persians who are gone to the land of Hellas, and guardians of their wealthy, gold-rich dwellings...'). Phrynichus's eunuch presumably described the Persian counsellors in similar terms. Nothing more is known of Glaucus's book *On Aeschylus's Plots*. He may be Glaucus of Rhegium, who produced a better-known work *On the Earliest Poets and Musicians* near the end of the fifth century.

F 9, F 10

The citations of these fragments have been condensed and muddled in transmission (on the text of the *Wasps* scholion see Koster 1973). **F 9** resembles the opening words of entering choruses in Aeschylus's *Suppliant Women* (4f., 'leaving the land of Zeus that borders on Syria') and Euripides' *Phoenician Women* (202, 'leaving the Tyrian sea', perhaps a reminiscence of Phrynichus), so these are usually thought to have been the first words of Phrynichus's entering chorus. But if Hesychius had (e.g.) ἐν ᾧ τὸ ἀπὸ τῆς θυμέλης ἄρχεται οὕτως, 'in which the (song) from the altar begins as follows', it might be the opening of a song following an anapaestic parodos (as in Aeschylus's *Persians*, *Suppliant Women* and *Agamemnon*). The supposed alternative opening **F 10** is hard to explain, especially since **And forsaking Sidon's temple** can hardly be a song's first words. The phrase might have occurred later in the same play and referred again to the chorus (cf. Koster, preferring the feminine participle **προλιποῦσα** to masc. προλιπόντα), or it might have originated elsewhere and been cited for comparison with **F 9**.

Sidon and **Arados** were wealthy Phoenician maritime centres. Arados (now Arwad or Rouad in Syria) is an offshore island, hence **δροσερὰν, watery** (δρόσος can denote sea-water: A. *Eum.* 904, E. *IT* 255, 1192). The women may have named other Phoenician cities and presumably went on to explain their presence in Susa, perhaps as hostages or slaves like the choruses in A. *Cho.*

75ff., E. *IT* 130ff., *Pho.* 202ff. **Sidon's temple** is probably the great temple of Eshmun, patron god of Sidon, whose construction was begun by the Sidonian king Eshmun'azar II in the early 5th century as recorded by an inscription on his sarcophagus (Pritchard 1969, 662). Extensive remains have been excavated.

F 9 metre: – – ᴗ ᴗ – ᴗ ᴗ – x – ᴗ ᴗ – ᴗ ᴗ – (= – D x D, initial anceps plus 'choerilean', cf. Choerilus **T 6** with note). »» Dale 1968, 175f., 179.

F 10 metre: – – – – ᴗ ᴗ – ᴗ – – (initial long + hipponactean)

F 10a

From a papyrus text of a commentary on the *Iliad* composed probably in the first century AD (the identity of Ammonius is uncertain). The commentator cites from Phrynichus two alternatives to the Attic form δείλη, **afternoon** (thus Erbse's reconstruction of the defective papyrus text: Erbse 1977, 83). The metre in the second citation is probably trochaic tetrameter, which would suit a narrative report of the Battle of Salamis.

F 11

From a discussion of stringed instruments. Athenaeus quotes Aristoxenus (above, p. x) as citing Pindar (fr. 125 Snell) to illustrate the playing of different kinds of finger-plucked instrument in concert, and adds (from a different source?) our fragment and Sophocles' *Mysians* F 412. See further below on Diogenes **F 1**.

F 13

In Ion's anecdote Sophocles recalls Phrynichus's verse while admiring a handsome slave-boy at a symposium. πορφύρεος ('purple', here **crimson**) could denote a range of colours from deep red to deep blue and was used with a variety of emotive connotations, here erotic. Grand-Clément 2009 discusses the nuances of Phrynichus's phrase and Ion's anecdote.

Metre: – – ᴗ ᴗ – ᴗ ᴗ – x – ᴗ – ᴗ – – ('archilochean': Dale 1968, 176, 181).

F 14

Hephaestion cites the couplet without a context, to illustrate catalectic ionic tetrameters (ᴗ ᴗ – – ¦ ᴗ ᴗ – – ¦ ᴗ ᴗ – – ¦ ᴗ ᴗ –). Webster (1970, 113) notes that this might suggest an Asian chorus, and suggests that the subject was the daughters of Danaus killing the sons of Aegyptus on their wedding night, i.e. *Danaides* (cf. Del Rincón Sánchez 2007, 253). But the wording (**to give hospitality**, and singular **κεφαλάν, his head**) is a little inappropriate for this.

F 16a

Cf. Ion **F 8a** with note.

PRATINAS
(*TrGF* 4)

Texts etc. *TrGF* 1².79–84 with *addenda* 1².345, 5.1105, 1115; *MusTr* 49–53, 272f.; Del Rincón Sánchez 2007, 267–323.

Discussions. Lloyd-Jones 1966, 13–18; Lesky 1972, 62–64 (= 1983, 35f.); West 1989; Scullion 2002a, 81f. Satyr-plays: *GrSat* 74–87; Cipolla 2003, 29–77; (F 3) O'Sullivan–Collard 2013, 242–47.

*Our information comes mainly from the Suda's notice **(T 1)**, which is subject to the same uncertainties as those for Thespis, Choerilus and Phrynichus. He was contemporary with the latter two, and presumably died a little before 467 when his son Aristias **(T 7** and TrGF no. 9 below) produced a satyr-play composed by his father in competition with Aeschylus and Phrynichus's son Polyphrasmon **(T 2)**. He is the first non-Athenian poet known to have competed at the City Dionysia, coming from Phlious **(T 1, T 7)**, just 20 km. upriver from Sicyon (above, p. 12).*

*Pratinas was famous for his satyr-plays **(T 1, T 7)** and was later said to have been 'the first to write satyr-plays' **(T 1)**, which may only mean that he was the earliest notable composer of satyr-plays for the City Dionysia, or the earliest one for whom some documentation was still available in the fourth century.*[1] *He was also remembered as an accomplished dancer **(T 3)**, a composer in non-dramatic genres, and a writer of at least one treatise on music (T 4, F 7–9). The few fragments in* TrGF *are all concerned with music and dance, and probably all come from satyr-plays or non-dramatic works.*[2] *Nothing is known of his tragedies, unless those named in **T 2(b)** were his (see note there).*

---

[1] The need for an 'inventor' of satyr-drama is due to later theorizing. Aristotle and his successors thought that tragedy had evolved from (Dionysiac) dithyrambs which at first gave it a 'satyric' character (cf. p. 1 above), and that satyr-plays were added to the festival programme when tragedy had become more dignified and lost its 'satyric' element. This seems to underrate the role of mimetic satyr-dances as cult-performances in their own right in the sixth century and earlier. On this whole issue see Seaford 1984, 10–16; Scullion 2002b, 106–9; 2005, 25f., 27f.; Hedreen 2007; Janko 2011, 368f.; O'Sullivan–Collard 2013, 22–25; Csapo–Wilson 2015, 350.

[2] The fragments are included in *PMG* pp. 367–69, and translated and discussed in Campbell 1988, 11, 318–27, as well as in *TrGF* etc. *Dymainai or Karyatides*,

Testimonia

T 1 Suda π 2230

Πρατίνας, Πυρρωνίδου ἢ Ἐγκωμίου, Φλιάσιος, ποιητὴς τραγῳδίας· ἀντηγωνίζετο δὲ Αἰσχύλῳ τε καὶ Χοιρίλῳ ἐπὶ τῆς ο΄ Ὀλυμπιάδος, καὶ πρῶτος ἔγραψε σατύρους. ἐπιδεικνυμένου δὲ τούτου συνέβη τὰ ἰκρία, ἐφ' ὧν ἑστήκεσαν οἱ θεαταί, πεσεῖν, καὶ ἐκ τούτου θέατρον ᾠκοδομήθη Ἀθηναίοις. καὶ δράματα μὲν ἐπεδείξατο ν΄, ὧν σατυρικὰ λβ΄· ἐνίκησε δὲ ἅπαξ.

T 2

(a) P. Oxy. 20.2256 (c. 200 AD), fr. 2, 3–7

ἐπὶ ἄρχοντ(ος) Θεαγ]ε̣νί̣δου Ὀλ̣[υ]μ̣πιάδος [οη΄ ἔτει] α[΄
ἔνικα Αἰσχύλ]ος Λαΐωι Οἰδ̣[ί]ποδι Ἑπτ̣ὰ̣ ἐπὶ Θήβας
Σφίγγι σατυ(ρικῆι)] δεύτερος Ἀ̣ριστίας ταῖς τοῦ πα-
τρὸ(ς) Πρατίνο]υ τραγῳδ[ί]α̣ις τρί[τ]ο̣ς̣ [Πο]λυ-
φράσμων] Λυ̣κουργε̣[ίαι] τ̣[ετρ]αλογία̣ι̣.

(b) Hypoth. Aesch. *Septem*

ἐδιδάχθη ἐπὶ Θεαγένους Ὀλυμπιάδι οη΄. ἐνίκα Λαΐῳ, Οἰδίποδι, Ἑπτὰ ἐπὶ Θήβας, Σφίγγι σατυρικῇ. β΄ Ἀριστίας Περσεῖ, Ταντάλῳ, 〈 〉, Παλαισταῖς σατύροις τοῖς Πρατίνου τοῦ πατρός. γ΄ Πολυφράσμων Λυκουργείᾳ τετραλογίᾳ.

T 3 *see Thespis* ***T 11***

T 7 Pausanias 2.13.6

ἐνταῦθά ἐστι καὶ Ἀριστίου μνῆμα τοῦ Πρατίνου· τούτῳ τῷ Ἀριστίᾳ σάτυροι καὶ Πρατίνᾳ τῷ πατρί εἰσι πεποιημένοι πλὴν τῶν Αἰσχύλου δοκιμώτατοι.

---

cited by Athenaeus for the adjective ἁδύφωνος 'sweet-voiced' applied to a quail (F 1), might have been tragedy, satyr-play or dithyramb. The names refer to a group of Spartan maidens performing ritual dances, especially for Dionysus. »» Del Rincón Sánchez 2007, 202–8; D'Alessio 2013, 127f.; Battezzato 2013, 107.

Testimonia

T 1 Suda, 'Pratinas'
Pratinas, son of Pyrrhonides or Enkomios, from Phlious, tragic poet; he competed with Aeschylus and Choerilus in the 70th Olympiad (500/499–497/6 BC), and was the first to write satyr-plays. When he was presenting a performance it happened that the bleachers on which the spectators were standing collapsed, and as a result of this a theatre was built for the Athenians. He presented 50 dramas, of which 32 were satyr-plays; and he won one victory.

T 2

(a) Oxyrhynchus papyrus 2256
*(In the archonship of Theag)*enides, the 1st *(year of the 78th)* Olympiad (468/7 BC), *(the winner was Aeschyl)*us with *Laius*, *Oedipus*, *Seven against Thebes*, *(satyric Sphinx)*. Second Aristias with his fa*(ther Pratinas's)* tragedies. Third Poly*(phrasmon)* with a t*(etr)*alogy *Lycurgeia*.

(b) Hypothesis to Aeschylus' *Seven against Thebes*
It (i.e. *Seven against Thebes*) was produced in Theagenes' archonship in the 78th Olympiad (468/7–465/4 BC). He (i.e. Aeschylus) was the winner with *Laius*, *Oedipus*, *Seven against Thebes*, and satyric *Sphinx*. Second Aristias with *Perseus*, *Tantalus*, *(a title missing)* and his father Pratinas's satyr-play *Wrestlers*. Third Polyphrasmon with a tetralogy *Lycurgeia*.

T 3 *see Thespis **T 11***

T 7 Pausanias, *Description of Greece*
Here (i.e. in the agora of Phlious) there is a memorial for Aristias, son of Pratinas. This Aristias and his father Pratinas composed satyr-plays that are the most famous except for those of Aeschylus.

Notes on Pratinas

T 1

son of Pyrrhonides or Enkomios: both names are probably fictitious, 'Redhead-son' and 'Kômos-man'. **competed with Aeschylus and Choerilus etc.:** perhaps derived from a didascalic record but more likely a rough synchronism (»» Scullion 2002a, 81f. arguing that there were no detailed didascalic records from the 490s and 480s). **first to write satyr-plays:** see introduction above, p. 49.

the bleachers *(ikria)***...collapsed...a theatre was built:** the anecdote is found only here and reflects a tradition that performances took place in the Athenian agora before a theatre was constructed in the sanctuary of Dionysus Eleuthereus.[3] The tradition however resulted from a confusion between the temporary *ikria* used in the agora and elsewhere for spectators watching Dionysiac and other processions and the *ikria* used for seating in the Theatre of Dionysus before it was rebuilt in stone in the mid-4th century. »» Papastamati-von Moock 2014; Csapo 2015, 99f. with n. 143.

50 dramas, of which 32 were satyr-plays: the number of satyr-plays is remarkable if this refers to productions at the City Dionysia. Either the rules were much looser in the early fifth century than they were in 472 and later (above, pp. xi–xii), or the numbers are in some way inaccurate or incomplete.

T 2

Both statements reflect the didascalic record for the City Dionysia of 467 BC. **T 2b** appears in some medieval manuscripts of *Seven against Thebes*, and **T 2a** in a papyrus text of one of Aeschylus's other plays of that year (»» Hutchinson 1985, 17f.). The hypothesis presumably omits the title of a third tragedy in Aristias's production. It seems natural to read it as ascribing only the satyr-play to Pratinas (**with...his father Pratinas's satyr-play *Wrestlers*** rather than 'with his father Pratinas's *Perseus*, *Tantalus*... and satyr-play *Wrestlers*'). If so, the record is misinterpreted in the papyrus text (**with his father Pratinas's tragedies**).

T 7

Aristias: *TrGF* no. 9 (below, p. 54).

---

[3] Photius ι 95, '*ikria:* those in the agora from which they viewed the Dionysiac contests before the theatre in the sanctuary of Dionysus was built'; ο 543, '*orchestra*: first so called in the agora...' (cf. Plato, *Apology* 26d with Timaeus, *Lexicon to Plato,* 'ὀρχήστρα').

POLYPHRASMON
(*TrGF* 7)

Texts etc. *TrGF* 1^2.84f.; *MusTr* 55, 273; Del Rincón Sánchez 2007, 327–35.

*Phrynichus's son Polyphrasmon is known from the Suda's notice about his father (Phrynichus **T 1**) and from three other testimonia derived from the records of the City Dionysia. The Victors Lists inscription gives a first victory between 482 (two years after Aeschylus's first victory) and 470 (two years before Sophocles' first victory: Polyphrasmon T 2). The Fasti inscription records a victory in 471 (T 1),*[1] *which could therefore have been this first one. The Didascaliae showed a* Lycurgeia *tetralogy placed third in 467 behind Aeschylus and Aristias (Pratinas **T 2**); this presumably had similar subject-matter to Aeschylus's* Lycurgeia, *i.e. the story of Dionysus's establishment of his worship in Thrace.*[2] *No individual play-titles survive, nor any fragments.*

[1] Only]ν is preserved in the Fasti inscription, but the name Polyphrasmon is the only relevant one that can be restored.

[2] See Aeschylus's *Edonians, Bassarai* (Thracian maenads), *Neaniskoi ('Youths')* and satyric *Lycurgus*: *TrGF* 3, 178–85, 138–40, 259–61, 234–36.

ARISTIAS
(*TrGF* 9)

Texts etc. *TrGF* 1^2.85–87 with *addenda* 1^2.346; *MusTr* 55, 273; Del Rincón Sánchez 2007, 343–80.

Satyr-plays. GrSat 213–23, Cipolla 2003, 79–102.

*The records of the City Dionysia listed a production by Aristias in 467, including a satyr-play by his father Pratinas who had probably died recently (T 1 = Pratinas **T 2**), and a first victory in the later 460s after those of Sophocles (468) and Mesatus (Aristias's name is incomplete but reliably restored in the Victors Lists inscription). The* Life of Sophocles *names him as a competitor of Sophocles (T 3 = Choerilus **T 5**). Like his father he was celebrated chiefly as a composer of satyr-plays (T 4 = Pratinas **T 7**). Most if not all of the preserved titles (*Antaeus, Atalanta, Kêres, Cyclops, Orpheus*) and the minimal remnants of his texts are satyric. Sansone 1985 argued that* Orpheus *could have been a tragedy and could have originated the myth of Orpheus's unsuccessful attempt to retrieve his wife from the Underworld (cf. Welcker 1841, 966,* GrSat *223, Cipolla 2003, 99f., Rincón Sánchez 2007, 372–74).*

EUPHORION, EUAEON
(*TrGF* 12, 13)

Texts etc. TrGF 1^2.88f. with *addenda* 1^2.346, 5.1105; Del Rincón Sánchez 2007, 390–95.
Discussion. West 2000 (Euphorion).

*Notices in the Suda (**T 1**) record that Aeschylus's sons Euphorion and Euaeon were both tragedians (*tragikoi*) and that Euphorion won four victories (*sc.* at the City Dionysia) with plays composed by his father but not yet produced when he died. There is no record of plays by Euaeon, who may have been a performer rather than a poet. Dramatic production became a long-lived tradition in this family (see Philocles I **T 1–2** with notes).*[1]

Euphorion is documented only in the record of his victory over Sophocles and Euripides in 431. The Suda's statement about his four victories is problematic: Aeschylus could hardly have left four new tetralogies for his son to use in this way. Several explanations can be considered: (1) The statement should refer to four plays, *i.e. one tetralogy. (2) The qualification 'that he had not yet exhibited' is mistaken: Euphorion actually produced* revivals *of his father's plays. This would be consistent with a later tradition that revivals of Aeschylus's plays were freely admitted at the City Dionysia after his death, but the tradition may be based on mistaken inferences from the texts of Aristophanes and confusion with the admission of a single 'old drama' in the competitions from 386 onwards.*[2] *(3) Euphorion produced plays or tetralogies of his*

---

[1] Sutton 1987a is a general survey of such theatrical families.

[2] E.g. *Life of Aeschylus* (*TrGF* 3, T 1), 48f., 'The Athenians so loved Aeschylus that they voted after his death that anyone who wanted to produce his plays should get a chorus . . . (51f.) and he won not a few victories after his death'; also *TrGF* 3, pp. 56–58 with T 72–77. Biles 2006–7 questions the historicity of this decree. Lamari 2015 defends it in a full review of the evidence for 5th-century reperformances of Aeschylus; cf. Revermann 2006, 72f., Lamari 2017, 62–77. One wonders how reperformances by 'anyone who wanted to produce his plays' could have been accommodated in the programme of the City Dionysia before 386. Reperformances at other venues are much more likely, but a special decree permitting them would hardly have been needed.

own under his father's name, as suggested especially by West;[3] *but despite West's reasoning it is again hard to account for four separate productions in this way, or to see why Euphorion would have persistently credited his own work to his dead father when he was capable of winning prizes in his own right. (4) Euphorion included a few previously unproduced plays of his father in tetralogies produced in his own name, and the records were misinterpreted as they may have been in the case of Aristias's production of 467 (note also the confusion over the posthumous production of Euripides' plays, p. 75 n. 2); but once more this can hardly account for four separate productions. (5) The statement is a fiction, perhaps originating in comedy, alleging that Euphorion's successful plays were really composed by his father (cf. below on Sophocles' son Iophon, p. 119). Of these explanations the first and the fifth are perhaps the most plausible.*

Testimonia

TrGF 12 T 1

(a) Suda αι 357

Αἰσχύλος, Ἀθηναῖος, τραγικός· υἱὸς μὲν Εὐφορίωνος, ἀδελφὸς δὲ Ἀμεινίου, Εὐφορίωνος καὶ Κυναιγείρου, τῶν εἰς Μαραθῶνα ἀριστευσάντων ἅμα αὐτῷ. ἔσχε δὲ καὶ υἱοὺς τραγικοὺς δύο, Εὐφορίωνα καὶ Εὐαίωνα.

(b) Suda ε 3800

Εὐφορίων, υἱὸς Αἰσχύλου τοῦ τραγικοῦ, Ἀθηναῖος, τραγικὸς καὶ αὐτός· ὃς καὶ τοῖς Αἰσχύλου τοῦ πατρός, οἷς μήπω ἦν ἐπιδειξάμενος, τετράκις ἐνίκησεν. ἔγραψε δὲ καὶ οἰκεῖα.

***TrGF* 12 T 2** Hypothesis to Euripides' *Medea*

ἐδιδάχθη ἐπὶ Πυθοδώρου ἄρχοντος ὀλυμπιάδος πζ΄ ἔτει α΄. πρῶτος Εὐφορίων, δεύτερος Σοφοκλῆς, τρίτος Εὐριπίδης Μηδείᾳ, Φιλοκτήτῃ, Δίκτυι, Θερισταῖς σατύροις.

---

[3] West 1979 and 1990, 68–72 on the Prometheus plays, 2000 on a possible Memnon trilogy

Nothing more is known of Euaeon, except that the inscription ΕΥΑΙΩΝ ΚΑΛΟΣ ΑΙΣΧΥΛΟ, *'Euaeon son of Aeschylus (is) handsome', appears on four mid-5th century Attic vases,* ΕΥΑΙΩΝ ΚΑΛΟΣ *on seven others, and simply* ΕΥΑΙΩΝ *on two more. Three of these vases show mythical scenes and might possibly allude to Euaeon's acting in related plays. For details of all the vases see Beazley 1963 II, 1579 and Carpenter et al. 1989, 394f.* Kalos-*inscriptions, usually with homoerotic connotations, were at home in upper-class symposia and were becoming rather old-fashioned in the third quarter of the fifth century: see e.g. Lissarague 1999, Braund and Hall 2014, 5–9. The vases with mythical scenes are discussed by Krumeich 2002 with full bibliography; Taplin 2007, 175 doubts that the scenes are dramatic. Euaeon's name is not necessarily connected with the scenes it accompanies.*

Testimonia

TrGF 12 T 1

(a) Suda, 'Aeschylus'

Aeschylus, Athenian, tragedian: son of Euphorion and brother of Ameinias, Euphorion and Kynaigeiros, who distinguished themselves along with him at Marathon. He also had two tragedian sons, Euphorion and Euaeon.

(b) Suda, 'Euphorion'

Euphorion, son of the tragedian Aeschylus, Athenian, himself also a tragic poet. He won four victories with his father Aeschylus's plays that he (i.e. Aeschylus) had not yet exhibited (i.e. when he died). He wrote plays of his own as well.

TrGF 12 T 2 Hypothesis to Euripides' *Medea*

It (i.e. *Medea*) was produced in the archonship of Pythodorus, in the 1st year of the 87th Olympiad (i.e. in 431 BC): first Euphorion, second Sophocles, third Euripides with *Medea, Philoctetes, Dictys,* and satyr-play *Theristai ('Harvesters').*

ARISTARCHUS
(*TrGF* 14)

Texts etc. *TrGF* 1^2.89–92 with *addenda* 1^2.346; 5.1105; *MusTr* 57–61, 273f.; Del Rincón Sánchez 2007, 396–424.

*The Chronicle of Eusebius (*DID D 3*) has Aristarchus 'noted' in 453, which might mean that he won the first of his two Dionysiac victories mentioned in the Suda (**T 1**) in that year. The Suda also makes him contemporary with Euripides, perhaps because their names began to appear in the didascalic records about the same time (Euripides' first production at the Dionysia was in 455, the year after Aeschylus's death). He is*

Testimonia

T 1 (with **F 1**) Suda *α* 3893
Ἀρίσταρχος, Τεγεάτης, ὁ τῶν τραγῳδιῶν ποιητὴς, νοσεῖ τινα νόσον· εἶτα αὐτὸν ἰᾶται ὁ Ἀσκληπιὸς καὶ προστάσσει χαριστήρια τῆς ὑγείας. ὁ δὲ ποιητὴς τὸ δρᾶμα τὸ ὁμώνυμόν οἱ νέμει . . . οὗτος δὲ ὁ Ἀρίσταρχος σύγχρονος ἦν Εὐριπίδῃ· ὃς πρῶτος εἰς τὸ νῦν αὐτῶν μῆκος τὰ δράματα κατέστησε. καὶ ἐδίδαξε μὲν τραγῳδίας ο΄, ἐνίκησε δὲ β΄, βιοὺς ὑπὲρ ἔτη ρ΄.

T 4 *Glossarium Ansileubi* TR 66 (*Glossaria Latina* I.568 Lindsay)
tragoedias autem Ennius fere omnes ex Graecis transtulit, plurimas Euripidis, nonnullas Aristarchi.

ΑΣΚΛΗΠΙΟΣ

*See **T 1** above. This is the only known Greek tragedy on this subject. It may have been about Asclepius's death, killed by Zeus's thunderbolt for using his healing powers to restore mortals to life, and his deification as a healing god (»» Gantz 1993, 91f.; Fowler 2013, 74–78). If so, it may have involved Asclepius taking payment for raising the dead, a detail which Plato in* Rep. *408b7ff. attributes to 'the tragedians' as well as to Pindar (Pyth. 3.55–58): cf. Del Rincón Sánchez 2007, 406.*

never mentioned in what remains of Old Comedy, but that is not very significant; Sophocles is hardly mentioned either before his death. He might however have stayed away from Athens during much of the Peloponnesian War period and produced there mainly in the 450s through 430s. If he lived for over a hundred years as the Suda says, he can hardly have died before the end of the fifth century. Some of his plays remained well enough known for Ennius to produce Latin versions of them in the early second century BC. Of the seventy tragedies mentioned by the Suda we have only three titles and a handful of fragments.

Testimonia

T 1 (with **F 1**) Suda, 'Aristarchus'
Aristarchus, from Tegea, the composer of tragedies, suffered an illness, and then Asclepius healed him and required an offering in thanks for his health; and the poet devoted to him the drama that bears his name . . . This Aristarchus was contemporary with Euripides, and was the first to set dramas at their current length. He produced 70 tragedies, and won two victories, living more than 100 years.

T 4 *Glossary of Ansileubus*, 'Tragedy'
Ennius translated nearly all his tragedies from Greek ones, very many by Euripides, some by Aristarchus.

ASCLEPIUS

See opposite.

ΑΧΙΛΛΕΥΣ

Fragment 3 of Ennius's Achilles *(=* ***F 1(c)****) is attributed by Festus to 'Ennius in Aristarchus's* Achilles'*; Ennius's play, then, was one of those that he 'translated' from Aristarchus (****T 4****). The subject may have been the recalcitrant Achilles' prolonged refusal to fight and the death of Patroclus fighting in his place as in* Iliad *16–18, also dramatized in the* Myrmidons *of Aeschylus and (in Latin) Accius (»» Jocelyn 1967, 161f.). Plays called* Achilles *are attributed to Iophon (TrGF 22), Astydamas II (TrGF 60), Carcinus II (TrGF 70) and others, but nothing is known of their content.*

F 1a

(a) P. Petrie 2.49(b) (3rd C. BC, ed. J. P. Mahaffy, 1893; re-ed. F. Maltomini 2001, Lloyd-Jones 2005, 118–20), col. 1.10–14

ἐπὶ Ἀχιλ]λ̣έως τοῦ Ἀρισταρχου·

Ὁ]μηρείης ἀπὸ βύβλου
]τον ἀπεπλάσατο
]νονι καὶ τὸν ἄριστ . .
]ησαμενος

4 Ἀγαμέμ]νονι Keil   ἄριστον ed. pr.

(b) Plautus, *Poenulus* 1–4, 11 (= Ennius, *Achilles* fr. 1.1–4, 11 Jocelyn)

Prologus:
Achillem Aristarchi mihi commentari lubet;
inde mihi principium capiam, ex ea tragoedia.
sileteque et tacete atque animum advortite.
audire iubet vos imperator histricus
. . .
exsurge, praeco, fac populo audientiam. 11

c) Festus p. 282.9 Lindsay (= Ennius, *Achilles* fr. 3 Jocelyn)
'prolato aere astitit': Ennius in Achille Aristarchi cum ait, significat clipeo ante se protento.

ACHILLES

F 1a

(a) Petrie papyrus (epigrams on tragic poets and plays)

On Aristarchus's *Achilles*:

. . . from *Ho*mer's book . . . . . . fashioned . . . . . . to/for *(Agamem?)*non and . . . . . . the *best* . . . . . .

(b) Plautus, *The Little Carthaginian* 1–4, 11

Prologue. It's my pleasure to rehearse Aristarchus's *Achilles*; I'll take my opening from that tragedy. Be still, be silent, give your attention! Your actor-commander orders you to listen . . . . . . (11) Rise up, herald, and prepare the people to listen!

c) Festus, *On meanings of words*

'He stood with bronze held forth': when Ennius says this in Aristarchus's *Achilles* it means 'with his shield held out before him'.

ΤΑΝΤΑΛΟΣ

Tantalus, a son of Zeus, was punished for abusing the gods' hospitality in one way or another (»» Gantz 1993, 531–36); this does not suggest an obvious context for the only fragment of Aristarchus's play, although its topic is apt enough. Tantalus was also the subject of plays by Phrynichus (brief ***F*** *7) and Pratinas (****T*** *2) of which even less is known.*

F 1b Stobaeus 2.1.1

Ἀριστάρχου ἐκ Ταντάλου·

καὶ ταῦτ' ἴσον μὲν εὖ λέγειν, ἴσον δὲ μή·
ἴσον δ' ἐρευνᾶν, ἐξ ἴσου δὲ μὴ εἰδέναι.
πλέον γὰρ οὐδὲν οἱ σοφοὶ τῶν μὴ σοφῶν
εἰς ταῦτα γιγνώσκουσιν· εἰ δ' ἄλλου λέγει
ἄμεινον ἄλλος, τῷ λέγειν ὑπερφέρει.

Incertae Fabulae

F 2 Stobaeus 4.20.9

Ἀριστάρχου·

Ἔρωτος ὅστις μὴ πεπείραται βροτῶν,
οὐκ οἶδ' ἀνάγκης θεσμόν· ᾧ πεισθεὶς ἐγὼ
οὕτω κρατηθεὶς τάσδ' ἀπεστάλην ὁδούς.
οὗτος γὰρ ὁ θεὸς καὶ τὸν ἀσθενῆ σθένειν
τίθησι καὶ τὸν ἄπορον εὑρίσκειν πόρον.

F 3 Stobaeus 4.52b.21

Ἀριστάρχου·

ὦ θάνατε, σωφρόνισμα τῶν ἀγνωμόνων

F 4 Athenaeus 13.612f

ἐγὼ δὲ κατὰ τὸν Ἀρίσταρχον τὸν τραγικὸν ποιητήν

τάδ' οὐχ ὑπάρχων ἀλλὰ τιμωρούμενος

καταπαύσω τὸν πρὸς σὲ . . . λόγον.

Brief fragment. **F 5** Ταλαός (*vel* Καλαός)

TANTALUS

F 1b Stobaeus, *Anthology*, 'On those who explain divine matters etc.'
Aristarchus, from *Tantalus*:

> It's all the same to speak well on these matters and not to do so, all the same to investigate them and to be ignorant. Those who are wise know no more of them than those who are not; and if one man speaks better about them than another, he's just better at speaking.

Unidentified Plays

F 2 Stobaeus, *Anthology*, 'On Aphrodite, Eros etc.'
Aristarchus:

> The man with no experience of Eros does not know necessity's law. I obeyed him and, thus overpowered, was dispatched along these paths. This god makes even the strengthless man strong, and causes the man without means to find a way.

F 3 Stobaeus, *Anthology* 4.52b, 'Praise of death'
Aristarchus:

> O Death, chastener of the foolish!

F 4 Athenaeus, *Sophists at Dinner*
But I, as Aristarchus the tragic poet puts it,

> not initiating these things but seeking retribution,

shall end my . . . speech in reply to you.

Brief fragment. **F 5** Talaos (*or* Kalaos)[1]

---

[1] Named by both Aristarchus and Philocles I (**F 3**) as father of a Parthenopaeus different from the well-known son of Atalanta.

Notes on Aristarchus

T 1 (with **F 1**)
Brief biographical data typical of the Suda's notices on dramatists are combined with an extract from Aelian's *On Providence* (fr. 104 Domingo-Forasté). The extract includes a refutation (omitted here) of the idea that a god would demand a reward for his benevolence. The anecdote may be a fiction but is the only evidence for Aristarchus's *Asclepius*. **first to set dramas to their current length:** this can hardly mean the standard length of tragic texts since Aeschylus was usually credited with bringing tragedy to this level of maturity; possibly the restriction of a play's action to a single day (**μῆκος** as in Aristotle, *Poetics* 1449b12ff.), if Aristarchus practised this more strictly than his predecessors and contemporaries.

T 4
The information is in a glossary dated around AD 800 but probably derives from Roman scholarship of the late second or the first century BC, possibly Varro (»» Jocelyn 1967, 44, 52ff.). *Achilles* (**F 1a**) is the only play of Ennius now known to have been derived from Aristarchus.

F 1a
The items collected by Snell under this heading are a very mixed bag:

a) is from a papyrus fragment containing parts of nine literary epigrams celebrating famous dramatists, each with one of his most noted plays; these perhaps originated as epigraphs for texts of the plays (Lloyd-Jones). Other recognizable names are Pratinas (with almost none of the epigram), Astydamas II (*TrGF* 60 **T 9**), Sosiphanes (*TrGF* 92 **T 4**). »» Maltomini 2001.

b) Plautus's reference to Aristarchus's *Achilles* has persuaded some editors that lines 3–4 (except for *histricus* 'actor-') and line 11 of his play are quotations from Ennius's play and therefore quasi-fragments of Aristarchus's play. Jocelyn observes that they are more likely just comic lines for an actor striking a tragic pose (Jocelyn 1967, 164ff.). He concludes that there may well be reminiscences of Ennius's play in the *Poenulus* prologue but if so these are now unidentifiable.

c) Latin translations of Greek plays were not always exact, so it is not certain, though likely enough, that this phrase originated with Aristarchus. It may be from a messenger speech describing Ajax protecting the body of Patroclus with his massive shield as in *Iliad* 17.132ff.

F 1b
The subject is clear from the full title of Stobaeus's chapter, *On those who explain divine matters, and that humans cannot grasp the real truth about immaterial things*. Stobaeus cites many examples of this philosophical commonplace,

most notably Xenophanes B 34 DK, Pindar fr. 61, Eur. *Philoctetes* F 795, Iophon **F 2**, Xen. *Mem.* 1.1.11–13.

F 2

Eros irresistible (cf. e.g. Eur. *Hippolytus Veiled* F 430, Soph. *Trach.* 441ff.) and empowering (e.g. Eur. *Antigone* F 162, *Stheneboea* F 663); probably used here to justify some aberrant behaviour as in Eur. *Hipp.* 439ff., *Tro.* 946ff. etc.

F 4

Aristarchus's verse is the first known occurrence of what became a proverbial phrase, possibly coined by him: see further on Chaeremon **F 3** in Vol. 2.

NEOPHRON
(*TrGF* 15)

Texts etc. *TrGF* 1^2.92–94 with *addenda* 1^2.346, 5.1115; *MusTr* 60–63, 274; Del Rincón Sánchez 2007, 425–57.

Discussions. Page 1938, xxx–xxxvi; Giordano 1961; Snell 1971, 199–205; Barone 1978; Manuwald 1983; Michelini 1989; Mastronarde 2002, 57–64; Diggle 2008; Mossman 2011, 23–28; Librán Moreno 2011; Lucarini 2013, 189–93.

Neophron is recorded as the author of a Medea *of which three fragments are preserved (**F 1–3**), two in the scholia to Euripides'* Medea *noting differences in the two poets' handling of the story, and one in Stobaeus's anthology giving fifteen lines from a speech of Medea resembling those in which she nerves herself to kill her sons in Eur.* Medea *1056–80 and 1236–50.*[1] *In Aristotle's school it was alleged that Euripides' play was an adaptation of Neophron's (**T 2**), an opinion later exaggerated so that Neophron was held to be its real author (**T 1**, **T 3**). The opinion seems to have relied essentially on comparisons between the two texts (Euripides 'seems to have adapted the play from Neophron', **T 2**). There are several reasons for doubting it:*

(1) There is no documentary evidence for this or any other play by Neophron, and no reference to him in any source before the late 4th century. This is surprising if he was a prolific 5th-century poet who

[1] I omit two unlikely additions from papyri: (1) An extensive but very damaged text from a *Medea* drama in P.Lit.Lond. 77 (2nd–3rd C. AD) has sometimes been tentatively ascribed to Neophron's play but includes obscene and otherwise non-tragic language which precludes ascription to any proper tragedy, let alone one that might have been considered a model for Euripides' play. Kannicht included it as possibly satyric in *TrGF* 5, pp. 1137–42 (adesp. F 667a); see recently O'Sullivan–Collard 2013, 488–97. (2) A rhetorical display-piece in P. Oxy. 76.5093 (1st C. AD) alleges that Euripides responded to a public outcry by having Medea kill her children offstage rather than in front of the audience, and quotes two verses from the offending version. It is not clear whether Euripides is supposed to have revised his own work or (less probably) that of a predecessor who in that case might be Neophron, but the question is hardly relevant since the entire story is probably a fiction. On all this see Colomo 2011, 112–16.

influenced Euripides, and whose texts survived into the late fourth century.

(2) Some of the phrasing in **F 2** *resembles phrasing found in other parts of Euripides' play, and in parts of 1056–80 (especially the debate with her* thumos, Med. 1056–64*) which may be 4th-century interpolations even if the passage as a whole is not. It is unlikely that Euripides drew on Neophron's speech in several different parts of his own play, or that Euripides and his interpolator both drew on it.*[2]

(3) The exaggerated and rather confused rhetoric of **F 2** *(see note there) looks like an unsuccessful attempt to emulate the Euripidean (or sub-Euripidean) model.*

(4) The allegation probably arose from the literary researches of Dicaearchus, a learned but far from infallible scholar who appears to have mistaken the Rhesus *now in the Euripidean corpus for a genuine work of Euripides. In his milieu it was possible for Heraclides to circulate his own compositions under the name of Thespis (cf. Thespis* ***T 24*** *with note).*[3] *Dicaearchus may well have drawn the wrong conclusion about Neophron's* Medea *and its relationship with Euripides' play.*[4]

(5) Medea was a popular dramatic subject,[5] *and Euripides' play was both celebrated and controversial for its treatment of Medea's murder of her own sons. Euripides was a particular target for denigration and accusations of plagiarism and other misconduct in Greek*

---

[2] Phrasing found in other parts of Euripides' play: Mastronarde 2002, 63, Diggle 2008, 410f. *Med.* 1056–64 are deleted by Kovacs 1986; 1053–66 (with 1044–48) by Diggle 407–9.

[3] And for Heraclides to be fooled by a *Parthenopaeus* forged under the name of Sophocles, according to an anecdote in Diogenes Laertius 5.92 (see Spintharus, *TrGF* 40 T 3).

[4] See further below on **T 2**. Dicaearchus may have meant that Euripides adapted Neophron's play in the same sense that Aeschylus adapted Phrynichus's *Phoenician Women* (Phrynichus **T 5** = **F 8**). This could have degenerated into the allegation of plagiarism (**T 2**), and then of appropriation of the whole play (**T 1, T 3**). Barone (1978, 130) suggested that Dicaearchus merely compared Euripides' play unfavourably with Neophron's according to Aristotelian criteria.

[5] *Medea*s are ascribed to another Euripides (*TrGF* 17), Melanthius (*TrGF* 23: see p. 132 n. 8), Dicaeogenes (*TrGF* 52), Carcinus II (*TrGF* 70: see Vol. 2), Theodorides (*TrGF* 78) and the Cynic Diogenes (*TrGF* 88: also in Vol. 2). These and later Greek and Latin tragedies, and comedies from the fifth and fourth centuries, are listed by Colomo 2011, 113.

comedy and in later biographical and rhetorical traditions (»» Lefkowitz 2012, 87–103; Colomo 2011, 115f.; Librán Moreno 2011, 116–24). The allegation about Medea *fits this pattern.*

Scholars since Wilamowitz (1880) have for the most part concluded that Neophron's Medea *was modelled on Euripides' play and was composed in the fourth century, some time before Dicaearchus made his comparison (recent exceptions include Snell 1971, Manuwald 1983, Michelini 1989). If so, either it was ascribed, deliberately or mistakenly,*

Testimonia

T 1 Suda *ν* 218

Νεοφρῶν ἢ Νεοφῶν, Σικυώνιος, τραγικός· οὗ φασιν εἶναι τὴν τοῦ Εὐριπίδου Μήδειαν· ὃς πρῶτος εἰσήγαγε παιδαγωγοὺς καὶ οἰκετῶν βάσανον. ἐδίδαξε δὲ τραγῳδίας ρκʹ.

T 2 Hypoth. Eur. *Medea*

τὸ δρᾶμα δοκεῖ ὑποβαλέσθαι παρὰ Νεόφρονος διασκευάσας, ὡς Δικαίαρχος ⟨ἐν . . . . . .⟩ τοῦ τῆς Ἑλλάδος βίου (fr. 63 Wehrli, 62 Mirhady) καὶ Ἀριστοτέλης ἐν ὑπομνήμασιν (fr. 635 Rose).

⟨ἐν πρώτῳ⟩ Luppe (⟨ἐν αʹ⟩ Klotz   τοῦ τῆς Wecklein   τοῦ τε or περὶ τοῦ τε mss.

T 3 Diogenes Laertius 2.134

πταίουσιν οἱ λέγοντες μηδὲν αὐτὸν (*sc.* Μενέδημον) ἀνεγνωκέναι πλὴν τῆς Μηδείας τῆς Εὐριπίδου, ἣν ἔνιοι Νεόφρονος εἶναι τοῦ Σικυωνίου φασίν.

ΜΗΔΕΙΑ

F 1 Schol. Eur. *Medea* 666

Νεόφρων δὲ εἰς Κόρινθον τὸν Αἰγέα φησὶ παραγενέσθαι πρὸς Μήδειαν ἕνεκα τοῦ σαφηνισθῆναι αὐτῷ τὸν χρησμὸν ὑπ' αὐτῆς, γράφων οὕτω·

(Αιγ.) καὶ γάρ τιν' αὐτὸς ἤλυθον λύσιν μαθεῖν
σοῦ· Πυθίαν γὰρ ὄσσαν, ἣν ἔχρησέ μοι
Φοίβου πρόμαντις, συμβαλεῖν ἀμηχανῶ·
σοὶ δ' εἰς λόγους μολὼν ἂν ἤλπιζον μαθεῖν.

to a fifth-century Neophron whose works were no longer available, or there was no fifth-century Neophron. Mastronarde favours the first of these alternatives, arguing that there must have been official records of 5th-century productions by Neophron including a Medea *earlier than that of Euripides (the case would then be similar to that of* Rhesus*).*[6] *Given the total absence of any other record of Neophron and his works, the second alternative seems quite possible.*

Testimonia

T 1 Suda, 'Neophron'
Neophron, or Neophon, from Sicyon, tragic poet: said to be the author of Euripides' *Medea*; first to introduce tutors and interrogation of slaves by torture. He produced 120 tragedies.

T 2 Hypothesis to Euripides' *Medea*
He (Euripides) seems to have adapted the play from Neophron and presented it as his own, according to Dicaearchus *(in Book One?)* of *The Life of Greece* and Aristotle in his *Annotations*.

T 3 Diogenes Laertius, *Lives of the Philosophers*
Those who say that he (i.e. Menedemus of Eretria, cf. Achaeus **T 6**) read nothing except Euripides' *Medea*, which some say is by Neophron of Sicyon, are mistaken.

MEDEA

F 1 Scholia on Euripides' *Medea*
But Neophron says that Aegeus came to see Medea in Corinth in order to get the oracle explained to him by her, writing as follows:

> *(Aegeus.)* I've come, in fact, to find a solution from you. I cannot interpret the Pythian utterance that Phoebus's prophetess delivered to me, and hoped I might learn the meaning by talking with you.

---

[6] Similarly Lucarini 2013, 192, arguing that Eur. *Med.* 1056–80 originated in an earlier *Medea* composed by Euripides himself.

F 2 Stobaeus 3.20.33

Νεόφρονος ἐν Μηδείᾳ·

(Μηδ.) εἶέν· τί δράσεις, θυμέ; βούλευσαι καλῶς
πρὶν ἐξαμαρτεῖν καὶ τὰ προσφιλέστατα
ἔχθιστα θέσθαι. ποῖ ποτ᾽ ἐξῇξας, τάλας;
κάτισχε λῆμα καὶ σθένος θεοστυγές.
καὶ πρὸς τί ταῦτα δύρομαι, ψυχὴν ἐμὴν
ὁρῶσ᾽ ἔρημον καὶ παρημελημένην
πρὸς ὧν ἐχρῆν ἥκιστα; μαλθακοὶ δὲ δή
τοιαῦτα γιγνόμεσθα πάσχοντες κακά;
οὐ μὴ προδώσεις, θυμέ, σαυτὸν ἐν κακοῖς;
οἴμοι, δέδοκται· παῖδες, ἐκτὸς ὀμμάτων
ἀπέλθετ᾽· ἤδη γάρ με φοινία μέγαν
δέδυκε λύσσα θυμόν. ὦ χέρες χέρες,
πρὸς οἷον ἔργον ἐξοπλιζόμεσθα· φεῦ,
τάλαινα τόλμης, ἣ πολὺν πόνον βραχεῖ
διαφθεροῦσα τὸν ἐμὸν ἔρχομαι χρόνῳ.

13 ἐξοπλιζόμεσθα δή· (then φεῦ *extra metrum*) Meineke

F 3 Schol. Eur. *Medea* 1386

Νεόφρων δὲ ξενικώτερον ἀγχόνῃ φησὶ τελευτῆσαι· τὴν γὰρ Μήδειαν παράγει πρὸς αὐτὸν εἰποῦσαν·

(Μηδ.) τέλος φθερεῖς γὰρ αὐτὸν αἰσχίστῳ μόρῳ
δέρῃ βροχωτὸν ἀγχόνην ἐπισπάσας.
τοία σε μοῖρα σῶν κακῶν ἔργων μένει,
δίδαξις ἄλλοις μυρίας ἐφ᾽ ἡμέρας
θεῶν ὕπερθε μήποτ᾽ αἴρεσθαι βροτούς.

1 τέλος γὰρ αὐτὸν ἐχθίστῳ μόρῳ φέρεις Schol.: corr. Elmsley, Hermann
2 βροχωτὸν ἀγχόνης ἐπισπάσας δέρῃ Schol.: corr. Hermann, Nauck
4 διδάξεις τ᾽ ἄλλους μυρίους ἐφημέρους Schol.: corr. Elmsley, Wilamowitz

F 2 Stobaeus, *Anthology*, 'On anger'
Neophron in *Medea*:

(Medea) So, then: what will you do, my heart? Consider well before you go astray and make those dearest to you your greatest enemies. What is this impulse, reckless one? Restrain this violent temper that the gods abhor. And yet why voice these laments when I see my life desolate, dismissed by those who owe me most? Am I becoming soft though I suffer such mistreatment? No, my heart, don't betray yourself in these afflictions! Alas, it's decided: children, leave my sight. Now murderous rage has invaded my angry heart. O my hands, my hands, what a deed we are arming for! Ah, how wretched I am in my rashness! In one brief moment I am going to destroy my life's long labour.

F 3 Scholiast on Euripides, *Medea* 1386
But Neophron rather strangely says that he (Jason) died by hanging himself. He brings on Medea saying to him:

(Medea.) For in the end you will destroy yourself with a most shameful death, tightening a knotted noose around your neck. That is the fate that awaits you for your evil works, a lesson for others for thousands of days to come, that mortals should not raise themselves above the gods.

Notes on Neophron

T 1
first to introduce tutors: this is impossible if Neophron was a 4th-century poet, but the earliest known appearance of a tutor (*paidagôgos*) is in Euripides' *Medea*, so Neophron's *Medea* could have featured one which was wrongly thought to have anticipated Euripides. **interrogation of slaves by torture:** such violence was avoided on the fifth-century tragic stage and more appropriate to comedy. »» Librán Moreno 2011, 114–18.

The Suda's entry continues: 'Subsequently he accompanied Alexander of Macedon (i.e. on his campaigns), and because he was a friend of the philosopher Callisthenes he (i.e. Alexander) had him tortured to death along with him'.

Obviously a supposed predecessor of Euripides could not have been a victim of Alexander. The Suda's entry on Callisthenes of Olynthus, a pupil of Aristotle who wrote an account of Alexander's early campaigns and was executed in connection with the so-called Pages' Conspiracy in 328, names the tragedian executed with him as Nearchus (Suda *κ* 240).

T 2

For discussion of this claim see the introduction above. Dicaearchus's ***Life of Greece*** was a wide-ranging work of cultural history in three books (frs 47–66 Wehrli, 53–77 Mirhady, some of these uncertainly assigned to this work), with Saunders 2001, Schütrumpf 2001, Ax 2001. The miscellaneous ***Annotations*** (*Hypomnemata*) were probably compiled by one or more of Aristotle's successors; Diogenes Laertius (5.48) attributed them to 'Aristotle or Theophrastus'. In *Poetics* 1453b15ff. Euripides' *Medea* exemplifies a plot in which a mother kills her sons intentionally, with no mention of Neophron.

F 1

In the Athenian myth king Aegeus consulted the Delphic oracle about his childlessness but received only a warning 'not to untie the wineskin's foot' (i.e. not to have sexual intercourse) before his return to Athens; on his way home he visited Troezen and was enticed into sleeping with king Pittheus's daughter Aethra, who later gave birth to Theseus. In Euripides' *Medea* Aegeus passes through Corinth on his way to consult Pittheus about the cryptic oracle, and Medea, learning of his problem, persuades him to promise her refuge in Athens in return for using her medicinal powers to cure his infertility. Neophron differed in bringing Aegeus to Corinth specifically to consult Medea. If he wrote in the fourth century this might have been a 'correction' of Euripides' play, which is criticized in Aristotle's *Poetics* (1461b19ff.) for (it seems) failing to provide a reason for Aegeus's appearance.

F 2

The excerpt has obvious and well-known similarities with Medea's speeches in Eur. *Med.* 1028–80 and 1236–50, and especially her debate with her *thumos* in *Med.* 1056ff. In particular:

1 εἶέν· τί δράσεις, θυμέ 'Well then, what will you do, my *thumos*?' ~ *Med.* 1042 αἰαῖ· τί δράσω 'Alas, what shall I do?', 1056 μὴ δῆτα, θυμέ, μὴ σύ γ' ἐργάσῃ τάδε 'No, my *thumos*, do not do these things!'

3 τάλας ~ *Med.* 1057 ὦ τάλαν both 'reckless one' addressed to her *thumos*.

7f. μαλθακοὶ δὲ δή…γιγνόμεσθα 'Am I becoming soft' ~ *Med.* 1052 τὸ καὶ προσέσθαι μαλθακοὺς λόγους φρενί 'to admit soft arguments to my mind'.

9 οἴμοι, δέδοκται 'Alas, it is decided' ~ *Med.* 1064 πάντως πέπρακται ταῦτα 'These things are wholly done', 1236 φίλαι, δέδοκται τοὔργον 'Friends, the deed is decided'.

10f. παῖδες, ἐκτὸς ὀμμάτων ἀπέλθετ' 'Children, leave my sight' ~ *Med.* 1053 χωρεῖτε, παῖδες, ἐς δόμους 'Go, children into the house', 1076f. χωρεῖτε χωρεῖτ'· οὐκέτ' εἰμὶ προσβλέπειν οἵα τε †πρὸς ὑμᾶς† 'Go, go; I can no longer look *upon you(?)*'.

12–14 ὦ χέρες χέρες...τάλαινα τόλμης 'O my hands, my hands... wretched am I in my rashness' ~ *Med.* 1028 ὦ δυστάλαινα τῆς ἐμῆς αὐθαδίας 'O, wretched am I in my ruthlessness' ~ 1244 ὦ τάλαινα χεὶρ ἐμή 'O my wretched/rash hand'.

14f. πολὺν πόνον...διαφθεροῦσα 'about to destroy my life's long labour' ~ *Med.* 1030 ἄλλως δ' ἐμόχθουν καὶ κατεξάνθην πόνοις 'In vain I toiled and was worn down with labours'.

As a whole the speech is rather confused. In Eur. *Med.* 1056–80 (whether authentic or not) there is a simple opposition between Medea's more compassionate 'self' (her love for her sons etc.) and her angry *thumos* (which overpowers her compassion and impels her to kill them). In Neophron's speech Medea instructs her *thumos* to deliberate and control itself, i.e. not make her kill her sons (1–4); then she recalls how she has been abused and tells it not to betray itself by failing to make her kill them (5–8); and finally she announces that the matter is settled and her *thumos* has succumbed to murderous rage (10–12). Thus the *thumos* itself becomes the locus of deliberation and conflicting impulses, while Medea provides a sort of commentary on what is happening to it. This looks like a melodramatic exaggeration of the more restrained use of the *thumos* motif which we see in the Euripidean text.[7]

F 3

As the scholion explains, Jason was usually supposed to have been killed by a piece of his ship Argo falling on his head, an event alluded to in Eur. *Med.* 1386f. Neophron differed in making him hang himself (or at least in having Medea predict that he would), perhaps in order to make his death additionally humiliating as this was typically a female method of suicide. [The textual adjustments in vv. 1, 2 and 4 are needed for both metre and sense.]

---

[7] Snell (1971, 199–205) argued that the speech's conception of a 'two-sided' *thumos*, comprising both emotion and reason, was a step towards the idea of a conflict between emotion and reason which Euripides made explicit in *Med.* 1056–80. His argument seems to me to make the speech more coherent than it really is, and his analysis of *Med.* 1056–80 has itself been much criticized (»» e.g. Gill 1995, 29–41, 216–26; Mastronarde 2002, 343–45, 393–97).

EURIPIDES I and II
(*TrGF* 16, 17)

Texts etc. *TrGF* 1^2.94. *Discussion.* Sutton 1987a, 16.

Two brief notices from the Suda are the only evidence for the existence of these namesakes of the famous poet (Euripides III in TrGF*).*[1] *As Sutton says, there is no reason to think they were related to him; if they had been we would probably have heard of it. The name is not uncommon.*

Testimonia

Euripides I (*TrGF* 16) T 1 Suda ε 3693

Εὐριπίδης, Ἀθηναῖος, τραγικός, πρεσβύτερος τοῦ ἐνδόξου γενομένου. ἐδίδαξε δράματα ιβ´, εἶλε δὲ νίκας β´.

Euripides II (*TrGF* 17) T 1 Suda ε 3694

Εὐριπίδης, τραγικός, τοῦ προτέρου ἀδελφιδοῦς, ὡς Διονύσιος ἐν τοῖς χρονικοῖς. ἔγραψε δὲ Ὁμηρικὴν ἔκδοσιν, εἰ μὴ ἄρα ἑτέρου ἐστί. δράματα αὐτοῦ ταῦτα· Ὀρέστης, Μήδεια, Πολυξένη.

---

[1] The victory dedication IG I^3 969, noted as **16 T 2** in *TrGF*, probably refers to Euripides III. »» Ghiron-Bistagne 1976, 119–21.

*Euripides III's youngest son was named Euripides and was said to have produced his father's last plays (*Iphigenia at Aulis, Alcmeon in Corinth, Bacchae*) at the City Dionysia shortly after his death, i.e. in 405 BC.*[2] *He may have been responsible for completing the text of* Iphigenia at Aulis *and is added as Euripides IV in* TrGF *5 (p. 1106). There is no record of his having produced plays of his own.*

Testimonia

Euripides I (*TrGF* 16) T 1 Suda, 'Euripides' (1)
Euripides, Athenian, tragic poet, older than the one who became celebrated. He produced 12 plays, and won 2 victories.

Euripides II (*TrGF* 17) T 1 Suda, 'Euripides' (2)
Euripides, tragic poet, nephew of the above, according to Dionysius in his *Chronicle*. He wrote an edition of Homer (unless this is by another Euripides).[3] Plays of his are these: *Orestes, Medea, Polyxena.*

---

[2] Schol. Ar. *Frogs* 66f. cites the didascalic record. The *Life of Euripides* (*TrGF* 5 **T 1** §8, p. 47) repeats this vaguely (he 'produced some of his father's plays'). The Suda (ε 3695 = *TrGF* 5 **T 3**, pp. 53f.) mentions the son but attributes the posthumous production to a nephew of the same name.

[3] This edition is otherwise known only for its inclusion of two interpolated verses in the Catalogue of Ships, *Iliad* 2.848a (cf. Ammonius on *Iliad* 21.155f.) and 866a (cf. Eustathius *ad loc.*). Its author was very probably a Hellenistic scholar rather than a fifth-century tragedian. »» Bolling 1925, 38f., 77, 79; West 2001, 52 n. 17.

ION
(*TrGF* 19)

Texts etc. *TrGF* 1^2.95–114 with *addenda* 1^2.346f., 5.1106; *MusTr* 64–80, 274–77; von Blumenthal 1939; Leurini 2000.

Bibliographical survey (1960–2005). Leurini 2006.

Discussions. Huxley 1965; West 1985b; Dover 1986; Leurini 1990; Jennings–Katsaros 2007; Federico 2015, 1–78.

Satyr-play (Omphale, F 17a–33a, *59). *GrSat* 479–90; Cipolla 2003, 103–38; O'Sullivan–Collard 2013, 414–25.

*Ion was born in the 480s, a close contemporary of Euripides and Achaeus, and died a little before 421 (**T 2**). He came from an elite Chian family with close ties to Athens (it was probably his son Tydeus who was killed by pro-Spartan Chians during the island's defection from its alliance with Athens in 412/11: Thucydides 8.38.2). Ion was acquainted with Cimon as a young man in the 460s, and with other notable Athenian figures in the following decades. The famous anecdote about Sophocles visiting Chios in 441 (quoted by Athenaeus, and source of Phrynichus **F 13**) comes from Ion's* Epidemiai *('Visits'), a book of reminiscences*

Testimonia

T 1 (4, 9 Leur.) Suda ι 487
Ἴων, Χῖος, τραγικὸς καὶ λυρικὸς καὶ φιλόσοφος, υἱὸς Ὀρθομένους, ἐπίκλησιν δὲ Ξούθου. ἤρξατο δὲ τὰς τραγῳδίας διδάσκειν ἐπὶ τῆς πβ´ ὀλυμπιάδος. δράματα δὲ αὐτοῦ ιβ´, οἱ δὲ λ´, ἄλλοι δὲ μ´ φασιν…

— Harpocration ι 27: Ἴων· Ἰσοκράτης ἐν τῷ περὶ τῆς ἀντιδόσεως. Ἴωνος τοῦ τῆς τραγῳδίας ποιητοῦ μνημονεύοι ἂν νῦν ὁ ῥήτωρ, ὃς ἦν Χῖος μὲν γένος, υἱὸς δὲ Ὀρθομένους, ἐπίκλησιν δὲ Ξούθου. ἔγραψε δὲ μέλη πολλὰ καὶ τραγῳδίας καὶ φιλόσοφόν τι σύγγραμμα τὸν Τριαγμὸν ἐπιγραφόμενον, ὅπερ Καλλίμαχος ἀντιλέγεσθαί φησιν…

about his travels and acquaintances. Besides this and his dramas he composed a variety of other works which are now only sparsely represented in the fragments, including lyrics, dithyrambs and convivial elegies, a Foundation of Chios *(possibly an elegy rather than a prose work as widely supposed)*[1] *and the philosophical* Triagmos *(cf.* ***T 1*** *with note below).*

Ion's dramas seem (not surprisingly) to have been read more widely than the rest of his works in antiquity; sources sometimes refer to him as 'Ion the tragedian', and he appears in lists of famous tragedians preserved in some Byzantine manuscripts.[2] *Hellenistic and later scholars consulted and commented on his works.*[3] *More than half of the fragments in Leurini's comprehensive edition are dramatic, including seventeen from* Omphale*, the only play identified (once, F 18) as satyric. None is specifically identified as tragic, but the ten other preserved titles probably belong to tragedies (*Alcmene, Laertes *and* Mega Drama *are possible exceptions). Considering Ion's importance in the literary tradition it is unfortunate that the fragments yield so little. Only one tragic fragment (**F 38**) amounts to more than three verses, and most come from baldly lexicographical sources. There are however some tantalizing hints about plots: see introductions to the individual plays below.*

Testimonia

T 1 (4 Leur.) Suda, 'Ion'
Ion, Chian, tragedian, lyric poet and philosopher, son of Orthomenes, nicknamed son of Xuthus. He began producing tragedies in the 82nd Olympiad (452/1–449/8 BC). His plays number 12 — some say 30, others 40…*(three more sentences repeating the content of* ***T 2(b)*** *and* ***T 3****)*

— Harpocration, *Lexicon to the Ten Attic Orators*: 'Ion: Isocrates in the speech on the Antidosis (Isocr. 15.268). The orator would be referring to the tragic poet Ion, who was a Chian by birth, son of Orthomenes, nicknamed son of Xuthus. He wrote many songs (i.e. lyric and choral works), and tragedies, and a philosophical work entitled the *Triagmos*, which Callimachus says is disputed…

[1] Cf. Cerri 1977, Leurini 2000, 60–62, Valerio 2010, 159–61 with recent history of the question.

[2] Cf. T 7a–b (= CAT A 2–3) in *TrGF*, T 15–19 and frs 98, 115 Leurini. For the reception and recollection of Ion in antiquity see Henderson 2007, Olding 2007a.

[3] T 20–32 Leurini.

T 2 (7–8 Leur.)

(a) Aristophanes, *Peace* 832–37

Οικ. οὐκ ἦν ἄρ' οὐδ' ἃ λέγουσι, κατὰ τὸν αἰθέρα
ὡς ἀστέρες γιγνόμεθ', ὅταν τις ἀποθάνῃ;
Τρυ. μάλιστα.
Οικ. καὶ τίς ἐστιν ἀστὴρ νῦν ἐκεῖ;
Τρυ. Ἴων ὁ Χῖος, ὅσπερ ἐποίησεν πάλαι
ἐνθάδε τὸν Ἀοῖόν ποθ'· ὡς δ' ἦλθ', εὐθέως
Ἀοῖον αὐτὸν πάντες ἐκάλουν ἀστέρα.

(b) Schol.$^{RV\Gamma(Lh)}$ *Peace* 835–37 (~ Suda *δ* 1029 = T 11 Leur.)
Ἴων διθυράμβων ποιητὴς καὶ τραγῳδίας καὶ μελῶν. ἐποίησε δὲ ᾠδὴν ἧς ἡ ἀρχή· *ἀοῖον ἀεροφοίταν* | *ἀστέρα μείναμεν, ἀελίου* | *λευκῇ πτέρυγι πρόδρομον*. φαίνεται δὲ τετελευτηκὼς εἶναι ἐκ τούτων. παίζων οὖν ὁ Ἀριστοφάνης ἀοῖον αὐτόν φησιν ἀστέρα κληθῆναι . . . (*more in* ***T 3(b)***).

T 3 (12 Leur.)

(a) Athenaeus 1.3f (~ Suda *α* 731)
ὁ δὲ Χῖος Ἴων τραγῳδίαν νικήσας Ἀθήνησιν ἑκάστῳ τῶν Ἀθηναίων ἔδωκε Χίου κεράμιον.

(b) Schol.$^{V(\Gamma)}$ Ar. *Peace* 835–37
φασὶ δὲ αὐτὸν ὁμοῦ διθύραμβον καὶ τραγῳδίαν ἀγωνισάμενον ἐν τῇ Ἀττικῇ νικῆσαι, καὶ εὐνοίας χάριν προῖκα Χῖον οἶνον πέμψαι Ἀθηναίοις.

T 5 (6 Leur.) Hypoth. Eur. *Hippolytus*
ἐδιδάχθη ἐπὶ Ἐπαμείνονος ἄρχοντος ὀλυμπιάδι πζ´ ἔτει δ´. πρῶτος Εὐριπίδης, δεύτερος Ἰοφῶν, τρίτος Ἴων.

T 6 (17 Leur.) 'Longinus' 33.5
τί δέ; ἐν μέλεσι μᾶλλον ἂν εἶναι Βακχυλίδης ἕλοιο ἢ Πίνδαρος, καὶ ἐν τραγῳδίᾳ Ἴων ὁ Χῖος ἢ νὴ Δία Σοφοκλῆς; ἐπειδὴ οἱ μὲν ἀδιάπτωτοι καὶ ἐν τῷ γλαφυρῷ πάντη κεκαλλιγραφημένοι, ὁ δὲ Πίνδαρος καὶ ὁ Σοφοκλῆς ὁτὲ μὲν οἷον πάντα ἐπιφλέγουσι τῇ φορᾷ, σβέννυνται δ' ἀλόγως πολλάκις καὶ πίπτουσιν ἀτυχέστατα. ἢ οὐδεὶς ἂν εὖ φρονῶν ἑνὸς δράματος, τοῦ Οἰδίποδος, εἰς ταὐτὸ συνθεὶς τὰ Ἴωνος ⟨πάντ'⟩ ἀντιτιμήσαιτο ἑξῆς.

T 2 (7–8 Leur.)

(a) Aristophanes, *Peace*

Servant. So it's not true, what they say, that we become stars in the sky when one of us dies?

Trygaeus. It certainly is!

Servant. So who's a star there now?

Trygaeus. Ion of Chios — down here he composed *The Dawn Star*, and as soon as he got there, they all started calling him 'Dawn-Star'.

(b) Scholia on the above

Ion, a poet of dithyrambs, tragedy and lyric poems. He composed a song which begins, 'We awaited the air-roving dawn-star, sun's forerunner on pale wing'. This (i.e. Trygaeus's remark) shows that he had died. So Aristophanes jokingly says he has been named Dawn-star . . . *(more, partly unreliable, about Ion's works in numerous poetic and prose genres, followed in one ms. by **T 3(b)**)*.

T 3 (12 Leur.)

(a) Athenaeus, *Sophists at Dinner*

Ion of Chios, on winning the tragic competition at Athens, gave each of the Athenians a jar of Chian wine.

(b) Scholia on Aristophanes' *Peace*

They say that he (i.e. Ion) competed and won in both dithyramb and tragedy in Attica, and sent Chian wine as a goodwill gift to the Athenians.

T 5 (6 Leur.) Hypothesis to Euripides' *Hippolytus*

It (i.e. Euripides' *Hippolytus*) was produced in the archonship of Epameinon, the 4th year of the 87th Olympiad (429/8 BC). First Euripides, second Iophon, third Ion.

T 6 (17 Leur.) 'Longinus', *On sublimity of style*

Or again, in lyric poetry would you rather be Bacchylides than Pindar, and in tragedy Ion of Chios — by Zeus! — rather than Sophocles? Those two are faultless and consistently fine in the smoothness of their writing, whereas Pindar and Sophocles sometimes set everything alight with their intensity but often are unexpectedly doused and fall disastrously. Surely no one in his right mind would compare *(all)* of Ion's dramas with a single one, the *Oedipus*, and consider them of equal value!

ΑΓΑΜΕΜΝΩΝ

The title suggests a play like those of Aeschylus and Seneca: Agamemnon returning from Troy to be murdered by his wife Clytemnestra and his usurping cousin Aegisthus. ***F 1–3*** *have been tentatively connected with such a plot. No other Greek tragedies on this subject are recorded, except perhaps the ΑΓΑ[listed in the Didascaliae as victorious at the*

F 1 (1 Leur.) Athenaeus 11.468c (~ Hesychius δ 145, Eustathius on *Iliad* 23.270)

'δακτυλωτὸν ἔκπωμα' οὕτως καλούμενον παρὰ Ἴωνι ἐν Ἀγαμέμνονι·

οἴσῃ δὲ δῶρον ἄξιον δραμήματος
ἔκπωμα δακτυλωτόν, ἄχραντον πυρί,
Πελίου μέγ' ἆθλον, Κάστορος δ' ἔργον ποδῶν.

F 2 (2 Leur.) Stobaeus 4.52b.36

Ἴωνος Ἀγαμέμνονος·

κακῶν ἀπέστω θάνατος, ὡς ἴδῃ κακά.

Brief fragments. **F 3** (3 L.) ἱππικὸν χλίδος, **F 4** (4 L.) πεδανῷ ὕπνῳ, **F 5** (5 L.) αἰετοί

ΑΛΚΜΗΝΗ

The subject was probably the seduction of Alcmene by Zeus in the form of her absent husband Amphitryon, which resulted in the birth of Heracles, a story well known in early epic and treated in Euripides' Alcmene *(probably after Ion's death). Other tragedies with this title are attributed*

F 5a (6 Leur.) Photius α 544 ('*ἄϊδρα*')

καὶ μὴν ἅπαντα τίκτεται πρώταις γοναῖς
ἄϊδρα, πειραθέντα δ' ἐκδιδάσκεται.

πρώταις Phot.[z] πρῶτον Phot.[b]

Brief fragments. **F 6** (7 L.) καταφάρκτοις ψυχαῖς, **F 7** (8 L.) σάγη φερέσβιος, **F 8** (9 L.) αὐτάγητοι

AGAMEMNON

Lenaea of 419 BC, a few years after Ion's death.[4] *It was however treated in at least two Roman tragedies of the Republican period, Livius Andronicus's* Aegisthus *and Accius's* Clytaemnestra, *which were presumably modelled on a Greek exemplar, possibly Ion's play, and whose fragments show some similarities with Seneca's (»» Tarrant 1976, 11–14, 17f.)*

F 1 Athenaeus, *Sophists at Dinner*

The 'fingered cup', so named in Ion's *Agamemnon*:

> And you shall win a gift worthy of your running, a fingered drinking-cup unsullied by fire, a great prize from Pelias earned by Castor's feet.

F 2 Stobaeus, *Anthology*, 'Praise of death'

From Ion's *Agamemnon*:

> Of (all) evils let (only) death be absent, so he may see evils.

Brief fragments. **F 3** horseman's finery, **F 4** in light sleep, **F 5** pediment (lit. 'eagle's wings')

ALCMENE

to Aeschylus (doubtfully), Astydamas II and Dionysius of Syracuse. Plautus's Latin comedy Amphitryon *has the same subject: »» Collard–Cropp 2008a, 100–3. Some scholars locate* Alcmene *in a tetralogy with* Sons of Eurytus *and the satyric* Omphale*: see below on* Sons of Eurytus.

F 5a Photius, *Lexicon*

> Moreover, all things are born unknowing at their first birth, and acquire knowledge through experience.

Brief fragments. **F 6** with enclosed (i.e. unwitting) minds, **F 7** a victual-bag, **F 8** self-admiring

---

[4] *IG* II^2 2319–2323a.71 = *TrGF* 1 DID A 2b.71 = *TrGF* 2 adesp. F 1.

ΑΡΓΕΙΟΙ

The title may indicate a connection with the legend of the Seven against Thebes, or of their sons the Epigoni who avenged them. Aeschylus's Women (*or* Men) of Argos *(title ambiguously recorded) seems to have*

F 8a (10 Leur.) Photius *α* 1509 ('*ἀναιτίατος*')

οὐδεὶς ἀναιτίατος ἀγγέλλων κακά.

Brief fragments. **F 9** (11 L.) ὡς παλαιὸν †ακις† σάρον,[5] **F 9a** (12 L.) φαιδρός

ΕΥΡΥΤΙΔΑΙ

The title suggests the story of Heracles at Oechalia, best known now as the back-story of Sophocles' Women of Trachis *but told at length in the lost epic* Sack of Oechalia *and reflected with variations in other archaic and fifth-century literature and art (»» Gantz 1993, 434–47, 457f.; Fowler 2013, 329–33). Heracles quarrelled with king Eurytus and his sons, his hosts at Oechalia either during an archery contest, perhaps with the king's daughter Iole as prize, or after falling in love with Iole and having his demand for her refused. He proceeded to kill the sons, destroy the city, and take possession of Iole; or he was humiliatingly expelled, retaliated later by killing one of the sons, Iphitus, after receiving*

F 10 (13 Leur.) Athenaeus 11.495a–b

Κράτης δ' ἐν δευτέρῳ Ἀττικῆς Διαλέκτου γράφει οὕτως· οἱ χόες πελίκαι, καθάπερ εἴπομεν, ὠνομάζοντο. ὁ δὲ τύπος ἦν τοῦ ἀγγείου πρότερον μὲν τοῖς Παναθηναϊκοῖς ἐοικώς, ἡνίκα ἐκαλεῖτο πελίκη, ὕστερον δὲ ἔσχεν οἰνοχόης σχῆμα, οἷοί εἰσιν οἱ ἐν τῇ ἑορτῇ παρατιθέμενοι, ὁποίους δή ποτε ὄλπας ἐκάλουν, χρώμενοι πρὸς τὴν τοῦ οἴνου ἔγχυσιν, καθάπερ Ἴων ὁ Χῖος ἐν Εὐρυτίδαις φησίν·

ἐκ ζαθέων πιθακνῶν ἀφύσαντες ὄλπαις
οἶνον ὑπερφίαλον κελαρύζετε.

---

[5] Cited by Hesychius to illustrate the use of the word σάρον, so editors assume the preceding word is corrupt. However, '[t]he word *akissaros* is still the name of a bush in the villages of NE Chios, the branch of which is used as a broom' (Haviaras 2007, 70).

MEN OF ARGOS

been concerned with the aftermath of the deaths of the Seven, but very little is known about that play either.

F 8a Photius, *Lexicon*

No one escapes blame when he brings bad news.

Brief fragments. **F 9** like an old…broom (i.e. useless), **F 9a** radiant (with joy)

SONS OF EURYTUS

him as a guest, and so incurred a year's exile and servitude to the Lydian queen Omphale, after which he returned to destroy Oechalia and take Iole. Either way she would be the cause of his death through the jealousy of his wife Deianeira. Ion's plot is unknown, but it may well have centered on the banquet (see **F 10** *with note) and the quarrel between Heracles and the sons of Eurytus. Scholars have surmised that this and the satyr-play* Omphale *were produced together; if so, their plots must have been compatible, but nothing in the fragments of* Omphale *(»» O'Sullivan–Collard 2013, 414–25) sheds light on the matter. Some go further and assign* Alcmene *to the same tetralogy, but the connection is remote.*

F 10 Athenaeus, *Sophists at Dinner*

Crates in the second book of his *Attic Dialect* writes as follows: 'Pitchers (*choes*) used to be called *pelikai*, as we have said. The shape of the vessel was previously similar to the Panathenaic cups,[6] when it was called a *pelikê*; but later it took the form of a wine-jug (*oinochoê*) — those, that is, of the kind that are set out at the festival,[7] which at one time they called *olpai*, using them for decanting wine, as Ion of Chios says in *Sons of Eurytus*:

Draw potent wine from divinely scented casks in *olpai*, and pour it with a splash!

---

[6] A type of large drinking-cup associated with the Panathenaea festival; briefly described by Athenaeus in the same catalogue (11. 494f–495a).

[7] i.e. the Athenian–Ionian Anthesteria, a spring festival celebrating the opening of wine from the latest vintage and on its second day, the 'Choes', featuring drinking contests using special jugs (*choes*: »» Burkert 1985, 237–42, Parker 2005, 290–316).

Brief fragments. **F 11** (14 L.) ἀθίκτ⟨ους κ⟩όρας, **F 12** (15 L.) ἰήιος, **F 13** (16 L.) κυδρός, **F 13a** (17 L.) ψαλάσσων

ΛΑΕΡΤΗΣ

The events of the final book of the Odyssey *are a likely subject: Odysseus finds his aged father in his rural retreat, teases him by concealing his identity, and finally relents and is reunited with him; they and their allies then await an attack from the vengeful relatives of the Suitors, which proceeds until Zeus and Athena intervene and restore peace.* **F 14** *with its agitated metre might come from a scene in which Laertes anticipates the attack. An entirely different possibility (less easily related with* **F 14***) is the story of how the young Laertes married Anticlea, daughter of Autolycus, when she was already pregnant with Odysseus after being seduced by the trickster Sisyphus. The seduction was the subject of one of Euripides' two satyr-plays named* Autolycus

F 14 (18 Leur.) Athenaeus 6.267d

Ἴων δ' ὁ Χῖος ἐν Λαέρτῃ τὸν οἰκέτην ἐπὶ δούλου τέθεικεν εἰπών·

ἴθι μοι δόμον, οἰκέτα,
κλῇσον ὑπόπτερος,
μή τις ἔλθῃ βροτῶν.

ΜΕΓΑ ΔΡΑΜΑ

This cryptically named play is cited three times in lexicographic sources. Some have thought the narthêx *in F 15 might be the fennel-stalk in which Prometheus conveyed fire to mankind, or a wand (thyrsus) of the kind carried by Bacchants.*

Brief fragments. **F 15** (19 L.) ψαθαρὸν νάρθηκα, **F 16** (20 L.) μελαγχαίταν(?), **F 17** (21 L.) ὀνοταζομένη

F 17a–33a *are the fragments of the satyr-play* Omphale.

Brief fragments. **F 11** untouched girls, **F 12** a lament (*or* lamenting?), **F 13** proud, **F 13a** touching

LAERTES

(»» O'Sullivan–Collard 2013, 384f.) and possibly of other plays named Sisyphus. *Erika Simon (1995, modifying A. Furtwängler) detected a tragic representation of this story in a late 5th-century Apulian vase (Munich 3268:* LIMC I, *'Antikleia', no. 1). On her interpretation the vase shows Sisyphus exhibiting the pregnant bride Anticlea to his friends while Laertes learns of his predicament from Autolycus and (presumably) decides not to renounce her. If this is correct, Ion's* Laertes *is the only known candidate for the featured play and the vase provides significant information about its content.*

No other play about Laertes is known, but a composition (nome?) so named is attributed to Timotheus (Suda τ 620; PMG *784).*

F 14 Athenaeus, *Sophists at Dinner*

And Ion of Chios in *Laertes* has put 'servant' (*oiketês*) for 'slave' (*doulos*), saying:

Go, servant, fly and bar the house, that none may come.

THE BIG DRAMA

Brief fragments. **F 15** a fragile fennel-stalk (*or* rod), **F 16** black-haired(?), **F 17** demeaning

F 17a–33a *are the fragments of the satyr-play* Omphale.

ΤΕΥΚΡΟΣ

Teucer was the son of the Salaminian hero Telamon and half-brother to Ajax. He assisted Ajax at Troy and secured his burial there with Odysseus's support. On returning to Salamis he was exiled by Telamon for failing to prevent Ajax's suicide and bring home Ajax's son Eurysaces, from whom he had been separated during the wreck of the Greek fleet returning from Troy. In his exile he founded the city of Salamis in Cyprus (»» Gantz 1993, 224f., 694f.). His condemnation by Telamon was probably the subject of Aeschylus's Women of Salamis, *and certainly of Sophocles'* Teucer *and the Latin* Telamo *of Ennius and* Teucer *of Pacuvius (whose Greek models are uncertain: »» Schierl 2006, 468–74). The* Teucer *with which Euaretus won second prize at the Dionysia of 341, and another by the Hellenistic poet Nicomachus of Alexandria Troas, are known only as titles (*TrGF *85 T 1, 127 F 1).*

F 34 (39 Leur.) Photius *α* 543 ('*ἄϊδρος*': ~ Hesychius *α* 1795, '*ἄϊδροι*')

ἡμεῖς τ' ἄϊδροι πρὸς πέτραις ἐπταίομεν.

Brief fragment. **F 35** (40 L.) ἀμφιβῶτις (*or* -βώτης)

ΦΟΙΝΙΞ Η ΚΑΙΝΕΥΣ

*Three fragments are cited by Athenaeus (***F 38–40***), and a fourth in the scholia on Aristophanes'* Frogs *(***F 41***: see note there), from '*Phoenix or Caeneus*'. Four more are cited simply from '*Phoenix*' by Athenaeus (***F 36***), Pollux (***F 37***) and Photius (***F 41a–b***).* **F 42** *and* **F 43** *are cited from '*Phoenix B*' by Athenaeus and Hesychius respectively. Since Ion will hardly have produced three* Phoenixes, *the first two are presumably the same play; this is confirmed if* **F 38** *from '*Phoenix or Caeneus*' and* **F 36** *from '*Phoenix*' belong together as they seem to. None of the fragments is particularly informative, but one or both plays probably involved the Phoenix who appears as Achilles' tutor in the* Iliad *(rather than the Tyrian son of Agenor and brother of Cadmus who gave his name to the Phoenicians). In* Iliad *9.447–95 Phoenix tells Achilles how he seduced his father's concubine, was cursed by him with childlessness, and fled to Phthia. That story was retold in Euripides'* Phoenix, *but with*

TEUCER

F 34 *probably refers to a shipwreck; a likely context is the wreck of the returning Greek fleet, which was certainly reported in Pacuvius's play and probably in Sophocles'. Ion's play might have been similar to theirs, although it could have treated a later stage of Teucer's story and included a retrospective narrative of his earlier misfortunes.*

Aristotle twice cites examples of Teucer defending himself against accusations of treachery brought by Odysseus (at Troy?) in a play named simply Teucer *(*Rhet. *1398a3ff., 1416a37ff.). These are often attributed to Sophocles (Radt includes them as Soph. F **579a–b), although they seem quite inconsistent with what we know of it. It is however unlikely that Aristotle would have cited Ion's play without naming him. He does not cite him elsewhere at all.*

F 34 Photius, *Lexicon*

And we, unknowing, ran upon the rocks.

Brief fragment. **F 35** famous

PHOENIX OR CAENEUS

Phoenix falsely accused of the seduction and blinded by his father, to be healed later by Cheiron. Other Phoenix *tragedies by Sophocles (perhaps identical with his* Dolopians*), Astydamas II and Ath?]enodorus (*TrGF *no. 154) may have been similar. Euripides' play seems to have been the basis of Ennius's Latin* Phoenix. »» *Gantz 1993, 618; Collard–Cropp 2008b, 405–7.*

The title Phoenix or Caeneus *is however puzzling. Caeneus was the transgendered and invulnerable Lapith hero whom the Centaurs killed by hammering him into the ground. His only known connections with Phoenix are that both belong to Thessalian legend and both are named (with thirty-four others) in Ovid's list of the Calydonian Boarhunters (*Metamorphoses *8.300ff.). How both could have been leading figures in the same play is a mystery.*

F 38 (44 Leur.) Athenaeus 3.91d (~ Zenobius 5.68 and others; vv. 4–5 Plut. *Mor.* 971f; only Athenaeus names the play)

ὅτι δὲ οἱ ἐχῖνοι, λέγω δὲ καὶ τοὺς χερσαίους καὶ τοὺς θαλαττίους, καὶ ἑαυτῶν εἰσι φυλακτικοὶ πρὸς τοὺς θηρῶντας, προβαλλόμενοι τὰς ἀκάνθας ὥσπερ τι χαράκωμα, Ἴων ὁ Χῖος μαρτυρεῖ ἐν Φοίνικι ἢ Καινεῖ λέγων οὕτως·

ἀλλ᾽ ἔν τε χέρσῳ τὰς λέοντος ᾔνεσα
ἢ τὰς ἐχίνου μᾶλλον οἰζυρὰς τέχνας·
ὃς εὖτ᾽ ἂν ἄλλων κρεισσόνων ὁρμὴν μάθῃ,
στρόβιλος ἀμφ᾽ ἄκανθαν εἱλίξας δέμας
κεῖται δακεῖν τε καὶ θιγεῖν ἀμήχανος.

F 36 (45 Leur.) Athenaeus 7.318e

τοῦ πολύποδος μνημονεύει καὶ ὁ τραγικὸς Ἴων ἐν Φοίνικι λέγων·

καὶ τὸν πετραῖον πλεκτάναις ἀναίμοσι
στυγῶ μεταλλακτῆρα πουλύπουν χροός.

F 37 (46 Leur.) Pollux 9.37

καλοῖτο δ᾽ ἂν καὶ κῶμαι ταῦτα, ὅθεν καὶ κωμήτας τοὺς γείτονας καὶ κωμήτιδας ὠνόμαζον . . . Ἴων δὲ ἐν Φοίνικι σαφέστερον·

ἀλλ᾽ ὦ θυρέτρων τῶνδε κωμῆται θεοί

F 39 (42 Leur.) Athenaeus 4.184f (with **F 42** and **F 45**)

Ἴων δ᾽ ἐν Φοίνικι ἢ Καινεῖ ἀλέκτορα τὸν αὐλὸν καλεῖ ἐν τούτοις·

ἐπὶ δ᾽ αὐλὸς ἀλέκτωρ
Λύδιον ὕμνον ἀχέων

F 40 (43 Leur.) Athenaeus 10.451d

Ἴων δὲ ἐν Φοίνικι ἢ Καινεῖ δρυὸς ἱδρῶτα εἴρηκε τὸν ἰξὸν ἐν τούτοις·

δρυός μ᾽ ἱδρώς
καὶ θαμνομήκης ῥάβδος ἥ τ᾽ Αἰγυπτία
βόσκει λινουλκὸς χλαῖνα, θήραγρος πέδη.

F 41 (41 Leur.) Schol. Ar. *Frogs* 706

εἰ δ᾽ ἐγὼ ὀρθὸς ἰδεῖν: τοῦτο Ἴωνός ἐστιν ἐκ Φοίνικος ἢ Καινέως·

εἰ δ᾽ ἐγὼ ὀρθὸς ἰδεῖν βίον ἀνέρος, ⟨ὦ⟩ πολιῆται

Καινέως Bentley καὶ Οἰνέως schol.

F 38 Athenaeus, *Sophists at Dinner*

And that *echinoi*, both land and sea types (i.e. hedgehogs and sea-urchins), are also very protective of themselves against predators, projecting their spines like a sort of palisade, is confirmed by Ion of Chios in *Phoenix or Caeneus*, saying:

> But on dry land I approve the lion's arts rather than the low tricks of the hedgehog, who when he discerns the onset of stronger creatures wraps his spikes around his body in a ball and lies impervious to bite or touch.

F 36 Athenaeus, *Sophists at Dinner*

The octopus is mentioned by the tragedian Ion in *Phoenix*, saying:

> I loathe also the octopus, rock-clinging with bloodless tentacles, that changes the colour of its skin.

F 37 Pollux, *Dictionary*

These (neighbourhoods) could also be called *kômai* ('villages'), and hence they called neighbours *kômêtai* and (fem.) *kômêtides* ('villagers') . . . (*two examples from Aristophanes*) . . . and Ion in *Phoenix* more clearly:

> Come, gods, you neighbours of these portals . . .

F 39 (42 Leur.) Athenaeus, *Sophists at Dinner* (with **F 42** and **F 45**)

And Ion in *Phoenix or Caeneus* calls the aulos 'cockerel', in these words:

> And with it the cockerel aulos sounding a Lydian song

F 40 Athenaeus, *Sophists at Dinner*

And Ion in *Phoenix or Caeneus* has called birdlime 'oak-sweat', in these words:

> Oak-sweat, a bush-length rod, and this cloak of Egyptian linen, my hunting-net, are my sustenance.

F 41 (41 Leur.) Scholia on Aristophanes' *Frogs*

If I am correct in seeing: this is Ion's, from *Phoenix or Caeneus*:

> If I am correct in seeing a man's life, *(O)* citizens . . .

F 41b (48 Leur.) Photius *α* 1294 (‘*ἀμφαδόν*’)

ὡς ἀμφαδὸν πέπραγα πανταχῇ καλῶς.

Brief fragment. **F 41a** (47 L.) ἐκ τῶν ἀΐδρων

ΦΟΙΝΙΞ Β΄

See above on Phoenix or Caeneus.

F 42 (49 Leur.) Athenaeus 4.185a (with **F 39** and **F 45**)

ἐν δὲ τῷ β΄ Φοίνικι ὁ αὐτὸς Ἴων φησίν·

ἐκτύπουν ἄγων βαρὺν
αὐλὸν τρέχοντι ῥυθμῷ,

οὕτω λέγων τὸν Φρύγιον· βαρὺς γὰρ οὗτος.

ἐκτύπουν Bentley ἔκτυπον Ath.

Brief fragment. **F 43** (50 L.) τιμαλφής

ΦΡΟΥΡΟΙ

*The title and the inclusion of a conversation between Helen and Odysseus (***F 44***) suggest that the play was about the episode near the end of the Trojan War in which Odysseus entered Troy as a spy, disguised as a beggar or deserter, and was recognized but not betrayed by Helen (thus Welcker 1841, 948ff.). In* Odyssey *4.240ff. Helen, now long returned to Sparta, recalls how after recognizing Odysseus she bathed, clothed and exchanged information with him, and let him escape killing many Trojans as he went. In the* Little Iliad *(as summarized by Proclus p. 123* GEF *= F **43a) Odysseus and Helen made an agreement ‘about the taking of the city’, and Odysseus returned later to steal the Palladion; presumably the theft and Helen’s ‘rescue’ from Troy had been the subject of their agreement. Besides* **F 44***, a few other fragments of Ion’s play (***F 43b, 45, 46***, possibly* **53b***) are at least compatible with this scenario (see notes on these). The episode is variously summarized in later sources, some combining the spying mission and the theft of the Palladion in a single exploit (e.g. Apollod.* epit. *5.13) as Sophocles seems to have done in his* Laconian Women *(Soph. F 367–369a: »» Gantz 1993, 641–43). The list of tragic plots yielded by the* Little

F 41b Photius, *Lexicon*

For plainly I've fared well in every way.

Brief fragment. **F 41a** from the unknowing

PHOENIX B

See above on Phoenix or Caeneus.

F 42 (49 Leur.) Athenaeus, *Sophists at Dinner* (with **F 39** and **F 45**)
And in the second *Phoenix* the same Ion says:

I made the deep-voiced aulos sound with a running beat,

meaning the Phrygian aulos, which is deep-toned.

Brief fragment. **F 43** esteemed (lit. 'honour-gathering')

GUARDS

Iliad *which is interpolated in Aristotle,* Poetics *1459b5f. includes both a* Ptôcheia *(*'Beggar episode'*) and a* Laconian Women.

*The play's presumed subject raises some interesting questions of dramatization. Was it set in darkness, or near-darkness (***F 45**, **F 53b?***)? If the Guards were the chorus, what were they guarding and how did Odysseus interact with them? Did they arrest him and bring him to Helen (Welcker 948f.)? Did Helen converse with him (***F 44***) before she recognized him, with or without the Chorus present? How was the recognition handled, and how much of the interaction between Odysseus and Helen took place indoors, i.e. offstage (***F 43b***)? What other characters were involved (see on* **F 44** *concerning Hecuba)? Some possibilities are suggested by the extant* Rhesus *(a fourth-century play wrongly attributed to Euripides), which is set at night with a chorus of Trojans guarding their camp outside the city; they leave the scene for some time, thus allowing Odysseus and Diomedes to enter unwitnessed, meet and get guidance from the goddess Athena (who distracts a suspicious Paris by impersonating his ally Aphrodite), slaughter the newly arrived Thracian king Rhesus and many of his men, and dodge the returning chorus as they escape. Ion's play might have featured some similarly adventurous staging, but as things stand this is all matter for conjecture.*

F 43b (51 Leur.) Herodian, *Περὶ καθολικῆς προσῳδίας* fr. 24 Hunger (‘*εὐναῖος*’)

καὶ πῶς παρῆλθεν θάλαμον εὐναῖον ξένος;

ξένος West ξένον Hdn.

F 43c (52 Leur.) Herodian, *Περὶ καθολ. προσῳδ.* fr. 25 Hunger (‘*τροπαῖος*’)

τροπαῖος αὖ με παρεφόβησεν αὔρα.

τροπαῖος Cropp –ον Hdn. αυρα or αβρα read by Hunger

F 44 (53 Leur.) Schol. Ar. *Frogs* 1425 (~ Suda *σ* 511, ‘*σιγῶ*’)

ποθεῖ μέν, ἐχθαίρει δέ: παρὰ τὰ ἐκ τῶν Ἴωνος Φρουρῶν, ὅπου ἡ Ἑλένη πρὸς τὸν Ὀδυσσέα φησί·

σιγᾷ μέν, ἐχθαίρει δέ, βούλεταί γε μήν

F 45 (54 Leur.) Athenaeus 4.185a (with **F 39** and **F 42**)

ἐν δὲ Φρουροῖς τὸν ἀλεκτρυόνα Ἰδαῖον εἴρηκε σύριγγα διὰ τούτων·

ῥοθεῖ δέ τοι σῦριγξ Ἰδαῖος ἀλέκτωρ.

ῥοθεῖ Nauck προθεῖ Ath.

F 46 (55 Leur.) Hesychius *ν* 601 (~ Photius *ν* 230)

νιφόεσσ᾽ Ἑλένη

νιφόεσσα σελήνη Phot.

Brief fragments. **F 47** (56 L.) πυργείαν ⟨σ⟩κοπήν, **F 48** (57 L.) στέφανοι χειρῶν, **F 49** (58 L.) κλητῆρα, **F 49a** (59 L.) προσφοραῖος

Incertae Fabulae

F 50 (*60 Leur.) Athenaeus 1.21a

ἔταττον γὰρ τὸ ὀρχεῖσθαι ἐπὶ τοῦ κινεῖσθαι καὶ ἐρεθίζεσθαι. Ἀνακρέων (fr. 45 *PMG*) *καλλίκομοι κοῦραι Διὸς ὠρχήσαντ᾽ ἐλαφρῶς.* Ἴων·

ἐκ τῶν ἀέλπτων μᾶλλον ὤρχησαι φρένας.

F 43b (51 Leur.) Herodian, *General Prosody*

And how did the stranger reach the marital chamber?

F 43c (52 Leur.) Herodian, *General Prosody*

And now a veering wind has moved me to fear.

F 44 (53 Leur.) Scholia on Aristophanes' *Frogs*

It longs for him, loathes him: imitating the passage in Ion's *Guards*, where Helen says to Odysseus:

He (she?, it?) keeps silent but loathes him (me?), yet wishes…

F 45 (54 Leur.) Athenaeus, *Sophists at Dinner* (with **F 39** and **F 42**)

And in *Guards* he (Ion) has termed the cockerel 'Idaean syrinx', in these words:

And hark, the cockerel crows, the Idaean syrinx.

F 46 (55 Leur.) Hesychius, *Lexicon*

Snow-white Helen

Brief fragments. **F 47** a high watch-tower, **F 48** 'arm-garlands' (i.e. bracelets), **F 49** a herald (*or* summoner?), **F 49a** beneficial (*or* appropriate)

Unidentified Plays

F 50 (*60 Leur.) Athenaeus, *Sophists at Dinner*

They used 'dancing' for 'moving oneself' and 'being excited'. Anacreon, 'the lovely-haired daughters of Zeus moved nimbly'. Ion:

These unexpected events have set your heart dancing more.

F 53 (*63 Leur.) Philo, *Quod omnis probus liber sit* 134

τοῦ δὲ περὶ τοὺς ὄρνιθας ἐναγωνίου μέμνηται καὶ ὁ τραγικὸς Ἴων διὰ τούτων·

οὐδ' ὅ γε σῶμα τυπεὶς διφυεῖς τε κόρας ἐπιλάθεται ἀλκᾶς,
ἀλλ' ὀλιγοδρανέων φθογγάζεται·
θάνατον δ' ὅ γε δουλοσύνας προβέβουλε.

F 53b (65 Leur.) Photius α 1167 ('*ἀμβλὺς ὄρθρος*')

νῦν δ' ἐγγὺς ἠοῦς ἡνίκ' οὐδέπω φάος
οὐδ' ἀμβλὺς ὄρθρος.

F 53e (*67 Leur.) Photius α 2032 ('*ἄνοπλοι*')

ἀπροσδόκητοι κἄνοπλοι πορθούμεθα.

F 54 (*69 Leur.) [Plutarch], *Mor.* 113b

τούτων γὰρ (*sc.* τῶν Αἰγυπτίων κτλ) τοὺς μὲν εἰς βόθρους τινὰς καταδύντας ἱστοροῦσιν ἐπὶ πλείους ἡμέρας μένειν, μηδὲ τὸ τοῦ ἡλίου φῶς ὁρᾶν βουλομένους, ἐπειδὴ καὶ ὁ τετελευτηκὼς ἀπεστέρηται τούτου. Ἴων γοῦν ὁ τραγικὸς ποιητής, οὐκ ἀνήκοος ὢν τῆς τούτων εὐηθείας, πεποίηκέ τινα λέγουσαν·

ἐξῆλθον †οἱ μωνῆται καί τ' ἡμῶν† τροφὸς
παίδων, βόθρους λιποῦσα πενθητηρίους.

1 variously corrupted in Plut. mss. (οἱ μωνῆται καί τ' ἡμῶν *vel sim.* Φ, ἡμωνῆται καί τοὺς ἡμῶν Πυ, ἡμῶν καί τα ἤμ D, ἡμῶν καί τὰ ἡμῶν Z) ὑμῶν ἱκέτις ἡβώντων ms. B (15th C.)

F 55 (*70b Leur.) [Plutarch], *Mor.* 116d (~ Olympiodorus on Pl. *Alcib.* 129a and Schol. *ibid.*, both without attribution)

ἔν τε γὰρ τῷ γιγνώσκειν ἑαυτὸν περιέχεται τὸ μηδὲν ἄγαν, καὶ ἐν τούτῳ τὸ γιγνώσκειν ἑαυτόν. διὸ καὶ περὶ μὲν τούτου φησὶν ὁ Ἴων οὕτως·

τὸ γνῶθι σαυτὸν τοῦτ' ἔπος μὲν οὐ μέγα,
ἔργον δ' ὅσον Ζεὺς μόνος ἐπίσταται θεῶν.

F 56 (*71 Leur.) Plutarch, *Mor.* 466d

καὶ γὰρ ἡ γυνὴ λυπεῖ καὶ τὸν ἰατρὸν αἰτιῶνται καὶ δυσχεραίνουσι τὸ κλινίδιον,

φίλων δ' ὅ τ' ἐλθὼν λυπρὸς ὅ τ' ἀπιὼν βαρύς,

ὡς ὁ Ἴων φησίν.

F 53 (*63 Leur.) Philo, *That every good man is free*

Cock-fighting is also mentioned by the tragedian Ion, in these words:

> Nor, though stricken in body and both his eyes, does he forget his courage, but failing in strength gives voice. He for his part has preferred death over slavery.

F 53b (65 Leur.) Photius, *Lexicon*

> Now it is close to dawn, when it is not yet daylight nor dull twilight.

F 53e (*67 Leur.) Photius, *Lexicon*

> Unprepared and unarmed, we are (*or* were) overwhelmed.

F 54 (*69 Leur.) [Plutarch], *Consolation to Apollonius*

It is reported that some of them (i.e. Egyptians and other orientals, when mourning) descend into pits and stay there for several days, not wishing to see the sun's light themselves when the deceased has been deprived of it. At any rate the tragedian Ion, being not unacquainted with this silliness of theirs, has portrayed a woman saying:

> I have come out † . . . . . . † nurse of (*your?*) sons, leaving the pits of mourning.

F 55 (*70b Leur.) [Plutarch], *Consolation to Apollonius*

For 'Knowing oneself' encompasses 'Nothing too much', and 'Nothing too much' encompasses 'Knowing oneself'. Hence Ion says on this subject:

> This 'know yourself' is no great saying, but a practice so great that Zeus alone of the gods has mastered it.

F 56 (*71 Leur.) Plutarch, *On calmness of spirit*

For their wife irritates them, they criticize their doctor and complain about their bed, and

> a friend arriving pains them, one leaving depresses them,

as Ion says.

F 57 (*72 Leur.) Plutarch, *Mor.* 658c

τὴν δὲ σελήνην ἀδρανεστέρας ἀφιέναι τὰς αὐγάς·

μέλας γὰρ αὐταῖς οὐ πεπαίνεται βότρυς

κατὰ τὸν Ἴωνα.

— Plut. *Mor.* 929a: αὐγῆς (Sandbach: αὐτῆς mss.) δὲ νώθειαν καὶ τάχους ἀμβλύτητα καὶ τὸ θερμὸν ἀδρανὲς καὶ ἀμαυρόν, ᾧ κατὰ τὸν Ἴωνα *μέλας οὐ πεπαίνεται βότρυς*, εἰς τί θησόμεθα πλὴν ἀσθένειαν αὐτῆς καὶ πάθος;

F 58 (*70a Leur.) Plutarch, *Demosthenes* 3.1

Διὸ καὶ γράφοντες ἐν τῷ βιβλίῳ τούτῳ . . . περὶ Δημοσθένους καὶ Κικέρωνος, ἀπὸ τῶν πράξεων καὶ τῶν πολιτειῶν τὰς φύσεις αὐτῶν καὶ τὰς διαθέσεις πρὸς ἀλλήλας ἐπισκεψόμεθα, τὸ δὲ τοὺς λόγους ἀντεξετάζειν καὶ ἀποφαίνεσθαι . . . ἐάσομεν·

κακὴ γὰρ, ὥς φησιν ὁ Ἴων, δελφῖνος ἐν χέρσῳ βία.

F 59 (*73 Leur.) Pollux 7.60

ὁ δὲ κύπασσις λίνου ἐπεποίητο, σμικρὸς χιτωνίσκος, ἄχρι μέσου μηροῦ, ὡς Ἴων φησὶ·

βραχὺν λίνου κύπασσιν ἐς μηρὸν μέσον
ἐσταλμένος

F 60 (*74 Leur.) Schol. Eur. *Phoenissae* 209

ἀκάρπιστα δὲ πεδία τὴν θάλασσάν φησιν, ἐπεὶ πεζεύειν αἱ νῆες δοκοῦσιν ὀχήματος τρόπον· ὡς καὶ Ἴων λέγει·

ὅταν δὲ πόντου πεδίον Αἰγαῖον δράμω

F 63 (*76 Leur.) Critolaus fr. 34 Wehrli in Sext. Emp. *adv. math.* 2.20 (v. 3 cited by schol. *Iliad* 2.273 attrib. Ion, 7.152f. unattrib.; as a proverb by Eustathius on *Iliad* 7.161ff. and in *Or.* 16, p. 286 Wirth)

ἐκ μέσων μέντοι γε καὶ τὸν Χίων πρεσβευτὴν περὶ ἐξαγωγῆς πυροῦ δεόμενον, ἐπεὶ μακρῶς ἡρμήνευε τὴν δέησιν, ἄπρακτον ἐξαπέστειλαν, ἑτέρου δὲ πεμφθέντος συντομωτέρου, ἤπειγε γὰρ ἀνάγκη τοὺς Χίους, ἔδοσαν· κενὸν γὰρ θύλακον αὐτοῖς οὗτος ἀνατείνας ἀλφίτων αὐτὸν ἔφη δεῖσθαι. ὅμως δ᾽ οὖν καὶ τοῦτον ὡς ἀδολέσχην ἐμέμψαντο, ἀποχρώντως γὰρ κενὸς δειχθεὶς ὁ θύλακος ἐσήμηνε τὴν τῶν Χίων αἴτησιν. ἔνθεν ὁ τραγικὸς Ἴων κινηθεὶς εἶπεν ἐπ᾽ αὐτῶν·

οὐ γὰρ λόγοις Λάκαινα πυργοῦται πόλις,
ἀλλ᾽ εὖτ᾽ ἂν Ἄρης νεοχμὸς ἐμπέσῃ στρατῷ,
βουλὴ μὲν ἄρχει, χεὶρ δ᾽ ἐπεξεργάζεται.

F 57 (*72 Leur.) Plutarch, *Sympotic Questions*

. . . whereas the moon emits its rays with less effect:

For the dark grape-cluster is not ripened by them,

as Ion has it.

— Plutarch, *On the face in the moon's orb*: 'And the slowness and sluggishness of its (i.e. the moon's) rays, and the ineffectiveness and faintness of their heat by which, as Ion puts it, 'the dark grape-cluster is not ripened' — to what shall we attribute these if not to its weakness and passivity?'

F 58 (*70a Leur.) Plutarch, *Life of Demosthenes*

Therefore in writing in this book . . . about Demosthenes and Cicero we will study their natures and dispositions, in relation to each other, in the light of their actions and policies, and will refrain from comparing and appraising their speeches . . . for as Ion says,

A dolphin's strength is worthless on dry land.

F 59 (*73 Leur.) Pollux, *Dictionary*

The *kypassis* was made of linen, a little tunic reaching to the middle of the thigh, as Ion says:

dressed in a short kypassis of linen to mid-thigh

F 60 (*74 Leur.) Scholia on Euripides' *Phoenician Women*

He calls the sea 'unharvested plains' (*pedia*), because ships seem to 'trek' (*pezeuein*) over it like wagons. Similarly Ion says:

And when I run over the Aegean sea's plain . . .

F 63 (*76 Leur.) Critolaus fr. 34

Moreover they (the Spartans) dismissed from their midst unsatisfied the ambassador of the Chians who was requesting an export shipment of grain, because he explained the request at length; but when another was sent who spoke more concisely (for the Chians' need was very pressing) they granted it — he just held out an empty sack in front of them and said it needed grain. Even so, they criticized this one too for being talkative, since the sack displayed empty sufficiently indicated the Chians' request. Hence the tragedian Ion was moved to say of them:

The Spartan state is not fortified by words. When Ares falls anew
upon its host, counsel determines, action accomplishes.

Brief fragments from unidentified plays.[8] **F 51** (*61 L.) κότυλον οἴνου πλέον,[9] **F 52** (*62 L.) Νυμφαῖον ὄχθον, **F 53a** (*64 L.) ἀμβλώψ, **F 53d** (*66 L.) ἀναρσίας, **F 53f** (*68 L.) αὐτοφρόνων καὶ ὁμοσπόνδων, **F 61** (*75 L.) τύπτου τὸν αὐτοῦ κρᾶτα, **F 63a** (122 L.) ἀπτέρως, **F 63b** (*81 L.) ἁρμάτειον μέλος, **F 66** (*78 L.) ῥᾶ, **F 67** (*79 L.) τραχεῖ (*dual form*), **F 68** (*80 L.) φοινικόλεγνον

Notes on Ion

T 1

The statements about Ion's varied literary production here and in **T 2(b)** (and in parts of the scholia on Ar. *Peace* 835–37 not reproduced here) are derived from Callimachus's *Pinakes* (»» Leurini 1985, cf. Henderson 2007). Callimachus singled out Ion as a precedent for his own use of a variety of poetic forms (*polyeideia*).[10] The date of Ion's first tragic production will have come from the Athenian competition records. The numbers **12**, **30**, **40** might mean that those records showed him competing ten times at the Dionysia (30 tragedies and 10 satyr-plays), while the texts of twelve plays were available in Alexandria (we hear of eleven).

T 2

In Ar. *Peace* 828–31 Trygaeus, returning to earth from his ride to Olympus on a dung-beetle, tells his servant how he saw the souls of dithyrambic poets collecting 'aerial-breeze-swimming preludes'. The reference to Ion suggests (as noted in the scholia) that he had died not long before the production of *Peace* in 421 BC.

T 3

Athenaeus mentions Ion's gift of wine to the Athenians in a list of famous instances of magnificent generosity (*megalopsychia*). The assertion in the Aristophanes scholia that he had won dithyrambic and tragic victories simultaneously

---

[8] Omitting **F 53c** (120 L.), **53dd** (*TrGF* 1^2, p. 346; 121 L.), **64** (*77 L.), **65** (124 L.) and **66a** (*TrGF* 1^2, p. 347; *95 L.) which are probably not tragic.

[9] Or πλέων (Dindorf, cf. Stephanopoulos 2014, 195); but Ion may have used the Ionic form which is found in *Odyssey* 20.355.

[10] See the papyrus *Diegesis* (summary) of Callimachus, *Iamboi* 13. The relevant text (*Iamb.* 13.41–49) is very incomplete but mentioned at least Ion's tragedies, elegies and lyrics (not his prose works as Callimachus's argument was about poetry). »» Pfeiffer 1949, 205–9; Kerkhecker 1999, 250–70.

Brief fragments from unidentified plays. **F 51** a cup filled with wine, **F 52** the hill of the Nymphs, **F 53a** dim *or* dim-sighted, **F 53d** hostile, **F 53f** like-minded and joined in friendship (lit. 'sharing libations'), **F 61** beat your head (in mourning), **F 63a** 'winglessly', i.e. swiftly, **F 63b** the chariot-song, **F 66** easy, **F 67** rough, **F 68** red-striped (of a bird's plumage)[11]

is not supported by the other sources and is probably an exaggeration of Ion's versatility. Stevens 2007, 243–46 discusses the donation's cultural significance.

T 6

'Longinus' argues that a 'sublime' (exalted) style, as of Homer, Archilochus, Pindar and Sophocles, may inevitably be prone to embarrassing lapses but is nevertheless superior to a flawless style that never achieves sublimity, as of Apollonius, Theocritus, Eratosthenes, Bacchylides and Ion. The comment is disparaging but suggests that Ion was best known as a tragedian, and a fairly highly regarded one.

F 1

The fragment is cited by Athenaeus in a catalogue of terms for drinking-cups which occupied nearly all of his Book 11 and includes other tragic fragments (Ion **F 10**, **F 51**, Critias(?) **F 2**) and many satyric fragments from Ion and Achaeus. Athenaeus's speaker offers several competing explanations of the phrase **ἔκπωμα δακτυλωτόν**, the most plausible coming from Didymus's commentary on the play. Didymus noted that Ion's description of the cup recalls Homer's ἀμφίθετον φιάλην ἀπύρωτον ('two-handled dish unmarked by fire') offered by Achilles as fifth prize in the horse-race at the funeral games for Patroclus (*Iliad* 23.270), and explained **δακτυλωτόν** as 'having finger-like indentations around the inside' (κύκλῳ…κοιλότητας ἔχουσαν ἔνδοθεν οἷον δακτύλων); this is reflected in some of the other glosses cited by Athenaeus and clarified by Hesychius's term ξυστρωτόν, i.e. 'fluted' or 'ribbed' (and so easier to hold than a smooth-surfaced cup). The suffix –ωτός here has nothing to do with ὦτα 'ears' (or ear-shaped handles) as some of the ancient explanations assumed. »» Leurini 1973–74, 239–42, and on Ion's adaptation of the Homeric phrase Stevens 2007, 259f.

---

[11] Perhaps 'alluding to the Wigeon's chestnut-red head and neck': Arnott 2007, 189.

The recollection of the Homeric context continues in **a great prize from Pelias earned by** (lit. 'achievement of') **Castor's feet**, i.e. a prize won by Castor in the footrace at the funeral games for the Thessalian king (or usurper) Pelias, in which all the great heroes of the time competed. These games were probably the subject of a lost epic poem which is reflected with variations in later extant accounts. Castor's victory in the footrace appears only in Hyginus, *Fab.* 273; elsewhere he and/or his twin brother Polydeuces compete in the chariot-race (»» Gantz 1993, 191–94).

In Ion's play the cup may have featured as a reward offered to the lookout set by Clytemnestra (Castor's sister) and Aegisthus to report Agamemnon's arrival on the Argive shore, like the reward of two talents of gold offered by Aegisthus in *Odyssey* 4.423–25. If so, the lookout was presumably required to match Castor's speed when running from the shore to the palace.

F 2

The meaning of this slightly cryptic fragment is suggested by its inclusion in Stobaeus 4.52b 'Praise of death', which with 4.53 'Life and death compared' gives many examples of the sentiment that death is a welcome release from the troubles of life. Thus the speaker wishes on his enemy all evils short of such a release. The idea recurs in Seneca, *Agamemnon* 996 (*Electra:* 'Is any punishment worse than death?' — *Aegisthus:* 'Life, if you desire to die'). Stackmann (1950, 218f.) suggested that Seneca's verse reflects Ion's, and that Ion's play like Seneca's included a scene in which Electra defied her father's murderers and was threatened with harsh punishments by Aegisthus. But the similarity is not compelling and the idea appears elsewhere in Greek tragedy, Seneca and others (»» Tarrant 1976 on Sen. *Ag.* 994f., 996).

F 5a

Context unknown. On text and sense see Leurini 1984, 164f. The adjective ἄϊδρος recurs in F 34 and F 41a.

F 8a

Context unknown. The speaker was probably someone apologizing for reporting bad news (such as the deaths of the Seven?), as in Aesch. *Pers.* 253, Soph. *Ant.* 277, and probably Phrynichus **F 16a**.

F 10

Again from Athenaeus's discussion of drinking-vessels (cf. **F 1** above), here the term *pelikê*, though Crates' discussion started from the term *chous*. This is probably Crates of Mallos who worked at Pergamum in the 2nd century BC, rather than the much less well-known Crates of Athens (*FGrH* 362), author of an *On sacrifices at Athens* (»» Broggiato 2000).

The fragment can presumably be related to the fatal banquet at Oechalia. Its lyric metre suggests it may come from a choral song accompanying the banquet, which must have taken place inside the palace, i.e. offstage. The scene is vividly evoked by the verses' dactylic rhythm and epic–poetic vocabulary (**ζαθέων**, **ἀφύσαντες**, **ὑπερφίαλον**, **κελαρύζετε**) and phrasing (cf. e.g. *Iliad* 3.295 οἶνον δ' ἐκ κρητῆρος ἀφυσσόμενοι δεπάεσσιν | ἔκχεον, 'Drawing wine from the mixing-bowl in cups they poured libations'; *Hom.Hymn.* 7.35f. οἶνος μὲν πρώτιστα θοὴν ἀνὰ νῆα μέλαιναν | ἡδύποτος κελάρυζ' εὐώδης, 'First of all wine, fragrant and sweet to drink, began splashing over the dark ship').

[**potent:** ὑπερφίαλος often means 'overbearing, hybristic' but also simply 'mighty, high-achieving' (»» LSJ); here obviously the latter, though with a suggestion of the wine's alcoholic effect. An ancient etymology ὑπερ-φιάλην 'overflowing the bowl', 'beyond measure' (*Etym.Gen.* s.v.) is implausible though favoured by Wilamowitz 1921, 389 n. 1. **divinely scented:** ζάθεος means simply 'divine' but here refers to the wine's character, primarily its scent (the word is glossed as εὐώδης in Hesychius ζ 18, *Etym.Magn.* s.v.: cf. *Hom. Hymn.* 7.36 quoted above). It does not imply a religious ceremony as von Blumenthal and Snell supposed.]

Metre: – ⏑ ⏑ – ⏑ ⏑ – ⏑ ⏑ – ⏑ – – | – ⏑ ⏑ – ⏑ ⏑ – ⏑ ⏑ – ⏑ ⏑ , i.e. 'praxillean' (Dale 1968, 161) *plus* dactylic tetrameter.

F 14

From Athenaeus's discussion of the history and terminology of slavery. οἰκέτης was a common word for a house-slave (though the plural sometimes includes other retainers), so Ion's use of it in this context is not really remarkable. This is however the only known literary use of its vocative singular form. For the context see above, p. 84. Metre: ⏖ – ⏑ ⏑ – ⏑ – | – ⏑ ⏑ – ⏑ – | – ⏑ – – ⏑ – (telesillean, dodrans, 2 cretics).

F 34

Probably from a report of a shipwreck: cf. Plato, *Rep.* 553b1, a politician πταίσαντα ὥσπερ πρὸς ἕρματι πρὸς τῇ πόλει, 'running upon the city as upon a reef', and thus meeting his downfall. For possible contexts see the introduction to *Teucer* above.

F 38, F 36

These two fragments are generally thought to come, probably in sequence (38.1 τε…36.1 καὶ…), from the same speech in which a heroic character recommends bold aggression and denigrates the defensive craft proverbially typified (often with approval) by the hedgehog (e.g. Archilochus fr. 201 *IEG*) and the octopus (e.g. *Odyssey* 5.432f., *Thebais* fr. 8 *GEF*, Theognis 212–17, Pind. fr. 43, Soph.

F 307). Rostagni (1927, 378) thought that **F 55** and **F 58** might come from the same context, but the connection is tenuous.

F 39

Quoted with **F 42** (from *Phoenix B*) and **F 45** (from *Guards*) by Athenaeus at the end of a long discussion of different types of aulos and other musical instruments (4.174f–185a: »» West 1992b, 89–94 on aulos types). Ion's **cockerel** metaphor alludes to the raucous sound of the aulos (and the syrinx, **F 45**). Auloi were typically characterized as oriental (so e.g. Diogenes **F 1.10f.**), partly with reference to their actual origins and partly because their music was emotive, whether of grief or celebration. Metre (aeolic): ⏕ – ⏑ ⏑ – – | – ⏑ ⏑ – ⏑ – ⏑ – (reizianum + 'choriambic dimeter').

F 40

Athenaeus quotes the fragment in a long discussion of *griphoi* or riddles (Ath.10.448b–459c: see further on Agathon **F 4**). **oak-sweat** here means bird-lime (prepared from oak-gum). The speaker is obviously a bird-catcher describing his equipment, probably a minor character reporting a dramatically important event.

F 41

The fragment is quoted in the scholia on Aristophanes' *Frogs* as the model for the opening of a choral interlude at *Frogs* 706 ('If I am correct in seeing a man's life…'). It may come from a similar reflection on the central character's fate in Ion's play, or perhaps his mistakenly expected fate (cf. Soph. *OT* 1086ff., 'If I am a seer and knowledgeable in my judgement…'). The citation in the scholia ἐκ Φοίνικος ἢ καὶ Οἰνέως is obviously a corruption of ἐκ Φοίνικος ἢ Καινέως, rather than the reverse as von Blumenthal preferred. Metre: dactylic hexameter.

F 41b

Photius cites the verse for the word ἀμφαδὸν, a mainly epic form of the commoner ἀναφανδόν 'plainly', 'openly'. The speaker could be someone about to discover that he had not in fact fared well (cf. **F 41**?).

F 42

See above on **F 39**. **the deep-voiced aulos:** cf. Eur. *Hel.* 1351 βαρύβρομον αὐλόν. Auloi varied in pitch, like recorders: roughly 'soprano, treble, tenor, baritone, bass' (West 1992b, 89). The 'Phrygian' aulos or *elymos* (a pair of narrow-bore pipes, one with a curved horn attached) was used in the music of ecstatic cults such as those of Cybele, Rhea and Dionysus (»» Bélis 1986, West 91f.). **with running beat** suggests the urgent rhythm of such music (Bélis 25), perhaps specifically the trochaic ('running') rhythm reflected in this fragment.

[**ἐκτύπουν ἄγων...αὐλὸν:** lit. 'I sounded the aulos, making it sound' (ἄγων supplementary participle), cf. Eur. *Or.* 183 κτύπον ἀγάγετ' (with LSJ 'ἄγω' IV.3) 'you've made a noise', *Alc.* 430 αὐλῶν...κτύπος 'the sound of auloi'; *Ba.* 129 κέρασαν ἡδυβόαι Φρυγίων | αὐλῶν πνεύματι..., κτύπον εὐάσμασι βακχᾶν, 'they (the Corybantes) mingled it (the *tympanon*) with the sweet-voiced breath of Phrygian auloi..., (making) sound for the bacchants' joyful songs'.]

Metre: iambo-trochaic, – ⏑ – ⏑ – ⏑ ⏑ | – – ⏑ – ⏑ – – (cf. e.g. Eur. *Hel.* 338f., 345f., 360f.).

F 43b

The grammarian Herodian cites this with **F 43c** and the brief **F 49a** to illustrate the accentuation of the adjectives εὐναῖος, τροπαῖος and προσφοραῖος. The speaker may have been asking how Odysseus reached Helen's chamber, where presumably he conversed with her as in *Odyssey* 4.250ff.

F 43c

See previous note. The text is uncertain, but **veering wind** is probably the wind of fortune, a common metaphor in tragedy, e.g. Eur. *El.* 1147 μετάτροποι πνέουσιν αὖραι δόμων, 'the house's winds are shifting' (»» Cropp 2013, 225; LSJ 'τροπαία'). [The Herodian palimpsest has either αβρα or αυρα (»» Hunger 1967, 8), i.e. ἅβρα/ἄβρα (aspiration disputed) or αὔρα. The first option can safely be discarded: ἅβρα/ἄβρα is a rare word, perhaps of Semitic origin, denoting a lady's maid, first attested in Menander as cited by Attic lexicographers (»» Francis 1975); if it had occurred in tragedy they would have said so. Metaphorical **αὔρα** is far more plausible, but the palimpsest's τροπαῖον gives poor sense ('a wind has scared me, making me turn') and is easily corrected to **τροπαῖος** (adjectives in –ιος frequently occur with two terminations, e.g. Eur. *Alc.* 99, 102, 246, 805: »» KB 1.536f., esp. 537(γ) -αιος). αὔρα as 'impulse', 'emotion' (cf. Collard on Eur. *Supp.* 1028–30) seems less likely here.]

Metre: ⏑ – ⏑ – ⏑ ⏑⏑ ⏑ – ⏑ – – (i.e. lyric iambic trimeter; there is no need to turn this into a dialogue trimeter as West 1968, 201 proposed.)

F 44

Cited as the model for Ar. *Frogs* 1425, 'It (the city of Athens) yearns for him (the exiled Alcibiades), loathes him, and wants to possess him'. Ion's context may or may not have been similar, e.g. Helen describing Troy's resentment of Paris (von Blumenthal) and/or herself (cf. *Iliad* 3.154ff.). Wilamowitz supposed a conversation about Hecuba's willingness to help Odysseus escape from Troy, as Hecuba herself claims to have done in Eur. *Hec.* 239–50 (Wilamowitz 1927, 287 n. 1 = 1962, 414 n. 1; cf. Welcker 1841, 950), but that claim was very probably an *ad hoc* invention as schol. *Hec.* 241 implies; it makes little sense except as a basis for Hecuba's plea for a reciprocal benefit from Odysseus.

F 45

See above on **F 39.** The subject is the cock-crow signalling the approach of dawn, as Athenaeus indicates: perhaps a sign that it is time for Odysseus to leave Troy? It is tempting to connect **F 53b** with the same moment (see note there). [Kaibel altered Athenaeus's text to mean 'Ion has termed the syrinx 'Idaean cockerel'' (cf. **F 39**). This is unjustified though accepted by Nauck, Snell (quoting Wilamowitz in his apparatus) and *MusTr* amongst others. Leurini prints Athenaeus's text but still translates 'strepita per te la zampogna, il gallo dell' Ida'.] Metre, dactylo-epitrite: ⏑ – ⏑ – – ¦ – – – ⏑ ⏑ – – (× *e* × ¦ *D* –).

F 46

Snow-white may simply allude to Helen's complexion. Fine female complexions are often 'white' (λευκός) in Greek poetry (and Latin, cf. Nisbet–Hubbard on Horace, *Odes* 2.4.3, Briseis *niveo colore*); Helen's would be supremely so. Without a context it is difficult to say if the epic word **νιφόεσσ(α)**, which properly describes snow-covered mountain-tops, might have implied more than that (bleak, looming, chilling) as it does when Hector is likened to a 'snow-covered mountain' in *Iliad* 13.754f. (»» Dodds on Eur. *Ba.* 661f.; Stevens 2007, 257–59).

F 50

Cf. Aesch. *Cho.* 167 ὀρχεῖται δὲ καρδία φόβῳ, 'my heart dances with fear'.

F 53

Quoted by Philo as an example of refusal to submit to slavery (δοῦλος 'slave' seems to have been a term for cocks defeated in cockfights: »» Dunbar 1995, 158 on Ar. *Birds* 70).

Metre, dactylic: – ⏑ ⏑ – ⏑ ⏑ – ⏑ ⏑ – ⏑ ⏑ – ⏑ ⏑ – ⏑ ⏑ – – | – ⏑ ⏑ – ⏑ ⏑ – – – ⏑ – | ⏑ ⏑ – ⏑ ⏑ – ⏑ ⏑ – ⏑ ⏑ – – – (D^5 – | *D* – *e* | ⏑ ⏑ D^2 –). Metre and vocabulary together give the description a Homeric tone: **τυπείς (stricken)**, cf. *Iliad* 11.433 etc. (8x). **οὐδ'…ἐπιλάθεται ἀλκᾶς (nor does he forget his courage)**, *Iliad* 16.601f. οὐδ' ἄρ' Ἀχαιοὶ ἀλκῆς ἐξελάθοντο (~ λάθοντο…ἀλκῆς *Iliad* 3x, ἀλκῆς λάθωμαι 2x). **ἀλλ' ὀλιγοδρανέων etc. (but failing in strength gives voice)**, τὸν δ' ὀλιγοδρανέων προσέφη(ς) *Iliad* 15.246 (Hector felled by Ajax's boulder addresses Apollo), 16.843 (Patroclus dying addresses Hector), 22.337 (Hector dying addresses Achilles). **προβέβουλε (preferred)**, *Iliad* 1.113.

F 53b

A reworking of *Iliad* 7.433 ἦμος δ' οὔτ' ἄρ πω ἠώς, ἔτι δ' ἀμφιλύκη νύξ, 'while it was not yet dawn, but still twilit night' (cf. Reitzenstein 1907, XVI; on the Homeric ἀμφιλύκη, West 2013c, 262–64). **dim twilight** matches the Atticist

Phrynichus's (2nd C. AD) definition of **ὄρθρος** as 'the time before the beginning of day in which one can still use a lantern' (*Selection of Attic Verbs and Nouns*, 240) and 'the hour of the night at which the cocks crow' (*Sophistic Preparation*, 93). Von Blumenthal's ascription of this fragment to *Guards* (cf. **F 45**, 'the cockerel crows…') is plausible. »» Leurini 1984, 166f.

F 53e
Probably part of a report narrative, in which case the present-tense verb refers to the past. Von Blumenthal (1939, 30) ascribed it to *Agamemnon,* for no sufficient reason.

F 54
Cited in the *Consolation to Apollonius* to illustrate excessive oriental indulgence in grief. None of Ion's known titles provides a likely context. [The first verse is incurably corrupt. The (conjectural?) reading in the late ms. B ('I have come out as a suppliant, nurse of your vigorous sons'?) is uncompelling, as are several modern conjectures listed by Leurini.]

F 55
Again from the *Consolation to Apollonius* supporting the argument that we should accept our mortality and not grieve excessively over our own or others' deaths (»» Kassel 1958, 93). [Rostagni's (1927) suggestion that **F 55** and **F 58** are from the same speech is unconvincing: see below on **F 58.**]

F 56
Plutarch (quoting also Eur. *Orestes* 232, 'Sick men are hard to please because of their helplessness') likens the inability of unreasoning men to reconcile themselves with their circumstances to the inability of sick men to bear their condition with good spirits.

F 57
Context unknown. [**γὰρ αὐταῖς** might be Plutarch's words rather than Ion's. Sandbach implausibly suggested that the phrase αὐγῆς…ἀμβλύτητα in *Mor.* 929a might reflect Ion's text (αὐγῆς δ' ἀμβλύτητα καὶ τάχους | νώθειαν).]

F 58
Plutarch states that he is not competent to compare Demosthenes and Cicero as orators. Ion's verse was probably ⟨⏑ – ⟩ κακὴ δελφῖνος ἐν χέρσῳ βία, not κακὴ ⟨⏑ – ⟩ δελφῖνος ἐν χέρσῳ βία as Snell and Leurini print it.

Snell and Leurini print **F 58** and **F 55** together as belonging to the same speech, following Rostagni 1927, but the connection is implausible. After citing **F 58** Plutarch goes on to say that the Sicilian rhetorician Caecilius of Calacte (1st

C. BC) naively attempted such a comparison, and adds that his failure was not really surprising: 'But perhaps, if it was easy for everyone to *Know Thyself*, the injunction would not seem to be divine'. Rostagni took this to be an allusion to the content of **F 55**, and proposed that **F 58** and **F 55** should therefore be combined. He also proposed that, given the 'zoological' content of **F 58**, these three verses should be combined with **F 38** and assigned to *Phoenix or Caeneus*. But when Plutarch calls *Know Thyself* 'divine' he means that it is a pronouncement of the Delphic Apollo, not that it is a unique attribute of Zeus as in **F 55**. Nor can both citations be attributed to Plutarch as Rostagni assumed, since Plutarch was not the author of the *Consolation to Apollonius*.

F 59

Context unknown. The fragment is often attributed (first by Meineke) to the satyr-play *Omphale*: »» *GrSat* 487, O'Sullivan–Collard 2013, 416 with refs.

F 60

For 'plain' as poetic metaphor for 'sea' (explained rather too elaborately by the Euripidean scholiast) see LSJ 'πεδίον' I.1.b; also Eur. *Helen* 1117 ἔδραμε ῥόθια πεδία 'ran over the foaming plains'.

F 63

The anecdote might derive from a prose work of Ion such as the *Epidemiai* but is probably apocryphal. A very similar story is told by Herodotus (3.46) about the Spartans' reception of Samian exiles seeking their aid against the tyrant Polycrates. Either way, the connection between the anecdote and Ion's verses is fanciful.

ACHAEUS
(*TrGF* 20)

Texts etc. *TrGF* 1^2.115–28 with *addenda* 1^2.347f., 5.1106; *MusTr* 80–89, 277–80.

Satyr-plays. *GrSat* 491–545; Cipolla 2003, 139–223; O'Sullivan–Collard 2013, 426–39.

*Achaeus, from Eretria on the island of Euboea, was a contemporary of both Euripides and Ion. Like Ion he remained relatively well known for some centuries after his own time, but our biographical data are limited to the Suda's very brief notice (**T 1**). He is not featured in what remains of Old Comedy, although Aristophanes used one of his phrases twice (*Wasps *1081,* Peace *356: cf.* Momos *F 29)*[1] *and a whole verse once (*Frogs *184 =* Aithon *F 11.1). He seems to have been remembered mainly for his satyr-plays (cf. **T 6**), which account for at least eight of the twenty extant titles and about two-thirds of the roughly fifty-five fragments. Nearly all of Athenaeus's twenty-one citations are from satyr-plays, as are two references in the Epicurean philosopher Philodemus (F 16b, 20). The tragic fragments, known or presumed, nearly all come from grammarians and lexica.*

The eight plays identified as satyric by testimonia and/or language are Athla ('Games'), Aithon, Alcmeon, Hephaestus, Iris, Linus, Moirai ('Fates') *and* Omphale. Erginus *(the king of Orchomenus punished by the young Heracles for his aggression against Thebes) and* Momos *(the spirit of fault-finding) were probably also satyr-plays.*[2] *Titles and language show that* Azanians *and* Philoctetes *were tragedies (see on these below), while* Adrastus, Alphesiboea, Theseus, Oedipus, Pirithous *and* Phrixus, *whose fragments amount to no more than three words each, are*

---

[1] On these allusions see Zogg 2014, 38–43.

[2] Erginus was probably the subject of Aeschylus's satyr-play *Kerykes ('Heralds')*: »» Gantz 1993, 379f.; Sommerstein 2008, 118f. Momos was born from Night (Hesiod, *Theogony* 214), and architect of Zeus's plan to reduce the earth's population, rather than destroy it entirely, by inducing the Trojan War (*Cypria* fr. 1 *GEF*). He was also featured in Aesop's fables (*Fab.* 102 Hausrath–Hunger) and became a byword for negative criticism. Sophocles' *Momos*, from which five words survive, was a satyr-play.

generally considered tragic on the strength of their titles (not a foolproof criterion, considering that Alcmeon *was a satyr-play).* Adrastus *was probably about some aspect of the disastrous expedition of the Seven against Thebes led by Adrastus of Argos,* Alphesiboea *about the daughter of Phegeus and her dealings with the matricide Alcmeon,*[3] Theseus *about the destruction of Hippolytus (see the brief* ***F 18, 18a****),* Oedipus *about the discovery of Oedipus's guilt,* Pirithous *about the*

Testimonia

T 1 Suda *α* 4683
Ἀχαιός, Πυθοδώρου ἢ Πυθοδωρίδου, Ἐρετριεύς, τραγικός· γέγονε κατὰ τὴν οδ´ Ὀλυμπιάδα καὶ δράματα ἐδίδαξε μδ´, οἱ δὲ λ´ ἱστορήκασιν, ἄλλοι κδ´· ἐνίκησε δὲ α´. ἦν δὲ νεώτερος Σοφοκλέους ὀλίγῳ τινί· ἐπεδείκνυντο δὲ κοινῇ σὺν καὶ Εὐριπίδῃ ἀπὸ τῆς πγ´ Ὀλυμπιάδος.

T 6 Diogenes Laertius 2.133
ἠσπάζετο δὲ (*sc.* ὁ Μενέδημος) καὶ Ἄρατον καὶ Λυκόφρονα τὸν τῆς τραγῳδίας ποιητὴν καὶ τὸν Ῥόδιον Ἀνταγόραν· μάλιστα δὲ πάντων Ὁμήρῳ προσεῖχεν· εἶτα καὶ τοῖς μελικοῖς· ἔπειτα Σοφοκλεῖ, καὶ δὴ καὶ Ἀχαιῷ, ᾧπερ καὶ τὸ δευτερεῖον ἐν τοῖς σατύροις, Αἰσχύλῳ δὲ τὸ πρωτεῖον ἀπεδίδου.

T 7 Athenaeus 10.451c
Ἀχαιὸς δ' ὁ Ἐρετριεὺς γλαφυρὸς ὢν ποιητὴς περὶ τὴν σύνθεσιν ἔσθ' ὅτε καὶ μελαίνει τὴν φράσιν καὶ πολλὰ αἰνιγματωδῶς ἐκφέρει . . . *(F 19).*

---

[3] A frequent tragic subject, sometimes under the title *Alcmeon*: »» Collard–Cropp 2008a, 80f. on Euripides' *Alcmeon in Psophis*. The title *Alphesiboea* was also used by Timotheus (*TrGF* no. 56) and Chaeremon (*TrGF* 71 **F 1**). One could imagine a tetralogy by Achaeus including *Adrastus*, a tragedy about Alcmeon's matricide, *Alphesiboea*, and the satyric *Alcmeon* (probably about his quest for relief from madness after killing his mother).

hero's imprisonment and rescue from the Underworld, and Phrixus *about the rescue of Phrixus from the schemes of his stepmother Ino and his transportation to Colchis on the golden-fleeced ram.* Katapeira ('The Attempt/Test') *is an obscure title, possibly referring to Agamemnon's disastrous testing of his army's mettle in* Iliad *2.*[4] Cycnus *is difficult to classify: see on this below.*

Testimonia

T 1 Suda, 'Achaeus'
Achaeus, son of Pythodorus or Pythodorides, from Eretria, tragic poet. He was born in the 74th Olympiad (484/3–481/0 BC), produced 44 plays (some have recorded 30, others 24), and won one victory. He was a little younger than Sophocles; they presented their plays together, and with Euripides as well, from the 83rd Olympiad (448/7–445/4 BC).

T 6 Diogenes Laertius, *Lives of the Philosophers*
He (i.e. the philosopher-politician Menedemus of Eretria, 3rd–2nd C. BC) enjoyed Aratus and Lycophron the tragic poet and Antagoras of Rhodes; but he was attached to Homer most of all, then to the lyric poets, then to Sophocles, and also to Achaeus, to whom he also awarded second place in satyr-drama, while awarding the first to Aeschylus.

T 7 Athenaeus, *Sophists at Dinner*
Achaeus of Eretria, an elegant poet in terms of composition, sometimes darkens his expression and produces much in riddling style . . . *(an example from his satyr-play* Iris, *F 19)*

---

[4] Latte 1968, 668 pointed out that *Apopeira* and *Diapeira* were regularly used as titles of *Iliad* 2.

ΑΖΑΝΕΣ

The Azanes were one of the three main peoples of Arcadia, inhabiting its northern regions. Their tribal identity was fading in the fifth century, and their name was sometimes used to denote all Arcadians. The land of Arcadia was proverbially barren, and its mythical history was complicated and variable. According to one genealogy (Pausanias 8.2ff.) their mythical progenitor Azan was one of the three sons of Arcas and thus a grandson of Zeus and Callisto and great-grandson of Callisto's father Lycaon. Lycaon was notorious for having offered a human child as a sacrifice to Zeus, who reacted by turning him into a wolf and destroying most of his family while restoring the child to life (or in some accounts sending the Great Flood). The only fragment of Achaeus's tragedy shows that it was concerned with this episode: the Chorus (presumably of Azanian men, and probably at the beginning of the play since the

F 2 Schol. Eur. *Orestes* 383

τὸ δὲ 'ἐξάπτων' ἔφη παρόσον οὓς ἱκέτευον, τούτοις παρετίθεσαν τὰς ἱκετηρίας. Ἀχαιὸς Ἀζᾶσι·

〈Χο.〉 νῦν οὖν ἡμεῖς ἱκέτας θαλλοὺς
στεφέων τε σέβας τίθεμεν πρὸ ποδῶν
τῶν σῶν, λῆξαι
τῆς ἀστόργου Ζηνὸς θυσίας

1 ἱκέτας Stephanopoulos ἱκέται schol. 2 στεφέων Wilamowitz τε θεῶν schol.
4 ἀστόργου Wilamowitz ἀστερόπου Schol.

AZANIANS

metre is anapaestic) begs Lycaon to desist from his cruel sacrifice. The play's title is however puzzling, firstly because Lycaon and his story were associated with Mt. Lykaion and the cult of Zeus Lykaios in south-western Arcadia, an area with which the Azanians of historic times were only tenuously connected (cf. Nielsen–Roy 33–36), and secondly because a people named after a descendant of Lycaon should not have existed in Lycaon's time.[5] *Possibly the title referred to primitive Arcadians in general (see above).*[6] *»» (history) Nielsen–Roy 1998; (mythology) West 1985a, 91–94; Gantz 1993, 728f.; Fowler 2013, 103–12.*

Only titles survive from plays named Lycaon *by Xenocles (*TrGF *33) and probably Astydamas II (*TrGF *60: title restored in the Didascaliae inscription for 340 BC).*

F 2 Scholiast on Euripides' *Orestes*

He has said 'attaching' inasmuch as they used to place their suppliant branches before those whom they were supplicating. Achaeus in *Azanians*:

> So now we place suppliant branches and sacred garlands before your feet, beseeching you to cease from your cruel sacrifice to Zeus . . .

[5] One version of Lycaon's story apparently made Azan his son and the victim of the human sacrifice (schol. Pind. *Ol.* 9.49ff. [9.78d Drachmann], cf. schol. Lycophron, *Alexandra* 73), but this still does not allow for the existence of Azanians at the time.

[6] Azania was sometimes considered an alternative name for Arcadia, etymologized from ἄζειν 'to parch': Schol. Ap. Rhod. 2.52f. Cf. the oracle given to the Phigaleians of SW Arcadia in Pausanias 8.42.6 ('Arcadians, acorn-eating Azanians...') and probably Eur. *Orestes* 1646f., Callimachus, *Aetia* fr. 190a Harder (= *SH* 276), 11.

ΚΥΚΝΟΣ

Greek myths included three Cycnuses: (1) a son of Ares who killed travellers as they passed his home near the sanctuary of Apollo at Pagasae and was in turn killed by Heracles; this episode was popular in early Greek poetry and art and treated extensively in the Hesiodic Shield of Heracles *and Stesichorus's* Cycnus (cf. Pind. *Ol.* 10.15f., Eur. *Heracles* 389–93)*; (2) a son of Poseidon who resisted the Greek landing at Troy and was killed by Achilles: again a well-known episode, told for example in the epic* Cypria *and Sophocles'* Poimenes *(*'Shepherds'*); (3), sometimes conflated with (2), another son of Poseidon who expelled his son Tennes from the Troad to the island of Tenedos; this was the subject of*

F 24 + 43 Hephaestion, *Enchiridion* 1.9

. . . τὸ 'ἐλήλυμεν' ἐδείξαμεν καὶ ἐν ἄλλοις μέτροις συνήθως αὐτοῖς λεγόμενον, ὡς παρὰ Ἀχαιῷ ἐν Κύκνῳ·

Κύκνου δὲ πρῶτα πρὸς δόμους ἐλήλυμεν,

παρ' ᾧ καὶ τὸ δεύτερόν ἐστιν ἀκολούθως πρόσωπον·

τοιοῦδε φωτὸς πρὸς δόμους ἐλήλυτε.

F 25 Athenaeus 6.270e–f

διὸ παραχωρῶ σοι...τῆς τοιαύτης ἐμφορεῖσθαι σιτήσεως·

πεινῶντι δ' ἀνδρὶ μᾶζα τιμιωτέρα
χρυσοῦ τε κἀλέφαντος,

κατὰ τὸν τοῦ Ἐρετριέως Ἀχαιοῦ Κύκνον.

CYCNUS

the tragedy Tennes *(see pp. 212–17). »» LIMC VII, 'Kyknos I'; Gantz 1993, 421–23, 594; Zardini 2009, 125–40; Fowler 2013, 292, 534f.; Davies–Finglass 2014, 462–69; Finglass 2015a, 83–87.*

*The fragments of Achaeus's play, referring to travellers arriving at Cycnus's home (**F 24 + 43**) and to someone's (Heracles'?) hunger (**F 25**), point strongly towards the Heracles–Cycnus episode. This kind of story (Heracles eliminating a hybristic villain) was well suited to satyr-drama, and in the fourth century Eubulus and Alexis produced comedies with this title.*[7] *But it is quite possible that Achaeus used it for a tragedy (or a hybrid like Euripides'* Alcestis*?) following the poetic tradition cited above and perhaps Stesichorus in particular.*

F 24 + 43 Hephaestion, *Handbook on Metres*
. . . we have shown that they routinely said ἐλήλυμεν (instead of ἐληλύθαμεν) in other metres as well (as in dactylic hexameters), as for example with Achaeus in *Cycnus*:

And first we have come to Cycnus's halls,

with whom also the second person occurs similarly:

To such a man's halls have you come.

F 25 Athenaeus, *Sophists at Dinner*
So I give you leave . . . to load yourself with that kind of (verbal) food.

But for a hungry man barley-cake is worth more than gold and ivory,

as Achaeus of Eretria's *Cycnus* puts it.

[7] *GrSat* 543f. and Cipolla 2003, 209 include it as probably satyric.

ΦΙΛΟΚΤΗΤΗΣ

Aeschylus, Sophocles and Euripides all produced plays about the Achaeans' retrieval of Philoctetes from the island of Lemnos. They had abandoned him there because the smell of his gangrenous leg was intolerable but later discovered that they could not take Troy without him and the bow he had inherited from Heracles. His retrieval was also the subject of Theodectas's Philoctetes *(*TrGF *72* ***F 5b****) and Accius's Latin* Philocteta *based on Euripides. For Philocles I we have only a title. On reaching Troy, according to the epic* Little Iliad, *Philoctetes' leg was healed by Machaon and he killed Paris in single combat; he then went on to participate in the sack of Troy. Sophocles'* Philoctetes at Troy *was about this later stage of the story, including presumably his arrival at Troy, healing, and reconciliation with the Greek leaders.* ***F 37****, which is all we have of Achaeus's* Philoctetes, *shows that it too treated this*

F 37 Schol. *Ar.* Birds 364 (~ Suda ε 786, which alone preserves the quotation)

ἐλελελεῦ· ἐπίφθεγμα πολεμικὸν τὸ ἐλελεῦ. οἱ προσιόντες γὰρ εἰς πόλεμον τὸ ἐλελεῦ ἐφώνουν μετά τινος ἐμμελοῦς κινήσεως. καθὸ καὶ Ἀχαιὸς Ἐρετριεὺς ἐν τῷ Φιλοκτήτῃ ποιεῖ τὸν Ἀγαμέμνονα παραγγέλλοντα τοῖς Ἀχαιοῖς·

ὥρα βοηθεῖν ἐστ'· ἐγὼ δ' ἡγήσομαι.
προσβαλλέτω τις χεῖρα φασγάνου λαβῇ,
σάλπιγγι δ' ἄλλος ὡς τάχος σημαινέτω·
ὥρα ταχύνειν, ἐλελελεῦ . . .

PHILOCTETES

episode. It may come from near the end of the play when the curing and reconciliation have been completed and Agamemnon is ready to lead his men confidently into battle (cf. Euripides' Telephus F 727c*).*

A papyrus fragment from the second century AD containing parts of twenty-seven lines of a 5th/4th-century tragic text (P. Oxy. 45.3216) is printed in TrGF *as adesp. F 654 under the heading* Philoctetes(?). *The apparatus there notes the proposed reconstruction of M. L. West (1977, 40–42) and the suggestion that the play might have been a* Philoctetes at Troy *(presumably that of Sophocles or Achaeus). West's reconstruction can more plausibly be linked with a play set in Lemnos, with Philoctetes still refusing to accept the necessity of going to Troy.*[8] *The possibility of a connection with Achaeus's play is therefore very remote.*

F 37 Scholia on Aristophanes' *Birds*

Eleleleu: *eleleu* was a martial cry. Those advancing into war used to cry *eleleu*, with some rhythmic movement. Thus Achaeus of Eretria in his *Philoctetes* makes Agamemnon proclaim to the Achaeans:

> It's time to join the fray, and I shall lead. Let one man put his hand to his sword's hilt, another haste to make the trumpet-signal. It's time to press on, *eleleleu* . . .

---

[8] In West's reconstruction the chorus tells Philoctetes that he can either relieve his suffering by doing what is required of him or continue it by persisting in his refusal; Philoctetes protests that Apollo has proclaimed that Troy must be taken 'by the spear' (so that his bow cannot be needed); and someone from the Achaean army insists that a new oracle requires the bow. West adds that the very fragmentary vv. 21–27 'might be an order to a body of soldiers' and tentatively compares Agamemnon's instruction to his men in Achaeus **F 37**, but this argument is very tenuous. Mette and Jouan–Van Looy treat the fragment as possibly Euripidean (without reference to a *Philoctetes*) because it includes the word ἀλίαστον which Byzantine lexica attribute to Euripides (fr. 1459b? Mette, fr. dub. *1123a Jouan–Van Looy).

Incerta Fabula

F 44 Lucian, *Pro lapsu inter salutandum* 6

πολὺ δ' ἂν καὶ ἐν τῇ τραγῳδίᾳ καὶ ἐν τῇ ἀρχαίᾳ κωμῳδίᾳ εὕροις τὸ ὑγιαίνειν πρῶτον εὐθὺς λεγόμενον . . . ὁ δὲ Ἀχαιός,

ἥκω πεπραγὼς δεινά, σὺ δ' ὑγίαινέ μοι.

Brief fragments:[9] **F 1** (*Adrastus*) ἀργᾶς, **F 16** (*Alphesiboea*) ἔναστρος ὥστε μαινάς, **F 18** (*Theseus*) Σαρωνία, **F 18a** (*Theseus*) ὀξυπρῴρῳ, **F 23a** (*Katapeira*) δίχολοι γνῶμαι, **F 30** (*Oedipus*) ἀκάθαρτον, **F 31** (*Oedipus*) ἐκλωτίζεται, **F 36** (*Pirithous*) ἀμφερκῆ πίθον, **F 38** (*Phrixus*) Πελεός, **F 40** Ταραντῖναι βαφαί, **F 45** τὰ μὴ νοσοῦντα . . . συναλγεῖν, **F 46** *τὰς Ὑάδας εἶναι τέσσαρας*, **F 48** αἰόλη, **F 50** κύτταροι, **F 51**? μάλευρον, **F 53**? πανόπτης Ζεύς, **F 54**? ἁλιάποδα, **F 55**? δραχμῇ παχείᾳ

Notes on Achaeus

T 1

44 plays…30…24: perhaps totals of documented titles (44) and of texts available to Hellenistic scholars (30 or 24): cf. Ion **T 1**. Twenty titles are still known (above, pp. 107–9).

T 6

For Aeschylus's pre-eminence in satyr-drama cf. Pratinas **T 7** (Pausanias 2.13.6), although there Pratinas and his son Aristias are the runners-up. Menedemus may have favoured Achaeus because both were both from Eretria.

F 2

The scholiasts's explanation is slightly inappropriate: in *Or.* 382f. Orestes grasps Menelaus's knees and 'attaches' his prayers (like suppliant garlands) to them, whereas Achaeus's chorus lays its branches and garlands before Lycaon's feet. [Stephanopoulos's **ἱκέτας** for ms. ἱκέται gives clearer sense and better balanced phrasing, **we place suppliant branches and sacred garlands** (lit. 'awesomeness

---

[9] **F 41, 42, 47, 52** are clearly satyric and therefore not included here. **F 40** and **F 50** are included but are more likely satyric than tragic. Attributions of **F 51** and **F 53–55** to Achaeus are uncertain.

Unidentified Play

F 44 Lucian, *In defence of his error in salutation*

And in tragedy and old comedy you will find 'good health' often said first of all . . . *(two examples)* . . . and Achaeus,

> I come here having fared terribly, but I wish you good health.

Brief fragments: **F 1** (*Adrastus*) a serpent, **F 16** (*Alphesiboea*) like an enstarred maenad,[10] **F 18** (*Theseus*) Saronian,[11] **F 18a** (*Theseus*) sharp-horned,[12] **F 23a** (*The Attempt*) differing opinions, **F 30** (*Oedipus*) mad (*lit.* 'uncleansed'), **F 31** (*Oedipus*) decked with flowers, **F 36** (*Pirithous*) an enclosed (rounded) urn, **F 38** (*Phrixus*) Peleos,[13] **F 40** Tarentine dyes, **F 45** (making) what is not ailing also feel the pain,[14] **F 46** *(according to Achaeus) the Hyades numbered four*, **F 48** quick, **F 50** honeycomb-cells, **F 51**? barley-meal, **F 53**? all-seeing Zeus, **F 54** a petrel, **F 55** with a thick drachma (i.e. a didrachm)

of garlands': LSJ 'σέβας' II.1) rather than 'we suppliants place branches and sacred garlands'.]

F 24 + 43, F 25

See the introduction to *Cycnus* above. **F 25** is quoted by Athenaeus's representative of Cynic philosophy (Cynulcus) to make the point that he would rather eat some modest but real food than listen to the elaborate comic descriptions of abundant food which another speaker has just recited.

F 37 *See above, introduction to* Philoctetes

---

[10] Hesychius gives this as an example of 'maenad' meaning 'Hyad', one of the rain-nymphs who in one tradition were nurses of Dionysus before being translated to the heavens as the constellation Hyades (»» Fowler 2013, 371–77).

[11] An epithet of Artemis at Troezen on the Saronic Gulf.

[12] Referring to a bull, either the one that Theseus killed at Marathon or (more likely in view of **F 18**?) the one that killed his son Hippolytus.

[13] A place, probably in Thessaly.

[14] Quoted (or paraphrased) in the *Consolation to Apollonius* to characterize people who harm themselves physically by over-reacting to misfortunes.

IOPHON
(*TrGF* 22)

Texts etc. *TrGF* 1^2.132–35 with *addenda* 5.1106f.; *MusTr* 88–93, 280f. *Satyr-play* (*Aulodoi/Aulos-singers*, F 1), *GrSat* 546–51; Cipolla 2003, 271f., 278f., 296–98.

Biographical data for Iophon come mostly from the Suda and the Life of Sophocles *(**T 1**). He was a legitimate son of Sophocles, who also had at least one son, Ariston, who was illegitimate (*nothos*) because his mother came from Sicyon and was therefore not an Athenian citizen (Sophocles may have lived with her after his first wife's death). From **T 1b** it looks as if Leosthenes was a second legitimate son, while Stephanus and Menecleides were further* nothoi. *Iophon and Ariston each had a son named Sophocles.*[1] *Ariston's son produced* Oedipus at Colonus *(with plays of his own?) at the Dionysia of 401 BC, four years after his grandfather's death, and built a successful career as a tragedian (Sophocles II, no. 62 in* TrGF*: see Vol. 2). Iophon's son is otherwise known only from official inscriptions;*[2] *nothing suggests that he had a theatrical career.*

Iophon was a prolific and successful playwright, credited in the Suda with fifty plays. There is no complete record, but the Fasti inscription lists a victory at the Dionysia in 435, and a hypothesis to Euripides' Hippolytus *records that he came second after Euripides, with Ion third, in 428 (T 2b = Ion **T 5**). He must have been born in the 460s, and his dramatic career overlapped with his father's for at least thirty years, which may have included most of his productions; he was already about sixty years old when his father died aged ninety. The titles listed in the Suda (**T 1a**) are familiar ones except for* Dexamenos, *which probably dealt with Heracles killing the centaur Eurytion as the latter tried to rape or abduct the daughter of Dexamenos ('Welcomer'), a story told by*

---

[1] Sutton 1987a, 15f. collects the relevant data and supplies a family tree.

[2] IG II^2 1445.37 (= *TrGF* 22 T 9), and restored in IG II^2 1374.3 and 1375.4.

Bacchylides and summarized with variations by later mythographers (»» Gantz 1993, 423f.; also Pausanias 7.18.1).[3] *Four more tragic titles should probably be added from the Suda's entry for Cleophon (see note on **T 1a**). There was also a satyr-play* Aulos-players *of which a line-and-a-half are preserved (F 1). Of the tragedies only* Bacchae *leaves any traces: see on this below.*

Most of what we are told about Iophon's relationship with his father originates in comic jokes and the increasingly implausible interpretations of them which emerge in the Life of Sophocles, *the Aristophanes scholia, and elsewhere.*[4] Frogs *71ff.* ***(T 5(a))*** *suggests that the true quality of Iophon's work could not be known before his father's death because he might have had help from him. In the scholia this innocuous suggestion (which actually implies that Iophon was quite highly regarded) has become 'Dionysus wonders whether he might have produced a tragedy* (or *tragedies?) of Sophocles as his own'* ***(T 5(b))****, and then, as if this were a fact, 'Iophon is lampooned in comedy . . . for having his own name put on his father's tragedies'* ***(T 5(c))****. The story of Iophon's jealousy of Ariston's son and his failed attempt to have his father declared senile has a similar background (see below on* ***T 1(c)****). The* Life of Sophocles *included Iophon in a list of poets with whom Sophocles competed (**T 4**); this may be true, or it may only reflect the fact that their careers overlapped for a long time (cf.* ***T 5(b)****); they could easily have avoided competing with each other.*

---

[3] The title *Dexamenos* is recorded for the 5th-century Sicilian comic playwright Epicharmus (*PCG* I, test. 36.12), and *Kentauros or Dexamenos* for the 4th-century comic playwright Timocles (fr. 21 *PCG* from Athenaeus 240d).

[4] Cf. Lefkowitz 2012, 75–87, esp. 82f. on Iophon.

Testimonia

T 1

(a) Suda ι 451

Ἰοφῶν, Ἀθηναῖος, τραγικός, υἱὸς Σοφοκλέους τοῦ τραγικοῦ γνήσιος ἀπὸ Νικοστράτης· γέγονε δὲ αὐτῷ καὶ νόθος υἱὸς Ἀρίστων ἀπὸ Θεοδωρίδος Σικυωνίας. δράματα δὲ Ἰοφῶν ἐδίδαξε ν´· ὧν ἐστιν Ἀχιλλεύς, Τήλεφος, Ἀκταίων, Ἰλίου Πέρσις, Δεξαμενός, Βάκχαι, Πενθεύς, καὶ ἄλλα τινὰ μετὰ τοῦ πατρὸς Σοφοκλέους.

4 Βάκχαι ἢ Πενθεύς Valckenaer μετὰ Porson κατὰ Sud.

(b) Suda σ 815 ('Σοφοκλῆς')

. . . παῖδας δὲ οὓς ἔσχεν οὗτοι, Ἰοφῶν, Λεωσθένης, Ἀρίστων, Στέφανος, Μενεκλείδης.

(c) *Life of Sophocles* 13 (*TrGF* vol. 4, pp. 34f.)

φέρεται δὲ καὶ παρὰ πολλοῖς ἡ πρὸς τὸν υἱὸν Ἰοφῶντα γενομένη αὐτῷ δίκη. ἔχων γὰρ ἐκ μὲν Νικοστράτης Ἰοφῶντα, ἐκ δὲ Θεωρίδος Σικυωνίας Ἀρίστωνα, τὸν ἐκ τούτου γενόμενον παῖδα Σοφοκλέα τοὔνομα πλέον ἔστεργε. καί ποτε †ἐν δράματι† εἰσήγαγε ⟨. . .⟩ τὸν Ἰοφῶντα αὐτῷ φθονοῦντα καὶ πρὸς τοὺς φράτορας ἐγκαλοῦντα τῷ πατρὶ ὡς ὑπὸ γήρως παραφρονοῦντι· οἱ δὲ τῷ Ἰοφῶντι ἐπετίμησαν. Σάτυρος δέ φησιν αὐτὸν εἰπεῖν 'Εἰ μέν εἰμι Σοφοκλῆς, οὐ παραφρονῶ· εἰ δὲ παραφρονῶ, οὐκ εἰμὶ Σοφοκλῆς', καὶ τότε τὸν Οἰδίποδα παραναγνῶναι.

(d) *Life of Sophocles* 11 (*TrGF* vol. 4, pp. 33f.)

ἔσχε δὲ (*sc.* ὁ Σοφοκλῆς) καὶ τὴν τοῦ Ἅλωνος ἱερωσύνην, ὃς ἥρως μετὰ Ἀσκληπιοῦ παρὰ Χείρωνι ⟨. . .⟩ ἱδρυνθεὶς ὑπὸ Ἰοφῶντος τοῦ υἱοῦ μετὰ τὴν τελευτήν.

T 2b *see Ion* ***T 5***

T 4 = Choerilus **T 5**

T 5

(a) Ar. *Frogs* 71–79

Δι. δέομαι ποιητοῦ δεξιοῦ.
οἱ μὲν γὰρ οὐκέτ' εἰσίν, οἱ δ' ὄντες κακοί.
Ηρ. τί δ'; οὐκ Ἰοφῶν ζῇ;
Δι. τοῦτο γάρ τοι καὶ μόνον
ἔτ' ἐστὶ λοιπὸν ἀγαθόν, εἰ καὶ τοῦτ' ἄρα·
οὐ γὰρ σάφ' οἶδ' οὐδ' αὐτὸ τοῦθ' ὅπως ἔχει.
Ηρ. εἶτ' οὐ Σοφοκλέα πρότερον ὄντ' Εὐριπίδου
μέλλεις ἀναγαγεῖν, εἴπερ ἐκεῖθεν δεῖ σ' ἄγειν;

Testimonia

T 1

(a) Suda, 'Iophon'
Iophon, Athenian, tragic poet, legitimate son of Sophocles by Nicostrate (he also had an illegitimate son Ariston by Theodoris of Sicyon). Iophon produced 50 plays, including *Achilles, Telephus, Actaeon, The Sack of Troy, Dexamenos, Bacchae*, *Pentheus*, and some others with his father Sophocles.

(b) Suda, 'Sophocles'
His (i.e. Sophocles') sons were these: Iophon, Leosthenes, Ariston, Stephanus, Menecleides.

(c) *Life of Sophocles*
Many record the lawsuit which was brought against him (i.e. Sophocles) by his son Iophon. Iophon was Sophocles' son by Nicostrate, but Sophocles had another son, Ariston, by Theoris of Sicyon, and he favoured the latter's son who was named Sophocles. Once †in a play† *(. . .)* introduced Iophon being jealous of him (i.e. Ariston's son) and bringing a complaint against his father on the grounds that he was mentally deranged because of his great age; but they fined Iophon. According to Satyrus Sophocles said, 'If I'm Sophocles I'm not deranged, and if I'm deranged I'm not Sophocles', and then gave them a reading of the *Oedipus*.

(d) *Life of Sophocles*
He (i.e. Sophocles) also held the priesthood of Halon, a hero *(educated)* along with Asclepius by Cheiron *(. . .)* established by his son Iophon after his death.

T 2b *see Ion T 5*

T 4 = Choerilus T 5

T 5

(a) Aristophanes, *Frogs*

Dionysus. I'm in need of a skilful poet: 'For some no longer live, and those that live are bad.'

Heracles. What? Isn't Iophon living?

Dionysus. Yes, that's the only good thing left — if it *is* a good thing; I'm not really sure what to say how that goes either.

Heracles. Then aren't you going to bring up Sophocles, who's ahead of Euripides, if you have to bring someone from there?

Δι. οὐ πρίν γ' ἂν Ἰοφῶντ', ἀπολαβὼν αὐτὸν μόνον,
ἄνευ Σοφοκλέους ὅ τι ποιεῖ κωδωνίσω.

(b) Schol.$^{VMG\Theta}$ Ar. *Frogs* 73–74

ἠγωνίσατο γὰρ (*sc.* ὁ Ἰοφῶν) καὶ ἐνίκησε λαμπρῶς ἔτι ζῶντος τοῦ πατρὸς αὐτοῦ. διὸ ἀμφιβάλλει μήποτε τοῦ Σοφοκλέους εἴη εἰσηχὼς τραγῳδίαν.

εἰσηχὼς Michaelis εἰρηκὼς Schol. τραγῳδίας Schuringa

(c) Schol.$^{VM\Theta}$ Ar. *Frogs* 78

Ἰοφῶν οὐ μόνον ἐπὶ τῷ ταῖς τοῦ πατρὸς τραγῳδίαις ἐπιγράφεσθαι κωμῳδεῖται, ἀλλ' ἐπὶ τῷ καὶ ψυχρὸς καὶ μαλακὸς εἶναι.

ΒΑΚΧΑΙ

The title suggests a plot similar to that of Euripides' Bacchae *and (probably) Aeschylus's* Pentheus. *What we know of the play is at least consistent with this: see the notes below on **F 2** and **F 3**.*

F 2 Stobaeus 2.1.9

Ἰοφῶντος Βακχῶν·

(Ἀγαύη?)

ἐπίσταμαι δὲ καὶ τάδ', οὖσά περ γυνή,
ὡς μᾶλλον ὅστις εἰδέναι τὰ τῶν θεῶν
ζητεῖ, τοσούτῳ μᾶλλον ἧσσον εἴσεται.

Fabula Incerta

F 3 Schol.^{V} Ar. *Frogs* 330

ἡ μυρσίνη ᾠκείωται τοῖς χθονίοις θεοῖς, Διονύσου δεδωκότος ὅτε ἀνήγαγε τὴν Σεμέλην. τρία γὰρ αὐτῷ ᾠκείωται, κισσὸς ἄμπελος μυρσίνη. μυθολογοῦσι δ' ἐν Σάμῳ θεῖον μη⟨χάνημα⟩ προσφέρεσθαι τῇ Ἥρᾳ. ἐπεὶ γάρ, ὥς φασιν, ἐξητεῖτο τὴν ψυχὴν τῆς Σεμέλης τοὺς κάτω θεοὺς καθάπερ ἦν ἐπηγγελμένον, ὑποσχέσθαι λέγουσιν αὐτῇ τὸν Ἅιδην τοῦτο δράσειν, τοῦ Διονύσου τῶν μάλιστα τερπόντων αὐτῷ ἀντίψυχον ἀντ' ἐκείνης πέμψαντος· τὸν δὲ Διόνυσον πυθόμενον τὰ παρὰ τῶν κάτω θεῶν ἐπεσταλμένα σοφίσασθαι πρὸς ταῦτα, καὶ τριῶν ὄντων αὐτῷ μάλιστα ἠγαπημένων, τοῦ τε κισσοῦ καὶ τῆς ἀμπέλου καὶ τῆς μυρσίνης, ἀποστεῖλαι τοῖς κάτω θεοῖς αὐτήν. δηλοῖ δὲ καὶ Ἰοφῶν ὁ τραγικός.

θεῖον μη⟨χάνημα⟩ προσφέρεσθαι Holwerda (see note below)

Dionysus. Not before I get hold of Iophon on his own and sound out what he composes without Sophocles.

(b) Scholia on *Frogs* 73

He (Iophon) competed (in the tragic contests) and won notable victories while his father was still alive. Hence he (i.e. Dionysus) wonders whether he (i.e. Iophon) might have produced a tragedy (*or* tragedies?) of Sophocles as his own.

(c) Scholia on *Frogs* 78[5]

Iophon is lampooned in comedy, not only for having his own name put on his father's tragedies, but for being frigid and soft.

BACCHAE

F 2 Stobaeus, *Anthology*, 'On those who explain divine things etc.'
From Iophon's *Bacchae*:

> *(Agave?)* I know this too, although I am a woman: the more we seek to know about the gods, the more our knowledge of them will be less.

Unidentified Play

F 3 Scholia on Aristophanes' *Frogs*

Myrtle belongs to the underworld gods, having been given to them by Dionysus when he retrieved Semele. Three things belong to him personally: ivy, grape-vine, and myrtle. In Samos they tell the story that Hera was the victim of a divine *(ruse)*. For, they say, when she asked the gods below to return the life of Semele, as had been commanded, they told her that Hades had promised to do this provided that Dionysus sent him as compensation a life from those that were most pleasing to him; and Dionysus, learning what the gods below had required, and cherishing three things especially — ivy, vine, and myrtle — sent them myrtle. The tragic poet Iophon also makes this known.

---

[5] Snell's **T 5(c)** includes two further scholia which duplicate the information printed here.

Notes on Iophon

T 1

(a) *Achilles, Telephus,* etc.: the Suda in a brief notice (κ 1730) ascribes all these titles except *Pentheus*, along with four others (*Amphiaraus, Erigone, Thyestes, Leucippus*) to Cleophon. Cleophon was included by Snell in *TrGF* as no. 77 but is otherwise known only from a few remarks in Aristotle's *Poetics* (1448a11f., 1458a18ff. = T 2, 3) and *Rhetoric* (1408a10ff. = T 4) which imply that he was an epic poet rather than a tragedian.[6] Probably, as Snell suggests, the Suda's tragedian Cleophon is actually Iophon, to whom the four additional titles can then be ascribed (»» Janko 2011, 333–35). Valckenaer's suggestion that ***Pentheus*** was identical with ***Bacchae*** is plausible but uncertain. Euripides' own *Bacchae* was sometimes referred to as *Pentheus*. The Suda's entry for Cleophon has only *Bacchae*.

(b) See above, p. 118.

(c) The citation of Satyrus (3rd–2nd C. BC) is telling; his *Lives* of famous men of the past were full of such gossipy anecdotes, e.g. that Sophocles expired after running out of breath while reading an emotional passage from the end of *Antigone*. **Once †in a play† etc.:** the missing subject of **introduced** was probably the name of a comic poet; the relevant play may also have been named. Radt in *TrGF* 4, p. 35 lists an array of emendations and interpretations proposed by 19th-century scholars. **If I'm Sophocles etc.:** a play on the name Sophocles, 'Famed for wisdom'. **a reading of the *Oedipus*:** Plutarch, *Mor.* 785a (= *TrGF* T 8a) has Sophocles more plausibly reading the 'parodos' (actually the first stasimon) of *Oedipus at Colonus*, a eulogy of Attica.

T 5(a)–(c)

See above, p. 119. *Frogs* 72 is borrowed from Euripides' *Oeneus* (F 565).

F 2

This gnomic comment is cited by Stobaeus under the same heading as Aristarchus **F 1b** (see note there). The female speaker may have been Agave, who in Euripides' *Bacchae* (1301ff.) admits to having shared her son's impiety. In Iophon's play she may have mocked acceptance of divine mysteries in much the same way as Pentheus in the first episode of Euripides' play. (Iophon's may have been the earlier, of course.)

---

[6] The Cleophon named in Aristot. *Soph. El.* 174b23ff. (= *TrGF* 77 T 5) as a speaker in Speusippus's dialogue *Mandroboulos* was perhaps the late 5th-century democratic politician.

F 3

This quaint story is based on the belief that Semele was deified and lived on Olympus after being blasted by Zeus in the form of a lightning-bolt and giving birth to Dionysus. Either she was immortalized by the bolt itself, or Dionysus on reaching maturity redeemed her from Hades and took her to Olympus (»» Frazer 1921, I.332f. on Apollodorus 3.5.3; West 1966, 416 on Hesiod, *Theogony* 942; Gantz 1993, 476f.; *LIMC* VII, 'Semele', nos. 19–26). The anodos was associated with several locations: Delphi (Plutarch, *Mor.* 293c), Troezen (Pausanias 2.31.2), Lerna (Pausanias 2.37.5). Iophon's story presumably came from the priests at the great archaic sanctuary of Hera on Samos, where it doubled as an *aition* for the fact that myrtle was associated both with Dionysiac ritual and with death and the underworld. Here uniquely it is Hera who has to negotiate Semele's release (**commanded** by Zeus, presumably, as a penance for causing Semele's death). Iophon may have used the story in a choral ode in his *Bacchae* (less likely in *Actaeon*, as Actaeon was usually supposed to have died before the incineration of Semele and birth of Dionysus). There is no need to think (with Steffen 1979, 75f.) that it might have been the plot of an unknown satyr-play.

[**that Hera was the victim of a divine ruse:** text and sense are as proposed by Holwerda 1997 (cf. *TrGF* 5, p. 1107). The scholion includes intrusive words between Σάμῳ and μὴ προσφέρεσθαι which seem to have been part of a hymn to Dionysus, probably not from Iophon's play, and originally quoted in a separate note (schol. 330d in Chantry 1999).]

PHILOCLES I
(*TrGF* 24)

Texts etc.. TrGF 1^2.139–42 with *addenda* 1^2.348; *MusTr* 94–97, 281f.

*Philocles, another contemporary of Euripides (**T 1**) is of interest as one of a prolific family of tragedians which included his uncle Aeschylus and his great-grandson the younger Astydamas,*[1] *as an active tragedian himself (**T 1, 2**), and as winner of first prize at the City Dionysia ahead of a production by Sophocles that included* Oedipus Tyrannus *(**T 3**). All that survives of his work is the seven play-titles listed in the Suda (**T 1**), another title* Tereus *with that of the tetralogy which included it,* Pan-

Testimonia

T 1 Suda *φ* 378

Φιλοκλῆς, Φιλοπείθους, Ἀθηναῖος, τραγικός, τοῖς χρόνοις κατ' Εὐριπίδην. ἐπεκαλεῖτο δὲ Χολὴ διὰ τὸ πικρόν. ἔγραψε τραγῳδίας ρ', ὧν ἐστι καὶ ταῦτα· Ἠριγόνη, Ναύπλιος, Οἰδίπους, Οἰνεύς, Πρίαμος, Πηνελόπη, Φιλοκτήτης. Αἰσχύλου δὲ τοῦ τραγικοῦ ἦν ἀδελφιδοῦς καὶ ἔσχεν υἱὸν Μόρσιμον τὸν τραγικόν, οὗτινος γίνεται Ἀστυδάμας ὁ τραγικός, τούτου δ' ἕτερος Φιλοκλῆς, τραγικός.

1 Φιλοπείθους schol. *Birds* (**T 2**) Πολυπείθους Sud.

T 2 Schol.$^{V\Gamma_2 Lh}$ Ar. *Birds* 281c (following **T 6c** below)

ἔστι δὲ ὁ Φιλοκλῆς τραγῳδίας ποιητὴς καὶ Φιλοπείθους υἱὸς ἐξ Αἰσχύλου ἀδελφῆς. ὅσοι δὲ Ἀλμίωνος αὐτόν φασιν ἐπιθετικῶς λέγουσι διὰ τὸ πικρὸν εἶναι· ἅλμη γὰρ ἡ πικρία. γεγόνασι δὲ Φιλοκλεῖς δύο τραγῳδιῶν ποιηταί, εἷς μὲν ὁ ‹Φιλοπείθους υἱός, ἕτερος δὲ ὁ› Φιλοκλέους ἀπόγονος· ἐκείνου μὲν γὰρ υἱὸς Μόρσιμος, τούτου δὲ Ἀστυδάμας, ἐκ τούτου δὲ Φιλοκλῆς καὶ ἕτερος ‹Ἀστυδάμας› ὁ κατὰ τὴν αὐτὴν ἡλικίαν περιπεπτωκὼς τῷ νεωτέρῳ Φιλοκλεῖ.

4, 5f. supplements: Boeckh   4 υἱός Dindorf ἄρης schol.   γὰρ ἦν Μόρσιμος ‹υἱός› Holwerda

---

[1] Cf. p. 55 above on Euphorion, and notes below on **T 1** and **T 2**.

dionis *(**T 6**), two mythical details (**F 2, 3**), and a handful of unrevealing words (**F 1, 4, 5**). The eight titles are unexceptional; all but* Penelope *(and perhaps* Priam*) were also treated by Sophocles, and* Penelope, Oedipus *and* Philoctetes *by Aeschylus. Comic jokes evoked various guesses about Philocles' personal and poetic qualities from later commentators on Aristophanes (T 5–9, see below on **T 6** and* Tereus*). The citations of **F 1–3** and **F 5** suggest that a few of his plays were known to Hellenistic literary scholars.*

Testimonia

T 1 Suda, 'Philocles'
Philocles, son of Philopeithes, Athenian, tragic poet, contemporary with Euripides. He was nicknamed 'Bile' because of his bitterness. He wrote 100 tragedies, including these: *Erigone, Nauplius, Oedipus, Oeneus, Priam, Penelope, Philoctetes.* He was a nephew of the tragic poet Aeschylus and had a son Morsimus the tragic poet, who fathered Astydamas the tragic poet, who fathered another Philocles, also a tragic poet.

T 2 Scholia on Aristophanes' *Birds* (following **T 6c** below)
Philocles is the tragic poet, son of Philopeithes by a sister of Aeschylus. Those who call him son of Halmion ('Salty') are using a nickname because of his being bitter; for bitterness is saltiness. There have been two tragic poets named Philocles, one *(the son of Philopeithes, the other)* Philocles' descendant; for he (i.e. Philocles I) had a son Morsimus, who had a son Astydamas, who had sons Philocles and another Astydamas, the one who coincided in age with the younger Philocles.

T 3

(a) Hypoth. II Soph. *Oedipus Tyrannus* (= Dicaearchus fr. 80 Wehrli, 101 Mirhady)

χαριέντως δὲ Τύραννον ἅπαντες αὐτὸν ἐπιγράφουσιν ὡς ἐξέχοντα πάσης τῆς Σοφοκλέους ποιήσεως, καίπερ ἡττηθέντα ὑπὸ Φιλοκλέους, ὥς φησι Δικαίαρχος.

(b) Aelius Aristides *Or.* 46, p. 334 Dindorf

καὶ οὐκ ἐπὶ μὲν τῶν ἀθλητῶν οὕτως συμβαίνει, τὰ δὲ τῆς μουσικῆς ἑστηκυῖαν ἔχει τὴν νίκην τοῖς κρείττοσιν, ἀλλὰ κἀνταῦθα τὸ τοῦ Πινδάρου κρατεῖ. πάνυ γὰρ μετ' ἀληθείας τοῦτ' ἐκεῖνος ὕμνησεν (fr. 38 Snell–Maehler), *ἐν ἔργμασιν δὲ νικᾷ τύχα, οὐ σθένος*. Σοφοκλῆς Φιλοκλέους ἡττᾶτο ἐν Ἀθηναίοις τὸν Οἰδίπουν, ὦ Ζεῦ καὶ θεοί, πρὸς ὃν οὐδ' Αἰσχύλος εἶχε λέξαι τι. ἆρ' οὖν διὰ τοῦτο χείρων Σοφοκλῆς Φιλοκλέους; αἰσχύνη μὲν οὖν αὐτῷ τοσοῦτον ἀκοῦσαι, ὅτι βελτίων Φιλοκλέους.

T 6

(a) Aristophanes, *Birds* 279–83

Πε. ἕτερος αὖ λόφον καθειληφώς τις ὄρνις οὑτοσί.
Ευ. τί τὸ τέρας τουτί ποτ' ἐστίν; οὐ σὺ μόνος ἄρ' ἦσθ' ἔποψ,
ἀλλὰ χοὖτος ἕτερος;
Επ. οὑτοσὶ μέν ἐστι Φιλοκλέους
ἐξ ἔποπος, ἐγὼ δὲ τούτου πάππος, ὥσπερ εἰ λέγοις
'Ἱππόνικος Καλλίου κἀξ Ἱππονίκου Καλλίας.'

(c) Schol. Ar. *Birds* 281a–c (preceding **T 2** above)

οὗτος ὁ Φιλοκλῆς ἔποπα ἐσκεύασεν ἐν τῇ Πανδιονίδι τετραλογίᾳ, οὗ ἡ ἀρχὴ *σὲ τῶν πάντων δεσπότην λέγω* (**F 1**).

ἄλλως· Φιλοκλεῖ ἐστι δρᾶμα Τηρεὺς ἢ Ἔποψ.

ἄλλως. ὁ Σοφοκλῆς πρῶτον τὸν Τηρέα ἐποίησεν, εἶτα Φιλοκλῆς. διὰ τοῦτο δὲ εἶπεν *ἐγὼ δὲ πάππος* ἀντὶ τοῦ *πρὸ αὐτοῦ ἐγράφην* . . .

ἄλλως. ἐν ἐνίοις ὑπομνήμασιν, ὅτι προκέφαλός ἐστιν ὁ Φιλοκλῆς ὡς ὁ ἔποψ· ἀλλ' οὐδαμοῦ κεκωμῴδηται. εἴη ἂν οὖν τὸν ἔποπα ἐσκευοποιηκὼς τῇ Πανδιονίδι τετραλογίᾳ, ἣν καὶ Ἀριστοτέλης ἐν ταῖς Διδασκαλίαις ἀναγράφει.

T 3

(a) Hypothesis to Sophocles' *Oedipus Tyrannus*
It is aptly titled *Tyrannus* by everyone, as being outstanding amongst all of Sophocles' compositions, even though it was defeated by Philocles, as Dicaearchus says.

(b) Aelius Aristides, *A Response to Plato on behalf of the Four*
And this (i.e. this unexpected defeat) does not just occur for athletes while music holds victory secure for the best competitors, but there too the words of Pindar prevail; he was absolutely right when he sang that 'in action fortune wins, not strength'. Sophocles saw his *Oedipus* worsted amongst the Athenians by Philocles (O Zeus and gods!), and that was a play to which even Aeschylus had no response. Was Sophocles, then, worse than Philocles? It shames him, indeed, just to be said to have been better than Philocles!

T 6

(a) Aristophanes, *Birds*
Peisaeterus. Here's another bird that's also got a crest.
Euelpides. Whatever can this apparition be? You weren't the only hoopoe, then, and this is another one?
Hoopoe. This one is from Philocles' hoopoe, and I'm his granddad — just as if you said 'Hipponicus son of Callias, and Callias son of Hipponicus'.

(c) Scholia on the above (preceding **T 2** above)
This Philocles fitted out a hoopoe in his *Pandionis* tetralogy which begins (*or* began?), 'I call you lord of all' (**F 1**).

also: Philocles has a play called *Tereus or Hoopoe.*

also: Sophocles composed his *Tereus* first, then Philocles. So he (i.e. Aristophanes' hoopoe) has said 'I'm his granddad' instead of 'I was written before him' . . .

also: some commentaries say that Philocles was dome-headed like a hoopoe; but nowhere in comedy is he lampooned as such. So maybe he put the hoopoe on the stage in his *Pandionis* tetralogy, which Aristotle lists in the *Didascaliae*.

ΤΗΡΕΥΣ

The story of the Thracian king Tereus ended with Tereus transformed into a hoopoe as he sought vengeance on his wife Procne (who became a nightingale) and her sister Philomela (a swallow). He had raped Philomela and cut out her tongue to conceal his crime, and they had retaliated by killing his and Procne's son Itys and serving him the boy's flesh. The story was treated in tragedies by Sophocles (of which we have a hypothesis and seventeen fragments),[2] *by Philocles (attested only in **T 6**), and perhaps by the younger Carcinus (see his **F 4** in Vol. 2). The facts that can be inferred from **T 6** are that Philocles produced a Tereus some time after Sophocles'* Tereus, *that it was part of a tetralogy about*

F 1 Schol. Ar. *Birds* 281 (see **T 6(c)** above)
(Tereus?) σὲ τῶν ἁπάντων(?) . . . δεσπότην λέγω

Fabula Incerta

F 2 Schol. Eur. *Andromache* 32
Φιλοκλῆς δὲ ὁ τραγῳδοποιὸς καὶ Θέογνις προεκδοθῆναί φασιν ὑπὸ Τυνδάρεω τὴν Ἑρμιόνην τῷ Ὀρέστῃ καὶ ἤδη ἐγκυμονοῦσαν ὑπὸ Μενελάου δοθῆναι Νεοπτολέμῳ καὶ γεννῆσαι Ἀμφικτυόνα· ὕστερον δὲ Διομήδει συνοικῆσαι.

Brief fragments from unidentified plays: **F 3** Ταλαός (*vel* Καλαός), **F 4**? δορυφόνον, **F 5** οὐδ' ἂν ἐγκέφαλον ἔσθων λίποι

[2] F 583 of Sophocles' play is now substantially enlarged by a papyrus fragment, P. Oxy. 82.5292: see Slattery 2016, Finglass 2016. On the attribution of Sophocles F 581 (ten lines announcing the transformation of Tereus) to Sophocles rather than Philocles see Sommerstein *et al.* 2006, 189f.

TEREUS

Pandion and his daughters,[3] *and that both productions were prior to the production of* Birds *in 414. Further details in the scholia are simply misguided guesswork: 'some commentators think Philocles was dome-headed' (because the hoopoe has a rounded crest); Philocles 'maybe' put Tereus on the stage in the form of a hoopoe (as Aristophanes did); his play was alternatively titled Hoopoe (as Aristophanes seems to imply).*[4] *»» Dunbar 1995, 233–35 on Birds 279–83; Gantz 1993, 239–341 and Sommerstein et al. 2006, 141–195 on the story of Tereus and Procne in Sophocles and elsewhere.*

F 1 Scholia on Aristophanes' *Birds* (see **T 6(c)** above)
(Tereus?) You I call lord of all . . .

Unidentified Play

F 2 Scholia on Euripides' *Andromache*
Philocles the tragedian and Theognis (*TrGF* 28 F 2) say that Hermione was previously given by Tyndareus to Orestes and when she was already pregnant was given by Menelaus to Neoptolemus and gave birth to Amphictyon; and that later she lived with Diomedes.

Brief fragments from unidentified plays: **F 3** Talaos (*or* Kalaos),[5] **F 4**? spear-slaying,[6] **F 5** nor would he desist from eating brains.[7]

---

[3] It is not easy to see how the story of king Pandion and his daughters could have filled an entire tetralogy. Welcker (1841, 1967f.) suggested a first play in which Tereus married Procne after assisting Pandion in a war against Labdacus of Thebes (cf. Apollodorus 3.14.8), a second about Tereus's abuse of Philomela, and a third about the sisters' revenge.

[4] The title is still given In *TrGF* as ΤΗΡΕΥΣ Η ΕΠΟΨ (*TEREUS OR HOOPOE*).

[5] Cf. Aristarchus **F 5** with footnote.

[6] Attributed to 'Philoctetus' in Hesychius δ 2241.

[7] Considered as possibly satyric by Cipolla 2003, 273, 280f., 298.

Notes on Philocles I

T 1, T 2

The four generations are (1) Philocles I, (2) Morsimus (*TrGF* 29), (3) Astydamas I (*TrGF* 59), (4) Philocles II (*TrGF* 61) and Astydamas II (*TrGF* 60). An Astydamas III (*TrGF* 96), also a tragic poet but known only as an ambassador for the Athenian Artists of Dionysus to the Delphic Amphictiony in 277 BC, was probably a further descendant. The Suda (**T 1**) here omits Astydamas II but has two separate entries for Astydamas father and son (see on these in Vol. 2). In **T 2**, line 4 Boeckh's supplement makes good sense of the transmitted text: simply changing Φιλοκλέους to Φιλοπείθους (Boeckh's earlier suggestion, preferred by Snell) is less likely as ἀπόγονος normally means **descendant**, not 'son'. The information that Astydamas II **coincided in age with the younger Philocles** was probably meant to distinguish the son from their father (both would have been simply 'Astydamas' in the didascalic records).

Both testimonia give Philocles one tragedian son, Morsimus. Some scholars (e.g. Sutton 1987a, 13, Sommerstein 2005 on *Peace* 807–9) think that Melanthius I (*TrGF* 23)[8] was also a son of Philocles since in *Peace* 802–12 Aristophanes attacks first 'Morsimus and Melanthius' and then 'Melanthius and his brother', but the inference is unnecessary and Melanthius is conspicuously not named as a son of Philocles or brother of Morsimus in the Aristophanes scholia.

T 3(b)

An example of the classicizing prejudices of the 2nd century AD. Aristides knew little or nothing about Philocles' plays, or about the criteria by which these productions were judged. Aelian is similarly indignant at the thought of Xenocles being preferred to Euripides in 415 (Xenocles I **T 3**).

T 6

In Aristophanes' *Birds* the heroes Peisetaerus and Euelpides find Tereus in his hoopoe form and are introduced by him to other birds including a second hoopoe. In the rather contorted joke that follows this second hoopoe is identified as the son of the hoopoe (formerly Tereus) in Philocles' *Tereus*; he is 'grandson' of the first because at Athens names usually passed from grandfathers to grandsons rather than from fathers to sons; thus 'Hoopoe grandson of Hoopoe'

---

[8] *TrGF*'s numbering makes the tragedian Melanthius an older contemporary of Philocles I, but the mid-5th century poet mentioned in *TrGF* 23 T 1 must be a different man. The tragedian was very probably the author of the verses from a *Medea* parodied in Ar. *Peace* 1013f. and tentatively ascribed by Snell (following Fritzsche 1845) to Morsimus (*TrGF* 29 F 1?, cf. *TrGF* 23 T 4). On all this see Olson 1998, 229, 263 on *Peace* 803–8, 1009–15; Zogg 2014, 169–75.

corresponds with 'Callias grandson of Callias', the subject of the next joke. On the information (and misinformation) about Philocles' play contained in the scholia see the introduction to *Tereus* above.

F 1

The verse is quoted not quite metrically in **T 6(c)** and seems to have been the first line of *Tereus* rather than the whole tetralogy. It was probably an invocation of Helios, the Sun-god, who was important in Thracian cult. Sophocles' *Tereus* may have begun with the similar invocation, Soph. F 582 (»» Sommerstein *et al.* 2006, 175–77).

F 2

Schol. Eur. *Andr.* 32 is a confused and textually corrupt collection of traditions about Hermione's childlessness while married to Neoptolemus, her later history, and his children by Andromache and Leonassa of Argos. These traditions were continually manipulated for political and poetic reasons which are now hard to penetrate (see also on Antiphon's *Andromache* in Vol. 2). The marriage of Helen's daughter to Neoptolemus is mentioned without complications in *Odyssey* 4.3–14, but in Sophocles' *Hermione* (summarized in the *Odyssey* scholia and Eustathius's commentary: »» Radt in *TrGF* 4.192f.) she was betrothed to her cousin Orestes as a child and given to him by her grandfather Tyndareus while Menelaus was retrieving her mother from Troy; Menelaus meanwhile had promised her to Neoptolemus in return for his help at Troy, so she was given to him on their return and only after his death to Orestes, to whom she bore Tisamenus. In Euripides' *Andromache* Orestes comes to Phthia to retrieve Hermione, complaining of Menelaus's duplicity (*Andr.* 966–70). In the 'happy ending' of his *Orestes*, on the other hand, Apollo announces that Hermione's expected marriage to Neoptolemus will not take place (*Or.* 1653–55). Philocles and Theognis apparently adjusted the story so that Hermione was pregnant with Orestes' son, Amphictyon, when she married Neoptolemus. The son's name might suggest a connection with the Delphic Amphictiony, but the motivation for all this is obscure (perhaps some connection with Neoptolemus's death at Delphi?), as are the dramatic contexts in which Philocles and his contemporary Theognis might have used it. Hermione's final marriage with **Diomedes** is mentioned in the scholia on Pindar, *Nem.* 10.7 in connection with Diomedes' immortalization 'with the Dioscuri', Hermione's uncles; it seems to be attributed there to Ibycus (fr. 13 *PMG*) although the text is ambiguous.

XENOCLES I
(*TrGF* 33)

Texts etc. TrGF 1^2.151–53.

*Xenocles is now known chiefly as the poet whose plays were preferred to Euripides' Trojan trilogy at the City Dionysia of 415 BC (**T 3**). Other than that (from Aelian), our information about him comes entirely from comic allusions in plays of Aristophanes and the scholia on these (**T 1** below, T 2, 4, 5) and Carcinus I T 2–4.*[1] *Xenocles himself, his father Carcinus I (TrGF 21), and his son Carcinus II (TrGF 70) were nevertheless significant tragedians, as well as belonging to the Athenian élite.*[2] *Their deme, Thorikos in southeast Attica, was the site of the earliest known stone theatre and one of the earliest rural Dionysia festivals in Attica.*[3] *Carcinus I was a trierarch (therefore wealthy) around 450 and a general (*stratêgos*, therefore politically influential) at the beginning of the Peloponnesian War, so he was probably born in the 480s;*[4] *we have*

Testimonia

T 1

(a) Aristophanes, *Clouds* 1259–66

Χρ. β′ ἰώ μοί μοι.
Στ. ἔα.
τίς οὑτοσί ποτ' ἔσθ' ὁ θρηνῶν; οὔ τι που
τῶν Καρκίνου τις δαιμόνων ἐφθέγξατο;

---

[1] Stewart 2016 suggests some possible inferences from this evidence about the dramatic careers of Carcinus I and his sons.

[2] Cf. Davies 1971, 283–85.

[3] See Csapo–Wilson 2015, 321 with comments on pp. 323 ('the oldest known theater built almost entirely of stone, and the only theater of fifth-century date to have survived to any significant degree'), 324, 328.

[4] See Carcinus I T 5–7 including Thuc. 2.23.2. The inscriptions listed as T 5 and T 7 are now IG I^3 365 and 874. To the dedication by Carcinus listed in T 7 (IG II^2 1498.67ff.) add one by his son Xenotimos listed in 4th-century inscriptions (IG II^2 1388 etc.; for Xenotimos cf. Isocrates 17.52). Neither this Carcinus nor his grandson Carcinus II should be identified with the Carcinus of Acragas (*TrGF* no. 235) named in Suda *κ* 394 (= Carcinus II **T 1**: see further in Vol. 2).

almost no details of his tragic career, and just one fragment of a play, but the Fasti inscription may include a tragic victory for him in 446 (the name is restored: DID A 1.81 = Carcinus I T 1). His three sons[5] *make their first comic appearance in Philocleon's famous dancing scene at the end of* Wasps, *when they were presumably young men (*Wasps *1501ff.,* 422 BC, *cf. Phrynichus* ***T 10(f)****). Xenocles was still active as a playwright in 405 (*Frogs *86 = T 5); he could have been still living and producing when his son Carcinus II made his début in the 380s.*

It is impossible to get any impression of Xenocles' qualities as a tragedian,[6] *except that he did win the prize in 415. The only known titles are those of 415 listed by Aelian (****T 3****, from the Didascaliae) and the* Licymnius *named in the scholia on* Clouds *1264f. (****T 1(b)****), so produced before 417 if not before the first production of* Clouds *in 423.*

Testimonia

T 1

(a) Aristophanes, *Clouds*

Second Creditor. O me, O me!

Strepsiades. Uh-oh: who's this doing a lament? Not one of Carcinus's daemons giving voice?

---

[5] The Aristophanes scholia are confused about the number and names (see Snell's note on Carcinus I T 3b), but the number was probably three and the names Xenocles and Xenotimos (cf. n. 1 above) are certain. »» Davies 1971, 285.

[6] Aristophanes comments equivocally on his speechwriting in *Women at the Thesmophoria* 440ff. (= T 4b). Comic allusions to his versatility with 'contrivances' (μηχαναί) are variously explained in the scholia on Aristophanes' *Peace* 791 (= Carcinus T 3c: »» Farmer 2017, 28f.).

Χρ. τί δ', ὅστις εἰμί, τοῦτο βούλεσθ' εἰδέναι;
ἀνὴρ κακοδαίμων.
Στ. κατὰ σεαυτόν νυν τρέπου.
Χρ. ὦ σκληρὲ δαῖμον, ὦ τύχαι θραυσάντυγες
ἵππων ἐμῶν, ὦ Παλλάς, ὥς μ' ἀπώλεσας.
Στ. τί δαί σε Τληπόλεμός ποτ' εἴργασται κακόν;

(b) Scholia on the above:

1261: ἐπεὶ τραγικῶς ἀνεφώνησε τὸ *ἰώ μοι μοι*. οἱ δὲ Καρκίνου παῖδες Ξενοκλῆς, Ξενότιμος καὶ Δημότιμος· καὶ οἱ μὲν χορευταί, Ξενοκλῆς δὲ τραγῳδίας ποιητής.

Ξενοκλῆς... καὶ οἱ μὲν χορευταί Schol.$^{\mathrm{E\Theta MA}}$ Ξενοκλῆς (-κλείδης Schol.^{R}) καὶ Ξενότιμος· καὶ ὁ μὲν χορευτής Schol.^{RV}

1264–65, Schol.$^{\mathrm{RV(E)}}$: *ὦ σκληρὲ δαῖμον*: τοῦτο Ξενοκλέους ἐστιν ἐκ τοῦ Λικυμνίου, λέγεται δὲ ὑπ' Ἀλκμήνης ⟨ ⟩ Λικύμνιον τεθνηκέναι ὑπὸ Τληπολέμου.

1264–65, Schol.^{ENp}: Εὐφρόνιος τὸ *ὦ Πάλλας, ὥς μ' ἀπώλεσας* Ξενοκλέους εἶναί φησιν ἐκ τοῦ Λικυμνίου λεγόμενον ὑπ' Ἀλκμήνης τοῦ Λικυμνίου ὑπὸ Τληπολέμου ἀνῃρημένου· διὸ καὶ ἐπήνεγκεν αὐτὸς *τί δὲ σε Τληπόλεμός ποτ' εἴργασται κακόν;* καὶ τὸ *θραυσάντυγες* ⟨ἐκ τοῦ⟩ *χρυσάμπυκες* παραπεποιῆσθαι.

T 3 Aelian, *Var. Hist.* 2.8

Κατὰ τὴν πρώτην καὶ ἐνενηκοστὴν Ὀλυμπιάδα . . . ἀντηγωνίσαντο ἀλλήλοις Ξενοκλῆς καὶ Εὐριπίδης. καὶ πρῶτός γε ἦν Ξενοκλῆς, ὅστις ποτὲ οὗτός ἐστιν, Οἰδίποδι καὶ Λυκάονι καὶ Βάκχαις καὶ Ἀθάμαντι σατυρικῷ. τούτου δεύτερος Εὐριπίδης ἦν Ἀλεξάνδρῳ καὶ Παλαμήδει καὶ Τρωσὶ καὶ Σισύφῳ σατυρικῷ. γελοῖον δὲ (οὐ γάρ;) Ξενοκλέα μὲν νικᾶν, Εὐριπίδην δὲ ἡττᾶσθαι, καὶ ταῦτα τοιούτοις δράμασι. τῶν δύο τοίνυν τὸ ἕτερον· ἢ ἀνόητοι ἦσαν οἱ τῆς ψήφου κύριοι καὶ ἀμαθεῖς καὶ πόρρω κρίσεως ὀρθῆς, ἢ ἐδεκάσθησαν. ἄτοπον δὲ ἑκάτερον καὶ Ἀθηναίων ἥκιστα ἄξιον.

Cred. Why wish you to know this, who I am? An ill-starred man!
Streps. Look after yourself, then!
Cred. O cruel daemon, O my horses' rail-shattering accident, O Pallas, how hast thou destroyed me![1265]
Streps. And what harm has Tlempolemus done to you?

(b) Scholia on the above:

1261: (Strepsiades says this) because he (i.e. the Creditor) has cried 'O me, O me' in tragic style. Carcinus's sons were Xenocles, Xenotimos and Demotimos; these two were actors, and Xenocles a tragic poet.

1264–65(a): 'O cruel daemon': this is Xenocles', from the *Licymnius*. It is said by Alcmene . . . *(on learning)* . . . that Licymnius has been killed by Tlepolemus.

1264–65(b): Euphronius says that 'O Pallas, how hast thou destroyed me!' is Xenocles', from the *Licymnius*, said by Alcmene when Licymnius has been killed by Tlepolemus, and accordingly he (i.e. Aristophanes) has added 'And what harm has Tlempolemus done to you?'; and that 'rail-shattering' is adapted *(from)* 'gold-frontleted'.

T 3 Aelian, *Historical Miscellany*

In the ninety-first Olympiad (416/5–413/2 BC) . . . Xenocles and Euripides competed with each other. And the winner was Xenocles, whoever he was, with *Oedipus, Lycaon, Bacchae,* and the satyr-play *Athamas*. Second came Euripides with *Alexander, Palamedes, Women of Troy* and *Sisyphus*. Ridiculous, is it not, that Xenocles won and Euripides was defeated — and with such plays, at that! Well, one of these must be the case: either those responsible for the voting were ignorant and far from able to judge correctly, or they were bribed. Either of these is extraordinary and quite unworthy of the Athenians.

ΛΙΚΥΜΝΙΟΣ

*The scholia on Clouds 1264f. (**T 1(b)**) make it clear that the play was about the killing of Licymnius (son of Electryon and half-brother of Heracles' mother Alcmene) by Tlepolemus, one of Heracles's many sons and thus Licymnius's great-nephew. As a result of the killing Tlepolemus was expelled from the Argolid and led the Dorian settlement of Rhodes (»» Gantz 1993, 466; Fowler 2013, 340f.). The story is summarized in* Iliad *2.653–69. The killing occurred at Tiryns (cf. Pindar,* Ol. *7.27ff.), and the story reflects (amongst other things) the fact that Licymna was the name of the acropolis of Tiryns (Strabo 8.6.11). There was a sanct-*

F 2 Ar. *Clouds* 1264f. (see **T 1** above)

Ἀλκμήνη. ὦ σκληρὲ δαῖμον . . .
. . . ὦ Παλλάς, ὥς μ' ἀπώλεσας.

LICYMNIUS

uary of Licymnius in nearby Argos (Plutarch, Life of Pyrrhus *34.4; Pausanias 2.22.8). In ancient summaries of the story Tlepolemus kills the elderly Licymnius by striking him with his staff, either accidentally or 'in anger' (Pindar). This has some bearing on the interpretation of our minimal evidence for its content: see the note on* ***F 2****.*

Euripides' Licymnius *was probably about an earlier episode in which Licymnius's son Argeus was killed while campaigning with Heracles at Troy (»» Collard–Cropp 2008a, 560f.).*

F 2 Aristophanes, *Clouds* (see **T 1** above)

Alcmene. O cruel daemon . . . O Pallas, how hast thou destroyed me!

Notes on Xenocles I

T 1

See below on **F 2**.

T 3

Cf. Philocles **T 3(b)** with note.

F 2

If the scholia on *Clouds* 1264–65 are correct, the Alexandrian commentator Euphronius (3rd/2nd C. BC)[7] identified these two phrases as coming from Xenocles' *Licymnius* and spoken by Alcmene on hearing that Licymnius had been killed by Tlepolemus. Some scholars infer that all of lines 1264–65 come from Xenocles' play (cf. Rau 1967, 191), but if so they cannot have been spoken by Alcmene, who could not have referred to 'my horses'. Perhaps they were the dying Licymnius's words reported *to* Alcmene in a messenger-speech, but if so, the phrase 'O my horses' rail-shattering accident' must be a mock-tragic invention of Aristophanes (or imported from a different tragic source?) since no known account of Licymnius's death involves horses or chariots. The information also attributed to Euphronius, that the word θραυσάντυγες 'rail-shattering' was modelled on Homeric χρυσάμπυκες 'gold-frontleted' seems to be a separate matter

[7] Cf. Montanari *et al.* 2015, 126f.

unrelated to Xenocles' text ('O my horses' gold-frontleted fortunes' is nonsense). A further scholion stating that in *Clouds* 1272 the phrase ἵππους ἐλαύνων ('driving my chariot-team') 'is also parodic' probably has nothing to do with Xenocles either.

AGATHON
(*TrGF* 39)

Texts etc. *TrGF* 1^2.155–68 with *addenda* 1^2.349, 5.1107; *MusTr* 97–109, 282–83.

Discussions. Schmid 1940, 843–50; Lévêque 1955; Machìna 1955; Waern 1956; Lesky 1972, 523–25 (= 1983, 394–96); Muecke 1982; Wright 2016, 59–90.

*Agathon is in some ways the best known of all the 'lost' Greek tragedians. Aristophanes (**T 4** etc., **T 7**) and Plato (**T 2–3**) give us fairly detailed impressions of his impact on his contemporaries, although these need to be handled with care (see especially on **T 4** below), as do the later biographical traditions which stemmed largely from them. These authors reflect the novelty of Agathon's poetic and (in the case of Aristophanes) his musical style, which became the subjects of more objective study so long as his texts and perhaps scores were available. His plays were of interest to Aristotle, who commends the elegance of his* gnômai *(**F 5–9**) and the invented plot of* Anthos/Antheus *(**F 2a**) while criticizing at least one episodic plot (**T 17**) and his introduction of* embolima *(choral songs unrelated to their dramatic contexts, **T 18**). Agathon is virtually the only fifth-century tragedian whom Aristotle cites besides Aeschylus, Sophocles and Euripides,*[1] *and is cited by him more often (or rather less rarely) than any fourth-century tragedian.*[2] *All that being so, it is frustrating that we know nothing substantial about the content of Agathon's plays.*

Agathon came from a wealthy and well-connected Athenian family[3] *and lived approximately from the mid-440s to the last year or two of the fifth century (»» Lévêque 28–31, 73–77). In the* Protagoras*, set towards the end of the 430s, Plato presents him, perhaps a little anachronistic-*

[1] The only exceptions are Sthenelus (*TrGF* 32), cited in the *Poetics* as an example of a 'low' style using too many common words, and perhaps Dicaeogenes (late 5th/early 4th C., in Vol. 2).

[2] In the *Poetics*, *Rhetoric* and ethical works together: Agathon 9x, Antiphon 3x, Astydamas II 1x, Carcinus II 5x, Chaeremon 4x, Theodectas (dramatic works) 7x.

[3] References in *TrGF*'s T 13; cf. Lévêque 25–27, 32–34, 40–48.

*ally, as a 'young lad' (*neon meirakion*) already attached to his long-term lover Pausanias (**T 3**).*[4] *He was old enough not only to compete but to win the first prize at the Lenaea of 416 (**T 1**). In the* Symposium *(**T 2**) Plato's speakers exaggerate his youth (*neos *'young' 175e,* neaniskos *'youth' 198a2,* meirakion *'lad' 223a1), partly to flatter his success and partly because of his youthful looks and his continuing relationship with Pausanias, which Plato idealizes. Aristophanes could still satirize him as youthful, effeminate and promiscuously homosexual in* Women at the Thesmophoria *(spring 411, **T 4**).*[5]

Plato's Symposium *is set on the day after the formal celebration of Agathon's victory with his first production at the Lenaea of 416 (**T 1**, **T 2**). He was presumably still in Athens when* Women at the Thesmophoria *was staged but had left for the court of king Archelaus in Macedonia before the production of* Frogs *in 405 (**T 7**).*[6] *The scholiast on* Frogs *85 says he lived the rest of his life at Archelaus's court (**T 7b**), which if taken literally implies that he died before the death of Archelaus himself in 399. Reasons for his leaving Athens are easy to imagine (oligarchic connections, comic mockery, political and military instability at Athens, generous patronage from Archelaus), but the evidence is circumstantial and it is not certain that he left Athens with no intention of returning.*

*Agathon's dramatic career was quite short. No records of his productions at Athens are preserved except for his famous first victory (with plays unknown), and nothing is known about his poetic activity in Macedonia. Titles of six plays survive, of which three (*Anthos/Antheus,

---

[4] The *Protagoras* is best understood as being set in the late 430s, but with a few distinct anachronisms: »» e.g. Nails 2002, 309f. For Pausanias see Nails 222.

[5] See especially *Thesm.* 31–35, 49f., 97f., 130–45. Other references to, and implausible anecdotes about, Agathon's appearance and sexuality are collected in *TrGF* as T 14, 15, 19, 22, 25; cf. Lévêque 35–40.

[6] Other evidence does not help to narrow the interval: (1) the narrator of the *Symposium*, supposedly speaking while Socrates was still living, i.e. before early 399, says that Agathon had not lived in Athens for 'many years' (see **T 1**). (2) Aristophanes' *Gerytades*, which lampooned Agathon (**T 11**, **T 20a**) presumably while he was still in Athens, may perhaps have been staged in 407, but the arguments for that date are very slight: »» Lévêque 61f., 67f. (3) Anecdotes about Agathon associating with Euripides in Macedonia (Aelian, *Miscellany* 13.4, ps.-Plutarch, *Mor.* 177a etc. = Agathon T 22 = Euripides, *TrGF* 5 T 79–82) would put him there before Euripides' death in 406, but these are largely if not completely fictitious (»» e.g. Scullion 2003, 396–98).

Thyestes, Telephus*) are discussed below.*[7] *The others —* Aerope *(brief* ***F 1****),* Alcmeon *(brief* ***F 2****),* Mysians *(****F 3a****: below, pp. 158f.) — drew on mainstream epic and tragic legends.*[8] Aerope *and* Thyestes *could have belonged in a single trilogy, as could* Mysians *and* Telephus, *but there is no evidence that they did so. The great majority of the thirty preserved quotations from his plays are either gnomic (****F 18–28*** *are all from Stobaeus) or lexical or rhetorical examples which without explicit identification cannot be ascribed to any particular play. If he competed at the City Dionysia (as is very likely) he will have composed one or more satyric or prosatyric plays, but there is no obvious trace of them in the titles or fragments.*[9]

As mentioned above, Aristophanes and Plato provide some unique if somewhat distorted insights into Agathon's poetic and musical styles, which are frequently reflected in later criticism. His poetic style is parodied in Women at the Thesmophoria *(the servant's announcement, 39–57; Agathon's hymn, 101–29) and in Agathon's encomium of Eros in the* Symposium *(194e–197e).*[10] *Its hallmarks were ingenuity (*sophia*) and elegance of vocabulary and phrasing (*kalliepeia*), the latter emphasized in* Thesm. *49 and 60 and in Socrates' ironic praise of Agathon's*

---

[7] A further title, *Achilles*, was mistakenly inferred from the corrupt text of Aristotle, *Poetics* 1454b8ff. by Welcker 1841, 991 and e.g. Lévêque 1955, 100: see [**F 10**] with note below.

[8] For Aerope (errant daughter of Catreus of Crete, wife of Atreus and/or Pleisthenes of Mycenae, mother of Agamemnon and Menelaus, and adultress with Atreus's brother Thyestes) see Gantz 1993, 545–47, 554–56. She was the central character in Euripides' *Cretan Women* (see Collard 2005, 52–57, Collard–Cropp 2008b, 516–19 for the tangled evidence concerning its plot). Carcinus II produced a later *Aerope* (see in Vol. 2). For Alcmeon (the son of Amphiaraus who led the Epigoni successfully against Thebes and killed his mother Eriphyle to avenge her betrayal of his father) see Gantz 522–28. There were numerous dramatic treatments, including the *Alcmeon*s of Astydamas II and Theodectas in the 4th century (see introduction to Astydamas's *Alcmeon* in Vol. 2; Collard–Cropp 2008a, 81).

[9] Snell's F 33 rather optimistically takes Ar. *Thesm.* 157 ('Well, when you're creating satyrs, give me a call') as positive evidence. See also below, p. 159 with n. 23 on *Telephus*.

[10] Other relevant testimonia are collected as *TrGF* T 16. For discussions see Lévêque 1955, 125–37; Machìna 1955, 28–32; Waern 1956, 95–100; Wright 2016, 70–77.

*speech (*Symp. *198b–c) comparing him with the rhetorician Gorgias. Most of the surviving fragments are cleverly phrased* gnômai *displaying a variety of verbal tricks (see especially* ***F 6–9, 11, 12, 14, 20, 27, 29*** *with notes). As a composer Agathon participated in the 'New Music' movement which involved advances in the design of instruments (cithara and aulos), a corresponding elaboration of musical styles, and an increased emphasis on virtuoso and professional solo performance.*[11] *In* Thesm. *99–133 (see* ***T 4****) Aristophanes satirizes Agathon's music, as well as the words of his hymn, as* avant-garde *nonsense, violating the traditions of properly structured song-making (*melopoiia*) and pandering to the base sexual instincts of his audience and himself (cf.* ***T 19,***

Testimonia

Note. *T 5, 9–16, 22 and 24–26, omitted here, comprise later comments and anecdotes about Agathon's life, family and associates, wealth, appearance, sexuality, poetic style, and relationships with Pausanias, Euripides and Archelaus.*

T 1 Athenaeus 5.216f–217a
Ἀριστίων . . . πρὸ τεσσάρων ἐτῶν Εὐφήμου πρότερος ἦρξεν, καθ' ὃν Πλάτων τὰ Ἀγάθωνος νικητήρια γέγραφεν . . . ὁ μὲν γὰρ ἐπὶ ἄρχοντος Εὐφήμου στεφανοῦται Ληναίοις . . .

T 2 Plato, *Symposium* 172c–173a, 175d–e, 194a–b
'Πόθεν', ἦν δ' ἐγώ, 'ὦ Γλαύκων; οὐκ οἶσθ' ὅτι πολλῶν ἐτῶν Ἀγάθων ἐνθάδε οὐκ ἐπιδεδήμηκεν, ἀφ' οὗ δ' ἐγὼ Σωκράτει συνδιατρίβω . . . οὐδέπω τρία ἔτη ἐστίν;' . . . 'Μὴ σκῶπτ',' ἔφη, 'ἀλλ' εἰπέ μοι πότε ἐγένετο ἡ συνουσία αὕτη.' κἀγὼ εἶπον ὅτι 'Παίδων ὄντων ἡμῶν ἔτι, ὅτε τῇ πρώτῃ τραγῳδίᾳ ἐνίκησεν Ἀγάθων, τῇ ὑστεραίᾳ ἢ ᾗ τὰ ἐπινίκια ἔθυεν αὐτός τε καὶ οἱ χορευταί.'

(175d–e) 'εἰ γὰρ οὕτως ἔχει καὶ ἡ σοφία, πολλοῦ τιμῶμαι τὴν παρὰ σοὶ κατάκλισιν· οἶμαι γάρ με παρὰ σοῦ πολλῆς καὶ καλῆς σοφίας πληρωθήσεσθαι. ἡ μὲν γὰρ ἐμὴ φαύλη τις ἂν εἴη, ἢ καὶ ἀμφισβητήσιμος ὥσπερ ὄναρ οὖσα, ἡ δὲ σὴ λαμπρά τε καὶ πολλὴν ἐπίδοσιν ἔχουσα, ἥ γε παρὰ σοῦ νέου ὄντος οὕτω σφόδρα ἐξέλαμψεν καὶ ἐκφανὴς ἐγένετο πρῴην ἐν μάρτυσι τῶν Ἑλλήνων πλέον ἢ τρισμυρίοις.

---

[11] For Agathon's music and the New Music context see Lévêque 1955, 145–51; Barker 1984, 93–95 and 2014, 97–102; West 1992b, 351–66; Csapo 2004; Hagel 2010, 444–48; Power 2012, 500–16 (including discussion of *Thesm.* 101–29).

***T 20, F 3a** with notes). Agathon here is made to resemble the solo citharodes and auletes who pioneered the New Music and dramatized their subjects with extreme mimetic effects (bodily movement, cross-dressing, exotic costumes), inviting reactions like the Kinsman's in* Thesm. *130–45 (»» Power 2010, 136–43, 512–16). This no doubt exaggerates and distorts both Agathon's personality and his musical practice, which may have been no more extreme than that of Euripides in his latest plays (contemporary with Agathon's) such as* Helen *and* Orestes. *Some later sources hint at more balanced assessments (**T 20b**) and mention specific innovations in tragic music with which his name was associated (**T 20(c), F 3a**).*

Testimonia

See note opposite.

T 1 Athenaeus, *Sophists at Dinner*
Aristion . . . was archon (421/0) four years before Euphemus (417/6), in whose archonship Plato sets Agathon's victory party . . . He was crowned at the Lenaea in Euphemus's archonship . . .

T 2 Plato, *Symposium*
'Where (did you get that idea) from, Glaucon?', said I (i.e. Apollodorus). 'Don't you know that it's many years since Agathon lived here, but not yet three years since I started spending time with Socrates . . . 'Don't tease me', said he, 'but tell me when this gathering took place.' And I said, 'When we were still boys, when Agathon had won with his first tragedy, the day after he and his chorusmen made their victory-offering.'

* * *

(Socrates) 'For if wisdom too is like that (i.e. capable of flowing from one person to another in close proximity), I value lying next to you (i.e. Agathon) greatly; for I reckon I'll be filled with much fine wisdom from you. My wisdom would be slight, or even of doubtful reality like a dream, whereas yours would be brilliant and would offer a great deal, seeing that it shone out from you so strongly, young as you are, and became conspicuous just lately with more than thirty thousand Hellenes as witnesses.'

* * *

(194a–b) 'Φαρμάττειν βούλει με, ὦ Σώκρατες', εἰπεῖν τὸν Ἀγάθωνα, 'ἵνα θορυβηθῶ διὰ τὸ οἴεσθαι τὸ θέατρον προσδοκίαν μεγάλην ἔχειν ὡς εὖ ἐροῦντος ἐμοῦ'.

'Ἐπιλήσμων μεντἂν εἴην, ὦ Ἀγάθων', εἰπεῖν τὸν Σωκράτη, 'εἰ ἰδὼν τὴν σὴν ἀνδρείαν καὶ μεγαλοφροσύνην ἀναβαίνοντος ἐπὶ τὸν ὀκρίβαντα μετὰ τῶν ὑποκριτῶν, καὶ βλέψαντος ἐναντία τοσούτῳ θεάτρῳ, μέλλοντος ἐπιδείξεσθαι σαυτοῦ λόγους, καὶ οὐδ' ὁπωστιοῦν ἐκπλαγέντος, νῦν οἰηθείην σε θορυβήσεσθαι ἕνεκα ἡμῶν ὀλίγων ἀνθρώπων.'

T 3 Plato, *Protagoras* 315d

παρεκάθηντο δὲ αὐτῷ ἐπὶ ταῖς πλησίον κλίναις Παυσανίας τε ὁ ἐκ Κεραμέων καὶ μετὰ Παυσανίου νέον τι ἔτι μειράκιον, ὡς μὲν ἐγᾦμαι καλόν τε κἀγαθὸν τὴν φύσιν, τὴν δ' οὖν ἰδέαν πάνυ καλός. ἔδοξα ἀκοῦσαι ὄνομα αὐτῷ εἶναι Ἀγάθωνα, καὶ οὐκ ἂν θαυμάζοιμι εἰ παιδικὰ Παυσανίου τυγχάνει ὤν.

T 4 with **T 21**, **T 23,** cf. **T 16** Aristophanes, *Thesmophoriazusae* 29–57, 95–100, 146–67

Ευ. ἐνταῦθ' Ἀγάθων ὁ κλεινὸς οἰκῶν τυγχάνει
ὁ τραγῳδοποιός.
Κη. ποῖος οὗτος Ἀγάθων;
Ευ. ἔστιν τις Ἀγάθων—
μῶν ὁ μέλας, ὁ καρτερός;
Ευ. οὔκ, ἀλλ' ἕτερός τις. οὐχ ἑόρακας πώποτε;
Κη. μῶν ὁ δασυπώγων;
Ευ. οὐχ ἑόρακας πώποτε;
Κη. μὰ τὸν Δί' οὔτοι γ' ὥστε κἀμέ γ' εἰδέναι.
Ευ. καὶ μὴν βεβίνηκας σύ γ'· ἀλλ' οὐκ οἶσθ' ἴσως.
ἀλλ' ἐκποδὼν πτήξωμεν, ὡς ἐξέρχεται
θεράπων τις αὐτοῦ, πῦρ ἔχων καὶ μυρρίνας,
προθυσόμενος, ἔοικε, τῆς ποιήσεως.

ΘΕΡΑΠΩΝ
εὔφημος πᾶς ἔστω λαός,
στόμα συγκλῄσας· ἐπιδημεῖ γὰρ
θίασος Μουσῶν ἔνδον μελάθρων
τῶν δεσποσύνων μελοποιῶν.
ἐχέτω δὲ πνοὰς νήνεμος αἰθήρ,
κῦμά τε πόντου μὴ κελαδείτω
γλαυκόν . . .
Κη. βομβάξ.
Ευ. σίγα. τί λέγει;

'You want to bewitch me, Socrates', said Agathon, 'and disturb me with the idea that my audience has great expectations of my speaking well.'

'I would be forgetful indeed, Agathon', said Socrates, 'if after seeing your courage and boldness as you ascended the platform with your actors and faced such a great audience, ready to explain your subjects, and were not in the least daunted, I should now expect you to be disturbed on account of us few men.'

T 3 Plato, *Protagoras*

Sitting beside him (i.e. Prodicus) on the nearby benches were Pausanias from the deme Kerameis and with him a lad still young, of an admirable nature in my opinion, and certainly very admirable in appearance. I gathered his name was Agathon, and I shouldn't be surprised if he were Pausanias's boyfriend.

T 4 (etc.) Aristophanes, *Women at the Thesmophoria*

Euripides, accompanied by a kinsman, arrives at Agathon's house in the hope of persuading him to infiltrate the women gathered for the Thesmophoria and defend him against their charges of misogyny:

Euripides. This is where the famous Agathon lives, the tragic poet.

Kinsman. Which Agathon is that?

Eur. There's an Agathon —

Kin. Not the dark, tough one?

Eur. No, another one. You mean you've never seen him?

Kin. Not the thick-bearded one?

Eur. You mean you've never seen him?

Kin. No indeed, by Zeus — well, not so far as I know.

Eur. And yet you must have shagged him — though maybe you're not aware of it. But let's duck out of the way; some servant of his is coming out. He has a brazier and a myrtle-wreath, preparing to make an offering, I suppose, for poetic success.

(The servant enters)

Servant (chanting). Let all the people be silent, with fast-locked lips. There stays within our master's halls the sacred band of Muses, fashioning songs. Let aether windless hold in check its breezes, let the gray sea-swell not resound . . .

Kin. Rhubarb!

Eur. Keep quiet! What's he saying?

Θε. πτηνῶν τε γένη κατακοιμάσθω,
θηρῶν τ' ἀγρίων πόδες ὑλοδρόμων
μὴ λυέσθων.
Κη. βομβαλοβομβάξ.
Θε. μέλλει γὰρ ὁ καλλιεπὴς Ἀγάθων
πρόμος ἡμέτερος —
Κη. μῶν βινεῖσθαι;
Θε. τίς ὁ φωνήσας;
Κη. νήνεμος αἰθήρ.
Θε. δρυόχους τιθέναι δράματος ἀρχάς.
κάμπτει δὲ νέας ἁψῖδας ἐπῶν,
τὰ δὲ τορνεύει, τὰ δὲ κολλομελεῖ,
καὶ γνωμοτυπεῖ κἀντονομάζει
καὶ κηροχυτεῖ καὶ γογγύλλει
καὶ χοανεύει.

* * *

Ευ. σίγα.
Κη. τί ἐστιν;
Ευ. Ἀγάθων ἐξέρχεται.
Κη. καὶ ποῦ ⟨'στιν;
Ευ. ὅπου⟩ 'στίν; οὗτος οὐκκυκλούμενος.
Κη. ἀλλ' ἦ τυφλὸς μέν εἰμ'; ἐγὼ γὰρ οὐχ ὁρῶ
ἄνδρ' οὐδέν' ἐνθάδ' ὄντα, Κυρήνην δ' ὁρῶ.
Ευ. σίγα· μελῳδεῖν δὴ παρασκευάζεται.
Κη. μύρμηκος ἀτραπούς ἢ τί διαμινύρεται;

* * *

Αγ. ὦ πρέσβυ πρέσβυ, τοῦ φθόνου μὲν τὸν ψόγον
ἤκουσα, τὴν δ' ἄλγησιν οὐ παρεσχόμην·
ἐγὼ δὲ τὴν ἐσθῆθ' ἅμα γνώμῃ φορῶ.
χρὴ γὰρ ποιητὴν ἄνδρα πρὸς τὰ δράματα
ἃ δεῖ ποιεῖν, πρὸς ταῦτα τοὺς τρόπους ἔχειν.
αὐτίκα γυναικεῖ' ἢν ποιῇ τις δράματα,
μετουσίαν δεῖ τῶν τρόπων τὸ σῶμ' ἔχειν.
Κη. οὐκοῦν κελητίζεις, ὅταν Φαίδραν ποιῇς;
Αγ. ἀνδρεῖα δ' ἢν ποιῇ τις, ἐν τῷ σώματι
ἔνεσθ' ὑπάρχον τοῦθ'. ἃ δ' οὐ κεκτήμεθα,
μίμησις ἤδη ταῦτα συνθηρεύεται.

Serv. . . . and let the avian tribes settle to sleep, and wild wood-roaming beasts not stir abroad . . .

Kin. Rhubarb, rhubarb!

Serv. . . . for Agathon our elegantly-spoken leader prepares . . .

Kin. To get shagged?

Serv. Who's that who spoke?

Kin. Windless aether!

Serv. . . . to set out the props for the building of his play. He bends new verse-rims; some he turns and others he glues, and fashions maxims and finds new words, and pours the wax and rounds out the form and funnels in the bronze…

The Kinsman interrupts with an obscenity, but Euripides cuts him short and explains to the servant his need for Agathon's help. Then the doors of the house open and the eccyclema rolls out bearing Agathon, reclining on a couch and elaborately dressed in effeminate oriental style:

Eur. Be quiet!

Kin. What is it?

Eur. Agathon's coming out.

Kin. So where *(is he?*

Eur. Where) is he? He's the one being wheeled out right here.

Kin. Well, am I blind? I don't see any *man* here — I see Kyrene!

Eur. Be quiet! He's getting ready to sing.

Kin. What's this he's humming, ant-paths or what?

Agathon, accompanying himself with lyre-music in Asiatic style, sings an exotic but rather vacuous antiphonal hymn addressed to Apollo, Artemis and their mother Leto (101–29).[12] *The Kinsman responds with comments on the sexually arousing effect of Agathon's song and on his female costume (130–145). Agathon replies:*

Agath. Old man, old man, I heard your spite's derision but did not register its pain. I wear the clothing that befits my thought. A poet must do what is needful for his plays, accommodating his behaviour to them. For instance, if one's plays are all about women, one's body must engage in women's ways.

Kin. So you're the rider when you're creating a Phaedra?

Agath. And if it's about men, one's body has what's needed. But what we don't possess, these things must be pursued by imitation.

---

[12] On the content and character of the hymn see Muecke 1982, 46–48, Austin-Olson 2004, 86–88, Power 2010, 507–17.

Κη. ὅταν σατύρους τοίνυν ποίῃς, καλεῖν ἐμέ,
ἵνα συμποιῶ σοὔπισθεν ἐστυκὼς ἐγώ.
Αγ. ἄλλως τ᾽ ἄμουσόν ἐστι ποιητὴν ἰδεῖν
ἀγρεῖον ὄντα καὶ δασύν. σκέψαι δ᾽ ὅτι
Ἴβυκος ἐκεῖνος κἀνακρέων ὁ Τήιος
κἀλκαῖος, οἵπερ ἁρμονίαν ἐχύμισαν,
ἐμιτροφόρουν τε καὶ διεκλῶντ᾽ Ἰωνικῶς.
καὶ Φρύνιχος — τοῦτον γὰρ οὖν ἀκήκοας —
αὐτός τε καλὸς ἦν καὶ καλῶς ἠμπίσχετο·
διὰ τοῦτ᾽ ἄρ᾽ αὐτοῦ καὶ κάλ᾽ ἦν τὰ δράματα.
ὅμοια γὰρ ποιεῖν ἀνάγκη τῇ φύσει.

T 6 Aristotle, *Ethica Eudemia* 1232b6–9

καὶ μᾶλλον ἂν φροντίσειεν ἀνὴρ μεγαλόψυχος, τί δοκεῖ ἑνὶ σπουδαίῳ ἢ πολλοῖς τοῖς τυγχάνουσιν, ὥσπερ Ἀντιφῶν ἔφη πρὸς Ἀγάθωνα κατεψηφισμένος τὴν ἀπολογίαν ἐπαινέσαντα.

T 7

(a) Aristophanes, *Frogs* 83–85

Ηρ. Ἀγάθων δὲ ποῦ ᾽στιν;
Δι. ἀπολιπών μ᾽ ἀποίχεται,
ἀγαθὸς ποιητὴς καὶ ποθεινὸς τοῖς φίλοις.
Ηρ. ποῖ γῆς ὁ τλήμων;
Δι. εἰς μακάρων εὐωχίαν.

(b) Schol. Ar. *Frogs* 85

ἢ ὡς περὶ τετελευτηκότος λέγει, ὡς ἂν εἶπε τὰς μακάρων νήσους, ἢ ὅτι Ἀρχελάῳ τῷ βασιλεῖ μέχρι τῆς τελευτῆς μετὰ ἄλλων πολλῶν συνῆν ἐν Μακεδονίᾳ, καὶ ‘μακάρων εὐωχίαν’ ἔφη τὴν ἐν τοῖς βασιλείοις διατριβήν.

T 8 Plato, *Symposium* 172c

οὐκ οἶσθ᾽ ὅτι πολλῶν ἐτῶν Ἀγάθων ἐνθάδε οὐκ ἐπιδεδήμηκεν, ἀφ᾽ οὗ δ᾽ ἐγὼ Σωκράτει συνδιατρίβω . . . οὐδέπω τρία ἔτη ἐστίν;

T 17 Aristotle, *Poetics* 1456a10–25

χρὴ δὲ ὅπερ εἴρηται πολλάκις μεμνῆσθαι καὶ μὴ ποιεῖν ἐποποιϊκὸν σύστημα τραγῳδίαν — ἐποποιϊκὸν δὲ λέγω τὸ πολύμυθον — οἷον εἴ τις τὸν τῆς Ἰλιάδος ὅλον ποιοῖ μῦθον. ἐκεῖ μὲν γὰρ διὰ τὸ μῆκος λαμβάνει τὰ μέρη τὸ πρέπον μέγεθος, ἐν δὲ τοῖς δράμασι πολὺ παρὰ τὴν ὑπόληψιν ἀποβαίνει. σημεῖον δέ, ὅσοι πέρσιν Ἰλίου ὅλην ἐποίησαν καὶ μὴ κατὰ μέρος ὥσπερ Εὐριπίδης, ⟨ἢ⟩

Kin. Well, when you're creating satyrs, give me a call, so I can help you from behind with a big erection.

Agath. Besides, it's off-key to see a poet who's rustic and rough. Consider that the famous Ibycus, the Teian Anacreon and Alcaeus, who spiced up harmony, all wore fancy headgear and lay about Ionian-fashion. And Phrynichus — you've surely heard of *him* — was elegant himself and elegantly dressed; that's why his plays were elegant. Our poetry must always match our nature.

T 6 Aristotle, *Eudemian Ethics*
And a great-spirited man would rather consider the opinion of one virtuous man than of many ordinary ones, as Antiphon said to Agathon when he had been condemned and Agathon praised his defence-speech.

T 7

(a) Aristophanes, *Frogs*
Heracles. And where is Agathon?
Dionysus. He's gone away and left me, a good poet much missed by his friends.
Heracles. To what land has the poor man gone?
Dionysus. To the enjoyments of the blessed.

(b) Scholia on the above
Either he (i.e. Dionysus) speaks of him as having died, as though he had said 'the Isles of the Blessed', or (he says this) because he (i.e. Agathon) resided with king Archelaus in Macedonia, with many others, until his death, and by 'banquets of the blessed' he means living in the king's entourage.

T 8 Plato, *Symposium*
Don't you know that Agathon hasn't lived here (i.e. at Athens) for many years, whereas I've been spending time with Socrates . . . for less than three years?

T 17 Aristotle, *Poetics*
One should remember what we have often said and not make a tragedy an epic structure — by epic structure I mean one with many plots — as for example if someone made a plot from the whole of the *Iliad.* In that poem the parts get their appropriate size because of its length, but in dramas it turns out quite disappointingly. This is shown by the fact that all those who have dramatized the *Sack of Troy* as a whole, and not in parts as Euripides did, *(or)* a complete *Niobe* and not

Νιόβην καὶ μὴ ὥσπερ Αἰσχύλος, ἢ ἐκπίπτουσιν ἢ κακῶς ἀγωνίζονται (ἐπεὶ καὶ Ἀγάθων ἐξέπεσεν ἐν τούτῳ μόνῳ), ἐν δὲ ταῖς περιπετείαις καὶ ἐν τοῖς ἁπλοῖς πράγμασι στοχάζονται ὧν βούλονται θαυμαστῶς· τραγικὸν γὰρ τοῦτο καὶ φιλάνθρωπον. ἔστιν δὲ τοῦτο, ὅταν ὁ σοφὸς μὲν μετὰ πονηρίας ⟨δ'⟩ ἐξαπατηθῇ, ὥσπερ Σίσυφος, καὶ ὁ ἀνδρεῖος μὲν ἄδικος δὲ ἡττηθῇ. ἔστιν δὲ τοῦτο καὶ εἰκὸς ὥσπερ Ἀγάθων λέγει, εἰκὸς γὰρ γίνεσθαι πολλὰ καὶ παρὰ τὸ εἰκός.

T 18 Aristotle, *Poetics* 1456a25–32
καὶ τὸν χορὸν δὲ ἕνα δεῖ ὑπολαμβάνειν τῶν ὑποκριτῶν, καὶ μόριον εἶναι τοῦ ὅλου καὶ συναγωνίζεσθαι μὴ ὥσπερ Εὐριπίδῃ ἀλλ' ὥσπερ Σοφοκλεῖ. τοῖς δὲ λοιποῖς τὰ ᾀδόμενα οὐδὲν μᾶλλον τοῦ μύθου ἢ ἄλλης τραγῳδίας ἐστίν· διὸ ἐμβόλιμα ᾄδουσιν πρώτου ἄρξαντος Ἀγάθωνος τοῦ τοιούτου. καίτοι τί διαφέρει ἢ ἐμβόλιμα ᾄδειν ἢ εἰ ῥῆσιν ἐξ ἄλλου εἰς ἄλλο ἁρμόττοι ἢ ἐπεισόδιον ὅλον;

28 λοιποῖς Ξ πολλοῖς Σ (conj. Gomperz)

T 19 Philodemus, *On Music*, col. 128.18–42 (pp. 244f. Delattre)
[δι]ọ́περ οὐ διὰ [μ]ελῶν | ὁμοίων, ἀλλ' ὀνομάτων | καὶ διανοημ[ά]των ἀρέσκ-| εσθαι καὶ τοὺς ἐρωμένους, | εἰ θέλουσιν, ὁμολο[γ]ήσο|μεν, τὸν δ' Ἀριστοφάνην | τοὺς ἀρχαίους ἀποφαίνειν | ἐνκε[κλ]ασμένηι, καθάπ̣[ερ] | οἱ παλαιοί, τῆι φωνῆι χρῆ|σθαι καὶ *τοῖς ὀφθαλμοῖς πρ[ο]|αγωγεύειν ἑαυτọ́ụς*, ọụ̓ [τ]οῖς | μέλεσιν . . . ταῦτα γὰρ οὔτ' εἰς ἅ | φησιν, ὥσπερ ἀδίστακτα | ἔχων, ἐκκαλεῖθ', ὅσον ἐφ' αὐ|τ[οῖ]ς, οὔτε πρὸς συνουσίας | [κακ]ὰς καὶ ἄνδρας καὶ γυναῖ|[κα]ς, καὶ νέους ὡραίους | π[ρὸ]ς γυναικισμόν· οὔτε | γὰρ ο[ὗτ]ος οὔθ' οἱ κωμικοὶ | παρέδ[ε]ιξάν τι τῶν Ἀγά|θωνος καὶ Δημοκρίτου | τοιοῦτον, ἀλλὰ μόνον λέ|γουσι[ν] . . .

T 20
(a) Schol. Lex. Cyrill. (Reitzenstein 1897, 297: ~ Hesychius *α* 281, Photius *α* 83)
Ἀγαθώνειος· ει̅· αὔλησίς τις μαλακὴ παρ' Ἀριστοφάνει ἐν Γηρυτάδῃ· Ἀγάθων γὰρ ὁ τραγικὸς ἐπὶ μαλακίᾳ διεκωμῳδεῖτο.

(b) Suda *α* 125 (~ Zenobius 1.2, Diogenianus 1.6/1.7)
Ἀγαθώνιος αὔλησις· ἡ μαλακὴ καὶ ἐκλελυμένη· ἢ ἡ μήτε χαλαρὰ, μήτε πικρὰ, ἀλλ' εὔκρατος καὶ ἡδίστη.

(c) Psellus, *Περὶ τραγῳδίας* 5
ὁ δὲ Ὑποφρύγιος καὶ ὁ Ὑποδώριος σπάνιοι παρ' αὐτῇ εἰσιν, ὡς διθυράμβῳ προσήκοντες· πρῶτος δὲ Ἀγάθων τὸν Ὑποδώριον τόνον εἰς τραγῳδίαν εἰσήνεγκεν καὶ τὸν Ὑποφρύγιον.

T 21, T 23 Aristophanes, *Thesmophoriazusae* 99f., 149f., 155 f., 167
*See above under **T 4***

as Aeschylus did, either fall short or do badly in the competition (even Agathon fell short in this one thing), though in reversals and simple actions they target what they want admirably, i.e. something tragic and satisfying to human feeling. This is the case when someone clever *(but)* mischievous is deceived, like Sisyphus, or someone brave but unrighteous is worsted; and this is in fact a likely outcome, as Agathon says, for it is likely that many seemingly unlikely things should happen.

T 18 Aristotle, *Poetics* (directly after **T 17**)
As for the chorus, one should treat it as one of the actors; it should be a part of the whole and participate in the action not as in Euripides but as in Sophocles. In the rest the sung parts no more belong to the plot than to some other tragedy, and so they (i.e. choruses) sing intermezzos; the first to do this sort of thing was Agathon. Yet how does singing intermezzos differ from fitting a speech from one play into another, or a whole episode?

T 19 Philodemus, *On Music*
And so we will agree, if they (i.e. our opponents) consent, that it is not through suitable *melodies* but through words and thoughts that loved ones are won over, and that Aristophanes shows that men of old used a *subdued* voice, *as* men did in those days, and 'offered themselves with their eyes', not with melodies . . . For these (i.e. melodies) do not of *themselves* provoke people to the things that he (i.e. Diogenes) asserts, as though it were indisputable, that they do — not men and women to *immoral* unions, nor handsome youths *to* effeminate behaviour. Neither *he* nor the comic playwrights have demonstrated any such thing about the works of Agathon and Democritus — they merely state it . . .

T 20

(a) Scholia on the Cyril Lexicon (and other lexica)
Agathoneian (*sic*): an effeminate kind of aulos-music, in Aristophanes' *Gerytades* (F 178 *PCG*). The tragedian Agathon was mocked for being effeminate.

(b) Suda (and paroemiographers)
Agathonian aulos-music: one that is effeminate and relaxed; or one that is neither languid nor harsh, but well-blended and very pleasant.

(c) Psellus, *On Tragedy*
The Hypophrygian and Hypodorian (modes) are rare in it (i.e. in older tragedy), as being appropriate for dithyramb. Agathon was the first to bring the Hypodorian and the Hypophrygian into tragedy.

T 21, T 23 Aristophanes, *Women at the Thesmophoria* (further extracts)
*See above under **T 4***

ΑΝΘΟΣ *vel* ΑΝΘΕΥΣ

Discussions. Pitcher 1939; Corbato 1948; Machìna 1955, 23f.; Lévêque 1955, 105–14.

Nothing is known of this play except that Aristotle in ***F 2a*** *mentions it as an example, not apparently unique, of a tragedy in which 'events and names are all alike invented'. Even its name is uncertain. The Byzantine manuscripts give ἄνθει, dative of ἄνθος, hence* Anthos, 'The Flower', *but their accentuation could easily be wrong and ἀνθεῖ dative of Ἀνθεύς, the not uncommon personal name* Antheus, *is equally possible.*[13] *The latter seems at first sight more likely, and two romantic tales about handsome young men named Antheus ('Flower-lad') are known: (1) In the* Erôtika Pathêmata *of Parthenius (1st C. BC), a collection of sad love stories summarized from various sources, Antheus of Assesos, a hostage in Miletus, spurns the queen's advances, causing her to contrive his death and then hang herself in remorse (Parthenius 14). This however seems to have been a local Milesian legend and can hardly have been invented by Agathon.*[14] *(2) Lycophron,* Alexandra *132ff. alludes to a story in which (as the scholia there explain) the young Trojan Antheus was loved by both Paris and Deiphobus but was killed accidentally by Paris, who then fled with Menelaus to Sparta and later abducted Helen. This is obviously not a story with entirely invented characters. In addition to these, Pitcher (1939) argued for (3) Anthos, who in the* Metamorphoses *of Antoninus Liberalis (another mythographic collection, 2nd C. AD?) was devoured by his father's mares and transformed into a bird,* anthos

---

[13] Gudeman inferred from the Arabic translation of the *Poetics* that the Greek exemplar of the lost Syriac translation from which the Arabic derives had the reading ἄνθη. This is negligible since the Syriac translator had completely misunderstood the Greek (»» Tarán–Gutas 2102, 258, 362). The feminine Anthê ('one of the Alkyonids': Suda α 1298, 2505) is in any case impossible since the Greek name was masculine (ἐν τῷ...). The masculine Anthês, legendary founder of Halicarnassus, was obviously not invented by Agathon.

[14] Parthenius himself cites a variant of the story which he illustrates by quoting thirty-four verses from the Hellenistic poet Alexander Aetolus (fr. 3 Powell). A later note on this names 'Aristotle and writers on Milesian topics' (»» Lightfoot 1999, 454–57). Neither mentions Agathon. Corbato 1948 nevertheless argues for ascribing the story to him, as does Karamanou 2010, 506.

THE FLOWER *or* **ANTHEUS**

(the yellow wagtail) while the rest of his family became other birds (Ant. Lib. 7). The name Anthos is common enough, but besides requiring an emendation to ἄνθῳ in the text of the Poetics *this hardly amounts to a tragic plot (though Pitcher went to some lengths to imagine one).*

Failing these, the majority of scholars have settled for Anthos 'The Flower', *while admitting that we have no way of telling what such a play might have been about.*[15] *I suspect that it was after all* Antheus *(as printed in* ***F 2a*** *below) and concerned a young man whose story is now unknown precisely because he was an invented figure and had no mythical or folklore associations.*[16] *As for its character, the suggestion that this was a tragedy with an 'ordinary life' setting, anticipating in some respects the development of New Comedy, is no more than a conjecture. Aristotle says only that its events and names were invented, not that it had a contemporary setting or lacked the mythical elevation of conventional tragedies.*[17]

The word ἄνθος could denote the erotically charged bloom of youth and is conspicuously linked with the god Eros himself in Agathon's description of the god's beauty in Plato's Symposium *(196a7–b3: cf. Dover 1980, 126). This may allude to Agathon's play, though whether it shows that the play was part of Agathon's first production celebrated in the* Symposium *(as Lévêque 55f. suggests) is more doubtful. It might simply be an allusion to Agathon's most memorable tragedy.*

---

[15] In recent times Lévêque 1955, 111–13; Radt 1971, 192 with n. 2; Snell 1971, 48 n. 38; *MusTr* 283 n. 14.

[16] Cf. Lesky 1972, 524 (= 1983, 395); Lightfoot 1999, 457 n. 201.

[17] On this point see e.g. Welcker 1841, 996, Lesky (previous note). Lévêque 1955, 112f. argues for a 'drame bourgeois'.

F 2a Aristotle, *Poetics* 1451b5–25

διὸ καὶ φιλοσοφώτερον καὶ σπουδαιότερον ποίησις ἱστορίας ἐστίν· ἡ μὲν γὰρ ποίησις μᾶλλον τὰ καθόλου, ἡ δ' ἱστορία τὰ καθ' ἕκαστον λέγει . . . ἐπὶ μὲν οὖν τῆς κωμῳδίας ἤδη τοῦτο δῆλον γέγονεν· συστήσαντες γὰρ τὸν μῦθον διὰ τῶν εἰκότων οὕτω τὰ τυχόντα ὀνόματα ὑποτιθέασιν, καὶ οὐχ ὥσπερ οἱ ἰαμβοποιοὶ περὶ τὸν καθ' ἕκαστον ποιοῦσιν. ἐπὶ δὲ τῆς τραγῳδίας τῶν γενομένων ὀνομάτων ἀντέχονται . . . οὐ μὴν ἀλλὰ καὶ ἐν ταῖς τραγῳδίαις ἐν ἐνίαις μὲν ἓν ἢ δύο τῶν γνωρίμων ἐστὶν ὀνομάτων, τὰ δὲ ἄλλα πεποιημένα, ἐν ἐνίαις δὲ οὐθέν, οἷον ἐν τῷ Ἀγάθωνος Ἀνθεῖ· ὁμοίως γὰρ ἐν τούτῳ τά τε πράγματα καὶ τὰ ὀνόματα πεποίηται, καὶ οὐδὲν ἧττον εὐφραίνει. ὥστ' οὐ πάντως εἶναι ζητητέον τῶν παραδεδομένων μύθων, περὶ οὓς αἱ τραγῳδίαι εἰσίν, ἀντέχεσθαι.

10 Ἀνθεῖ Welcker ἄνθει mss.

ΘΥΕΣΤΗΣ

Discussions. Machìna 1955, 19–21; Lévêque 1955, 94–96.

At least eight tragedies named Thyestes *are known from the fifth and fourth centuries: two or three by Sophocles, one each by Euripides, Agathon, Apollodorus, Chaeremon, Cleophon (or Iophon? see on Iophon* **T 1**), *the Cynic Diogenes, and possibly Carcinus II.*[18] *A further eight Latin tragedies are recorded, including the extant* Thyestes *of Seneca. Thyestes' story offered several episodes suitable for tragic plots, including his attempt to usurp the kingdom of Mycenae from his brother Atreus by seducing Atreus's wife Aerope and stealing the Golden Lamb; Atreus's revenge, killing Thyestes' sons and feeding him with their flesh; the exiled Thyestes' incest with his daughter Pelopia leading to the birth of Aegisthus; and Thyestes' return to Mycenae and reunion with Aegisth-*

F 3 Athenaeus 12.528d (~ Eustathius on *Iliad* 23.141)

Ἀγάθων δ' ἐν τῷ Θυέστῃ τοὺς τὴν Πρώνακτος θυγατέρα μνηστεύοντας τοῖς τε λοιποῖς πᾶσιν ἐξησκημένους ἐλθεῖν καὶ κομῶντας τὰς κεφαλάς, ἐπεὶ δ' ἀπέτυχον τοῦ γάμου,

κόμας ἐκειράμεσθα, φησίν, μάρτυρας τρυφῆς,
ἦ που ποθεινὸν χρῆμα παιζούσῃ φρενί.
ἐπώνυμον γοῦν εὐθὺς ἔσχομεν κλέος
Κουρῆτες εἶναι, κουρίμου χάριν τριχός.

[18] These are conveniently surveyed with related material by Collard 2009.

F 2a Aristotle, *Poetics*
Thus poetry is actually more philosophical and more serious than history; for poetry is more concerned with relating generalized events, and history specific ones . . . This is already clear in the case of comedy; for they (i.e. comic poets) first put together the plot using probable events and then supply the names that happen to suit it, rather than making poems about individuals as iambic poets do. In tragedy they (i.e. tragic poets) do stick to the actual names (i.e. of mythical figures) . . . Yet even amongst tragedies there are some that include just one or two well-known names while the rest are invented, and some that have none at all, such as Agathon's *Antheus*; in this play events and names are all alike invented, and it is none the less pleasing for that. It is not, then, absolutely necessary to try to stick to the traditional stories that are (i.e. typically) the subjects of tragedies.

THYESTES

us leading to their revenge on Atreus (see also above on Aerope*). Our sole mention of Agathon's play leaves its subject unknown. According to Apollodorus (1.9.13) Pronax's daughter Amphithea was married to his brother (her uncle) Adrastus, who ruled successively at Sicyon and Argos and led the Seven against Thebes. How her marriage might have involved a contest of suitors, and why one of them should have recalled it in a play about Thyestes, are matters that remain unexplained.*[19]

F 3 Athenaeus, *Sophists at Dinner*
Agathon in his *Thyestes* (says that) the suitors of Pronax's daughter arrived decked out in every way, and in particular wearing fine long hair, but when they failed to win the bride,

> We cut our hair (he says), the evidence of our luxury, something a light heart surely desires to have. And so straightway we gained the appellation 'Kourêtes' ('Shorn ones'), because of our shorn (*kourimou*) hair.

---

[19] Machìna and Lévêque offer some unconvincing guesses. Adrastus, Amphithea and Thyestes appear together in a well-known Apulian vase-painting (Boston 1987.53) showing them at Sicyon with Thyestes' daughter Pelopia and the baby Aegisthus, whom she has borne after being raped by her father. Thyestes seems to be trying to save the baby from being exposed while concealing his own identity. This may reflect Sophocles' *Thyestes at Sicyon* (»» Taplin 2007, 105–7). It could conceivably be connected with Agathon's play, but again the presence of an Aetolian ex-suitor would be unexplained.

ΜΥΣΟΙ

F 3a is our only evidence for this play. See further below on Telephus.

F 3a Plutarch, *Moralia* 645d–e
θαυμάζω δὲ καὶ Ἐράτωνα τουτονί τὰς μὲν ἐν τοῖς μέλεσι παραχρώσεις βδελυττόμενον καὶ κατηγοροῦντα τοῦ καλοῦ Ἀγάθωνος, ὃν πρῶτον εἰς τραγῳδίαν φασὶν ἐμβαλεῖν καὶ ὑπομῖξαι τὸ χρωματικόν, ὅτε τοὺς Μυσοὺς ἐδίδασκεν, αὐτὸς δ' ἡμῖν ὁρᾶθ' ὡς ποικίλων χρωμάτων καὶ ἀνθηρῶν τὸ συμπόσιον ἐμπέπληκεν . . .

ΤΗΛΕΦΟΣ

Discussions. Lévêque 96–100; Musa 2005.

The Telephus *plays of Aeschylus, Sophocles and Euripides, and the Latin derivatives of Ennius and Accius, all dealt with the* Cypria*'s story of Achilles healing Telephus's grievously wounded leg as the Achaean army prepared to set sail for Troy for the second time. Telephus had been wounded by Achilles when they landed in Mysia on their abortive first expedition.*[20] *Moschion's* Telephus *may have been similar (see Vol. 2), while those attributed to Iophon and/or Cleophon (see on Iophon* ***T 1****) are known only as titles. Other episodes from Telephus's legend were dramatized under different titles: his birth in Arcadia as son of Heracles and Auge (Euripides'* Auge*); the killing of his uncles which in some accounts caused his exile in Mysia (Sophocles'* Sons of Aleus*); his arrival and acceptance by king Teuthras in Mysia leading to a distinguished military career there (Aeschylus' and Sophocles'* Mysians*).* [21]

F 4 Athenaeus 10.454d
τὸ δ' αὐτὸ πεποίηκε καὶ Ἀγάθων ὁ τραγῳδοποιὸς ἐν τῷ Τηλέφῳ. ἀγράμματος γάρ τις κἀνταῦθα δηλοῖ τὴν τοῦ Θησέως ἐπιγραφὴν οὕτως·

---

[20] See in general Gantz 1993, 428–31, 576–80; Collard–Cropp–Lee 2009, 17–25, 282.

[21] The title *Mysians* is also recorded for Nicomachus of Alexandria Troas (*TrGF* no. 127). See also adesp. F 327c in *TrGF* 5, 1125f. Sophocles' *Aleadai*, *Mysians* and *Telephus* could have formed the *Telepheia* recorded in *IG* II^2 3091.8 (= *TrGF* DID B 5.8): cf. on Sophocles II in Vol. 2.

MYSIANS

F 3a Plutarch, *Sympotic Questions*
I'm surprised that Eraton here abominates and condemns the 'colourings' in the songs of the handsome Agathon, who they say was the first to introduce and intermix the chromatic (scale) when he produced *Mysians*, and yet himself — see how he's intertwined our symposium with elaborate floral colours . . .

TELEPHUS

Hyginus, Fab. *100 tells of his near-marriage and reunion with his long-lost mother, now Teuthras's protégée: this was probably a tragic plot but its origin is unknown. The events that led to his being wounded by Achilles (Apollodorus* epit. *3.17, probably from the* Cypria*) are not known to have been treated in any tragedy but were significant in earlier poetry*[22] *and would have made a good tragic subject.*

The precedents suggest that Agathon's Mysians *might have been about Telephus's arrival in Mysia and his* Telephus *about the healing of his wound. The only fragment of either, however, does nothing to confirm this and might point in another direction: see further on* ***F 4****.*

There is no good reason to think that Agathon's Telephus *might have been a satyr-play.*[23]

F 4 Athenaeus, *Sophists at Dinner*
Agathon the tragedian does the same thing in his *Telephus*. There too an illiterate man explains the inscription of Theseus's name (ΘΗΣΕΥΣ) as follows:

---

[22] Beside the *Cypria*, the Hesiodic *Catalogue of Women* fr. 165 M.–W. (where Auge is said to have given birth to Telephus in Mysia), Pind. *Isthm.* 8.49f., and a new and much discussed fragment of Archilochus (Obbink 2006, West 2006; cf. Swift 2012, 2014).

[23] Sutton 1980, 75, Cipolla 2003, 300. Sutton supposed wrongly that Euripides' *Theseus* might have been a satyr-play, and that the imitations of his F 382 by Agathon and Theodectas would then have been in satyr-plays as well. A satyric *Telephus* is attested only in an inscription from Rome recording a performance by a Hellenistic actor (*IGUR* I 229 = *TrGF* DID A 5g).

γραφῆς ὁ πρῶτος ἦν μεσόμφαλος κύκλος·
ὀρθοί τε κανόνες ἐζυγωμένοι δύο,
Σκυθικῷ τε τόξῳ ⟨τὸ⟩ τρίτον ἦν προσεμφερές·
ἔπειτα τριόδους πλάγιος ἦν προσκείμενος,
ἐφ' ἑνός τε κανόνος †ἦσαν ἐζυγωμένοι† δύο·
ὅπερ δὲ τὸ τρίτον, ἦν τελευταῖον πάλιν.

Incertae Fabulae

F 5 Aristotle, *Nicomachean Ethics* 1139b5–11

οὐκ ἔστι δὲ προαιρετὸν οὐδὲν γεγονός, οἷον οὐδεὶς προαιρεῖται Ἴλιον πεπορθηκέναι· οὐδὲ γὰρ βουλεύεται περὶ τοῦ γεγονότος ἀλλὰ περὶ τοῦ ἐσομένου καὶ ἐνδεχομένου, τὸ δὲ γεγονὸς οὐκ ἐνδέχεται μὴ γενέσθαι· διὸ ὀρθῶς Ἀγάθων·

μόνου γὰρ αὐτοῦ καὶ θεὸς στερίσκεται,
ἀγένητα ποιεῖν ἅσσ' ἂν ᾖ πεπραγμένα.

F 6 Aristotle, *Nicomachean Ethics* 1140a10–20 (~ Simplicius on Aristotle, *Physics* 195b31)

ἔστι δὲ τέχνη πᾶσα περὶ γένεσιν καὶ τὸ τεχνάζειν καὶ θεωρεῖν ὅπως ἂν γένηταί τι τῶν ἐνδεχομένων καὶ εἶναι καὶ μὴ εἶναι . . . ἐπεὶ δὲ ποίησις καὶ πρᾶξις ἕτερον, ἀνάγκη τὴν τέχνην ποιήσεως ἀλλ' οὐ πράξεως εἶναι. καὶ τρόπον τινὰ περὶ τὰ αὐτά ἐστιν ἡ τύχη καὶ ἡ τέχνη, καθάπερ καὶ Ἀγάθων φησὶ·

τέχνη τύχην ἔστερξε καὶ τύχη τέχνην.

F 7 Aristotle, *Eudemian Ethics* 1229b39–1230a2

οὔτ' εἰ φεύγοντες τὸ πονεῖν, ὅπερ πολλοὶ ποιοῦσιν, οὐδὲ τῶν τοιούτων οὐδεὶς ἀνδρεῖος, καθάπερ καὶ Ἀγάθων φησὶ·

φαῦλοι βροτῶν γὰρ τοῦ πονεῖν ἡσσώμενοι
θανεῖν ἐρῶσιν.

F 8 Aristotle, *Rhetoric* 1392b5–8

καὶ εἰ ἄνευ τέχνης καὶ παρασκευῆς δυνατὸν γίγνεσθαι, μᾶλλον διὰ τέχνης καὶ ἐπιμελείας δυνατόν, ὅθεν καὶ Ἀγάθωνι εἴρηται·

καὶ μὴν τὰ μέν γε χρὴ τέχνῃ πράσσειν, τὰ δέ
ἡμῖν ἀνάγκῃ καὶ τύχῃ προσγίγνεται.

The first thing drawn was a circle with a central navel; then two upright rods yoked together, and *(the)* third shaped similarly to a Scythian bow; next to that was placed a trident lying sideways, and two †*were yoked*† upon a single rod; and as the third was, so again was the last.

Unidentified Plays

F 5 Aristotle, *Nicomachean Ethics*
Nothing that has already happened is subject to choice: for example, no one chooses to have sacked Troy, for one does not deliberate about what has happened but about what is to come and is capable of happening, whereas what has happened is not capable of not happening. Thus Agathon rightly (says):

> This power alone is denied even to a god, to make undone such things as have been done.

F 6 Aristotle, *Nicomachean Ethics*
Art (*technê*) as a whole is concerned with creation, with applying skill (*techn-azein*) and considering how to bring into existence something that is capable either of existing or of not existing . . . And since making is distinct from doing, art is a matter of making and not of doing. In a way, chance and art are concerned with the same things, as Agathon says:

> Art fosters chance, and chance art.

F 7 Aristotle, *Eudemian Ethics*
Nor if (they endure death) in order to escape suffering, as many do, is any of such people brave: as Agathon says,

> Weak men, when worsted by their suffering, desire to die.

F 8 Aristotle, *Rhetoric*
And if something is able to happen without artifice and preparation, it is more able to happen with art and application: thus Agathon says,

> And yet some things must be achieved by art, while others befall us through necessity and chance.

F 9 Aristotle, *Rhetoric* 1402a4–11 (~ *Poetics* 1456a24f. in **T 17** above, cf. *Po.* 1461b15)

ἔτι ὥσπερ ἐν τοῖς ἐριστικοῖς παρὰ τὸ ἁπλῶς καὶ μὴ ἁπλῶς, ἀλλὰ τί, γίγνεται φαινόμενος συλλογισμός . . . οὕτως καὶ ἐν τοῖς ῥητορικοῖς ἐστιν φαινόμενον ἐνθύμημα παρὰ τὸ μὴ ἁπλῶς εἰκὸς ἀλλὰ τὶ εἰκός. ἔστιν δὲ τοῦτο οὐ καθόλου, ὥσπερ καὶ Ἀγάθων λέγει·

τάχ' ἄν τις εἰκὸς αὐτὸ τοῦτ' εἶναι λέγοι,
βροτοῖσι πολλὰ τυγχάνειν οὐκ εἰκότα.

[F 10] *is improbably inferred from the text of Aristotle,* Poetics *1454b15. See note below.*

F 11 Athenaeus 5.185a (~ Clement Alex., *Stromata* 5.14.139.2)

ἡμεῖς γὰρ κατὰ τὸν καλὸν Ἀγάθωνα,

τὸ μὲν πάρεργον ἔργον ὣς ποιούμεθα,
τὸ δ' ἔργον ὡς πάρεργον ἐκπονούμεθα.

F 12 Athenaeus 5.211e

κατὰ γὰρ τὸν Ἀγάθωνα,

εἰ μὲν φράσω τἀληθές, οὐχί σ' εὐφρανῶ·
εἰ δ' εὐφρανῶ τί σ', οὐχὶ τἀληθὲς φράσω.

F 13 Athenaeus 10.445c

τούτων ἀκούσας ὁ Οὐλπιανὸς 'ὁ δὲ πάροινος', ἔφη, 'καλέ μου Ποντιανέ, παρὰ τίνι κεῖται;' καὶ ὃς ἔφη,

ἀπολεῖς μ' ἐρωτῶν (κατὰ τὸν καλὸν Ἀγάθωνα) καὶ σὺ χὠ
νέος τρόπος,
ἐν οὐ πρέποντι τοῖς λόγοισι χρώμενος.

F 14 Athenaeus 13.583e–584a

καὶ ἄλλαι δὲ ἑταῖραι μέγα ἐφρόνουν ἐφ' αὑταῖς, παιδείας ἀντεχόμεναι καὶ τοῖς μαθήμασι χρόνον ἀπομερίζουσαι . . . κατὰ γὰρ τὸν Ἀγάθωνα,

γυνή τοι σώματος δι' ἀργίαν
ψυχῆς φρόνησιν ἐντὸς οὐκ ἀργὸν φορεῖ.

τοι σώματος Porson (σώματος Grotius) τὸ σῶμα Ath.

F 16a Photius *α* 1137 (*'ἄμαρτυς'*)

ἀλλ' οὐκ ἄμαρτυς ἡ χάρις δοθήσεται.

F 9 Aristotle, *Rhetoric*

Again, just as in eristic arguments an apparent syllogism arises with respect to what is absolutely true and what is not absolutely true but true in a specific instance . . . so also in rhetorical arguments an apparent enthymeme arises with respect to what is not absolutely likely but is likely in a specific instance. The latter is not valid in general: thus Agathon says,

> Perhaps one could say that this itself is likely, that in human life
> much occurs that is unlikely.

[F 10] *See note opposite.*

F 11 Athenaeus, *Sophists at Dinner*

For, as the admirable Agathon puts it,

> We are treating what is incidental as our main task, and working
> at our main task as if it were incidental.

F 12 Athenaeus, *Sophists at Dinner*

For as Agathon puts it,

> If I tell the truth I shall not give you pleasure; and if I give you
> any pleasure I shall not be telling the truth.

F 13 Athenaeus, *Sophists at Dinner*

On hearing this Ulpian said, 'And the word *paroinos* ('drunk'), my fine Pontianus, in whom is it found?' And he replied,

> You'll kill me with your questions (as the admirable Agathon puts
> it), you and your modern way of using words inappropriately!

F 14 Athenaeus, *Sophists at Dinner*

Other *hetairai* too were very proud of themselves, laying claim to education and devoting time to their studies . . . For as Agathon puts it,

> A woman, though idle in body, does not on that account carry an
> idle intelligence within her soul.

F 16a Photius, *Lexicon*

> But this favour shall not be granted unwitnessed.

F 17 Schol. Soph. *Trach.* 638

ἔνθ' Ἑλλάνων ἀγοραί: ὅπου συνάγονται οἱ Ἀμφικτύονες εἰς τὴν λεγομένην Πυλαίαν περὶ ἧς Ἀγάθων φησὶ Πυλάδην τὸν Στροφίου πρῶτον συστήσασθαι ἐν τῇ Φωκίδι καθαιρόμενον τὸ ἐπὶ Κλυταιμήστρᾳ μύσος καὶ ἀπ' αὐτοῦ τὴν σύνοδον Πυλαίαν φησὶ προσαγορεύεσθαι.

F 18 Stobaeus 1.8.7

Ἀγάθων·

οὐ πώποτ' ἠξίωσα †χρήσασθαι τρόποις†

F 19? Stobaeus 1.8.14

Ἀγάθων·

σοφὸν λέγουσι τὸν χρόνον πεφυκέναι.

F 20 Stobaeus 3.3.15

Ἀγάθων·

οὐ τῇ φρονήσει, τῇ τύχῃ δ' ἐσφάλμεθα.

F 21 Stobaeus 3.29.39

Ἀγάθων·

ἰδίας ὁδοὺς ζητοῦσι φιλόπονοι φύσεις.

F 22 Stobaeus 3.31.17

Ἀγάθων·

ἀδικεῖν νομίζων ὄψιν αἰδοῦμαι φίλων.

F 23 Stobaeus 3.38.7

Ἀγάθων·

ὄλοιθ' ὁ τοῖς ἔχουσι τἀγαθὰ φθονῶν.

F 24 Stobaeus 3.38.12

Ἀγάθων·

οὐκ ἦν ἂν ἀνθρώποισιν ἐν βίῳ φθόνος,
εἰ πάντες ἦμεν ἐξ ἴσου πεφυκότες.

F 25 Stobaeus 3.38.23

Ἀγάθων·

σοφίας φθονῆσαι μᾶλλον ἢ πλούτου καλόν.

F 17 Scholia on Sophocles' *Women of Trachis*
where the gatherings of the Hellenes . . . : where the Amphictyons gather in the so-called Pylaea, concerning which Agathon says that Pylades son of Strophius first convened them when he was being purified from his pollution from the killing of Clytemnestra, and that the council was named Pylaea after him.

F 18 Stobaeus, *Anthology*, 'On the nature of time etc.'
Agathon:

> I have never thought fit †*to make use of habits?*†

F 19? Stobaeus, *Anthology*, 'On the nature of time etc.'
Agathon:

> They say that time is by nature wise.

F 20 Stobaeus, *Anthology*, 'On good judgement'
Agathon:

> Not our intelligence but fortune has laid us low.

F 21 Stobaeus, *Anthology*, 'On eagerness to strive'
Agathon:

> Natures that welcome toil seek their own paths.

F 22 Stobaeus, *Anthology*, 'On shame'
Agathon:

> When I think I am doing wrong, the sight of friends makes me feel shame.

F 23 Stobaeus, *Anthology*, 'On envy'
Agathon:

> Perish the man who resents those who have the good things of life!

F 24 Stobaeus, *Anthology*, 'On envy'
Agathon:

> There'd be no envy in human life if we were all born equal.

F 25 Stobaeus, *Anthology*, 'On envy'
Agathon:

> It's good to feel envy for wisdom rather than for wealth.

F 26 Stobaeus 4.11.2

Ἀγάθων·

νέων γὰρ ἀνδρῶν πολλὰ κάμπτονται φρένες.

F 27 Stobaeus 4.13.15

Ἀγάθων·

γνώμη δὲ κρεῖσσόν ἐστιν ἢ ῥώμη χερῶν.

F 28 Stobaeus 4.25.12

Ἀγάθων·

ὡς ἡδὺ τῷ φύσαντι πείθεσθαι τέκνα.

F 29 Zenobius Athous 2.54 attributed to Sthenelus (*TrGF* 32) or Agathon; Diogenianus 4.49 and others without attribution

ἐκ τοῦ γὰρ ἐσορᾶν ἐγένετ' ἀνθρώποις ἐρᾶν.

ἐκ τούτου and ἀνθρωπίνοις ὁρᾶν Zenob. (correctly other sources) ἐγένετ' Tucker γίνετ' Zenob. (γίνετ' or γίνεται others)

Brief and doubtful fragments: **F 1** (*Aerope*) εἰσῆσαν, **F 2** (*Alcmeon*) ἀθέμιστοι μοῦσαι, **F 15** ἐκφέρετε πεύκας φωσφόρους, **F 30?** ἀντεύφρασμα, **F 31?** ὕβριν ἢ ⟨Κύ⟩πριν †μισθῷ ποθὲν ἢ μόχθον πατρίδων†, **F 32?** ὦ λαμπρὸν ὄμμα τοῦ τροχηλάτου . . . , **F 34?** τὰς συμφορὰς γὰρ οὐχὶ τοῖς τεχνάσμασιν | φέρειν δίκαιον, ἀλλὰ τοῖς παθήμασιν.

F 26 Stobaeus, *Anthology*, 'On youth'

Agathon:

> Young men's minds often change direction.

F 27 Stobaeus, *Anthology*, 'On generalship'

Agathon:

> Good judgment is more powerful than strength of arm.

F 28 Stobaeus, *Anthology*, 'That parents should be properly honoured by their children etc.'

Agathon:

> How gratifying for a father when his children obey him!

F 29 Zenobius, *Proverbs*

> Looking begets loving in human kind.

Brief and doubtful fragments: **F 1** (*Adrastus*) they entered, **F 2** (*Alcmeon*) unlawful music, **F 15** bring out light-bearing torches, **F 30?** joy's contrary, **F 31?** Hybris or *(Cy)*pris †*for pay from somewhere or fatherlands' toil*†,[24] **F 32?** O bright-shining eye of the chariot-drawn *(god)*,[25] **F 34?** It's right to bear misfortunes not with invention but with resignation.[26]

---

[24] Quoted by Dionysius of Halicarnassus (*On Demosthenes' Style*, 26) to illustrate the misuse of the figure *parison* (antithesis of similar words) by authors such as Licymnius (a contemporary of Plato who wrote on rhetoric and also composed dithyrambs) and Agathon. These may have been two examples, Hybris 'lust' *vs.* Cypris 'love)', and μισθός 'reward' *vs.* μόχθος 'toil'. *TrGF* adesp. F 409 (from Plutarch, *Mor.* 768e) might be relevant: ὕβρις τάδ', οὐχὶ Κύπρις ἐξεργάζεται, 'Hybris, not Cypris brings this about'. See note there in *TrGF*.

[25] The first words of Aristophanes' *Ecclesiazusae (Assemblywomen)*, 'suspected to be from Agathon or Dicaeogenes' according to a suspiciously vague scholion.

[26] Verses spoken by Agathon and imitating his style in Aristophanes, *Women at the Thesmophoria* 198f., more likely parody than quotation: »» Rau 1967, 113.

Notes on Agathon

T 1

Part of a long catalogue of misrepresentations and historical errors committed by Plato and other philosophical writers. Athenaeus's speaker oddly suggests that Plato pretends to have been present at the Symposium himself. The date for Agathon's victory is presumably derived from the Athenian records. The same discussion sets Xenophon's *Symposium* and the production of Eupolis's first *Autolycus* in the archonship of Aristion, i.e. in summer 421 and early 420 respectively (though Xen. *Symp.* 1.2 itself implies 422 for his *Symposium*).

[Schol.[R] *Thesm.* 32 puts Agathon's first production 3 (*Γ´*) years before that play, i.e. before 411, but the number is probably corrupted from 6 (*Ϝ´*) which with inclusive counting would mean 416: »» Austin–Olson 2004, xxxv n. 17; Regtuit 2007, 20.]

T 2

For the biographical details see above, pp. 141f.. **it's many years etc.** is too vague (and somewhat exaggerated in any case) to help in dating Agathon's departure from Athens more exactly than the period 411–405. **thirty thousand Hellenes** is a flattering exaggeration. The Theatre of Dionysus at this time probably held around 8,000 people, and at the Lenaea in midwinter most would have been Athenians. **audience**: not 'theatre'; see LSJ 'θέατρον' 2, Critias(?) **T 1** with note. **you ascended the platform…to explain your subjects:** i.e. at the Proagon, a preliminary event held in the Odeion at which tragedians (and probably other competitors) announced the subjects of their forthcoming productions in the theatre: »» Pickard-Cambridge 1988, 67f.; Csapo–Slater 1995, 105, 109f.; Wilson 2000, 95f.

T 3

See above, pp. 141f. on Agathon's relationship with Pausanias.

T 4

The early scenes of *Women at the Thesmophoria*, abridged in **T 4**, give a comically distorted portrayal which virtually turns Agathon into a personification of his 'degenerate' art (»» Muecke 1982, Zeitlin 1996, 383f.). Sommerstein 1994 and Austin–Olson 2004 provide detailed commentaries, including the scenes' paratragic elements and parodies of Agathon's style.

36–38. let's duck out of the way etc.: a conventional dramatic move preparing an 'eavesdropping' scene, two characters hiding so as to observe the entrance of a third and/or the chorus (often, as here, performing a ritual). Cf. Aesch. *Cho.* 20ff., Eur. *El.* 107ff., Soph. *OC* 111ff. (in Soph. *El.* 77ff. Orestes decides *not* to stay), and in comedy Ar. *Ach.* 238ff., *Peace* 232ff., *Frogs* 312ff.

39–48. Let all the people be silent etc.: an exaggerated call for ritual silence, as if Agathon's poetry-making will be a religious event. He communes with **the sacred band of Muses**, the deities who inspire all music and song. All nature must join in the silence, as if hushed by their divine presence (»» Dodds on Eur. *Bacch.* 1084f., Austin–Olson on *Thesm.* 43–48)

52–57. Agathon's meticulous craftsmanship is conveyed in a jumble of metaphors from shipbuilding (the wooden **props** on which a ship's keel was laid), wheelmaking (**new verse-rims**), joinery (**some** verses **he turns etc.**), moulding or sculpting (**fashions maxims etc.**) and bronze-casting (**pours the wax etc.**: the 'lost-wax' technique involved making a wax-covered figure, covering it with clay, and firing it so that the wax melted away leaving a hardened clay mould into which molten bronze could be poured). Some of these terms were used metaphorically in sophistic analyses of poetry and rhetoric, which Aristophanes also seems to be satirizing here (»» Muecke 1982, 45f.).

98. Kyrene: a versatile prostitute, also named in *Frogs* 1327f. (and elsewhere by Aristophanes according to Schol.[R] here).

100. What's this he's humming etc.: Agathon hums along with the music while playing a prelude on his lyre (I think δια- in **διαμινύρεται** implies humming in 'dialogue' with, rather than 'singing through' as e.g. Austin–Olson's note and Power 2010, 507 take it). **ant-paths**: either of wandering ants (Schol.[R]) or the maze-like pathways inside anthills (as Austin–Olson prefer). If Agathon is humming the reference must be to his elaborate New Musical style (**T 19**, **F 3a** with notes) rather than to words. Commentators compare Pherecrates F 155.21ff. where Music complains that Timotheus has taken her 'along outlandish ant-paths' and dismantled her 'with his twelve strings' (cf. Hagel 2010, 269f. with note 26).

146–7. I heard your spite's derision but did not register its pain: i.e. it did not bother me. An Agathonian antithesis as in **F 14**, **20**, **25**, **27**.

148–56. Agathon justifies his effeminate behaviour by claiming that a poet can only create convincing female characters by impersonating a woman (not a very persuasive defence if Agathon is naturally effeminate: next note). **μίμησις** (**imitation**) here is essentially impersonation (»» Muecke 1982, 55; Austin–Olson 2004, 107f. with refs.: the Kinsman will later follow Agathon's example and 'impersonate' (μιμήσομαι) Euripides' Helen, *Thesm.* 850), but the use of the term anticipates the theorization of mimesis as representation (»» Zeitlin 1996 on the confusions of illusion and reality which pervade Aristophanes' play). **So you're the rider:** i.e. you 'mount' your sex-partner, as the notoriously shameless Phaedra of Euripides' first *Hippolytus* might have done.

159–67. Only an elegant poet can produce elegant poetry, and Agathon's effeminacy is now an expression of his **nature** (*phusis*); thus his imitations of female characters 'come naturally' after all (cf. Zeitlin 1996, 383f.; Farmer 2017, 158–62 argues that Agathon's point here complements rather than contradicts his previous point). The poets **Alcaeus**, **Ibycus** and **Anacreon** were associated with the luxury-loving elites of 6th-century Lesbos and Ionia (Ibycus came from Rhegium in southern Italy but spent time at the court of the tyrant Polycrates of Samos). For **Phrynichus** see above, pp. 23–48.

T 6

Antiphon of Rhamnous was one of the more extreme leaders of the oligarchic coup of 411 at Athens, subsequently tried and executed after refusing to flee into exile; Thucydides greatly admired him and his **defence-speech** (Thuc. 8.68, 8.90). A small part of the speech survives in a papyrus fragment (P. Genav. 264*bis*–267 ed. Nicole 1907). He is probably the author of the extant speeches bearing his name, and probably identical with 'Antiphon the Sophist' (author of now fragmentary works including *On Truth* and *On Concord*), but certainly not with the tragedian Antiphon (Vol. 2, *TrGF* no. 55). Agathon's praise of his speech suggests oligarchic sympathies which may have been relevant to his leaving Athens after 411.

T 7

The date of the production of *Frogs*, Jan. 405, provides the lower limit for Agathon's departure to Macedonia and makes it look fairly recent; the question would be rather pointless if he had left more than a couple of years before. In Plato's *Symposium* (172c = **T 8**), set around 400, Apollodorus says that Agathon has lived away from Athens 'for many years', but even if this suggests more than seven or eight years it need not be taken literally. The reference in *Frogs* is certainly to Agathon's departure rather than his death, for *(a)* Heracles is asking about poets who are still living, and *(b)* if Agathon were dead we would expect him to be in Hades with the other dead poets whose loss Dionysus laments. The joke is that he has gone **to the enjoyments of the blessed** even though he is *not* dead. **μακάρων (of the blessed)** is a pun on Μακεδόνων 'of the Macedonians' (cf. Dover 1993, 201 on *Frogs* 85). **εὐωχίαν (enjoyments)** is literally 'having a good time', especially in feasting and relaxation.

T 8

Apollodorus, narrator of the *Symposium*, explains that he only knows about the event at second hand as he was a child at the time, and not directly from Socrates. For the chronological implications see on **T 7**.

T 17

From Aristotle's discussion of tragic plot-structures in *Poetics* 17–18. A tragedy, he asserts, should have a unitary plot involving a single 'action' (*praxis*), and should not include multiple narratives as epic does.[27] The tragedy (or tragedies) of Agathon that **fell short** in this respect cannot be identified, nor is it clear precisely how, or to what extent, the poet erred.[28] The cyclic *Sack of Troy* (in the extant summary, *GEF* pp. 142–47) told the Troy story from the Trojans' acceptance of the Wooden Horse to the burning of the city and departure of the Greek forces, thus including the material of such plays as Euripides' *Trojan Women* and *Hecuba*. Tragedies entitled *Sack of Troy* are recorded for Iophon (**T 1** with note) and probably Nicomachus of Alexandria Troas in the 3rd century. The reference to Niobe is puzzling since her story is not obviously epic material. The point may be that Aeschylus's *Niobe* (like Euripides' *Trojan Women*) dramatized the aftermath of her catastrophe (the slaughter of her children by Apollo and Artemis) rather than the series of events that brought it about.[29]

[**either fall short etc.:** i.e. fail to make a well-designed tragedy. The meaning 'are hissed off the stage' (LSJ 'ἐκπίπτω' 12, and some translators) is not possible. **ἐκπίπτουσιν** must have the same sense as **ἐξέπεσεν** in the next line. ἐκπίπτειν in *Poetics* 1459b31 is no different.]

a likely outcome, as Agathon says etc.: it is 'likely', though unexpected, when a clever man is deceived or a brave one worsted. Aristotle presumably had in mind **F 9**, which he quotes in the *Rhetoric*.

T 18

This is the *Poetics*' only comment on the management of the chorus: its role should be like that of an actor (**συναγωνίζεσθαι** here means 'be a συναγωνιστής, a fellow performer'). The comment on Sophocles and Euripides is a broad generalization: Sophocles' choruses (at least in the extant plays) tend to be more engaged with and affected by the dilemmas and decisions of the main characters, whereas Euripides' choruses, especially in his latest plays, are often sympathetic spectators and their songs more detached from, though not irrelevant to, the immediate dramatic situation (»» Mastronarde 2010, 88f., 126–52). Agathon's *embolima* (**intermezzos**) may have taken this tendency a step or two further, and

---

[27] In *Poetics* 23 and 26 Aristotle notes that the *Iliad* and the *Odyssey* do have unitary plots (i.e. the wrath of Achilles, the restoration of Odysseus) while achieving epic scale through digressive narratives, flashbacks etc. They are thus artistically superior to most epics, which are purely episodic, but they still lack the concentration of tragic dramas.

[28] Euripides adopted an epic expansiveness in some of his latest plays (*Phoenician Women*, *Orestes*, *Iphigenia at Aulis* »» Michelini 2009), but not the episodic plot-structure that Aristotle implies here.

[29] Gudeman's suggestion that the Arabic translation of the *Poetics* implies the reading Θηβαΐδα (*Thebaid*) rather than Νιόβην (*Niobe*) is denied by Gutas in Tarán–Gutas 2012, 410.

are perhaps the specific target of Aristophanes' parody in *Thesm.* 101–29. Aristotle's wording is vague but suggests that in his case this was an experiment (perhaps connected with the experimental *Anthos/Antheus*?), and that the practice caught on to some extent. That **the rest** (i.e. Euripides' and Sophocles' successors) habitually used *embolima* is surely an overstatement: the only extant 4th-century tragedy, *Rhesus*, has a very active and engaged chorus (which may be one reason why the second hypothesis to *Rhesus* says the play has 'the stamp of Sophocles', τὸν Σοφόκλειον χαρακτῆρα). But the use of *embolima* may have made it possible for choruses to be detached from the drama entirely, without a significant *persona* and perhaps on stage only for its songs as in New Comedy.

[The Arabic text of the *Poetics* suggests that the Greek source of the Syriac text from which the Arabic was translated had τοῖς...πολλοῖς, 'most (of them)' rather than the Byzantine tradition's **τοῖς...λοιποῖς the rest** (»» Tarán–Gutas 2012, 411). This would make Aristotle's statement a little less sweeping but πολλοῖς is more likely a corruption of λοιποῖς than the other way round (cf. Tarán–Gutas 281).]

T 19

From a carbonized roll containing Book 4 of the treatise *On Music* by the Epicurean philosopher Philodemus (1st C. BC), found in the Villa of the Papyri at Herculaneum; the other books have not been found. For full introduction, text and French translation see Delattre 2007. Book 4 contained an extensive critique of the views on music of Diogenes of Babylon, a leading Stoic philosopher of the 3rd–2nd century. The Stoics shared the view, common in music theory since the mid-5th century, that music has a profound moral and educational importance because of its effect on the soul and on human behaviour (cf. Plato, *Rep.* 398c–400c). This view is already criticized in P. Hibeh 13, a papyrus fragment of a probably 4th-century sophistic text which denies that melodies can have any moral effect, and in particular that musical 'colouring' (*chrôma*) makes men cowardly or unmanly (cf. **F 3a** n.: »» West 1992a, 16–23; Csapo 2004, 230–32). Philodemus takes a similar, probably orthodox Epicurean position, arguing that melodies are merely one of many irrational sources of pleasure which one may or may not choose to enjoy for their own sake. In **T 19** the focus is on erotic behaviour in particular, lines 23–27 quoting somewhat obliquely from the Stronger Argument's description of old-fashioned education in Aristophanes' *Clouds* 979f. Lines 34–40 (**not men and women etc.**) repeat the terms of Philodemus's summary of Diogenes' views earlier in Book 4 (col. 43.11–17).

T 20

Details of Agathon's musical style, cf. **T 4** (Ar. *Thesm.* 99f.), **T 19**, **F 3a**, and above, pp. 144f. The testimonia give similar information transmitted in **(a)** lexica (the scholion on Cyril Lexicon cites the 5th-6th grammarian Timotheus of Gaza:

» Kaster 1997, 368–70, Dickey 2007, 100f.) and **(b)** proverb-collections. **(a)** indicates that Aristophanes coined the term **Agathoneian (Ἀγαθώνειος**, a metrically convenient form) denoting **an effeminate kind of aulos-music**. The play *Gerytades* (*Singer-son?*, F 156–190 *PCG*: »» Farmer 2017, 197–212) involved three Athenian poets visiting the underworld and conversing with dead poets, thus providing a forum for criticizing contemporaries such as Agathon. **(b)** interestingly adds a different evaluation (**neither languid nor harsh etc.**); this might reflect a debate within Aristophanes' play (the New Music pioneer Cinesias was one of its three poets) or a later commentator's response. On positive evaluations of the New Music see West 1992b, 371f., Barker 2014, 92, Ieranò 2013, 383–86 with Antiphanes F 207.4ff. *PCG* ('how well are [Philoxenus's] melodies blended with modulations and colourings…'). On the controversial role of the aulos in the New Music: Wilson 1999–2000, Csapo 2004, 216–29.

(c) is from a paragraph on tragic musical styles in the treatise *On Tragedy* now ascribed to Michael Psellus (cf. above, p. 45 on Phrynichus **T 12**). For definitions of the Hypophrygian and Hypodorian modes see West 1992a, 183, Hagel 2010, 430–35. A discussion in the Aristotelian *Problems* (19.48) states that in tragedy they were used only for solo songs and were suitable for heroes and men of action — the opposite of the languid, effeminate music commonly associated with Agathon (»» West 1992b, 184 with n. 94, 352; Barker 2014, 94f.).

F 2a

See the introduction to *Anthos/Antheus* above, pp. 154f.

F 3

Athenaeus discussing types of luxurious self-indulgence cites Aeschylus (F 313) as deriving the name of the Curetes (warriors from Pleuron in Aetolia, cf. *Iliad* 9.529ff.; Phrynichus, *Women of Pleuron*, pp. 36f. above) from their 'girlish' long hair (κούρη, 'girl'), and Agathon as relating it to the cutting (κουρά) of their hair after their failure to win the hand of Pronax's daughter. Ancient sources offered several other explanations of the name based on these two words, and several suggested connections between the Curetes of Aetolia and the Cretan Curetes, mythical guardians of the baby Zeus: see especially Strabo 10.3.6–8 with Henrichs 1975, 16f. Agathon's explanation gives a unique twist to the etymology from 'cutting'.

F 3a

Plutarch's speaker attributes to Agathon the use of 'colourings' and the introduction of 'the chromatic', lit. 'the coloured', in tragedy (the innovation is attributed to Euripides by Psellus, *On Tragedy* 5, the source of **T 20(c)** above). These were 'the subtle effects produced by the use of microintervals' (Csapo

2004, 227) associated with the theatrical 'New Music' and its development of virtuoso instrumental playing. Traditionalists condemned them as undisciplined (the 'ant-paths' of Ar. *Thesm.* 100 in **T 4**) and immoral (**T 19**, **T 20a–b** with notes): see further above, pp. 144f. Technical details, »» Barker 1984, 63, 184 n. 8, 225 n. 132; West 1992b, 161–66, 250; Hagel 2010, 44–52, 446–48.

F 4

Athenaeus cites this in a long discussion (10.448b–459c) of various kinds of riddle (*griphos*), here those playing with letters of the alphabet (»» Gagné 2013 for these and similar phenomena).[30] According to Athenaeus, Euripides in his *Theseus* (F 382), Agathon in his *Telephus*, and Theodectas in an unnamed play (**F 6**) all presented illiterate characters describing the inscribed name 'Theseus'. Athenaeus identifies Euripides' and Theodectas's speakers (a herdsman and a 'rustic') but not Agathon's, and he does not identify the inscribed items or the dramatic contexts. For Euripides these are easy enough to guess at (perhaps the herdsman saw Theseus's ship approaching Crete with his name displayed on its sail), but why should something bearing an inscription of the name Theseus be featured in a play about Telephus, when Theseus was a generation older than Telephus and had no connection with his legend? Two long-standing guesses can be mentioned: (1) Agathon may have drafted Athens's national hero into the story of Telephus's healing, or (2) the inscription may have been on a shield carried by one of Theseus's sons, Acamas and Demophon, who did participate in the Trojan war.[31] The first of these is favoured by Lévêque, though he does not offer an exact context for the inscribed item and its description. The second (recommended most recently by Musa 2005, 131f.) would make good sense if the play concerned not the healing of Telephus but his wounding by Achilles during the Achaeans' landing in Mysia; we might then have a rustic character describing the Achaean leaders and their accoutrements as they landed or prepared for battle, like the 'messengers' in Aeschylus's *Seven against Thebes* (375ff.) and Euripides' *Phoenician Women* (1104ff., whether authentic or not), or the Herdsman reporting the arrival of Rhesus and his army in *Rhesus* 284ff.; cf. Antigone surveying the Argive leaders in *Phoenician Women* 119ff., and the

---

[30] Riddles were a popular feature of Greek poetry and symposia. Athenaeus's examples are drawn mainly from the work *On Riddles* by Aristotle's pupil Clearchus of Soloi in Cyprus. Many are from comedy and satyr-drama (e.g. Achaeus F 19). This fragment with Euripides F 382, Ion **F 40**, Theodectas **F 4**, **F 6**, **F 18** are from tragedy. Other riddling fragments: Carcinus **F 1g**, Chaeremon **F 41**. »» M. L. West in *OCD*[4] 'riddles', and for fourth-century drama Xanthakis-Karamanos 1980, 97–102.

[31] A third suggestion, that *Telephus* is a corruption of *Tlepolemus* (Meineke) or *Temenos* (Walker), is rightly dismissed by Lévêque 1955, 98 n. 3.

maiden chorus describing the Achaean leaders in Eur. *Iphigenia at Aulis* 185ff. But all this remains speculative.

Euripides' *Theseus* was produced before 422, so Agathon was certainly emulating Euripides' word-riddle (see in Vol. 2 for Theodectas's use of both). Agathon's description is more succinct (six lines against eleven) and more neatly phrased. Euripides' herdsman mostly sticks to abstract descriptions of shapes, while Agathon's speaker offers material comparisons (rods, bow, trident; in the first line **μεσόμφαλος κύκλος**, **circle with a central navel**, could suggest a shield with a central boss). Musa notes that the military comparisons would be apt if the speaker was describing a shield.

F 5

A commonplace, perhaps used by Agathon as by [Plutarch], *Consolation to Apollonius* 115a: 'Endless grief is futile, for even a god cannot undo what has come to pass (τὸ μὲν γὰρ γεγενημένον οὐδὲ θεῷ δυνατόν ἐστι ποιῆσαι ἀγένητ-ον)'. Other nuances are possible, e.g. Soph. *Trach.* 742f. 'The harm you have done is irretrievable, for who could make what has happened undone (τὸ γὰρ φανθὲν τίς ἂν δύναιτ' ἂν ἀγένητον ποεῖν;'), cf. Simonides fr. 98 *PMG*); Pindar, *Ol.* 2.15ff., 'Even Time cannot undo the outcomes of past deeds (τῶν…πεπραγ-μένων…ἀποίητον οὐδ' ἄν Χρόνος…δύναιτο θέμεν ἔργων τέλος), yet a happy fortune may make them forgotten'; Plato, *Laws* 934a (cf. *Protagoras* 324b), 'Punishment should not be retributive, for what has been done will never be undone (οὐ γὰρ τὸ γεγονὸς ἀγένητον ἔσται ποτέ)'.

F 6

Good outcomes depend on both chance (the right conditions) and human devising: cf. e.g. Hippocrates, *De Arte* 4, Plato, *Laws* 709. The antithesis *technê/tuchê* (skill or calculation *vs.* chance), as in **F 8** below, is very common in 5th-century and later rationalistic thought; cf. also **F 20** (intelligence *vs.* fortune).

F 7

Perhaps an argument against suicide in Agathon's context, though this is not specifically Aristotle's point: cf. e.g. Eur. *Heracles* 1248, 1347–50, *Orestes* 415, F 1070. Note the balanced πονεῖν ~ θανεῖν (*paronomasia*), as in **F 6**, **F 27**, **F 29**.

F 8

See above on **F 6**. **necessity and chance:** hendiadys for 'irresistible/uncontrollable chance' (ἀναγκαία τύχη, cf. Soph. *Aj.* 485, 803, *El.* 48).

F 9

Similar paradoxes: Eur. *Thyestes* F 396 (if some falsehoods are persuasive, some truths may be unpersuasive), Soph. F 860 (there's a first time for everything).

[F 10]

In *Poetics* 1454b8–15 Aristotle states that the tragic poet should follow the example of portrait-painters who create likenesses of their subjects but make them look better than they really are. The poet 'should portray men as being hot-tempered, lazy and having other such character-traits but nevertheless make them admirable (ἐπιεικεῖς)…'. In the transmitted text the sentence ends as follows: παράδειγμα σκληρότητος οἷον τὸν Ἀχιλλέα ἀγαθὸν (*or* ἀγαθῶν *or* Ἀγάθων) καὶ Ὅμηρος (the alternative readings are all attested: »» Tarán–Gutas 2012, 268f.). The words παράδειγμα σκληρότητος ('an example of harshness') should probably be deleted as an explanatory addition to the text. Reading Ἀγάθων would then give, '…make them admirable, as Agathon and Homer make Achilles'. This is recommended by Tarán–Gutas, but a reference to 'Agathon and Homer' is unlikely. Homer was the archetypal example of the complex characterization of Achilles. Agathon, if he portrayed Achilles at all, would have been just one of many poets who followed his example. More likely the word comes from another explanation pointing out that Achilles was ἀγαθόν 'noble', and the correct reading is just οἷον τὸν Ἀχιλλέα καὶ Ὅμηρος, 'as Homer portrayed Achilles'. For οἷον καὶ used in this way see Denniston 1954, 296(iv); Pl. *Phaedo* 94d6 οἷόν που καὶ Ὅμηρος ἐν Ὀδυσσείᾳ πεποίηκεν, 'as Homer has put it in the *Odyssey*'.

F 11, F 12

Extreme examples of Agathon's antithetical style, with rhyming verbal contrasts (πάρεργον ~ ἔργον, ποιούμεθα ~ ἐκπονούμεθα, φράσω ~ εὐφρανῶ) and inverted phrasing (chiasmus: πάρεργον ἔργον ~ ἔργον…πάρεργον; φράσω τἀληθές, οὐχί σ' εὐφρανῶ ~ εὐφρανῶ…σ', οὐχὶ τἀληθὲς φράσω). For the dilemma in **F 12** cf. Euripides F 1036.

F 13

Ulpian is the provocative symposiarch (director) of Athenaeus's symposium (Athen. 1d–e, cf. Olson 2006, x). Here he has interrupted Pontianus's discourse on the perils of drunkenness with a demand to know where in Attic literature the word πάροινος is attested (Pontianus responds by quoting Antiphanes fr. 144 *PCG*).

F 14

Cf. Eur. *Wise Melanippe* F 482 ('I'm a woman, but I have intelligence [*nous*]'), *Antiope* F 199 (a woman's physical weakness unimportant if she has a sound mind [*eu phronein*]). Physical idleness is assumed to be normal for women unless they are poor. Phaedra in Euripides' *Hippolytus* famously sees it as a constraint (*Hipp.* 378ff.): 'Many of us have intelligence (*eu phronein*) but fail to act accordingly, through idleness (*argia*) or a taste for the pleasures of leisure.'

F 16a

Context unknown. Photius cites the fragment for the unique form **ἄμαρτυς, unwitnessed** (usually ἀμάρτυρος or ἀμαρτύρητος).

F 17

Sophocles' chorus calls on the people living around the Malian Gulf to welcome Heracles as he returns from Euboea, including the place 'where the gatherings of the Hellenes are held that are called Pylaean'. The place is Anthela near Thermopylae (or simply Pylae), the gatherings those of the Pylaea, the amphictyonic council which controlled the sanctuary of Demeter Pylaea there and, at least from the early sixth century, the sanctuary of Apollo at Delphi (Sophocles' ***ἀγοραί, gatherings*** evokes the title Pylagorai, delegates to the Pylaea). The story that the Pylaea was first convened by Orestes' comrade Pylades in connection with his purification from the murder of Clytemnestra, and so named after him, is an obvious fiction (derivation *from* Pylae is one suggested explanation of his name). It presumably served to reinforce the claim of the Phocians (Pylades' people) to the much-disputed control of Delphi, which Athens sometimes supported (Thuc. 1.112, cf. 3.95.1);[32] this may have influenced Agathon's mention (or invention?) of the story. None of the plays whose titles we know provides an obvious context. [The fragment has occasionally been attributed to the obscure Hellenistic historian Agathon of Samos, *FGrH* no. 843, who may or may not be identical with another Agathon, *FGrH* no. 801). A Sophoclean commentator is much more likely to have cited the tragedian.]

F 18

The sentence is obviously corrupt (or incomplete?). Grotius changed τρόποις to χρόνῳ ('to make use of time'). Others have preferred χρόνοις, with χρήσασθαι 'to make use of' (Meineke) or χαρίσασθαι 'to gratify' (Wachsmuth) or ἀποχρῆσθαι 'to abuse' (Waern 1956, 92 n. 1), but the plural 'periods of time' seems inappropriate.

F 19?

Time is **by nature wise** because it sees all and brings what is hidden to light sooner or later, a commonplace well illustrated in this chapter of Stobaeus, e.g. Soph. *Ajax* 646f., *OT* 1213, F 301, F 918, Eur. *Hippolytus Veiled* F 441. [Attribution to Agathon is uncertain because the lemmata in Stobaeus 1.8.13–16 are confused. Wachsmuth in his edition of Stobaeus transferred the lemma Ἀγάθωνος to this excerpt (1.8.14) from 1.8.16.]

[32] On the origin of the mythical Pylades see Forrest 1956, 42–44.

F 20

fortune: *tuchê* here is the force that shapes events beyond human control (less random than the 'chance' of **F 6** and **F 8**): cf. Gorgias, *Helen* 19, 'blame *tuchê*, not human calculation', *Tuchê* more powerful than human intelligence: Soph. *OT* 977f., Chaeremon **F 2**, Diogenes Sinop. **F 2**, Menander fr. 372 *PCG*. For an opposing statement see Critias(?) **F 10**.

F 21

Philoponia (devotion to toil) is required for the achievement of *aretê* (virtue) and glory (*eukleia*). This basic tenet of Greek morality is illustrated by one hundred and twenty quotations in Stobaeus 3.29 ('On *philoponia*') and 3.30 ('On *argia*/idleness'). Cf. especially Hesiod, *Works* 286–92 (the paths of *aretê*/virtue and *kakotês*/vice), Xenophon, *Mem.* 2.1.18–34 (Socrates quotes Hesiod and relates Prodicus's fable of Heracles' choice of toil and *aretê* over pleasures and *kakia*); in tragedy e.g. Eur. *Hcld.* 625 ('*aretê* proceeds through toils'), F 134, F 236–237, Theodectas **F 11**. Agathon's verse stresses the independence, self-reliance and perseverance of the *philoponoi*, cf. Socrates in Xen. *Mem.* 2.18f. **Natures (φύσεις)** suggests their capacity for *aretê* is innate, cf. Virtue addressing Heracles in *Mem.* 2.27.

F 22

the sight of friends makes me feel shame: the judgement of others was a fundamental consideration in ancient Greek morality. The opinions of those close to oneself (*philoi*) mattered most, not only because they had to be respected but because their own reputations would be affected by association. »» Dover 1974, 226–29, 236f., and 1980, 91 on Plato, *Symp.* 178d2–4.

F 23, 24, 25

Phthonos (envy/resentment) for the better off is natural but harmful: a common sentiment, e.g. Soph. *Ajax* 157ff., Eur. F 294–295, F 403, F 551, Dionysius **F 8** (in Vol. 2), and others in Stobaeus 3.38.

F 26

A commonplace as old as *Iliad* 3.108, 'Younger men's minds are always up in the air'. Cf. Plato, *Laws* 929c5–6.

F 27

A neat formulation of a commonplace idea, e.g. Xenophanes fr. 2.11f. *IEG*, Soph. *Ajax* 1250–52, F 939, Eur. F 199, F 200. For the *gnômê*/*rhômê* antithesis cf. Gorgias, *Epitaphios* (B 6 D–K) 11 and 15, Ar. *Birds* 636f., Xen. *Oecon.* 21.8, Isocr. 2.32, 4.45.

F 28

Respect for parents a cardinal virtue: Stobaeus 4.25 has fifty-four excerpts including Dicaeogenes **F 4**, **F 5**, Chaeremon **F 33** (see these in Vol. 2), Soph. *Ant.* 639 ff., many Euripidean fragments, and at length Xen. *Mem.* II.ii, Plato, *Laws* 717b–718a, 930e–932d.

F 29

A common idea formulated with an elegance (ἐσορᾶν ~ ἐρᾶν) which made this verse proverbial. For simple 'love at first sight' cf. e.g. Eur. *Hipp.* 24–28. The lover's eyes may be pierced by rays (or missiles) projected from the loved one's eyes, e.g. Pindar fr. 123.2–4, Soph. *Ant.* 795f., F 157, F 474. Plato makes this reciprocal, *erôs* generated through the lover's eyes flowing back into the loved one's eyes (*Phaedrus* 255b–d). These ideas are endlessly elaborated in later erotic contexts: »» e.g. Pearson 1909, Walker 1992.

[Attribution to Agathon is more likely than to his slightly older contemporary Sthenelus (*TrGF* no. 32); this would be Sthenelus's only extant tragic verse, and Aristotle commented on his mundane style (*Poetics* 1458a18–21). Tucker's **ἐγένετ'** (gnomic aorist) is preferable to the usually printed γίγνετ' (elision of -ται or -σθαι is not reliably attested in tragedy: Diggle 1994, 313, disputed unpersuasively by Hose 1994, 32–43).]

CRITIAS?
(*TrGF* 43)

Texts. etc. *TrGF* 1^2.170–84 with *addenda* 1^2.349–51, 5.1107f.; *MusTr* 108–25, 283f.; Battegazzore 1962; Collard–Cropp 2008b, 627–77.

Discussions. Wilamowitz 1875, 159, 161–6; Schmid 1940, 176–81; Hoffmann 1951, 138–45; Lesky 1972, 525f. (= 1983, 396); Pančenko 1980; Kannicht 1995; Pechstein 1998, 185–91; Wright 2016, 50–58.

See also the bibliography for *Pirithous*, p. 186.

Under this heading TrGF *includes testimonia and fragments for four named plays (*Pirithous, Rhadamanthys, Sisyphus, Tennes*) along with four gnomic fragments (**F 22–25**) which Stobaeus ascribes simply to Critias. The attributions of the named plays to Critias are disputed: essentials and history of the question are briefly summarized in Collard–Cropp 2008b, 629–35. Critias (Plato's uncle) was a leader of the pro-Spartan oligarchs who governed Athens after its fall in 404; he was killed in the counter-revolution of 403. He certainly wrote on political, moral and cultural subjects in both verse and prose. That he composed tragedies is attested only in the ascriptions of **F 2**, F 19 and **F 22–25**. It is usually but questionably inferred from two allusions in Plato's* Critias *and* Charmides *(see **T 1** with note).*

The book-fragments of the four named plays are all ascribed by their sources to Euripides,[1] *with two exceptions. **F 2** is ascribed by its only source, Athenaeus, to '[t]he author of Pirithous, whether this is Critias the tyrant or Euripides'. F 19, forty-two lines of a speech asserting that the gods are a human invention, is quoted in full by the philosopher Sextus Empiricus (2nd* c. *AD) and ascribed by him to Critias without naming either the speaker or the play; other sources ascribe parts of it to Euripides, and the pseudo-Plutarchan* Placita Philosophorum *(an epitome of a 1st-century doxographical work usually ascribed to Aetius) names Sisyphus as its speaker, still without naming the play.*[2]

---

[1] The *Pirithous* cited without a poet's name in Stobaeus 3.37.15 (**F 11**) is presumably the one he ascribes elsewhere to Euripides.

[2] It is therefore not certain that the play was named *Sisyphus*. F 19 is usually though again uncertainly thought to have come from a satyr-play (cf. note 14

*The papyrus fragments **F 4a**, **5**, **7–9**, all from the same roll (2nd C. AD), carry no identification but are reasonably ascribed to a* Pirithous, *presumably the one that was being read and usually ascribed to Euripides when this text was written. The verses ascribed by Stobaeus simply to Critias (**F 22–25**) are probably from one or more of the plays in question.*[3] *Other testimonia include the papyrus hypothesis-fragments of* Rhadamanthys *(**F 15**) and* Tennes *(**F 20**); these come from a well-known collection of narrative hypotheses, the so-called 'Tales from Euripides', as does the hypothesis-fragment printed as Euripides'* Sisyphus *test. iii in* TrGF *5. Lastly,* Sisyphus *and* Tennes *are listed in a fragmentary papyrus list of Euripides' plays (2nd* C. *AD),*[4] *while* Sisyphus *and probably the first one or two letters of* Pirithous *are included in an inscribed list of Euripides' plays known as the 'Piraeus Catalogue' (c. 100 BC).*[5] *That Euripides produced a satyr-play* Sisyphus *with the Trojan trilogy of 415 is known from Aelian's complaint about his being passed over for the prize in that year.*[6]

*These data make it clear that all four of the plays in question were included in the Euripidean corpus which was established at the Alexandrian Library in the third century BC, and that all were normally ascribed to Euripides thereafter. The uncertainty suggested by the ascriptions of **F 2** and F 19 is however compounded by the information found in two redactions of an ancient* Life of Euripides *which are found in some medieval manuscripts (**T 2**). Taken together, these indicate that the Alexandrian corpus comprised seventy tragedies (including the prosatyric* Alcestis*) and eight satyr-plays from a total of ninety-two*

---

below). For text, translations, notes and bibliography see *GrSat* 552–61; Cipolla 2003, 225–68; Collard–Cropp 2008b, 670–77; O'Sullivan–Collard 2013, 440–47. For discussion of the content see most recently Whitmarsh 2014, also with translation. For Aetius see Diels 1879 (relevant sections) and e.g. Runia 1996, Bremmer 1998 (questioning the author's name), Mansfeld 2016.

[3] It seems unlikely that they came from some other completely unattested play(s) of Critias. Cf. Hoffmann 1951, 140.

[4] P. Oxy. 27.2456 = Euripides T 8 in *TrGF* 5, p. 60: the extant part covers only the letters Σ (including *Sisyphus*) to X.

[5] Euripides T 7a in TrGF 5, pp. 58f.: the parts that might have listed *Rhadamanthys* and *Tennes* are missing. The extant part of another inscribed list (T 6) covers only letters A to O.

[6] See Xenocles **T 3**, pp. 136f. above.

recorded titles, and that amongst these the authorship of the tragedies Tennes, Rhadamanthys *and* Pirithous *and one unnamed satyr-play was disputed (see note on **T 2**). This analysis of the sources (and some slightly confused derivatives) was established by Wilamowitz*[7] *and is confirmed by the detailed study of Kannicht,*[8] *who shows that the Alexandrians' seventy-eight 'preserved' plays can be exactly identified with the seventy-eight titles represented in our corpus of extant and fragmentary Euripidean texts, including* Tennes, Rhadamanthys, Pirithous *and the inauthentic* Rhesus *(which must have replaced Euripides' own, lost* Rhesus*).*

Wilamowitz inferred from this evidence that Tennes, Rhadamanthys, Pirithous *and the unnamed satyr-play must have constituted a single tetralogy, that Alexandrian scholars had found such a tetralogy under Critias's name in the records of the City Dionysia, and that Critias's authorship had been forgotten or suppressed after his death and the plays wrongly attributed to Euripides until Alexandrian scholars rediscovered the true attribution in the Didascaliae. He also inferred, in view of Sextus's ascription of the Sisyphus-fragment F 19, that the disputed satyr-play was a* Sisyphus *composed by Critias, the text of Euripides'* Sisyphus *having been lost like that of his* Rhesus *and some other plays (especially satyr-plays).*[9] *This hypothesis has been very influential and was reflected in Snell's inclusion of all four plays under Critias's name in* TrGF *1 (though a little inconsistently without the testi-*

---

[7] Wilamowitz 1875, 144f. As he pointed out, the Hellenistic origin of this information is confirmed by the 1st-century BC Roman scholar Varro's slightly inaccurate comment that Euripides won only five victories despite having written seventy-five tragedies (Varro fr. 298 Funaioli = Aulus Gellius, *Attic Nights* 17.4.3). Seventy-five is actually the total number of *plays* preserved at Alexandria (78) less *Tennes*, *Rhadamanthys* and *Pirithous*.

[8] Kannicht 1996 (summarized in *TrGF* 5.2.80, §d), with a few corrections of Wilamowitz's list (Wilamowitz had counted *Epeus* as a tragedy, excluded a second *Phrixus* and a second *Autolycus*, and unnecessarily posited an otherwise unknown satyr-play beginning with the letter Π in the Piraeus catalogue).

[9] Wilamowitz 1875, 159, 161–66. Following this logic he suggested that the one significant book-fragment attributed to Euripides' *Sisyphus*, F 673 *TrGF* addressed to Heracles, actually belonged to his *Syleus* (the only other fragment, F 674, is a single word cited by Hesychius). He was of course unaware of the papyrus hypothesis to *Sisyphus* published in 1962 (P. Oxy. 2455 fr. 7), which places it amongst Euripides' plays.

monia and fragments ascribed exclusively to Euripides' Sisyphus*).*[10] *It has however been questioned periodically, especially in recent years.*[11] *If this was a tetralogy produced at the City Dionysia by Critias and traceable under his name in the Didascaliae, it is difficult to see how the plays came to be attributed to Euripides, for whom no such tetralogy was recorded and whose own* Sisyphus *was recorded as part of a different tetralogy.*[12] *It is also difficult to see why the plays should have continued to be almost universally ascribed to Euripides even after Alexandrian scholars had noticed that they actually belonged to Critias.*[13] *The biographical statements (**T 2**) are no doubt much abbreviated, but as they stand they suggest that if the plays were not by Euripides their real author was unknown, not that it was known to be Critias.*[14]

---

[10] These are therefore included under the name of Euripides in *TrGF* 5.2.657–59, although Kannicht there explains that he thinks they really belong to Critias: cf. Kannicht 1995, 27f. The four plays were also attributed to Critias in Diels–Kranz's collection of the fragments of the Presocratic philosophers (88 B 12–29 DK). Three recent historical studies of Critias (Centanni 1997, Caire 1998 [cf. Caire 2016], Bultrighini 1999) take Wilamowitz's theory for granted and treat the dramatic fragments as evidence for Critias's moral and political thought, as do Angiò 1989 and (on *Tennes*) Wilson 2003.

[11] See e.g. Kuiper 1907, 354–65 (following Kuiper 1888, 362–65); Schmid 1940, 180; Hoffmann 1951, 142f.; Dihle 1977, 28–30; *MusTr* 109; Pechstein 1998, 185–91; Egli 2003, 49; Collard–Cropp 2008b, 630–35, with Page, Mette, Sutton, and Collard 2007 in the bibliography for *Pirithous* below. Nauck in his 1889 edition assigned the Sisyphus-fragment to Critias but left the three tragedies with Euripides, noting their disputed status but not accepting Wilamowitz's tetralogy theory.

[12] Wilamowitz thought that Critias's authorship had been forgotten or suppressed because of his oligarchic record (1875, 166), but this does not explain the attribution to Euripides. In 1920 (I.118 n. 1) he suggested that 4th-century booksellers used Euripides' name in order to improve their sales. In 1927 (292) he suggested that the Didascaliae might have named someone other than Critias as the producer of the tetralogy (which negates the basis of his original hypothesis, that Alexandrian scholars found Critias's name in the Didascaliae). Kannicht suggests some unexplained confusion in the Didascaliae (*TrGF* 5.2.659, cf. Kannicht 1995, 27).

[13] Wilamowitz's assertion (in 1875) that Alexandrian scholars unanimously assigned the three tragedies to Critias was inappropriate: see below on **T 2**.

[14] The second hypothesis to *Rhesus*, which raises the question of its authenticity, is similarly vague. It should be kept in mind that the atheist speech F 19 is not

The tetralogy theory cannot be disproved but is at least questionable. Without it there is no reason to treat the four plays as belonging either all to Euripides or all to Critias, and no reason to think of Critias as a possible author of Tennes *and* Rhadamanthys*; if not by Euripides these might, like the extant* Rhesus, *have been fourth-century works that*

Testimonia

T 1

(a) Plato, *Critias* 108b3–7
προλέγω γε μήν, ὦ φίλε Κριτία, σοὶ τὴν τοῦ θεάτρου διάνοιαν, ὅτι θαυμαστῶς ὁ πρότερος ηὐδοκίμηκεν ἐν αὐτῷ ποιητής, ὥστε τῆς συγγνώμης δεήσει τινός σοι παμπόλλης, εἰ μέλλεις αὐτὰ δυνατὸς γενέσθαι παραλαβεῖν.

(b) Plato, *Charmides* 162c6–d3
ὁ μὲν οὖν Χαρμίδης βουλόμενος μὴ αὐτὸς ὑπέχειν λόγον ἀλλ' ἐκεῖνον τῆς ἀποκρίσεως, ὑπεκίνει αὐτὸν ἐκεῖνον, καὶ ἐνεδείκνυτο ὡς ἐξεληλεγμένος εἴη· ὁ δ' οὐκ ἠνέσχετο, ἀλλά μοι ἔδοξεν ὀργισθῆναι αὐτῷ ὥσπερ ποιητὴς ὑποκριτῇ κακῶς διατιθέντι τὰ ἑαυτοῦ ποιήματα.

T 2 *Life of Euripides* IA.9 (*TrGF* 5.1, p. 47)
τὰ πάντα δ' ἦν αὐτοῦ δράματα ϙβ´, σῴζεται δὲ οη´. τούτων νοθεύεται τρία, Τέννης Ῥαδάμανθυς Πειρίθους.

~ *Life of Euripides* IB.5 (*TrGF* 5.1, p. 49): τὰ πάντα δ' ἦν αὐτοῦ δράματα ϙβ´, σῴζεται δὲ αὐτοῦ δράματα ξζ´ καὶ γ´ πρὸς τούτοις τὰ ἀντιλεγόμενα, σατυρικὰ δὲ η´, ἀντιλέγεται δὲ καὶ τούτων τὸ α´.

---

known to come from a play named *Sisyphus* and may be unrelated to the fragments of Euripides' *Sisyphus* (Pechstein 1998, 191 suggests it may have come from one of Euripides' two satyr-plays named *Autolycus*; on the question of its satyric character see Davies 1989, 29–32, Whitmarsh 2014, 111f.).

were mistaken for, or passed off as, his. Without the theory it is also easier to assess the disputed ascriptions of Pirithous *and the Sisyphus-fragment on their merits: see the introductions to the three tragedies below and for the Sisyphus-fragment the references in note 2 above.*

Testimonia

T 1

(a) Plato, *Critias*

(*Socrates*) But, my dear Critias, I'll declare to you the opinion of the audience, that the previous poet has impressed them mightily; so you'll need a very large measure of indulgence if you're going to prove able to follow that.

(b) Plato, *Charmides*

(*Socrates*) So Charmides, wanting him (Critias) rather than himself to account for the answer, was provoking him and suggesting he had been refuted; and Critias could not bear it but seemed to me to have become angry with him, like a poet with an actor who has handled his compositions badly.

T 2 *Life of Euripides*, version IA

His (i.e. Euripides') plays totalled 92, of which 78 are preserved. Three of these are inauthentic: *Tennes, Rhadamanthys, Pirithous*.

~ version IB: His plays totalled 92, and 67 plays of his are preserved, plus 3 that are disputed; and 8 satyr-plays, and of these too 1 is disputed.

ΠΕΙΡΙΘΟΥΣ

Texts etc. *TrGF* 1².171–78 with *addenda* 1².349–51, 5.1107; *MusTr* 111–20, 283f.; Battegazzore 1962, 280–305; Battegazzore–Carlini 1989, 442–66; Collard–Cropp 2008b, 636–57. See further below under **F 1, F 4a, F 5**.

Myth. Herter 1973, 1158–83; Mette 1983; Gantz 1993, 277–82, 288–95; *LIMC* VII, 'Peirithoos', nos 69–91 (~ V, 'Herakles', nos 3515–19; VII, 'Theseus', nos 291–9).

Discussions. Wilamowitz 1875, 161–72; 1907b (response to Kuiper 1907, first published in Bremer–Calder 1994, 211–16; reprinted with commentary, Alvoni 2011); Kuiper 1907, 1908a; Page 1941, 120–23; Mette 1983; Sutton 1987b, 1–106; Dover 1993, 54f.; Dobrov 2001, 133–56; Collard 2007, 56–68.

Pirithous was a prince of the Thessalian Lapith people in the generation before the Trojan War, son of the sinner Ixion but also said to have been begotten by Zeus (e.g. Iliad *14.317f.). He was known in early Greek poetry and art for three exploits: leading the suppression of the Centaurs in the battle resulting from their disruption of his wedding with Hippodameia; helping the Athenian hero Theseus to abduct Helen from Sparta; and attempting with Theseus's aid to abduct Persephone from the Underworld, with the result that both were imprisoned there.*[15] *The outcome of this third episode varied in different versions of the story: either both heroes remained permanently trapped in Hades (as seems to be implied in* Odyssey *11.63f. and in Polygnotus's mural in the Lesche at Delphi as described by Pausanias 10.29.9), or Theseus was rescued by Heracles when he visited the Underworld to seize Cerberus,*[16] *or Heracles on this mission rescued both Theseus and Pirithous. The tragedy* Pirithous *is the first clear instance of the double rescue, and may well have introduced it.*[17] *The play focused on the obligations of*

---

[15] Theseus was also associated with the Centauromachy at least as early as the 6th century. *Iliad* 1.265 refers to it but may be an interpolation.

[16] First explicitly in Euripides, *Heracles* 618ff., 1169f. 1221f. etc. (where Pirithous is not mentioned at all) but probably already in the 6th century: »» Lloyd-Jones 1967, 185f.; Herter 1973, 1177, 1181; Gantz 1993, 292; cf. Apollodorus 2.5.12, epit. 1.24.

[17] So already Wilamowitz 1875, 167f. Gantz (292, 294) suggests that the double rescue might be implied in an early 6th-century bronze shield-band from Olympia (*LIMC* 'Peirithoos' no. 84) and a mid-5th century vase-painting now in New York (*LIMC* no. 73). Manakidou in *LIMC* VII.i.241 considers it unattested

PIRITHOUS

*friendship (*philia*) which bind Heracles and Theseus (**F** 7.15ff.) and cause Theseus to refuse to abandon Pirithous when he has the opportunity (**F 1** Hypothesis, **F 6**, **F** 7.6f.). It seems to have innovated further by having only Pirithous physically trapped, so that Theseus is free to leave Hades if he so chooses; in the Hypothesis only Pirithous is 'seated and motionless', and in **F 4a** Theseus is apparently not present as Heracles converses with Pirithous.*[18]

The fragments of the play that can be located come from its early scenes. It was set in Hades,[19] *with Pirithous fastened to a rock and therefore present from the outset, like Prometheus in the Aeschylean plays (where Heracles rescued him), and Andromeda in Euripides'* Andromeda *(where Perseus rescued her). The text in **F 1**, in which Heracles arrives and meets Aeacus, must precede **F 4a** in which he and the Chorus have heard a speech from Pirithous describing his torments, Pirithous recognizes Heracles' voice but is prevented from seeing him by a 'mist' spread before his eyes, and Heracles asks why he is so tormented. **F 5**, in which Pirithous describes his father Ixion's crime and punishment, is probably part of his answer to Heracles' question (see further below on **F 4a–F** 7), and these two fragments presumably preceded **F** 7, in which Heracles has now met Theseus, hears of Theseus's refusal to abandon Pirithous, and declines his offer of help against Cerberus. **F 6**, a single verse describing Theseus's loyalty to Pirithous, is plausibly but by no means certainly placed in the vicinity of **F** 7. As for the entry of the Chorus, probably including **F 2–4**, this must have preceded the dialogue in **F 4a** with its comment from the Chorus-leader, and probably followed Heracles' arrival (**F 1** Text) which otherwise has*

---

in archaic and classical iconography. It never became standard but surfaces in Diodorus 4.26.1 and Hyginus, *Fab.* 79 (Diod. 4.63.4 records both the other alternatives). Tzetzes' comment on *Chil.* 4.912, 'In Euripides both are rescued', derives from the *Pirithous* hypothesis.

[18] Two immobile characters permanently on stage would have been very inconvenient in a production where the rules allowed only three speaking characters to be present at one time.

[19] Wilamowitz suggested implausibly that it was set partly in the upper world, at Aphidna in Attica, and included Eur. F 955c with its reference to the hero Aphidnus (Wilamowitz 1907a, 7; doubted by himself, 1907b, 214). Others have supposed a setting partly at Eleusis, in view of **F 2–4** (see note there).

to be fitted between the parodos and the dialogue represented by **F 4a**.[20] *The simplest structure for the prologue, then, would be a speech by Aeacus ending with* **F 1**.*1–4 followed by Heracles' arrival and self-introduction, some dialogue between him and Aeacus, and then the entry of the Chorus. In his reply to Aeacus Heracles probably described both his descent and his previous initiation into the Eleusinian Mysteries, which will gain him the favour of Persephone and permission to rescue Theseus and Pirithous. If the dialogue preceded the chorus entry he would witness the song of his fellow-initiates, as Dionysus–Heracles hears the initiates' song in Aristophanes,* Frogs *312ff.*

*The remaining fragments (***F 9–14***) are unplaceable, and for the rest of the plot we have just two pieces of evidence. A scholion of Tzetzes on* Frogs *142 states that after the imprisonment of Theseus and Pirithous, 'when Heracles made his descent for Cerberus, Theseus informed him very exactly about everything there, as Euripides informs us in his dramas'.*[21] *This probably preserves a detail from* Pirithous*; a description of the underworld by Theseus might fit either before or after his discussion with Heracles represented by* **F 7**. *As for the later content, the Hypothesis (***F 1***) states that Heracles 'both overcame the beast by force and by the grace of the underworld gods released Theseus and his comrade from their plight'. The grace of the underworld gods was no doubt obtained by an appeal to Heracles' initiation at Eleusis (cf. Eur.* Heracles *610–13, Apollod. 2.5.12, Diod. 4.25f.). Apollodorus adds that Heracles was required to master Cerberus without weapons, i.e. by wrestling (cf. Eur.* Heracles *612f., 'in a fight'), and this was probably the case in* Pirithous. *The fight must have been offstage, perhaps witnessed and reported by Theseus. Heracles will in any case have returned to complete the rescue of Pirithous.*

The play's known characters are Pirithous, Theseus, Heracles, Aeacus, and the chorus of initiates (see on **F 2–4***). Persephone and/or Hades might perhaps have appeared as speaking characters, but they*

---

[20] Some place the text in **F 1** after **F 2–4**, including Collard–Cropp 2008b, 637f., 644ff.

[21] ὕστερον δὲ Ἡρακλεῖ κατελθόντι διὰ τὸν Κέρβερον πάντα Θησεὺς τὰ ἐκεῖ αὐτῷ ἀκριβέστατα ὑποτίθησιν, ὡς Εὐριπίδης διδάσκει τοῖς δράμασιν. In *Frogs* 143ff. Heracles describes to Dionysus the terrors of the Underworld that Theseus had previously described to him. Koster *ad loc.* discusses the probable reference of Tzetzes' comment to *Pirithous*, and its accuracy; cf. Meccariello 2014, 101f.

were usually imagined as enthroned in their palace, and post-Aeschylean tragedy did not normally include major deities as participants (let alone those of the underworld), except in prologues and deus *scenes;*[22] *so it seems more likely that Heracles' negotiation with them was conducted within the palace or through a third party such as Aeacus. Four is not an unusually low number for the major characters in a Greek tragedy, and the underworld setting offered little scope for incidental characters or events. So far as we can tell from our limited knowledge,* Pirithous *consisted largely of mythical narrative, ethical discourse, reports of events within the drama, and the mystic songs of the chorus. Cockle (1983, 32) thought that the play, if Euripidean, must have been prosatyric, but a happy ending is no guarantee of that and (as Sutton 1987, 11 noted) nothing in the fragments suggests that it shared the humour or lightness of touch of Euripides'* Alcestis.

Some of ***F 22–25*** *could be from* Pirithous *(see above, p. 181 and* ***F 23*** *n.). Several other fragments from unidentified plays of Euripides have been assigned to it at one time or another,*[23] *some merely because they refer to the Underworld or the dead (in ways that hardly suit the context of* Pirithous*: F 865, 868, 912) or come from a speech by Theseus (F 964). F 936 ('No, I was still alive when Hades received me') suits someone who has already completed a visit to Hades, as the context of its quotation in Lucian's* Menippus *strongly suggests.*[24] *For F 955c see note 19 above.*[25]

Two very incomplete papyrus fragments from a single roll (P. Köln 2, PSI inv. 3021) have been tentatively attributed by some scholars to a

[22] Athena in the 4th-century *Rhesus* is an exception, but with the chorus absent. Hera in Aeschylus's *Semele* (or *Xantriai*) and Dionysus in Eur. *Bacchae* are disguised as mortals.

[23] For references see *TrGF* 1^2.178 (apparatus), 5.1107 (addenda for p. 173), and 5.934 for F 936.

[24] It might have been spoken by Heracles in Euripides' satyr-play *Eurystheus*: cf. Pechstein 1998, 349.

[25] All these and more (Eur. F 910, F 913, adesp. F 658) are discussed somewhat erratically by Sutton 1987, 89–106 (doubted by Egli 2003, 53 n. 2); see also Mette 1983, 15–17 and Dobrov (below, n. 30). A prose sentence of Critias quoted by a rhetorician of the 3rd century AD (Critias B 49 DK) was reconstructed a little fancifully as tragic iambics by Usener, and is suggested for *Pirithous* by Battegazzore–Carlini 1989, 461.

Pirithous, *and by some of these to the* Pirithous *of Euripides or Critias; they are printed in* TrGF *2 as adesp. F 658 frs* a *and* b. *If they belong to a* Pirithous, *fr.* a *involves Heracles preparing to confront Cerberus, and fr.* b *Persephone anticipating a meeting between Heracles and her husband Hades. All this however is very uncertain, and some see (more plausibly in my opinion) a confrontation between Heracles' wife and a hostile figure, such as Eurystheus at Mycenae or Lycus at Thebes, as they await his return, or failure to return, from the Underworld. Whatever the subject, some of the language of the fragments suggests a post-classical composition rather than a late 5th-century tragedy.*[26]

H.-J. Mette suggested that Pirithous *was closely connected with Euripides'* Heracles, *in which Heracles returns to Thebes from the Underworld having captured Cerberus and rescued Theseus with the benefit of his initiation at Eleusis, and that it must have been composed by Euripides, perhaps in the same tetralogy.*[27] *This is unlikely since in* Heracles *there is no mention of Pirithous or of Theseus's friendship with him; this would hardly have been irrelevant as Mette claimed.* Heracles *seems in fact to assume that only Theseus has been rescued and, understandably, to pass over the fact that Pirithous has been left behind (cf. Battegazzore–Carlini 1989, 452). If the double rescue was introduced in* Pirithous, *whether by Euripides or not, that might suggest that it was produced later than* Heracles, *which probably belongs to the period 421–416.*

A more contentious question is the relationship between Pirithous *and Aristophanes'* Frogs. *In* Frogs *Dionysus, accompanied by his slave Xanthias, disguises himself as Heracles in order to replicate the hero's successful descent to the Underworld and so retrieve Euripides for the benefit of Athens and its theatre. On reaching the palace of the underworld gods he knocks at the door and is confronted by a servant who in*

---

[26] See especially Carlini 1968 (the first publication of PSI inv. 3021) and 2012 (history of the question and bibliography). Carlini is inclined to attribute the fragments to a post-classical *Pirithous*. For the alternative see especially Luppe 1980.

[27] Mette 1983, 18f. For Heracles' initiation at Eleusis see *HF* 612f., where Mette wrongly took τὰ μυστῶν δ' ὄργι' ηὐτύχησ' ἰδών ('I benefited from seeing the initiates' rites') as referring to rites performed in the underworld as in *Frogs* 316ff. Initiates are properly described as 'seeing the orgia' at Eleusis: cf. *Hom. Hymn.* 2.476–82 with Richardson 1974, 302, 311, 314.

*most manuscripts is identified as Aeacus but in some simply as 'Servant'. This character threatens him with a series of underworld punishments for having abducted Cerberus on his previous visit, and re-enters the palace to fetch the Gorgons (*Frogs *460–78). A little later he emerges with some additional slaves, has both Dionysus and Xanthias (who by now has donned the Heracles disguise) soundly beaten, and eventually takes them into the palace to meet Hades and Persephone (*Frogs *605–73). Wilamowitz argued that these scenes must have been modelled on the scene of Heracles' arrival in* Pirithous ***(F 1)*** *since both plays featured Aeacus confronting Heracles, each had a mystic chorus, and the language of* Frogs *470–77 is paratragic. He also inferred that* Frogs *had imitated* Pirithous *in demoting Aeacus (the Aeginetan hero, son of Zeus and grandfather of Achilles and Ajax) from his established role as a judge amongst the dead*[28] *to the position of Gatekeeper of Hades, and in showing him obstructing and brawling with Heracles;* Pirithous *must then have been produced soon before* Frogs, *between 411 and 405.*[29]

Wilamowitz's opinion has been widely accepted and in some recent accounts elaborated on the assumption that Pirithous *was systematically reflected in* Frogs *and can be reconstructed accordingly.*[30] *But his dating of* Pirithous *close to* Frogs *relies on a circular argument, and the similarities between* Frogs *and what we know of* Pirithous *are in fact very limited. A tradition of Heracles'* katabasis *including his initiation at Eleusis and rescue of Theseus was probably current from the sixth century onwards,*[31] *and there is nothing in* Frogs *that is not sufficiently explained in terms of this tradition rather than dependence on* Pirithous; *references to the plot of* Pirithous *are in fact notably absent from*

---

[28] This role is first mentioned explicitly by Plato (*Apology* 41a, *Gorgias* 523–4) and Isocrates (9.13–15). Pindar makes him a judge of divine disputes (*Isthm.* 8.23f.).

[29] Wilamowitz 1875, 171, cf. 1895, 157f.; 1907b, 214; 1927, 446f. The connection had been suggested by Fritzsche 1845, 206–8 on *Frogs* 470–78.

[30] This was briefly suggested by Wilamowitz himself (1875, 172). Dobrov 2001, 133–56 (following Mette and Sutton) interprets *Frogs* as a comic 'contrafact' of *Pirithous*, including all of Euripides F 868, 910, 912, 913, 964 and adesp. F 658 in the latter and assuming that its opening was set at Eleusis. Such arguments are almost entirely circular.

[31] See above, n. 16 and especially Lloyd-Jones 1967.

Frogs.[32] *The chorus of initiates which greets Heracles/Dionysus in each play was probably part of this earlier tradition. Wilamowitz made much of the fact that each play featured an encounter with Aeacus, but the name Aeacus does not appear in the text of* Frogs;[33] *it seems to have been supplied to identify the play's comic doorkeeper in manuscripts of the late Hellenistic or Roman period, when the naming of originally unnamed characters in dramatic texts was common.*[34] *This might even be true of Aeacus in* Pirithous *since that name is known only from the early Byzantine commentary underlying* ***F 1****, but probably this really was Aeacus and his role quite different from that of the comic doorkeeper. The encounter in* Pirithous *takes place near the entrance to Hades and the site of Pirithous's punishment, whereas the encounter in* Frogs *is at the door of Hades' palace.* Frogs *has a typical comic doorkeeper scene, whereas in* Pirithous *Aeacus is already present when Heracles arrives, has probably delivered the prologue-speech, and may have continued to play an important part in the play. Wilamowitz's assumption that the paratragic language in* Frogs *465ff. implies a similar scene in* Pirithous, *i.e. an altercation between Aeacus and Heracles, is unfounded.*[35] *With-*

---

[32] The 'allusions' detected by Centanni 1997, 195–99 are uncompelling, e.g. that when Aristophanes' Innkeeper complains that Heracles stole her mattresses (*Frogs* 567) this 'alludes' to his absconding with Theseus and Pirithous.

[33] Wilamowitz was of course aware of this (cf. Hiller 1874, 453–56). He argued, again circularly, that the ancient scholars who gave the name Aeacus to Aristophanes' doorkeeper must have inferred it from the text of *Pirithous*. This is actually denied by Hiller, not affirmed as Wilamowitz implies.

[34] See Dover 1993, 52–55. Dover infers that *Pirithous* must have been produced after *Frogs*, at the Lenaea of 403, or not produced at all, since '[i]f *Peirithoos* was produced before *Frogs*, we could not reasonably resist the hypothesis that in the Doorkeeper Aristophanes means us to see the tragic Aiakos, even though the dialogue between Aiakos and Herakles in *Peirithoos* is courteous'. I do not think the hypothesis is so hard to resist.

[35] The scholia on *Frogs* 465ff. suggest that the doorkeeper's verbal assault on Dionysus was derived from Minos's threats against Theseus in Euripides' *Theseus*. Since that is unlikely, Wilamowitz guessed that the play parodied was not *Theseus* but *Pirithous* (Wilamowitz 1875, 171f.; cf. Fritzsche 1845 *ad loc.*). The guess is unnecessary since the language of the *Frogs* passage resembles that of the *Theseus* passage only loosely and is not a parody of it: »» Rau 1967, 115–18; Kannicht in *TrGF* 5, 434f. on Eur. *Theseus* F 386c. Rau adds that Alexandrian scholars would have noted similarities between the *Frogs* and *Pirithous* scenes if they existed (cf. Hoffmann 1951, 144).

out it Aeacus in Pirithous *can readily be seen as a serious character acting as a judge and supervisor of punishments in the Underworld.*

Other Pirithous *plays are attributed to Euripides' contemporary Achaeus (perhaps a tragedy: above, pp. 107f. with brief* ***F 36****) and the Middle Comedy playwright Aristophon (F 7* PCG*: 4 verses naming a species of tuna, quoted by Athenaeus).*

The authorship of Pirithous *remains an open question. The frequency of words found here but nowhere else in the extant texts of Euripides is far from disproving Euripides' authorship (see notes on* ***F 1, F 2–4, F 4a–7, F 11****), nor do Euripidean features tell strongly in favour of it since Critias might well have used a broadly Euripidean style.*[36] *The low resolution-rate of the iambic fragments might suggest composition by Euripides in the 420s or earlier, or by Critias in a conservative manner, but the fragments are too few to allow confident inferences.*[37] *Perhaps more significant is that the style of the* Pirithous *fragments (especially* ***F 4, F 3, F 7****) seems more accomplished and more Euripidean than that of the laboured and monotonous Sisyphus-fragment (F 19); it is not easy to believe that the same poet produced both. As for content, the cosmology of* ***F 3–4****, the anti-democratic tone of* ***F 11****, and the emphasis on friendship in this version of the myth (****F 1*** *Hypothesis,* ***F 6, F 7****) could be aligned with what we know of Critias from other sources if we knew that Critias composed them, but they cannot serve to prove his authorship or disprove that of Euripides (see notes below on these and* ***F 10****).*

The question depends essentially on what we make of the scant evidence that Euripides' authorship was doubted in antiquity. If there was no official record of a production by Critias (cf. above, p. 183), the Hellenistic scholars who raised these doubts must have had some other reason(s) both to doubt Euripides' authorship and to ascribe the play to Critias — perhaps something in the play that echoed Critias's doctrines, or comic allegations that Critias helped Euripides with his work,[38] *or a*

---

[36] The few ancient discussions of Critias's style are concerned with rhetoric, not poetry. For these and other observations on his linguistic style see Garzya 1952.

[37] Cf. Cropp–Fick 1985, 14–25. **F 1, 4a, 5–7, 10–12** yield six resolutions in the equivalent of 67 whole lines, a rate of about 9 per cent (in Cropp–Fick's terms, 1.8 per 100 resolvable feet).

[38] Ancient biographies of Euripides repeated such allegations about Socrates and others: Diogenes Laertius 2.18 cited Teleclides F 41–42, Aristophanes F 392, and Callias F 15. The *Life of Euripides* (1A.3 and IV.1 *TrGF*) cites Teleclides

suggestion that Critias composed the play but had it presented by Euripides.[39] *We have no way of following up such possibilities, and even if we could we might not reach a definitive answer. As things stand, this could*

F 1 Ioannes Diaconus et Logothetes, Commentary on [Hermogenes], *Περὶ μεθόδου δεινότητος* 28 (ed. Rabe 1908, 144f.), ~ Gregory of Corinth on the same treatise (*Rhet. Gr.* VII.1312–13 Walz); re-ed. Page 1941, 122f. (text only), Diggle 1998, 172f., Alvoni 2006 (hypothesis), 2008 (text); Meccariello 2014, 93–99, 268–72. Ioannes quotes vv. 1–16 of the dramatic text, [Hermogenes] v. 9 only, Gregory vv. 6–10.

Ζεύς, ὡς λέλεκται τῆς ἀληθείας ὕπο· οὗτος ὁ στίχος ἐν δύσιν εὕρηται δράμασιν Εὐριπίδου, ἔν τε τῷ λεγομένῳ Πειρίθῳ καὶ ἐν τῇ Σοφῇ Μελανίππῃ. ὧν τὰς ὑποθέσεις καὶ τὰ χωρία οὐκ ἄκαιρον ἐκθεῖναι τοῖς ἀσπαζομένοις τὴν πολυμάθειαν. ἡ μὲν οὖν τοῦ Πειρίθου ὑπόθεσίς ἐστιν αὕτη·

Πειρίθους ἐπὶ τὴν Περσεφόνης μνηστείαν μετὰ Θησέως εἰς Ἅιδου καταβὰς τιμωρίας ἔτυχε τῆς πρεπούσης· αὐτὸς μὲν γὰρ ἐπὶ πέτρας ἀκινήτῳ καθέδρᾳ πεδηθεὶς δρακόντων ἐφρουρεῖτο χάσμασιν, Θησεὺς δὲ τὸν φίλον ἐγκαταλιπεῖν αἰσχρὸν ἡγούμενος βίον εἶχε τὴν ἐν Ἅιδου ζωήν. ἐπὶ δὲ τὸν Κέρβερον Ἡρακλῆς ἀποσταλεὶς ὑπὸ Εὐρυσθέως τοῦ μὲν θηρίου βίᾳ περιεγένετο, τοὺς δὲ περὶ Θησέα χάριτι τῶν χθονίων θεῶν τῆς παρούσης ἀνάγκης ἐξέλυσε, μιᾷ πράξει καὶ τὸν ἀνθιστάμενον χειρωσάμενος καὶ παρὰ θεῶν χάριν λαβὼν καὶ δυστυχοῦντας ἐλεήσας φίλους. εἰσάγεται γοῦν ἐν τούτῳ τῷ δράματι Αἰακὸς πρὸς Ἡρακλέα λέγων·

ἔα, τί χρῆμα; δέρκομαι σπουδῇ τινα
δεῦρ' ἐγκονοῦντα καὶ μάλ' εὐτόλμῳ φρενί.
εἰπεῖν δίκαιον, ὦ ξέν', ὅστις ὢν τόπους
ἐς τούσδε χρίμπτῃ καὶ καθ' ἥντιν' αἰτίαν.

εἶτα Ἡρακλῆς πρὸς αὐτόν·

οὐδεὶς ὄκνος πάντ' ἐκκαλύψασθαι λόγον·
ἐμοὶ πατρὶς μὲν Ἄργος, ὄνομα δ' Ἡρακλῆς,
θεῶν δὲ πάντων πατρὸς ἐξέφυν Διός·
ἐμῇ γὰρ ἦλθε μητρὶ κεδνὸν εἰς λέχος
Ζεύς, ὡς λέλεκται τῆς ἀληθείας ὕπο.
ἥκω δὲ δεῦρο πρὸς βίαν, Εὐρυσθέως

F 41 and Aristophanes F 596: cf. Lefkowitz 2012, 90. Clement of Alexandria, *Strom.* 6.2.9.1 accuses Critias (B 32 DK) of plagiarizing Euripides (F 525).

[39] For this practice, better attested for comedy than tragedy, see Pickard-Cambridge 1988, 84–86.

well be a play of Euripides, perhaps not produced at one of the major city festivals and therefore not in the didascalic records which would have confirmed its authenticity. A production at Eleusis is an attractive possibility in view of the play's subject-matter.[40]

F 1 Ioannes, Deacon and Logothete

Zeus, as is stated by true tradition: This verse is found in two plays of Euripides, in the one entitled *Pirithous* and in the *Wise Melanippe*. It would not be inappropriate to set out the hypotheses and the locations of these for those who love breadth of learning. The hypothesis of *Pirithous*, then, is this:

Pirithous went down to Hades with Theseus to woo Persephone, and met with the appropriate punishment; he himself was held fast, seated and motionless, upon a rock and guarded by the yawning mouths of serpents, while Theseus, thinking it shameful to abandon his friend, kept as his life the life in Hades. But Heracles, who had been sent by Eurystheus to get Cerberus, first by force overcame the beast, and then by the grace of the underworld gods released Theseus and his comrade from their plight, thus in a single action subduing his adversary and getting grace from the gods and exercising pity for friends suffering misfortune. In this play, then, Aeacus is introduced saying:

> Hey, what's this? I see someone hurrying towards me, and with an undaunted heart. It's right you should tell me, stranger, who you are that draw near this region, and for what cause you do so.

And then Heracles says to him:

> I'll not hesitate to tell you my whole story.[5] My homeland is Argos, my name is Heracles, and I am the offspring of Zeus, father of all the gods; for Zeus, as has been told with truth, came to my mother's noble bed. I have come here under compulsion,

[40] See Csapo–Wilson 2015, 324, 383, Finglass 2015b, 212–14 on productions at Eleusis.

ἀρχαῖς ὑπείκων, ὅς μ' ἔπεμψ' Ἅιδου κύνα
ἄγειν κελεύων ζῶντα πρὸς Μυκηνίδας
πύλας, ἰδεῖν μὲν οὐ θέλων, ἆθλον δέ μοι
ἀνήνυτον τόνδ' ᾤετ' ἐξηυρηκέναι.
τοιόνδ' ἰχνεύων πρᾶγος Εὐρώπης κύκλῳ
Ἀσίας τε πάσης ἐς μυχοὺς ἐλήλυθα.

Hypoth.: 4 βίον om. Greg. (see Alvoni 2006, 292f.) εἶχε mss. εἵλετο Nauck 7 δύο δυστυχοῦντας some mss.

Text: 7 θεῶν Reiske(?) (cf. Alvoni 2008, 43) θεοῦ mss. 8 κεδνὸν εἰς λέχος (*or* κεδνὰ πρὸς λέχη) Dobree κεδνῆ (i.e. -ῇ) πρὸς λέχος mss. 14 ἀνήνυτον Rabe ἀνήνυστον Ioann. τόνδ' ᾤετ' ἐξηυρηκέναι Wilamowitz τὸν δῶκεν ἐξηνυκέναι Ioann.

F 2 Athenaeus 11.496a–b (~ Pollux 10.74, Hesychius *π* 2570)

Πλημοχόη· σκεῦος κεραμεοῦν βεμβικῶδες ἑδραῖον ἡσυχῇ, ὃ κοτυλίσκον ἔνιοι προσαγορεύουσιν, ὥς φησι Πάμφιλος. χρῶνται δὲ αὐτῷ ἐν Ἐλευσῖνι τῇ τελευταίᾳ τῶν μυστηρίων ἡμέρᾳ, ἣν καὶ ἀπ' αὐτοῦ προσαγορεύουσι Πλημοχόας, ἐν ᾗ δύο πλημοχόας πληρώσαντες . . . ἀνατρέπουσιν . . . ἐπιλέγοντες ῥῆσιν μυστικήν. μνημονεύει αὐτῶν καὶ ὁ τὸν Πειρίθουν γράψας, εἴτε Κριτίας ἐστὶν ὁ τύραννος ἢ Εὐριπίδης, λέγων οὕτως·

(Χο.) ἵνα πλημοχόας τάσδ' εἰς χθόνιον
χάσμ' εὐφήμως προχέωμεν.

F 4 Clement of Alexandria, *Stromata* 5.14.112.4–114.4 (~ Eusebius, *Praep. Evang.* 13.13.40f.; parts of vv. 1–5 in Satyrus, *Life of Euripides* fr. 37.2; vv. 1–2 Schol. Eur. *Or.* 982; σὲ...ῥύμβῳ misquoted in Schol. Ap. Rhod. 4.143. Satyrus ascribes the verses to Euripides, the others all name Euripides' *Pirithous*. Cf. Hesychius α 1854, αἰθέριος ῥύμβος· οὐρανος, *ρ* 488 ῥύμβος· δῖνος).

Ναὶ μὴν καὶ ἡ τραγῳδία ἀπὸ τῶν εἰδώλων ἀποσπῶσα εἰς τὸν οὐρανὸν ἀναβλέπειν διδάσκει. ὁ μὲν Σοφοκλῆς . . . ἄντικρυς ἐπὶ τῆς σκηνῆς ἐκβοᾷ . . . *(TrGF adesp. F 618, falsely ascribed to Sophocles by Clement's source)* . . . Εὐριπίδης δὲ ἐπὶ τῆς αὐτῆς σκηνῆς τραγῳδῶν, ὁρᾷς, φησὶ . . . *(Eur. F 941 quoted)* . . . ἐν δὲ τῷ Πειρίθῳ δράματι ὁ αὐτὸς καὶ τάδε τραγῳδεῖ·

(Χο.) σὲ τὸν αὐτοφυῆ, τὸν ἐν αἰθερίῳ
ῥύμβῳ πάντων φύσιν ἐμπλέξανθ',
ὃν πέρι μὲν φῶς, πέρι δ' ὀρφναία
νὺξ αἰολόχρως ἄκριτός τ' ἄστρων
ὄχλος ἐνδελεχῶς ἀμφιχορεύει . . .

bowing to the authority of Eurystheus, who sent me with a command to bring the hound of Hades to the gates of Mycenae — not that he wants to see him, but he thought he had found in this a labour I could not fulfil. Such is my project; tracking it I have gone in a circuit into the recesses of all Europe and Asia.

F 2 Athenaeus, *Sophists at Dinner*
Plêmochoê ('full-pourer'): a ceramic vessel shaped like a spinning-top but fairly stable, which some people call *kotuliskos* ('small *kotylê*'), as Pamphilus says. They use it at Eleusis on the last day of the Mysteries, which they call Plêmochoai after it. On this day they fill two *plêmochoai . . . (details of the procedure)* . . . and upend them while reciting a mystic formula. The author of *Pirithous* mentions them — whether this is Critias the tyrant or Euripides — as follows:

> *(Chorus).* So that in silence we may pour forth these *plêmochoai* into earth's cleft.

F 4 Clement of Alexandria, *Stromata*
Indeed, tragedy too tears us away from images and instructs us to look up into the heaven. Sophocles . . . proclaims straight out on the stage . . . *(*TrGF *adesp. F 618, here ascribed to Sophocles)* . . . And Euripides on the same tragic stage, look you, says . . . *(Eur. F 941)* . . . And in the play *Pirithous* the same poet presents these tragic verses as well:

> *(Chorus).* You, the self-generated, you who wove the growth (*phusis*) of all things in aether's whirl, around whom daylight, around whom murky night with its glittering surface and the countless host of stars dances incessantly . . .

ἐνταῦθα γὰρ τὸν μὲν αὐτοφυῆ τὸν δημιουργὸν νοῦν εἴρηκεν, τὰ δ' ἑξῆς ἐπὶ τοῦ κόσμου τάσσεται, ἐν ᾧ καὶ ⟨αἱ⟩ ἐναντιότητες φωτός τε καὶ σκότους. ὅ τε Εὐφορίωνος Αἰσχύλος ἐπὶ τοῦ θεοῦ σεμνῶς σφόδρα φησίν . . . *(Aesch. F 70 quoted).*

F 3 Clement of Alexandria, *Stromata* 5.6.35.5–36.3 (v. 5 quoted loosely and attributed to Euripides' *Pirithous* by Schol. Ar. *Birds* 179 (~ Suda *π* 1922) illustrating the use of πόλος meaning 'heaven')

τά τε ἐπὶ τῆς ἁγίας κιβωτοῦ ἱστορούμενα μηνύει τὰ τοῦ νοητοῦ κόσμου τοῦ ἀποκεκρυμμένου καὶ ἀποκεκλεισμένου τοῖς πολλοῖς. ναὶ μὴν καὶ τὰ χρυσᾶ ἐκεῖνα ἀγάλματα, ἑξαπτέρυγον ἑκάτερον αὐτῶν, εἴτε τὰς δύο ἄρκτους, ὡς βούλονταί τινες, ἐμφαίνει, εἴτε, ὅπερ μᾶλλον, τὰ δύο ἡμισφαίρια, ἐθέλει δὲ τὸ ὄνομα τῶν Χερουβὶμ δηλοῦν ἐπίγνωσιν πολλήν. ἀλλὰ δώδεκα πτέρυγας ἄμφω ἔχει καὶ διὰ τοῦ ζῳδιακοῦ κύκλου καὶ τοῦ κατ' αὐτὸν φερομένου χρόνου τὸν αἰσθητὸν κόσμον δηλοῖ. περὶ τούτων οἶμαι καὶ ἡ τραγῳδία φυσιολογοῦσά φησιν·

(Χο.) ἀκάμας τε χρόνος περί τ' ἀενάῳ
ῥεύματι πλήρης φοιτᾷ τίκτων
αὐτὸς ἑαυτόν, δίδυμοί τ' ἄρκτοι
ταῖς ὠκυπλάνοις πτερύγων ῥιπαῖς
τὸν Ἀτλάντειον τηροῦσι πόλον.

1 τ' Schwartz γ' Clem.

F 4a P. Oxy. 50.3531 (2nd C. AD, from the same roll as P. Oxy. 2078 with **F 5** and **F 7–9**), ed. H. M. Cockle (1983); re-ed. Kannicht, *TrGF* 1^2.349–51, Diggle 1998, 174f.

(Πε.) δρακοντ̣[
τηνου[
ὀργην ̣ [
ἐπίσταμ̣[αι
Χο. ὀψὲ ξυνει ̣[̣ ̣ ̣ ̣]ο ̣ ̣[
θεοὺς σ̣έβεσθ ̣ ̣ ̣οτ[
Ηρ. Ἰ̣ξίονος πα̣[ῖ, πο]λ̣λ̣ὰ̣ δ[
εἶδον λόγωι τ' ἤ̣κουσα [
οὐδ' ἐγγὺς οὐδέν' η̣ι̣[
τῆι σῆι πελάζο̣ντ' ἀ̣λ̣[λ
δυσπραξίαι τοὺς π[
σκῆψιν τιν' ητι̣ ̣[
ἄτης ἀπρούπτως ̣[

Here by ‘the self-generating’ he means the Craftsman Mind, and the rest refers to the cosmos which contains *(the)* opposites of light and darkness. And Aeschylus son of Euphorion says very exaltedly of God . . . *(Aesch. F 70)* . . .

F 3 Clement of Alexandria, *Stromata*

The things recorded as being on the sacred ark point towards those things that belong to the world of thought, which is hidden and closed to the many. Those golden figures indeed, each of them six-winged, represent either the two Bears (as some choose to think) or more likely the two hemispheres; and the name of the Cherubim is meant to signify ‘abundant knowledge’. Together they have twelve wings, and through the cycle of the zodiac, and through time which is borne along in concert with it, they signify the sensible cosmos. It is about these, I think, that Tragedy, discoursing on Nature, says:

> *(Chorus).* And unwearying Time circles around, full in an ever-flowing stream, himself begetting himself; and the twin Bears on their swift-beating wings keep watch over the Atlantean heaven.

F 4a Oxyrhynchus Papyrus

(Pirithous.) . . . serpent*(s?)* . . . wrath . . . *(I)* know . . .

Chorus. (Having?) understood belatedly *(you are now prepared?)* to respect the gods…

Heracles. Son of Ixion, *many* . . . have I seen and heard told . . . *(but I have never learned of)* anyone *(ever?)* coming close to your *(misfortune?)* . . . ; *(you far surpass?)* those *(previously most unfortunate?)* in hardship . . . *some/what?* pretext *(which?)* . . . *(for this?)* destruction . . . incautiously . . .

Πε. ἤδ' οὐκέτ' ἐστ' ἄσ̣ημος [
ὀνειρατώδης ἀλλ' ο̣[
Ἕλλην· ἰδεῖν δὲ τὸν λ ̣[
οἷός τ' ἂν εἴην. πέπτατ̣[αι
ἀχλὺς πάροι̣θε τῶν ἐμῶ̣[ν
ἄθλους ἐρωτᾶις τοὺς ἐμο̣[ὺς
γλώσσης γὰ̣ρ ἠχὼ τῆσδ̣ε̣ πρ ̣ ̣[
Ηρ. οὐδέν τι πάντως θαῦμ[α
ἀπεστερῆσθαί ⟨σ'⟩ ἐστὶν α ̣ ̣[
καὶ φθέγμα καὶ σχῆμ' ̣[
πολλαὶ διῆλ̣θον τῆς ἐ[μῆς
καὶ σῆς· ἀναμνήσω δὲ̣ ̣[
Πε. σιγησιναρ[
φων[
τησ[

4 ἐπίσταμ̣[αι *or* ἐπίσταμ̣[εσθα 5 ξυνεὶς̣ [Cockle, Kannicht 6 σ̣έ̣βεσθ̣α̣ι̣ uncertain, Cockle 9 ηἰ[σθόμην τύχῃ ποτὲ Parsons 10 ἀλ̣[λ' ὑπερβάλλεις μακρῶι West ἄλ̣[λον, ἀλλ' ὑπερφέρεις Diggle 11 π[ρόσθε δυστυχεστάτους Diggle 12 τίν' ἢ τ̣ίν̣'[, τίν' ἥτ̣ι̣ς [*etc.* Cockle 14 [οὐδ(ε) Cockle 15 ὅ[σον γ' ἐπεικάσαι Diggle ὁ [φωνήσας τάδε Maehler 16 λέ̣[γοντα Handley, then οὐκ ἂν σαφῶς West (οὔπω σαφῶς Luppe) 17 γὰρ ὀμμάτων *or* 18 ἐμῶ̣[ν ὅσσων Cockle 18 end λέξον· τίς ὢν Diggle 23 σχημα ̣[P. Oxy. (perhaps σχῆμ' α ̣[ ) ἐ̣[ν μέσωι γὰρ ἡμέραι Diggle (ἡμέραι Parsons) 24 end ὁμιλίας Cockle ἀπαλλαγῆς Collard 26 σειγησιναρ[P. Oxy. σίγησον· ἆρ[(α) Mette

F 5 P. Oxy. 17.2078 (2nd C. AD: see above on **F 4a**) ed. A. S. Hunt (1927); re-ed. Körte 1932, 50–53; Pickard-Cambridge 1933, 148–51 (fr. 1.7–20 with supplements by Housman 1928; fr. 2.6–19); Page 1941, 122–25 (as Pickard-Cambridge); *TrGF*1².174–77; Diggle 1998, 175f.; new readings in Cockle 1983 (see **F 4a**), 30 notes 1, 2.

fr. 1

(Πε.) ἐσφηλα[
υ̣φ̣ ̣ ̣[
κατελ ̣[
ἐλθὼν ̣[
Ἕλλην[
βωμῶ ̣ ̣[

Pirithous. This *(voice)* is no longer unintelligible *(nor)* . . . dream-like, but *(so far as I can surmise?)* Greek. But I would *(not)* be able to see the *(speaker clearly, for?)* a . . . mist is spread before my *(eyes. Tell me, who are you who?)* ask about my ordeal? For the sound of this voice . . .

Heracles. It is not at all surprising that *(you)* have lost . . . *(and do not recall my?)* voice and appearance. Many *(days?)* have passed *(in the meantime? since my)* and your *(association?).* But I'll remind *(you)* . . .

Pirithous. . . . quiet(?) . . . *(voice?)* . . .

F 5 Oxyrhynchus Papyrus (almost immediately after **F 4a**)

Continuation of the dialogue:

(Pirithous.) . . . *(they?)* brought low . . . *(remnants of two verses)* . . . coming . . . . . . Greek . . . . . . altar(s?) . . . . . .

θεὸς δὲ μανία[
ἔπεμψεν ἄτῃ[ν
νεφέλην γυναικ̣[
ἔσπειρεν εἰς τοὺς θ ̣[
θυγατρὶ μίσγοιτ’ ἐ[
τοιῶνδε κόμπω[ν
ποινὰς θεοῖς ἔτεισεν̣[
μανίας τροχῷ περι̣[
οἰστρη[λ]άτοισιν ὤχ̣[
ἄπυστο[ς] ἀνθρώποι[σι
ἔκρυψεν, ἀλλὰ βορε̣[α
δι̣ε̣σπα̣[ρ]άχθη σ̣ῶ̣μ[α
πατὴ̣[ρ ἁ]μαρτὼν εἰς θε[οὺς
ἐγὼ [δ’ ἐκ]ε̣ί̣νου π[ή]ματ’ α[

8–9 ἁρπάσας δ’ ῃ̣κασμένην | νεφέλην γυναικ[ὶ δυσσεβέστατον λόγον Housman (λόγον Hunt) 10 Θε[σσάλους ὡς δὴ Κρόνου Hunt 11 ἐ[ν πτύχαισιν αἰθέρος? Snell 14 περί[δρομον Murray περι[φερὲς Housman 15 ᾤιχ̣[ετ(ο) Hunt 16 ἀνθρώποι[σιν, οὐδέ νιν τάφος Körte 17 βορε̣[άσιν πνόαις Housman βορε̣[άδων δίναις πνοῶν Körte (ῥιπαῖς ἅπαν Diggle) 18–19 ends τήνδε δὴ τίσιν…ἐκτήσατο Diggle 19 end ἀπώλετο Körte

F 6 Plutarch, *Mor.* 96c (verse quoted without ascription also in *Mor.* 482a, 533a, and ἀχαλκεύτοισιν…πέδαις in 763f with ascription to Euripides)

ὡς γὰρ τὸν Κρέοντα τῆς θυγατρὸς οὐδὲν ὁ χρυσὸς οὐδ’ ὁ πέπλος ὠφέλει, τὸ δὲ πῦρ ἀναφθὲν αἰφνιδίως προσδραμόντα καὶ περιπτύξαντα κατέκαυσε καὶ συναπώλεσεν, οὕτως ἔνιοι τῶν φίλων οὐδὲν ἀπολαύσαντες εὐτυχούντων συναπόλλυνται δυστυχοῦσι. καὶ τοῦτο μάλιστα πάσχουσιν οἱ φιλόσοφοι καὶ χαρίεντες, ὡς Θησεὺς τῷ Πειρίθῳ κολαζομένῳ καὶ δεδεμένῳ

αἰδοῦς ἀχαλκεύτοισιν ἔζευκται πέδαις.

F 7 P. Oxy. 2078 (as for **F 5**)

frs 2 + 3

ends of three lines including 3 πόνου, *then:*

. . . .] ̣σοι το ̣[. . . . .] ἡδὺ νῦ̣ν δοκεῖ.
(Θη.) . . . .]τ̣ος, Ἡράκλεις, [σὲ] μέμψομαι

But the god . . . madness . . . sent a fatal delusion . . . a cloud *(resembling a?)* woman . . . he sowed *(a most impious report?)* among the *(Thessalians? that)* he was having intercourse with *(Cronus's)* daughter . . . For such boasts . . . he made amends to the gods . . . *(whirled?)* on a wheel in frenzied *(fits?)* of madness *(he perished)* unobserved by men, *(nor did a tomb?)* cover *(him?*), but his body was torn apart *(by)* north *(winds' blasts)* . . . *(Thus my)* father *(paid)* for sinning against the gods, and I . . . his afflictions . . .

F 6 Plutarch, *On having many friends* (and elsewhere as a proverb)

For just as neither his daughter's gold nor her robe helped Creon, but the fire that had suddenly flared up, when he ran to her and embraced her, consumed him and killed him along with her, so some men, having had no benefit from their friends when they fared well, perish along with them when they fare ill. This happens especially to philosophical and high-minded men, just as Theseus, when Pirithous is imprisoned and being punished,

is bound (to him) by the fetters of shame, not forged from bronze.

F 7 Oxyrhynchus Papyrus (further fragments)

Ends of three dialogue lines, including 3 *(of/from?)* . . . labour, *then:*

(Heracles) . . . *(if the task?)* now seems pleasing *to you(?)*.

(Theseus) . . . I will *(not)* blame *(you)*, Heracles, . . . *(But I must*

........]η̣, πιστὸν γὰρ ἄνδρα καὶ φίλον
...... πρ]ο̣δοῦναι δυσμ[εν]ῶς εἰλημμένον.
(Ηρ.) σαυτῶι τε,] Θησεῦ, τῆι τ' Ἀθηναίων πό[λει
πρέποντ' ἔλεξας· τοῖσι δυσ[τυ]χοῦσι γὰρ
ἀεί ποτ' εἶ σὺ σύμμαχος· σκῆψιν [δ' ἐμ]οὶ
ἀεικές ἐστ' ἔχοντα πρὸς πάτρα̣ν̣ μολεῖν.
Εὐρυσθέα γὰρ πῶς δοκεῖς ἂν ἄσμενον,
εἴ μοι πύθοιτο ταῦτα συμπράξαντά σε,
λέξειν ἂν ὡς ἄκραντος ἤθληται πόνος;
(Θη.) ἀλλ' οὖ σὺ χρήιζεις π[.........] ἐμὴν ἔχεις
εὔνοιαν, οὐκ ἔμπλ[ηκτον, ἀλλ' ἐ]λ̣ευθέρως
ἐχθροῖσί τ' ἐχθρὰν̣ [καὶ φίλοισι]ν εὐμενῆ.
πρόσθεν σ' ἐμοὶ τ̣[............]ει λόγος,
λέγοις δ' ἂν [....] . [............]ους λόγους.
(Ηρ.) ὦ φ[ίλτατ(ε)
]ιας
ὑ]π̣ηρετῶ
]η̣ θν̣[η]τ̣ῶ[ν] φρένας
] γνώμης ἄτερ
τοῦ]τό σοι φίλον
]δ̣ι̣κώτ̣ατ' αἰτιᾶι θεούς
]η πᾶς [ἀ]νέρριπται κύβος
] . . οντα μὴ μάταιον ἦ
]ην ἔχω . εξα[.] δὲ χρή
]μαθεῖν ὅτου[

31–40: *line-ends including* 34]αλλ̣αγήν, 36 φ]ρενί, 37 θεῶι, 38 νερτέρων

4 το̣[ῦργον? Snell 5 beg. οὔτοι Körte 6 μένειν δὲ χρ]ή Körte 7 beg. αἰσχρὸν Hunt 10 [δ' ἐμ]οὶ Körte [δέ τ]οι Hunt 13 εἴ μοι...σε P. Oxy. (εμοι...σοι corr. to ειμοι...σε (*or* γε), cf. W. Cockle 1970; ἔμ' εἰ...σοι Hunt) 15 π[ανταχῆι γ'] Hunt π[αντελῶς] Page π[ροστύχοις· Maehler 18 τ̣[οιοῦτον ὄνθ' αἰρ]εῖ Murray, Hunt (αἰν]εῖ Körte, ᾔν]ει Snell) 19 [ἤδη καὶ σὺ τοὺς αὐτ]οὺς Murray, Hunt ([αὐτὸς *etc.* Körte, [αὖθις *etc.* Snell) 20 φ[ίλτατ(ε) Snell 22 *or* ὑ]πηρετῶ[ν] Hunt 26 ἐκ]δικώτατ' (Hunt) *or* ἐν]δικώτατ' Körte 29 λ̣έξα[ι]? Snell

remain?), for *(it is shameful)* to forsake a loyal man, my friend, caught as he is in hostile hands.

Heracles. What you have said, Theseus, is fitting *(for yourself)* and for the city of Athens; you are always an ally to those suffering misfortune. *(But)* it is unseemly *(that I)* should return to my homeland with a pretence. How gladly do you think Eurystheus would say, if he learned you had helped me accomplish this, that the labour had been incompletely contested?

Theseus. Well, *(may you accomplish?)* what you desire. You have my good will, not *thoughtlessly (but)* freely given, inimical to enemies *(and)* benevolent *(to friends)*. Word *(has reached?)* me in the past that you . . ., and you may say . . . words.

Heracles. O *(dearest friend)* . . . ,

then ends of twenty more lines, speaker-changes undetermined, including:

22 I serve . . . 23 . . . the minds of mortal men 24 without judgement 25 *(this)* . . . dear to you 26 . . . most justly *(or un*justly*?)* blames the gods 27 the die is wholly cast 28 lest it be in vain 29 I have . . . but I/you must *(say?)* . . . 30 . . . to learn of/from whom . . . 34 *release?* 36 to/for *(my/your)* mind 37 to/for the god 38 of/from the nether . . .

F 8, F 9 P. Oxy. 2078 (as for **F 5**), frs 4 and 5

Remains of seventeen and nine lines respectively with no complete words

F 10 Stobaeus 2.8.4

Εὐριπίδου Πειρίθῳ·

ὁ πρῶτος εἰπὼν οὐκ ἀγυμνάστῳ φρενὶ
ἔρριψεν, ὅστις τόνδ᾽ ἐκαίνισεν λόγον,
ὡς τοῖσιν εὖ φρονοῦσι συμμαχεῖ τύχη.

1 ὁ πρῶτος εἰπὼν del. Wilamowitz

F 11 Stobaeus 3.37.15

Πειρίθου·

τρόπος δὲ χρηστὸς ἀσφαλέστερος νόμου·
τὸν μὲν γὰρ οὐδεὶς ἂν διαστρέψαι ποτὲ
ῥήτωρ δύναιτο, τὸν δ᾽ ἄνω τε καὶ κάτω
λόγοις ταράσσων πολλάκις λυμαίνεται.

F 12 Stobaeus 4.53.23

Εὐριπίδου Πειρίθου·

οὔκουν τὸ μὴ ζῆν κρεῖσσόν ἐστ᾽ ἢ ζῆν κακῶς;

Brief fragments: **F 13** ἔφεξις, **F 14** θράξαι

F 8, F 9 Oxyrhynchus Papyrus (further fragments)

Remains of seventeen and nine lines respectively with no complete words

F 10 Stobaeus, *Anthology*, 'On what is within our power'

Euripides in *Pirithous*:

> The first to say it tossed it out with no unexercised mind, who invented this saying: fortune is on the side of those who have good sense.

F 11 Stobaeus, *Anthology*, 'On uprightness'

Pirithous:

> An upright disposition is more secure than the law. No orator could ever pervert it, though he often abuses the law and turns it upside down with words.

F 12 Stobaeus, *Anthology*, 'Comparison of life and death'

Euripides' *Pirithous*:

> Isn't not living, then, better than living badly?

Brief fragments: **F 13** a pretext, **F 14** to upset

ΡΑΔΑΜΑΝΘΥΣ

Texts etc. *TrGF* 1².178–80 with addenda 1².351, 5.1107; *MusTr* 120f. (F 17); Battegazzore 1962, 277–81; Collard–Cropp 2008b, 658–63.

Myth. Gantz 1993, 259f.; Davidson 1999; *LIMC* VII, 'Rhadamanthys'.

*The papyrus hypothesis-fragment **F 15** shows that the play culminated in the deaths of Zeus's sons Castor and Polydeuces (the Dioscuri) and an appearance* ex machina *of the goddess Artemis telling Helen to establish a cult for her brothers and announcing the deification of Rhadamanthys's daughters. The Dioscuri (or at least one of them) were usually said to have been killed in combat with their cousins Idas and Lynceus (sons of Aphareus) after abducting the latter's destined brides (another pair of cousins, daughters of Leucippus), and subsequently either heroized (as in our play, apparently) or partly or wholly deified. The story is mentioned in numerous sources with many variations (»» Gantz 1993, 323–28, Fowler 2013, 420–24), but none includes a role for Rhadamanthys*

F 15 (Hypothesis) PSI XII.1286 (2nd C. AD) col. ii.1–8, ed. V. Bartoletti (1951) after Gallavotti 1933; re-ed. Austin 1968, 92, van Rossum-Steenbeek 1998, 202, Meccariello 2014, 284f.

[Πο-
λυδεύκους, ἀνηιρέθη μονομαχήσας.
Ῥ]αδαμάνθυος δ' ἐπὶ μὲν τῆι νίκηι [χ]α̣ί̣-
ρ]οντος, ἐπὶ δὲ ταῖς θυγατράσιν ἀ[λ-
γ]οῦντος Ἄρτεμις ἐπιφανεῖσα π̣ρ̣[οσ-
ἐ̣]ταξε τὴν μὲν Ἑλένην ἀ[μφοτέροις
το̣ῖς ἀδελφοῖς τοῖς τεθνη̣[κόσιν
τιμὰς καταστήσασθαι, τ̣[ὰς θυγα-
τέρας δ' αὐτοῦ θεὰς ἔφησε γεν̣[ήσεσθαι.

———

7 τεθνη̣[κόσιν Diggle, Meccariello τεθνη̣[κόσι τὰς Gallavotti 8 γεν̣[ήσεσθαι Gallavotti γεν̣[έσθαι Latte *ap.* Bartoletti

RHADAMANTHYS

*who is usually known as one of the sons born by Europa to Zeus after he had carried her to Crete, and as a wise lawgiver who after his death dwelled in the Elysian Fields (*Odyssey *4.563–65) or the Islands of the Blessed (Pindar,* Ol. *2.75), or became one of the judges in the Underworld (first in Plato,* Gorgias *523e). No other source mentions his having daughters. Possibly the play made them, rather than the Leucippides, the brides abducted by the Dioscuri, and had them divinely rescued to become goddesses after the deaths of their abductors; their cult would then be similar to the better known Spartan cult of the Leucippides.*[41] *Whether or not that guess is correct, the play appears to have involved an abstruse local myth. This would be a little surprising in a tragedy produced by an Athenian playwright in the late fifth century, as Wilamowitz's tetralogy theory implies (above, pp. 182f., cf. below on* Tennes).

F 15 Papyrus hypothesis

. . . *(when? Po)*lydeuces *(had died?)* . . . he (i.e. Castor) was killed in single combat. And as *(Rh)*adamanthys was *(rejoic)*ing at the victory, but *(griev)*ing for his daughters, Artemis appeared and *(in)*structed Helen to establish rites honouring *(both)*[5] her *dead* brothers, and declared that *(his daugh)*ters *(would?)* become goddesses. *(end of hypothesis)*

---

[41] For the Leucippides and their cult see Larson 1995, 64–69, Calame 2001, 185–91, Fowler 2013, 422. Steffen (1954) suggested implausibly that the play was about the abduction of Helen by Theseus, with Rhadamanthys taking custody of Helen, the Dioscuri retaliating by seizing his daughters, and Theseus killing the Dioscuri with his assistance. Gallavotti (1933) had suggested that it combined the abductions of Helen and the Leucippides.

F 16 Strabo 8.3.31

τινὲς δὲ πόλιν μὲν οὐδεμίαν γεγονέναι Πῖσαν φασίν . . . , Στησίχορον δὲ καλεῖν πόλιν τὴν χώραν Πῖσαν λεγομένην, ὡς ὁ ποιητὴς τὴν Λέσβον Μάκαρος πόλιν, Εὐριπίδης δ' ἐν Ἴωνι *Εὔβοι' Ἀθήναις ἐστί τις γείτων πόλις*, καὶ ἐν Ῥαδαμάνθυι

οἳ γῆν ἔχουσ' Εὐβοΐδα πρόσχωρον πόλιν

Σοφοκλῆς δ' ἐν Μυσοῖς *Ἀσία μὲν ἡ σύμπασα κλῄζεται, ξένε, πόλις δὲ Μυσῶν Μυσία προσήγορος.*

F 17 Stobaeus 2.8.12 (vv. 1–8 Stob. 4.20b.61 with ascription to Euripides' *Rhadamanthys*, v. 4 Schol. Eur. *Orestes* 1197)

Εὐριπίδου·

(Ῥαδαμανθυσ?)
ἔρωτες ἡμῖν εἰσὶ παντοῖοι βίου·
ὃ μὲν γὰρ εὐγένειαν ἱμείρει λαβεῖν,
τῷ δ' οὐχὶ τούτου φροντίς, ἀλλὰ χρημάτων
πολλῶν κεκλῆσθαι βούλεται πατὴρ δόμοις·
ἄλλῳ δ' ἀρέσκει μηδὲν ὑγιὲς ἐκ φρενῶν
λέγοντι πείθειν τοὺς πέλας τόλμῃ κακῇ·
οἱ δ' αἰσχρὰ κέρδη πρόσθε τοῦ καλοῦ βροτῶν
ζητοῦσιν· οὕτω βίοτος ἀνθρώπων πλάνη.
ἐγὼ δὲ τούτων οὐδενὸς χρῄζω τυχεῖν,
δόξαν ⟨δὲ⟩ βουλοίμην ἂν εὐκλείας ἔχειν.

F 18 'Antiatticista', *Anecdota Graeca* 1.93.31ff. Bekker ('*ἐξαιρεῖν*')

οὐδεὶς γὰρ ἡμᾶς ⟨ὅστις⟩ ἐξαιρήσεται.

⟨ὅστις⟩ Van Dam

F 16 Strabo, *Geography*

Some say there has never been a city *(polis)* of Pisa . . . , but that Stesichorus gives the name *polis* to the region known as Pisa,[42] as the poet (i.e. Homer) calls Lesbos 'Makar's *polis*',[43] and Euripides in *Ion* says 'There is a *polis* Euboea, neighbour to Athens',[44] and in *Rhadamanthys*,

> who possess the land of Euboea, an adjacent *polis*,

and Sophocles in *Mysians*, 'The whole area is called Asia, stranger, but the Mysians' *polis* is known as Mysia'.[45]

F 17 Stobaeus, *Anthology*, 'On what is within our power'
Euripides:

> *(Rhadamanthys?)* Our desires in life are of every kind. One man yearns to get nobility, another cares nothing for that but wants to be called the father of abundant possessions for his house. Another chooses to say nothing wholesome based on sound thinking[5] and to entice his fellows with vile audacity; while others again prefer base gains to honorable achievement. That's how diversely men's ways of life range. *(But)* I for my part want to get none of these things, and would rather have the credit of good repute.

F 18 'Antiatticist' Lexicon

> *(There is)* none *(who)* shall dispossess us.

---

[42] Stesichorus fr. 263 *PMGF* = 318 Finglass.

[43] *Iliad* 24.544 (but the text has ἕδος 'seat', not πόλιν).

[44] Eur. *Ion* 294.

[45] Sophocles F 411 *TrGF*.

ΤΕΝΝΗΣ

Texts etc. *TrGF* 1².182f. with *addenda* 5.1109; Collard–Cropp 2008b, 664–69.

Discussions. Jouan 1966, 303–8; Gantz 1993, 591f.; *LIMC* VII, 'Tennes'.

Myths and history of Tenedos. Halliday 1927; Specht 2001; Rutishauser 2001; Brown 2002, 201–7; Polito 2005.

Tennes was the eponymous hero of Tenedos, the small island located 5 km. off the coast of the Troad and 20 km. south of the entrance to the Hellespont (Dardanelles). His legend as known in the Hellenistic period and later is cryptically sketched in Lycophron, Alexandra *232–42 and summarized in several mythographic sources.*[46] *Tennes and his sister (usually named Hemithea) were children of Cycnus, who ruled the territory of Colonae on the mainland opposite Tenedos. Tennes was also said to have been sired by the god Apollo. After their mother's death Cycnus took a second wife who tried to seduce Tennes and, when rejected, accused him of assaulting her. Convinced by his wife and the false testimony of an aulos-player, Cycnus placed Tennes and his sister (who had defended her brother) in a chest and threw it into the sea. The chest floated to the island, the couple were rescued, and Tennes was later adopted as the island's ruler, changing its name from Leucophrys,*[47] *founding the polis of Tenedos, establishing its laws, and honoured with a cult after his death. In some accounts Cycnus later learned the truth, killed his wife and her accomplice (cf.* ***F 20****), and attempted a reconciliation with his son, but Tennes rejected him and cut the mooring-ropes of his boat with a double-axe (*pelekus*) when he tried to land on the island.*[48] *Tennes was eventually killed by Achilles while resisting the*

[46] Chiefly Conon, *Narratives* 28; Diodorus 5.83; Apollodorus *epit.* 3.24; Plutarch, *Mor.* 297d–e; Pausanias 10.14.2–4; Schol. D *Iliad* 1.38; Tzetzes on Lycophron 232. An ostracon from Kellis in Upper Egypt published in 1996 may have the beginning of a brief summary of the story but adds nothing to our knowledge of it (»» Huys 2005; Meccariello 2014, 320).

[47] The name means 'White-Brow', alluding to the island's geological profile. Its modern Turkish name is Bozcaada, 'Grey Island'.

[48] Lycophron however has Cycnus killed with his children by Achilles, and Tzetzes explains that they had been reconciled and then lived together on Tenedos. This seems to merge the traditional story of Cycnus's death (killed by Achilles while resisting the Achaeans' landing on the mainland: cf. above pp.

TENNES

Achaeans' landing on Tenedos in primitive style by hurling rocks at them, or while defending his sister from Achilles' pursuit (Plutarch). Some accounts add that Achilles had forgotten his mother's warning never to kill a son of Apollo, and that Apollo avenged Tennes' death by securing Achilles' death at Troy. Plutarch and Diodorus record that auletes and the naming of Achilles were both prohibited in the sanctuary of Tennes, which was centered on his tomb.

Proclus's summary of the epic Cypria *mentions the Achaean landing on Tenedos and a feast during which Philoctetes suffered his noxious snakebite, and the poem itself probably included the fighting there and Tennes' death at Achilles' hands as recounted by Apollodorus (»» West 2013b, 111f.;* Iliad *11.624–27 recalls Achilles' sacking of Tenedos). Aeschylus may have produced a* Tennes *about these events.*[49] *The hypothesis* ***F 20****, however, shows that our play concerned the false accusation, the casting adrift of Tennes and Hemithea, a report of their survival to a now regretful Cycnus, and a speech of Apollo confirming Tennes' innocence and ordering the renaming of the island and the execution of Cycnus's wife (and presumably the aulete). The speech probably looked ahead to Tennes' successes as a ruler and his heroization and cult. The question of reconciliation and the future deaths of Tennes, Hemithea and Cycnus may or may not have been included. If Cycnus renamed the island in honour of his son, as the hypothesis suggests, that suggests some kind of reconciliation.*

The story of Tennes employs a number of familiar mythical tropes: a divine father; the 'Potiphar's Wife' motif; a youth expelled from his homeland but surviving with divine aid to establish himself in a new land (his casting adrift in a chest is shared with the myths of Perseus and Telephus amongst others); his acceptance there and achievements leading to his recognition as the community's founder and eponymous hero. These motifs are blended with features specific to the context of Tenedos. The cults of Tennes and his sister probably originated in the worship of pre-Greek deities. The double axe with which Tennes severed his

---

112f. on Achaeus's *Cycnus*) with the story of Tennes' death (killed by Achilles while resisting the Achaeans' landing on Tenedos).

[49] Mette 1959, 143f.; 1963, 100–3; Radt in *TrGF* 3, 343 and 479–80 (F 451o = P. Oxy. 20.2256. frs 51–53).

father's mooring-ropes, thus declaring the independence of his new realm, is a Bronze-Age symbol of authority and a standard feature of Tenedian coinage. The story also differs significantly from another account of the settlement of Tenedos, which told that the island was subdued after the Trojan War by Aeolian Greeks led by Agamemnon's heir Orestes (Pindar, Nem. *11.33–37); this was part of a wider tradition, promoted by Hellanicus of Lesbos in particular, which attributed all the Aeolian settlements to Orestes or his descendants (»» Fowler 2013, 597–602). Tenedos was in fact generally regarded as Aeolian and long retained some degree of control over the coastal area opposite the island (cf. Strabo 13.1.46f.). The Tennes myth thus served to distinguish the island from the other Aeolian communities and to emphasize its autonomy, while also recognizing its kinship and connections with them. This peculiar status can be related to its position as an essential staging post for ships approaching the difficult passage through the Dardanelles into the Sea of Marmara and thence to the Black Sea. Between the 470s and the 330s Tenedos seems to have fended off local competitors and maintained a degree of independence by aligning itself with Athens, the dominant sea-power in most of this period (»» Rutishauser 2001).*

F 20 (Hypothesis) P. Oxy. 27.2455 (2nd C. AD) ed. E. Turner (1962), fr. 14 col. xiii; re-ed. Austin 1968, 97, Luppe 1989, 1993, Meccariello 2014, 319f.

. . ἀπ]ο̣θ̣αν̣[
. . . .]κλείσας [
[μ]ά̣ρτυρα τω̣ν[
σ̣ά̣μενος· τα[
μ̣ε̣τ̣εμελη[*c. 8 letters*] . . . .ι το̣ὺν Τ[έ]ν-
νην ἤκουσε̣ν ἐ̣π̣ὶ̣ τ̣ὴν̣ ἀ̣ντιπέρα νῆσον
σεσῶσθαι· προει̣πό[ν]τος δ' Ἀπόλλωνος
τὴν μὲν νῆσο̣ν Τ̣ένεδ̣ον π̣ροσηγόρευσεν,
τ]ὴν δὲ ψευσα[μέν]ην̣ γυ̣ν̣αῖκα ἀπέ̣κτεινεν.

———

1–2 ὡς ἀπ]ο̣θ̣αν̣[ούμενον/-ένους εἰς λάρνακα | κατα]κλείσας [ἔρριψεν εἰς τὴν θάλατταν Luppe 1989 2 κλείσας [εἰς λάρνακα Turner κλεισας not now legible: Meccariello 3–4 τῶν [διαβολῶν αὐλητὴν ποιη]σάμενος Turner τῶν [εἰρημέν-ων Μόλπον ἡγη]||σάμενος Luppe 1989 4 τά[ληθῆ δ'ἐπιγνοὺς ἐπὶ τούτῳ Luppe 1989 5 μ̣ε̣τ̣εμέλη[σε Turner -μελή[θη Luppe 1989] επ̣ε̣ι Turner ('most uncertainly')] δ̣ὲ̣ π̣ερὶ Luppe 1993 7 προει̣πό[ν]τος Lloyd-Jones προσ- P. Oxy.

The tragedy Tennes *is the oldest known account of Tennes' early life and his emergence as Tenedos's founding hero,*[50] *but its contribution to the development of the myth is unknown since we do not know when the myth was formed, nor when or by whom the play was composed. It could have been produced at Athens towards the end of the Peloponnesian War, emphasizing the autonomy of Tenedos but also promoting its loyalty to the Delian League, whose patron was Tennes' divine father Apollo.*[51] *Euripides or Critias would then be possible authors, but if Euripides produced such a play at a major Athenian festival there would have been little reason for Alexandrian scholars to doubt its authenticity, and without Wilamowitz's tetralogy theory (pp. 182f. above) there is no reason to think that Critias produced such a play at all. A production by Euripides at a lesser or non-Athenian festival cannot be ruled out, but neither can a production in Euripidean style by a local poet whose main interest was in promoting the myth of Tennes and the autonomy of Tenedos. This could place it anywhere between the late fifth and the late fourth century, perhaps most plausibly in the period from the mid-350s to the mid-330s when, as Rutishauser points out, Tenedos seems to have achieved a notable degree of independence and prosperity.*

F 20 Papyrus hypothesis
. . . *(having died?)*. . . shutting *(him/them up in a chest to die he threw it into the sea, having made an aulos-player?)* a witness of the *(slanders. But on learning the truth about this he?) relent(ed?)* . . . . . . he heard that Tennes[5] had safely reached the island opposite. At Apollo's command he named the island Tenedos and killed the wife who had deceived him. *(end of hypothesis)*

---

[50] If it was a 4th-century play it could have been later than Aristotle's *Constitution of Tenedos* (frs 593–594 Rose), but there is no reason to think that the *Constitution* mentioned the story told in the play. Its only relevant fragment (fr. 593 Rose) tells a quite different story to explain the proverb 'Tenedian axe' (*Tenedios pelekus*) and the use of the axe and the double head as symbols on Tenedian coinage: a king of Tenedos ruled that adulterers should be beheaded with an axe, and enforced this even when his own son was convicted of adultery. Polito (2005) argues unconvincingly that this was derived from the *Tennes* (which she ascribes to Euripides) and was the source of all later accounts of the myth. In fact the hypothesis to *Tennes* (**F 20**) makes it unlikely that the axe was mentioned in the tragedy where, as noted above, Apollo's final commands are likely to have included a reconciliation (above, p. 213).

[51] This is suggested by Jouan 1966, 308; Polito 2005, 196f.

F 20a? P. Hamb. 3.199 (2nd C. AD) ed. B. Kramer, D. Hagedorn (1984), col. ii, from a mythographic commentary on *Iliad* 1.38–39; re-ed. Kannicht, *TrGF* 5.1108, cf. Luppe 1984

τῆι ἀδελφῆι . (.)[
τα θάλατταν [ἡ δὲ
λάρναξ κατάγ[εται θείαι
γ̣ώμηι τῆι τό[τε μὲν ἐπικα-
λουμένηι νήσ̣[ωι Λευκόφρυϊ,
Τενέδωι δὲ ὕστ[ερον ἀπ' αὐτοῦ
προσαγορευθε̣[ίσηι. οὕτως
Μύρτιλος καὶ Ε̣[

———

7 οὕτως Luppe 8 ε[or θ[P. Hamb. Ε̣[ὐριπίδης or Θ̣[εόπομπος Kannicht Ἑ̣[λλάνικος Montanari (hence Hellanicus fr. **160B Fowler)

F 21 Stobaeus 3.2.15

Εὐριπίδου Τέννῃ·

φεῦ·
οὐδὲν δίκαιόν ἐστιν ἐν τῷ νῦν γένει.

Incertae Fabulae

F 22? Stobaeus 1.8.10

Κριτίου·

ὁ χρόνος ἁπάσης ἐστὶν ὀργῆς φάρμακον.

ὀργῆς ἁπάσης ὁ χρόνος ἐστὶ φάρμακον Bothe (ἐστὶ φάρμακον χρόνος Stephanopoulos 2013)

F 23 Stobaeus 3.14.2

Κριτίου·

ὅστις δὲ τοῖς φίλοισι πάντα πρὸς χάριν
πράσσων ὁμιλεῖ τὴν παραυτίχ' ἡδονὴν
ἔχθραν καθίστησ' εἰς τὸν ὕστερον χρόνον.

F 20a? Papyrus mythographic summary

. . . *(with?)* his sister . . . the sea . . . *(The)* chest *(was brought)* to land by *(divine)* decision on the *island then called (Leucophrys)* but *later named* Tenedos *(after him. Thus)* Myrsilus and *E* . . . . *(end of summary)*

F 21 Stobaeus, *Anthology*, 'On Vice'

Euripides' *Tennes*:

> Alas, there is no righteousness in the present generation.

Unidentified Plays

F 22? Stobaeus, *Anthology*, 'On the nature of time etc.'

Critias:

> Time is a cure for all anger.

F 23 Stobaeus, *Anthology*, 'On ingratiation'

Critias:

> Anyone who deals with his friends by doing everything for their gratification sets up the pleasure of the moment as enmity for later time.

F 24 Stobaeus 3.23.1

Κριτίου·

δεινὸν δ' ὅταν τις μὴ φρονῶν δοκῇ φρονεῖν.

F 25 Stobaeus 4.33.10

Κριτίου·

σοφῆς δὲ πενίας σκαιότητα πλουσίαν
κρεῖσσον σύνοικόν ἐστιν ἐν δόμοις ἔχειν.

Notes on Critias

T 1

These passages are usually supposed to allude to Critias's dramatic activity, but in the first (*Critias* 108b, cf. 108d) the word *theatron* means **audience** (cf. Agathon **T 2** with note); Socrates pretends that both Timaeus and Critias are giving poetic recitations (*not* dramatic productions) before a large public audience rather than their actual small and informal audience. In the second passage (*Charmides* 108c–d) Critias is merely said to have behaved *like* an anxious dramatist.

T 2

See introduction above, pp. 181f. These are two summaries of the same information derived from an Alexandrian *Life of Euripides* (cf. Wilamowitz 1875, 144f.): IA names the three disputed tragedies but omits the disputed satyr-play, while IB mentions the satyr-play but omits all the play-names (that the satyr-play was *Sisyphus* is Wilamowitz's inference from the sources' divided attribution of the long Sisyphus-fragment, F 19). The summaries differ on one point: IA says the plays **are inauthentic (νοθεύεται)**, whereas IB calls them **disputed (ἀντιλεγόμενα)**. Wilamowitz's assertion that Alexandrian scholars 'unanimously' (*uno ore*: 1875, 166) restored the three tragedies to Critias when they noticed a didascalic record of his tetralogy is therefore questionable, as is Snell's inclusion of only IA's statement as his Critias **T 2** (similarly 88 B 10 DK).[52] The Alexandrians' uncertainty in this case was probably similar to their uncertainty about *Rhesus*, which the second hypothesis says was 'suspected by some' of not

[52] Wilamowitz and Diels were of course not aware of the papyrus hypothesis-fragments, *Rhadamanthys* **F 15** and *Tennes* **F 20**, which were published in 1933 and 1962 and show that these two plays were still included in the Euripidean corpus in the second century AD.

F 24 Stobaeus, *Anthology*, 'On self-love'

Critias:

It's terrible when someone who's stupid thinks he's intelligent.

F 25 Stobaeus, *Anthology*, 'Poverty compared with wealth'

Critias:

It's better to have wealthy ignorance than wise poverty as a companion in your house.

being by Euripides (τοῦτο τὸ δρᾶμα ἔνιοι νόθον ὑπενόησαν, Εὐριπίδου δὲ μὴ εἶναι). The doubt may go back at least to Callimachus's *Pinakes*, which certainly noted questions of ascription and authenticity.[53]

[In IB **τὸ α´** means simply 'one (out of the eight)' (cf. Kannicht 1996, 27 n. 12), not 'the first' or 'the one beginning with α' as Cipolla 2003, 265 insists. The definite article is idiomatic where numbers are subdivided or compared, e.g. Xen. *Hell.* 7.5.10 ἀπῆσαν...τῶν λόχων δώδεκα ὄντων οἱ τρεῖς, 'of the twelve platoons three were absent' (»» Gildersleeve 1980, §535; Smyth 1920, §1125; KG I.638(ζ)).]

F 1, Hypothesis

The hypothesis of *Pirithous* is preserved in two Byzantine commentaries on the *Method for Forcefulness*, a treatise wrongly attributed to the influential rhetorician Hermogenes of Tarsus (2nd–3rd C.) and probably written near his time. The commentaries also preserve the hypotheses and some verses of Euripides' *Wise Melanippe* and *Stheneboea.* The treatise itself (§28) quotes the line **Zeus, as has been told with truth**, attributing it to Euripides, as an example of reinforcing a narrative statement by stressing its authority (**as is stated**) and reliability (**by true tradition**). The Byzantine commentaries must have drawn on an earlier commentary, probably of the 5th or 6th century.[54] The hypotheses that

[53] See especially Callimachus frs 437, 442–446, 449 (Ion's *Triagmos* 'disputed', ἀντιλέγεσθαι), 451 (the/a text of Euripides' *Andromache* carried the name Democrates).

[54] For Gregory of Corinth (11th–12th C.) see e.g. Dickey 2007, 82f., Pontani 2015, 373–75. Ioannes has been tentatively identified with figures from either the 8th or the 11th–12th centuries (»» Meccariello 2014, 94 n. 36). Whether

they quote are of a kind often found in Byzantine manuscripts of the extant tragedians, abbreviated from an ancient source such as the so-called *Tales from Euripides* (»» Meccariello 2014, esp. 3–18, 83–107, and on this hypothesis 268–72).

found in two plays of Euripides etc.: the verse is quoted as the opening line of a play of Euripides in Aristophanes, *Frogs* 1244, where Schol.^{v} identifies the source as *Wise Melanippe* (F 481.1).[55] Wilamowitz thought (1907b, 214) that Euripides could not have repeated himself in this way and so could not have been the author of *Pirithous*, but such repetitions are found elsewhere in Euripidean texts (»» Harsh 1937).

held fast, seated and motionless etc.: lit. 'in an unmoving sitting' (the abstract sense of καθέδρα, LSJ II.2). Literature and art regularly show Pirithous and Theseus seated, either on a rock or on chairs. The elevated phrasing of this sentence may reflect the tragic text but is not uncharacteristic of the tragic hypotheses themselves (as in the last sentence of this one). Pirithous's **seated** posture may have evoked the punishment of criminals (Battegazzore 1970, comparing Plato, *Laws* 855c). The **serpents** reappear in Apollodorus *epit.* 1.24, but there they hold the victims fast with their coils (even though they are already physically attached to the rock).

kept as his life (βίον) the life in Hades (τὴν ἐν Ἅιδου ζωήν): an oxymoron; 'life' in Hades is typically a living death, cf. **F 12** n. (Eleusinian initiates are an exception: **F 2–4** n., para. 1). **[βίον** is omitted in some mss., hence some confusion over the text and unnecessary 19th-century conjectures. Nauck's εἵλετο would give 'chose as his life', but the sentence describes an ongoing condition (**εἶχε** imperfect), not the initial choice (εἵλετο aorist). »» Alvoni 2006, 292f.; Meccariello 2014, 271.**]**

released Theseus and his comrade: see above, p. 186 with notes 16 and 17. **τοὺς περὶ Θησέα**, lit. 'those around Theseus', can hardly exclude Pirithous in this context, although 'those around *x*' is sometimes virtually equivalent to just '*x*': »» Alvoni 2006, 294f.; Meccariello 2014, 207, 271.

for friends suffering misfortune: or in some mss., 'for two friends…', δύο either mistakenly added or mistakenly omitted before δυσ-. Diggle and Meccariello prefer the latter, but the emphasis should be on 'exercising pity for friends' in general.

Gregory drew on Ioannes' commentary or directly on the earlier one is also uncertain (Meccariello 94 n. 38).

[55] Plutarch's claim in *Mor.* 756b–c that *Wise Melanippe* originally had a different opening line (*Zeus, whoever Zeus is, for I know not but by report*) is not credible: »» Collard–Cropp–Lee 2009, 266f.

F 1, Text
For the context and the role of Aeacus see above, pp. 190–93. A dialogue of this kind can hardly have been the play's opening. Wilamowitz and others (including Snell in *TrGF* 1) thought it was identified as such by Ioannes and Gregory,[56] but those scholars quote the passage because it includes the verse **Zeus, as has been told with truth** and do not identify it with the prologue of *Pirithous* (whereas they do identify their excerpt from *Wise Melanippe* as its opening). For the correction see Sutton 1987, 33f.; *MusTr* 110f.

[**7. offspring of Zeus etc.:** Ioannes' and Gregory's θεοῦ gives 'offspring of the god Zeus, father of all'. This is defended by Alvoni (2008, 43), who notes that Zeus is often called 'father of all' or 'father of gods and men'. But to say 'Zeus the father of all is my father' is tautologous. Heracles is asserting his semi-divine status (he will ultimately become a god himself).]

[**13–14. he thought he had found etc.:** Ioannes' corrupt text was corrected by Wilamowitz. Alvoni (2008, 43f.) defends Ioannes' ἐξηνυκέναι, but apart from the metrical anomaly (the υ of ἀνύω is normally short) the phrasing and the perfect infinitive are both awkward ('he gave me an unachievable labour to have achieved'). See now Irmici 2016.]

15–16. the recesses of all Europe and Asia: i.e. all the caves and chasms which might provide access to the underworld (cf. Seaford 1984, 158 on Eur. *Cyclops* 291; Alvoni 2008, 44f.). Such a grand tour is usually part of Heracles' journey to and from the Garden of the Hesperides.

[Wilamowitz considered the verb ἐγκονεῖν (v. 2) unEuripidean (but see Eur. *Hec.* 507, *HF* 521: Kuiper 1908a, 338), and πρὸς βίαν (v. 10) inappropriate as Heracles was not 'forced' to fetch Cerberus (but πρὸς βίαν need not imply force: cf. Eur. *Andr.* 730 with Stevens 1971, 183). His objections to vv. 3–4 ('vacuous'), vv. 7–10 ('trivial'), and the sense of v. 8 ('was ist κεδνὸν εἰς λέχος?') are highly subjective. On the repetition of v. 9 here and in *Wise Melanippe* see above on the Hypothesis.]

F 2–4
These three fragments in recitative anapaests probably all come from the play's choral parodos (though **F 2** might possibly have been introducing a later ritual moment in archaic style, as Aesch. *Pers.* 623ff., *Supp.* 626ff., *Ag.* 355ff., *Cho.* 306ff. etc.). Sutton (1987b, 90–99) suggested implausibly that Eur. F 868, 910, 912 and 913 might also come from this parodos; against this see Egli 2003, 63 n. 2. The libation-pouring **into earth's cleft** (**F 2**) and focus on the heavens (**F 4**, **F 3**) need not imply that this scene was set in the upper world; the initiates in the Underworld are replicating the rituals they performed in life, and in a similar

[56] Wilamowitz (1907b, 214) also thought such an opening impossible for Euripides and claimed it as evidence of Critias's authorship: »» Alvoni 2011, 124f.

environment. According to Sophocles F 837 Eleusinian initiates still *live* in the Underworld (τοῖσδε γὰρ μόνοις ἐκεῖ ζῆν ἔστι). In Ar. *Frogs* they alone enjoy sunlight, singing and dancing joyously day and night in meadows and flowery groves (*Frogs* 154–57, 324–53, 382–87, 440–59): »» Richardson 1974, 310–12 on *Hom.Hymn.* 2.480–82.

F 3 describes Time as an essential feature of the cosmos and relates it to the regular, cyclical motion of the heavens. In **F 4** the Chorus addresses an unnamed **You**, a **self-generated** entity which **wove the growth (*phusis*) of all things in the whirl of aether**, thus establishing the cosmos in its present state, i.e. a whirling mass of aether which carries day and night and the heavenly bodies on their courses, with **You** at its centre. Satyrus cited this passage as evidence of Euripides' adherence to the doctrines of Anaxagoras, with some reason: cf. especially Anaxagoras B 1 DK (the cosmos began as a mass of undifferentiated matter contained within aer and aether), B 9 DK (the mass began to rotate at tremendous speed, thus causing the undifferentiated matter to be shuffled and separated into its present forms), and B 12 DK (the process was initiated and controlled by an autonomous and intelligent Mind (*nous*) which pervades the universe, is inherent in all living creatures, and imparted order (*cosmos*) to the rotation of stars, Sun, Moon, aer and aether). Clement's identification of **You** in **F 4** as 'the Craftsman Mind' (*dêmiourgos nous*) cannot be exactly right since it includes the Platonic idea of the divine Craftsman who created and controls the cosmos from outside it, but it might point in the right direction. Wilamowitz took **You** as a direct reference to Anaxagoras's Mind (Wilamowitz 1875, 165; 1929, 464; cf. *MusTr* 283 n. 2); this too is questionable since Anaxagoras is not known to have thought of his Mind as a deity, but in this poetic context the idea is perhaps re-packaged in imaginative and religious terms. In Eur. *Troades* 884–86 (also cited by Satyrus as Anaxagoraean) Hecuba identifies Zeus as 'earth's sustainer…whether compelling force of nature (*phusis*) or mind (*nous*) of men'; and in Eur. F 941 (cited by Clement along with **F 4**) a speaker identifies the aether surrounding the Earth with Zeus. It seems likely, then, that our fragment implicitly associates Mind with the supreme god traditionally known as Zeus, although this supreme power may have remained purposefully unnamed. »» Egli 2003, 49–51; Schorn 2004, 204–8; Alvoni 2012, 484 (cf. Kuiper 1907, 385).

A different interpretation, much favoured in modern scholarship, makes the **You** of **F 4** identical with the subject of **F 3**, i.e. Time.[57] Time was sometimes identified as a primal cosmogonic force in early Greek philosophy and especially

[57] e.g. Nestle 1903, 105; Battegazzore 1962, 297; Defradas 1967; West 1983, 198, 231; Schorn 2004, 205f.; Assaël 2008; others in Alvoni 2012, 480 n. 23. Egli 2003, 51f. rejects the identification.

in Orphic doctrine.[58] The terms **ἀκάμας, unwearying** (**F 3**) and **αὐτοφυής, self-generated** (**F 4**) recur in Orphic texts, where the phrase αὐτοφυής ἀκάμας describes both the Sun (*Hymn* 8.3) and Heracles as father of Time (*Hymn* 12.9). **F 4**'s **whirl** (*rhumbos*) of aether is featured in *Hymn* 8.7, where the Sun 'drives its path in the whirlings (*dineumata*) of the boundless *rhombos*'. But it seems unlikely that the Chorus would have described the same entity twice, and the terms of these descriptions are rather dissimilar. The deity of **F 4** is a primal power containing its own *phusis* (**αὐτοφυῆ**) and generating the *phusis* of everything else in the cosmos. Time in **F 3** is described as **begetting himself** in a different sense: it renews itself continually, day by day and year by year, and thus seems to be a part of the functioning cosmos which the **You** of **F 4** has generated. If so, **F 3** should belong to the description of this cosmos which began with **F 4**.3–5. I have therefore printed **F 3** after **F 4**; it may be an immediate continuation of **F 4** as von Arnim and Wilamowitz supposed.[59]

The three fragments do not help to determine the authorship of *Pirithous*. Wilamowitz maintained that Euripides could not have been responsible for the cosmology of **F 4** because he would not have agreed with Anaxagoras, and because the cosmology here differs from that of *Wise Melanippe* F 484 which speaks of the separation of Sky from Earth resulting in the generation of living things;[60] but there is no reason to think that either of these cosmologies represented Euripides' personal beliefs.[61] Wilamowitz also noted many 'unEuripidean' words or usages in the *Pirithous* fragments generally and these especially,[62] but most of them are designed (some perhaps invented) for this peculiar mystic–scientific context and would be rare in any poet's vocabulary.[63]

---

[58] »» West 1983, 103–6, 108 and index, 'Time-cosmogony'. Cataudella 1932, 265–68 proposed to identify **You** in **F 4** as the Orphic Zeus.

[59] Von Arnim 1913, 42; Wilamowitz 1929, 463f. Each proposed to adjust the text of **F 3**.1 accordingly (see below). **F 4** and **F 3** are Nauck's frs 593 and 594.

[60] Wilamowitz 1875, 162; 1907b, 215f.

[61] Cf. Kuiper 1907, 381–85 and many others since. In 1907b, 216 Wilamowitz added arbitrarily that Euripides would not have known of the existence of the constellation Ursa Minor (which happens to be mentioned here for the first time in extant Greek literature), whereas Critias would.

[62] Wilamowitz *ibid.*, rebutted by Kuiper 1907, 371–73.

[63] A full list: **(F 2)** πλημοχόας, εὐφήμως (adverb), **(F 4)** αὐτοφυῆ, αἰολόχρως, ἐνδελεχῶς, ἀμφιχορεύει, **(F 3)** ἀκάμας, περίφοιτᾷ, ὠκυπλάνοις, Ἀτλάντειον, τηροῦσι. Some of these are discussed in the notes on each fragment below. Most are mentioned by Defradas 1967, who like Wilamowitz considered them un-Euripidean.

F 2

From the catalogue of cup-types which occupies most of Athenaeus Book 11 (cf. Ion **F 1** n.). Pamphilus (1st C. AD) was an Alexandrian grammarian and a seminal figure in the history of Greek lexicography, often cited by Athenaeus (»» Matthaios 2015, 227, 288f.). It is not clear whether the quotation from *Pirithous* and comment about its authorship are due to Pamphilus or to Athenaeus himself; probably the former. **we may pour... into earth's cleft:** see above on **F 2–4**.

F 4

Cited by Satyrus for its 'Anaxagorean' content (damaged papyrus text), and by Clement arguing that Greek ideas of the divine were taken from and agree with Jewish sources. See above on **F 2–4** for discussion of the content and the association with Anaxagoras. **1–2. You, the self-generated etc.:** the primal entity, self-generated (**αὐτοφυῆ**), activated the generation (**φύσιν**) of all other things in the material cosmos. Alvoni 2012 discusses the use of the term αὐτοφυής in later pagan and Christian theology. The word φύσις is hard to translate, referring basically to natural processes of birth or development and by extension to the products of these processes (natural forms, the natural world, Nature as a whole). Here both are suggested: the self-generated entity activated the process which produced the whole cosmos as we know it (»» Egli 2003, 50 n. 3), not of course from nothing but from an originally undifferentiated mass of matter (above, p. 222). The entity **wove** the cosmos, i.e. gave it an intricate and carefully planned design, an idea found in many Greek and oriental creation myths (»» West 1971, 54f.). In Critias F 19.33f. the starry sky is 'the beauteous handiwork of Time, that clever craftsman', but that does not make Time the subject of **F 4**.

in aether's whirl (ἐν αἰθερίῳ ῥύμβῳ): see above, p. 222, and for the *rhombos* ('bull-roarer') used in ecstatic rituals Diogenes **F 1**.1–5 with note (below, pp. 236–39). Here the image fits the idea of a generating entity **around whom** the material cosmos rotates. The whirling heavens embody the cycles of **daylight** and **night** and of the **stars** (including planets), here imaged as a dancing chorus as in e.g. Soph. *Ant.* 1146, Eur. *El.* 467: »» Cropp 2013, 173; Csapo 2008 (with pp. 273–75 on **F 4**). [The adjective **αἰολόχρως** is found only here and in *Orphic Hymn* 78.4, again describing Night, which is conventionally **ὀρφναία**, **murky** (*Iliad* 10.83 etc., *Od.* 9.143, *Hom.Hymn* 4.97, 578, Eur. *Or.* 1225).]

F 3

Cited by Clement in his gnostic interpretation of the design and decoration of the Ark of the Covenant (*Exodus* 25.10–22), which in part drew on Philo's *Life of Moses* 2.95–100: »» J. Kovacs 1997. The two six-winged Cherubim stood at either end of the Throne of Mercy, on top of the Ark itself. For Clement the Cherubim with their twelve wings signified the orderly structure of the material cosmos which is manifest in the cyclical, time-determined motion of the twelve-fold zodiac, as opposed to God's timeless, unmoving and immaterial world symbolically concealed within the Ark. **F 3** asserts a similar structure for the material cosmos (vv. 1–3). Its description of the two Bear constellations as winged (vv. 3–5) encouraged Clement's interpretation of the Cherubim, although he questions their actual identification with the Bears.

F 3 seems to belong to the description of the cosmos which **F 4** introduced, **Time** in this scheme being an essential part of the *phusis* which the **You** of **F 4** generated. Time **circles around, full in an ever-flowing stream**, a river without beginning or end, constantly replenishing itself (**himself begetting himself**). This cyclical fullness was reflected in the idea that the 'year' (*eniautos*) carries everything 'in himself' (*en hautôi*: Eur. F 862, Hermippus F 73 *PCG*, Pl. *Cratylus* 410d, cf. Heraclitus C 3.2 DK: »» Egli 2003, 52). The **twin Bears** are the constellations Ursa Major and Minor (Great and Little Bear) which are constantly prominent in the northern sky, the North Star (Polaris) being the brightest star in Ursa Minor. In *Iliad* 18.487–89 the Great Bear 'turns in its place and watches Orion, and alone has no part in Ocean's baths' (i.e. never sinks below the horizon). Here the Bears' **swift-beating wings** (lit. 'swift-pulsating wing-beats', the adj. ὠκυπλάνοις found only here) hold them continually aloft as they **watch over the Atlantean heaven**, so called because mythically upheld by Atlas.[64] I have translated **πόλον** as **heaven**, as suggested by the Aristophanes scholiast who quotes v. 5 (cf. *PV* 429, Eur. *Or.* 1685, F 839.11 etc.), although in this context it could have its basic sense 'axis', i.e. 'the polar axis around which the sky revolved' (West 2013a, 119f., 129; cf. West 1983, 197).

[In v. 1 **περί** belongs in tmesis with **φοιτᾷ**. The ms. reading περί γ' is hardly possible, but Schwartz's περί τ' with punctuation after χρόνος ('Time is unwearying; it circles around etc.') disturbs some carefully balanced phrasing ('Unwearying Time circles around…and the twin Bears keep watch…'): cf. Alvoni 2012, 482–84 (accepting περί γ'). I prefer to read περί τ' without punctuation, although this admittedly makes the τ' in περί τ' anomalous. Von Arnim and Wilamowitz, assuming **F 3** to be a direct continuation of **F 4**, proposed different but less plausible adjustments: von Arnim πέρι γ' (repeating πέρι from **F 4**.3), Wilamowitz περί σ' ('around you', i.e. the **You** of **F 4**).]

F 4a–F 7

F 4a, 5 and **7–9** all come from a single papyrus roll of the second century AD (**F 4a** connected with the rest by H. M. Cockle's publication in 1983). Only **F 4a, 5** and **7** offer coherent content. The play is clearly a *Pirithous*, and there is no obvious alternative to identifying it with the one that was preserved in the Euripidean corpus. Some scholars had been inclined to locate **F 5** in the prologue

---

[64] Metre required the rare form Ἀτλάντειον rather than Ἀτλαντικόν.

(e.g. Schmid 1940, 178; Page 1941, 120), but Cockle places it below **F 4a** in a single papyrus column (hence the numbering of **F 4a** in *TrGF* 1²). If that is correct, the two fragments belong probably in the first episode, but as Gauly in *MusTr* 111 points out, it is difficult to see how the end of **F 4a** (Heracles telling Pirithous about their previous acquaintance) could immediately precede the beginning of **F 5** (Pirithous telling the story of his father Ixion). Gauly suggested inverting the order, so that the first four lines of **F 4a** are the end of the speech contained in **F 5**, but that too is difficult since Heracles will then explain his identity to Pirithous only after hearing the latter's lengthy account of his father's crime. Possibly Pirithous's narrative in **F 5** follows **F 4a** less immediately than Cockle thought. **F 7** is reasonably placed in a subsequent scene of dialogue between Heracles and Theseus. The numbering of the book-fragment **F 6** implies that it comes from this sequence, but that is not certain (see note there).

[Several words in these fragments are not found elsewhere in extant texts of Euripides and have been claimed as evidence of Critias's authorship (e.g. Battegazzore–Carlini 1989, 459–61 on **F 4a**.13, 15, 17, 18, **F 5**.11). Most are simply very rare in archaic and classical texts, so it is just as likely that Euripides used them once as that Critias used them once; these include **F 4a**.13 ἀπρούπτως (virtually unique in this form, adj. ἀπρόοπτος *PV* 1074), **F 4a**.15 ὀνειρατώδης (only here), **F 5**.15 οἰστρήλατος (*PV* 580), **F 5**.16 ἄπυστος (*Odyssey* 3x, S. *OC* 489, Empedocles B 12 DK, Parmenides B 8.21 DK), **F 5**.18 διασπαράσσω (A. *Pers*. 195, F 451s.10, S. *Trach.* 782; διασπαρακτός E. *Bacch.* 1220), **F 6** ἀχάλκευτος (A. *Cho.* 493, Soph. F 158.1, 708.1). See also below on **F 4a**.17f. πέπταται…ἀχλὺς, **F 5**.11 μίσγοιτο.]

F 4a

Lines 1–4 are the end of a speech in which Pirithous has described his imprisonment and admits that he now recognizes his offence against the gods (4). The Chorus remarks that he has learned his lesson belatedly (5f.). Heracles comments on the unprecedented severity of his punishment (7–11) and asks how he incurred it (12f.). Pirithous has been only dimly aware of Heracles' presence but now realizes he is speaking Greek (14–18) and asks who he is (19), perhaps noticing something familiar about his voice (14–20 n.). Heracles agrees that they have met before, though long ago (21–25).

1. serpent*(s?)*: presumably as in the Hypothesis ('guarded by the yawning mouths of serpents').

5–6. *(Having?)* understood etc.: that sinners learn the error of their ways **belatedly** through suffering the consequences was proverbial (Hesiod, *Works* 218). Tragic wrongdoers are often reminded of it, e.g. Soph. *Ant.* 1270, *OC* 1264, Eur. *El.* 1111, *Or.* 99, *Bacch.* 1345. [One would expect ξυνείη[ς, i.e. ξυνίῃς 'you understand' (P. Oxy. has ιξει- for Ἰξι- in line 7, σειγ- for σιγ- in 26), but the traces seem not to allow η̣[(Cockle 34 *ad loc.*). For the participle ξυνεὶς Kannicht compares Soph. *Trach.* 934 ὄψ' ἐκδιδαχθείς, 'taught belatedly'.]

12–13. pretext...destruction: the words suggest a divinely imposed destruction (*âtê*), perhaps inflicted through a deception which created a **pretext** (the victim incriminates himself), like the *âtê* that destroyed Ixion (**F 5**.8): cf. Battegazzore–Carlini 1989, 453f..

14–17. This *(voice)* is no longer unintelligible etc.: Heracles has recognized Pirithous (v. 7) and heard his speech, but Pirithous has not seen Heracles and only now hears his voice distinctly. Probably he half-recognizes Heracles' voice (v. 20), thus prompting Heracles' reply in 21ff. (We need not imagine that **This** is a threatening Erinys as Cockle (35) tentatively suggested.)

17–18. a...mist is spread before my *(eyes)*: probably because of his near-death state rather than some divine interference, though Homeric usage covers both possibilities (»» LSJ or *DGE* 'ἀχλύς'). The phrase echoes the Homeric κατ' ὀφθαλμῶν κέχυτ' ἀχλύς, 'a mist poured down upon his eyes' (of dying warriors). **πέπταται (is spread)** is also a Homeric form, found only here in tragedy. [Critias used the word ἀχλύς in an elegy to describe a drunken daze (B 6.13 DK = 6.10 *IEG*), but this hardly favours his authorship of *Pirithous* as Battegazzore (1989, 459f.) suggests.]

21–25. It is not at all surprising etc.: this is the only suggestion in Greek literature that Heracles and Pirithous had met before their meeting in the Underworld, a plausible innovation as both were traditionally involved in conflicts with Centaurs and Amazons. It gives Heracles an additional motive for rescuing Pirithous. ***(association?)*:** or with Collard's conjecture, *(parting)*.

26–28. The sense is obscure, especially if these lines lead into Pirithous's narrative about Ixion in **F 5** (see above on **F 4a–F 7**). There seems to be a reference to silence, hence Mette's 'Be silent!...', but this is difficult to accommodate in the context.

F 5

Pirithous (v. 20) tells the story of his father Ixion's crimes and punishment, which foreshadowed his own. Ixion treacherously killed his wife's father Eioneus but was purified by Zeus (his own father: *Iliad* 14.317f.) and hospitably entertained on Olympus. He then lusted after Hera, but Zeus tricked him into mating with a cloud-figure resembling the goddess and punished his insolence by having him bound on a wheel revolving continually in the aether (or in some later accounts, the underworld). These essentials of what must have been an older story are seen first in Pindar, *Pyth.* 2.21–45. Pirithous's narrative is similar except in the detail of Ixion's punishment (see notes below). »» *LIMC* V, 'Ixion'; Gantz 1993, 718–21; Collard–Cropp 2008a, 460f.; Fowler 2013, 149–52.

7. madness: probably the madness that induced Ixion's attempt on Hera and the *âtê* that foiled it (Pind. *Pyth.* 2.26–29, cf. Schol. Eur. *Pho.* 1158), though

Hunt took it to be the madness resulting from his murder of Eioneus (cf. Pherecydes F 51a–b Fowler, Schol. *Iliad* 1.268, Tzetzes, *Chil.* 9.273.1–9) and Housman supplemented accordingly (θεὸς δὲ μανία[ς ἀρτίως ἐλευθέρῳ | ἔπεμψεν ἄτη[ν, 'the god sent a fatal delusion on him, lately freed from madness').

8–10. Housman's supplements convey the general sense: 'And having seized a cloud resembling a woman he (i.e. Ixion) sowed a most impious report …'. Hunt (followed by Körte and Battegazzore) printed Νεφέλην γυναικ̣[α, 'a woman (named) Nephelê'. Mythographers sometimes give this name to Ixion's cloud-woman (e.g. Diodorus 4.12.6, 4.70.1), but a name is out of place here.

11. Snell's conjecture gives 'in the folds of aether'. **[μίσγοιτο, he was having intercourse:** the verb μίσγω (more commonly μείγνυμι) is found elsewhere in tragedy only in Soph. F 271.4 (active 'mixes') but is the form normally used with reference to sexual intercourse in Homer and other early poetry (*Iliad* 2.232, *Odyssey* 6.288, 7.247, 15.430 etc.).]

12–13. For such boasts etc.: Ixion's boasting is mentioned in some later summaries as the cause of his punishment (Apollod. *epit.* 1.20, Servius on *Aeneid* 6.601, *Myth.Vat.* I.14, II.128; also Lucian's satire, *Dialogues of the Gods* 9).

15–16. *(he perished)* unobserved by men: Hunt compared *Od.* 1.242 οἴχετ' ἄϊστος ἄπυστος, 'he has perished unknown, unobserved' (Telemachus thinking Odysseus has died 'snatched away by harpies').

17–18. his body was torn apart etc.: like Pentheus in Eur. *Bacch.* 1220. In one version of the story Ixion was said to have been destroyed by 'the whirling (of the wheel) and wind-gusts' (ὑπὸ δίνης καὶ θυελλῶν Schol. Pind. *Pyth.* 2.21ff., perhaps derived from Pherecydes F 51a Fowler). The wheel propelled by winds through the aether: Apollod. *epit.* 1.20. I doubt if these winds are represented in South Italian vase-paintings as suggested by Simon 1955, 16–20 (cf. Cockle 1983, 30f. n. 2).

F 6

shame is the Greek *aidôs*, a feeling of inhibition. The fragment probably comes from an early scene (cf. **F 7**.6–10), but other contexts can be imagined (Schmid 1940, 178f. thought of Heracles addressing a plea to Persephone). [Third-person **ἔζευκται (is bound)** is probably correct but possibly determined by Plutarch's context. *Mor.* 763f has the infinitive ἐζεῦχθαι. First and second persons ἔζευγμαι, ἔζευξαι are also possible).]

F 7

Theseus, it seems, has asked for Heracles' help in releasing Pirithous, and has offered Heracles his help in subduing Cerberus; and Heracles has suggested that Theseus could return with him in any case if (or because?) Pirithous cannot be freed (»» Mette 1983, 17; Battegazzore–Carlini 1989, 456f.). Theseus accepts the suggestion courteously (5) but insists he will not desert his comrade (6–7).

Heracles with equal courtesy recognizes Theseus's noble choice (8–10) but declines his offer of help with Cerberus since this would allow Eurystheus to claim that he had not properly completed the labour (10–14). Theseus in turn accepts the rejection of his help and assures Heracles of his high regard and friendship nonetheless (15–19). The remainder (20–30) is probably part of a longer speech of Heracles, perhaps introducing the idea that he might seek Pirithous's release.

[The papyrus marks speaker-changes at 15 and 20 with paragraphi. Those at 5 and 8 are inferred as the beginnings are lost.]

5–7. The translation follows Körte's suggestions in 5 and 6. Hunt's αἰσχρὸν reflects the Hypothesis, 'Theseus, thinking it disgraceful…'.

8–10. What you have said etc.: the ideal of Athens as defender of the weak and unfortunate, embodied in its legendary kings Theseus and his son Demophon, was a theme of tragedies such as Euripides' *Children of Heracles* and *Suppliant Women* and Sophocles' *Oedipus at Colonus*, and of funeral speeches and other patriotic rhetoric (e.g. Lysias 2.12, Isocrates 4.52–60).

10–14. it is unseemly etc.: this seems to be an allusion to an idea otherwise found only much later in Apollodorus's account of Heracles' twelve labours. According to this, Heracles originally had to perform ten labours (2.4.12), but Eurystheus refused to count the killing of the Lernaean Hydra because Heracles' nephew Iolaus helped him cut off the heads (2.5.2), and the cleaning of the Augean Stables because Heracles had accepted a fee for it (2.5.5). This must reflect a compromise between differing traditions concerning the number of the labours. Both their number and their composition varied considerably in early literature and art and were only gradually standardized in the fifth century and later (»» Fowler 2013, 272; Bond 1981, 253–55 on Eur. *Heracles* 359ff.).

[**13.** Hunt's misreading of the papyrus, giving 'if he learned I had helped you accomplish this', was corrected by W. Cockle (see app. crit.). **14.** For the future infinitive **λέξειν** with ἄν in indirect discourse see Moorhouse 1946, Goodwin 1889, 68f., Kannicht 1969, II.134 on *Helen* 448.]

17. inimical to enemies etc.: Theseus formally declares that Heracles' enemies will be his enemies, and his friends his friends.

18–19. Word *(has reached?)* me in the past etc.: probably Theseus says that Heracles has confirmed his reputation for the kind of generous action that creates lasting friendships. [Hunt printed Murray's conjectures (see app. crit.: similarly Page) and translated, 'Report goes that in former times thou wert such to me, and now thou mayst tell the selfsame tale': thus Theseus says that Heracles has reaffirmed a friendship established (Hunt suggested) when he joined Heracles' expedition against the Amazons (cf. Eur. *Hcld.* 215–17). But αἱρ]εῖ would give either 'report convicts' or 'reason determines' (hence Körte αἰν]εῖ 'commends', Snell ᾔν]ει 'commended'), and if Theseus is referring to personal experience he has no need to appeal to a common report. In 6th/5th-century sources he is normally supposed to have made his own Amazon expedition. The specifics of his participation in Heracles' expedition alluded to in *Hcld.* 215ff. are unclear since the text is defective, but it may well have been an *ad hoc* invention there: »»› Gantz 1993, 282f., 398f., Fowler 2013, 485f.]

27. the die is wholly cast: proverbial for a risky and irrevocable decision: as in Julius Caesar's ἀνερρίφθω κύβος, 'Let the die be cast', Plut. *Caes.* 32.8, *Pomp.* 60.2 (πᾶς ἀνερρίφθω κύβος, *Mor.* 206c); cf. Aristophanes fr. dub. 929 *PCG*, Menander fr. 64.4 *PCG*, LSJ ἀναρρίπτω II.

F 10

Stobaeus's chapter 'On what is within our power' comprises excerpts stating that one's well-being depends as much or more on one's own decisions as on *tuchê* (**fortune**) or the gods. For the opposite view see Agathon **F 20** with note. This excerpt might be the opening lines of *Pirithous* (cf. on **F 17**, also from this chapter), especially if the speaker was Aeacus commenting on the outcome of Pirithous's foolish exploit. There is no need to see it as a boldly Socratic statement ('Only the virtuous man can be happy') as Wilamowitz asserted (1875, 165), adding that in that case Euripides could not have made it. **tossed it out:** see LSJ 'ῥίπτω' V. **with no unexercised mind:** cf. Eur. *Bacch.* 491 οὐκ ἀγύμναστος λόγων ('not unexercised in talk'), F 344 πόνοις…οὐκ ἀγύμναστος φρένας ('not unexercised in mind by toils'). **who invented this saying:** the verb καινίζω in pre-4th C. texts only in Aesch. *Ag.* 1071, *Cho.* 492, Soph. *Trach.* 867, Eur. *Tro.* 889.

[Wilamowitz (above) deleted **The first to say it** because of the repetition (**who invented this saying**), but this could be intentional in a portentous play-opening statement (see below on **F 17**). The phrase appears as a cliché in comedy, Alexis F 27 *PCG* (cf. Arnott 1996, 128), Com. adesp. F 859 *PCG*.]

F 11

An upright disposition is more secure etc.: cf. Eur. *Antiope* F 206 (good character guarantees truth, words do not) with Collard–Cropp–Gibert 2004, 310. The perverting power of rhetoric in legal or political contexts is a common topic in tragedy, e.g. **F 17**.5f. below, Eur. *Or.* 907f., F 56, 253, 439, 813a, 928b; often embodied in the person of Odysseus. Bultrighini (1999, 73–80, 106–16) notes that the fragment is phrased in elitist, anti-democratic terms found in other late 5th C. Athenian texts: a *chrêstos tropos* (**upright disposition**) is determined by good birth, Eur. *Hec.* 597f., *Hel.* 940ff., F 329, F 739; demagoguery suits a man who is not properly educated and not upright in his ways (*chrêstos tous tropous*), Ar. *Knights* 191ff.; by choosing the *tropos* of democracy Athens has allowed scoundrels (*ponêroi*) to do better than upright men (*chrêstoi*), [Xen.] *Ath. Pol.* 1.1, cf. Xen. *Hell.* 2.3.13, 14 etc.; upright and wise men (*chrêstoi, sophoi*) stay out of the turmoil of Athenian politics, Eur. *Ion* 598ff. The **orator** who **abuses**

the law and turns it upside down with words resembles one of the demagogues and sycophants who were accused of abusing Athens' democratic constitution with its proliferation of written laws and thus incurring the oligarchic reactions of 411 and 404. Bultrighini infers that our fragment was a programmatic statement of Critias's oligarchic principles, but without a dramatic context this is quite uncertain; it might have been part of a balanced debate like Eur. *Supp.* 238–47. Being *chrêstos*, or indeed 'noble' (*eugenês*), does not necessarily depend on noble birth: cf. e.g. Eur. *Andr.* 636–41, *El.* 366–72, *Ion* 834f., F 362.27; Collard–Cropp–Gibert 2004, 76f. on Eur. *Alex.* F 61b.

[Wilamowitz considered the words τρόπος (sing.) and ῥήτωρ meaning 'politician' un-Euripidean, on very slight grounds (1907b, 215). On τρόπος see Kuiper 1908b.]

F 12

Isn't not living...better than living badly: a commonplace in tragedy (Soph. *Aj.* 479f., Eur. *Hec.* 377f., *Tro.* 636 etc.) and elsewhere as illustrated in Stobaeus' chapter. Here probably Theseus explaining his decision to stay with Pirithous and accept the 'life in Hades' described in the Hypothesis.

F 15

See Introduction above, pp. 208f.

F 16

Strabo quotes the verse as an example of the word πόλις denoting a region rather than a city. The people **who possess the land of Euboea** and its cities were traditionally the Abantes (cf. *Iliad* 2.536–41). The mainland areas **adjacent** to Euboea are Locris (cf. *Iliad* 2.535), Boeotia, and Attica (cf. Eur. *Ion* 294 quoted by Strabo). Rhadamanthys had some mythical connections with Boeotia, especially as one of Heracles' teachers and second husband of Heracles' mother Alcmene (»» Davidson 1999, Fowler 2013, 267). His only connection with Euboea is in *Odyssey* 7.321–26, a mysterious reference to the Phaeacians having carried him there to visit Tityos (»» Garvie 1994, 231f., Davidson 250). None of this helps much in identifying a context for this fragment.

[Wilamowitz (1875, 162) claimed that the word πρόσχωρος was 'frequent' in Aeschylus and Sophocles but 'constantly avoided' by Euripides. In fact it occurs once in Aeschylus and three times in Sophocles.]

F 17

The statement has the form of a priamel ('preamble'), reviewing a series of alternatives before stating a preferred choice. Its content conforms with traditional Greek ethics as stated, for example, in Solon's *Hymn to the Muses*, which begins with a wish for wealth combined with good repute, the wealth being god-granted and not unjustly acquired (Solon fr. 13.3–8 *IEG*). Its ethical tone points to Rhadamanthys as speaker, perhaps in a prologue-speech but probably not its very first lines. Similar gnomic openings are formally introduced: Soph. *Trach.* 1 'There is a long-known saying amongst men', Eur. *Hcld.* 1 'This has long been my opinion', probably Eur. *Bellerophon* F 285 'I assert what is everywhere on men's tongues', possibly **F 10** above.

to get nobility: i.e. to become noble through e.g. marriage, wealth or political advancement. *Eugeneia* is literally 'good birth' and in traditional terms hereditary; this equation and other definitions of nobility and ways of acquiring it are frequently debated in Euripidean tragedy. **to be called the father of abundant possessions:** i.e. to build up a stable wealth which he can pass on to his heirs as χρήματα πατρῷα, 'ancestral possessions' (Snell, apparatus), unlike the wealth acquired unjustly, with disastrous consequences, of Solon fr. 13.11ff. **to say nothing wholesome etc.:** i.e. to spread corruption amongst his fellows; the emphasis on speaking (**λέγοντι**) suggests this refers primarily to corrupt politicians (cf. on **F 11** above). **μηδὲν ὑγιὲς ἐκ φρενῶν** is literally 'nothing healthy out of (his) mind', implying that the mind itself is unhealthy: cf. Aesch. *Eum.* 534ff. (health of mind brings prosperity), Eur. *Andr.* 448f., Eur. F 493.4f., Soph. *Phil.* 1006 (corrupt thinking 'unhealthy'). In Solon fr. 13.70 the wrong-doer suffers from *aphrosunê*, 'mindlessness'. **Base gains:** i.e. wealth acquired unjustly (see above) and dishonorably. **βροτῶν** is otiose, and depends on **οἱ δ'** ('others amongst men') rather than **τοῦ καλοῦ** ('men's honorable achievement'). **That's how diversely men's ways of life range:** perhaps an allusion to Solon's catalogue of men's uncertain ways of seeking a livelihood (βίοτον), fr. 13.43–62. **to have the credit of good repute: δόξαν...εὐκλείας ἔχειν** recalls Solon fr. 13.4 δόξαν ἔχειν ἀγαθήν, 'to have a good reputation'. In earlier Greek *eukleia* usually means 'glory', but in late 5th-century texts the meaning 'good repute' is more frequent. The sense here is best illustrated by Soph. *Ant.* 703f. ('What greater ornament is there for children than the *eukleia* of a flourishing father etc.'), Eur. F 853 ('Honour the gods, your parents and the law; then you will always have the finest crown, *eukleia*'), Antiphon B 49.25f. DK ('for the sake of prestige [*doxa*], moderation, *eukleia*, and being well spoken of'), Anon. Iamblichi B 2.12–14 DK ('But virtue [*aretê*] practised in the way I have set out engenders trust in itself and *eukleia*').[65]

---

[65] Bultrighini (1999, 86, 154–59) understands *eukleia* as 'glory' (p. 155) and reads the fragment as an assertion by Critias of the aristocratic values of hereditary birth and wealth (vv. 1–4) and 'glory' (of athletic victories etc.) against the corrupt values and practices of the Athenian democracy of his own day (vv. 5–8: similarly Centanni 1997, 173). This disregards the priamel structure, in which all the values listed in vv. 1–8 are dismissed in favour of a δόξα εὐκλείας in vv. 9–10. Bultrighini also misinterprets εὐγένειαν λαβεῖν in v. 2

F 18

Probably spoken by one of the parties to the conflict over the Leucippides. The sense **dispossess us** (*sc.* 'of them', cf. LSJ ἐξαιρέω III.3, ἀφαιρέω II.1) seems likelier than the simpler 'remove us'.

[The supplement ⟨ὅστις⟩ *('who')* is supported by identical phrasing in Eur. *Alc.* 848, *Med.* 793, *Hcld.* 977, Ar. *Peace* 316.]

F 20

See Introduction above, pp. 212–15.

F 20a?

This is simply a summary of the myth and probably does not refer specifically to the tragedy *Tennes*. **Myrsilus**, was a local historian from Methymna in Lesbos (a mere 50 km from Tenedos) writing in the early third century BC (*FGrH* no. 477). Kannicht tentatively restored the incomplete name of the second source as Euripides, thus connecting the summary with the tragedy, but as Montanari points out (1995, 151 n. 24), it is more likely to be the late fifth-century historian Hellanicus, also from Lesbos. Myrsilus may have cited Hellanicus as his authority, and the author of *Tennes* may himself have drawn on Hellanicus rather than *vice versa*.

F 21

Cycnus accusing his son, like Theseus in *Hippolytus*?

F 22?

The word-break after ὀργῆς (with long second syllable) breaches Porson's Law, so the verse as it stands is not tragic. Bothe and Stephanopoulos correct this, but Snell suggests the verse might be satyric (cf. Sutton 1980, 74 n. 244; Cipolla 2003, 268f.) or its attribution to Critias in the mss. of Stobaeus confused. For the sentiment cf. Aristotle, *Rhet.* 1380b6 (παύει γὰρ ὀργὴν ὁ χρόνος, 'time puts a stop to anger'), Theodectas **F 9** with note.

F 23

Possibly from the discussion of friendship in *Pirithous* (**F** 7), as noted by Kranz in the *addenda* to DK II[6], p. 427. The thought seems to be that doing everything your friends want will eventually turn them against you when they find that some of what they wanted was bad for them. Stobaeus quotes this in his chapter on ingratiation (*kolakeia*), where many excerpts discuss flattery in similar terms.

---

as 'to have nobility of birth' ('avere nobiltà di natali', p. 154). Caire 2016, 169f. misinterprets **F 17**.10 ('c'est une réputation de gloire que je voudrais posséder').

F 25

A poor wise man is worse off than a wealthy ignorant one because poor men are inevitably handicapped by their poverty (cf. Eur. F 327, F 362.16f.). σκαιότης includes moral as well as intellectual ignorance. Wealth and ignorance are often associated with each other (e.g. Theognis 683, Eur. F 235, F 776), or a damaging combination (e.g. Eur. F 96, F 163). In Eur. F 641 wisdom is naturally associated with poverty and the rich inclined to poor judgement.

The sentence is obviously phrased as a gnomic statement. Diels punctuated it as a question (B 29 DK), perhaps doubting that any dramatic character could state a preference for wealthy ignorance. Similarly Bultrighini 1999, 86 assuming that this expressed a personal opinion of Critias. Snell notes succinctly: 'ἔχειν; Diels, *sed contextus ignotus*'. The speaker might have been a poor man complaining that wealthy and ignorant men flourish, or a wealthy one justifying his ignorance. The content does not favour a satyric context as supposed by Sutton (1980, 74 n. 244) and Cipolla (2003, 269).

DIOGENES OF ATHENS
(*TrGF* 45)

Texts etc. *TrGF* 1^2.184f. with *addenda* 5.1109; *MusTr* 124–27, 284f.
Testimonia and chronology. Hoffmann 1951, 145–47.

*Our information about Diogenes is limited to the Suda's brief record (**T 1**), Plutarch's anecdote (**T 2**) and Athenaeus's comment and quotation (**F 1**). The Suda dates his activity near 400 BC; this is consistent with Plutarch's naming Melanthius as one of his critics, assuming this is Melanthius the tragedian (*TrGF *no. 23, cf. above, p. 132 with n. 8*).[1] *The seven titles which Meineke deleted from the Suda's entry are elsewhere attributed to the Cynic philosopher Diogenes of Sinope (*TrGF *88, in Vol. 2), and the name Oenomaus belongs to a later Cynic philosopher, Oenomaus of Gadara (2nd C. AD), who seems to have composed tragedies of his own (*TrGF *188 T 1–2). Two gnomic fragments and a lost excerpt in Stobaeus (F 2–4? Snell) probably belong to Dicaeogenes rather than Diogenes (see in Vol. 2). What remains is the title* Semele *with a single fragment quoted by Athenaeus.*

[1] Hoffmann, following Rohde's analysis of the use of the word γέγονε in the Suda, notes that γέγονεν in **T 1** probably refers to Diogenes' maturity rather than his birth. His inference that this means Diogenes' first production is less secure.

Testimonia

T 1 Suda *δ* 1142

Διογένης [ἢ Οἰνόμαος] Ἀθηναῖος, τραγικός· γέγονεν ἐπὶ τῆς τῶν λ΄ καταλύσεως. δράμα[τα] αὐτοῦ [Ἀχιλλεύς, Ἑλένη, Ἡρακλῆς, Θυέστης, Μήδεια, Οἰδίπους, Χρύσιππος,] Σεμέλη.

Deletions: Meineke

T 2 Plutarch, *Mor.* 41c

ἔχει δέ τι καὶ ἡ λέξις ἀπατηλόν, ὅταν ἡδεῖα καὶ πολλὴ καὶ μετ' ὄγκου τινὸς καὶ κατασκευῆς ἐπιφέρηται τοῖς πράγμασιν. ὡς γὰρ τῶν ὑπ' αὐλοῖς ᾀδόντων αἱ πολλαὶ τοὺς ἀκούοντας ἁμαρτίαι διαφεύγουσιν, οὕτω περιττὴ καὶ σοβαρὰ λέξις ἀντιλάμπει τῷ ἀκροατῇ πρὸς τὸ δηλούμενον. ὁ μὲν γὰρ Μελάνθιος, ὡς ἔοικε, περὶ τῆς Διογένους τραγῳδίας ἐρωτηθεὶς οὐκ ἔφη κατιδεῖν αὐτὴν ὑπὸ τῶν ὀνομάτων ἐπιπροσθουμένην.

ΣΕΜΕΛΗ

The play must have been about Semele's pregnancy and the birth of Dionysus. Semele, pregnant by Zeus, was tricked by Hera into inviting the god to visit her in his real form; his appearance as a lighting bolt incinerated her but the baby Dionysus was rescued from her womb. Other tragedies on this subject are known, notably Aeschylus's Semele or Hydrophoroi ('Water-Carriers') *in which the poet 'introduced Semele*

F 1 Athenaeus 14.636a

Διογένης δ' ὁ τραγικὸς διαφέρειν πηκτίδα μαγάδιδος, λέγων οὕτως ἐν τῇ Σεμέλῃ·

καίτοι κλύω μὲν Ἀσιάδος μιτρηφόρους
Κυβέλης γυναῖκας, παῖδας ὀλβίων Φρυγῶν,
τυπάνοισι καὶ ῥόμβοισι καὶ χαλκοκτύπων
βόμβοις βρεμούσας ἀντίχερσι κυμβάλων

Testimonia

T 1 Suda, 'Diogenes (of Athens)'
Diogenes, Athenian, tragic poet: he lived at the time of the overthrow of the Thirty (403 BC). A play of his (was) *Semele*.

T 2 Plutarch, *On the right way of listening*
Verbal style too can be deceptive, when it is attractive and copious and is applied to the subject-matter with some degree of grandeur and elaboration. For just as most of the mistakes of singers backed by auloi escape the audience's notice, so a profuse and lofty verbal style dazzles the listener and blinds him to what the speaker is actually saying. Thus Melanthius, when asked about Diogenes' tragedy, supposedly said that he had not seen it as it was obscured by the words.

SEMELE

pregnant and divinely possessed, and the women touching her belly likewise divinely possessed'.[2] *These women must have been Aeschylus's chorus, tending the pregnant Semele and (as a dramatic chorus) singing and dancing ecstatically. Our fragment of Diogenes' tragedy suggests a similar situation. For details see the notes below.*

F 1 Athenaeus, *Sophists at Dinner*
Diogenes the tragedian (indicates) that the *pêktis* differs from the *magadis*, saying in *Semele*:

> And yet I hear that Asian Cybele's mitra-wearing women, daughters of wealthy Phrygians, making a din with drums and rhomboi and hand-clashed clangour of bronze-hammered

[2] Schol. Ap. Rhod. 1.636. Spintharus's *Semele Keraunoumenê ('Semele Lightning-struck'*: *TrGF* 40 T 1, but see above, p. xv n. 26 on the date) and Carcinus II's *Semele* (*TrGF* 70 **F 2–3**, in Vol. 2) were presumably similar, and Sophocles' *Hydrophoroi* (F 672–674) may have been. A citharodic *Semele's Labour* by Diogenes' contemporary Timotheus is also recorded (*PMG* 792), and a 4th-century comedy *Semele or Dionysus* by Eubulus.

〈 〉
σοφὴν θεῶν ὑμνῳδὸν ἰατρόν θ' ἅμα.
κλύω δὲ Λυδὰς Βακτρίας τε παρθένους
ποταμῷ παροίκους Ἅλυϊ Τμωλίαν θεόν
δαφνόσκιον κατ' ἄλσος Ἄρτεμιν σέβειν
ψαλμοῖς τριγώνων πηκτίδων 〈τ'〉 ἀντιζύγοις
ὁλκοῖς κρεκούσας μάγαδιν, ἔνθα Περσικῷ
νόμῳ ξενωθεὶς αὐλὸς ὁμονοεῖ χοροῖς.

4 lacuna following: Wilamowitz 9 〈τ'〉 Casaubon

Notes on Diogenes of Athens

F 1

The fragment is quoted by Athenaeus in a long discussion of stringed instruments which includes many quotations from early poets and conflicting interpretations of them by later writers on music (14.634e–637e, cf. 4.182e–183f). It also bears out Melanthius's comment (**T 2**) about Diogenes' florid style. The speaker, probably an insightful figure like Tiresias in Euripides' *Bacchae*, justifies the ecstatic music and dancing of the Theban women, possessed by Dionysus from within the womb, by comparing it with the Asiatic rituals of Cybele/Cybebe (the Great Mother) and Artemis. For similar connections see especially Pindar fr. 70b.8–23 (the Olympian gods make music and dance for Dionysus 'in the presence of the Great Mother'), Aeschylus F 57 (Dionysus's rites assimilated to those of the Thracian mother-goddess Cotyto), Eur. *Bacchae* 55–167 (the Bacchants bring the rites of Dionysus *and* Cybele, along with their and Rhea's music, from Phrygia and Lydia to Thebes), Eur. *Helen* 1301–68 (Demeter identified with the Great Mother and charmed with Dionysiac music and dance). Such connections reflect the underlying commonalities of the cults of these deities. »» Kannicht 1969, 2.327–33 on *Helen* 1301–68 (with a full collection of similar material); Dodds on Eur. *Bacch.* 78f.; *New Pauly*, 'Cybele', 'Mother Goddesses'; Allan 2004, esp. 131–33, 138–48, cf. 2008, 294f.

The verse missing after v. 4 must have contained an infinitive parallel with **σέβειν** in v. 8; thus there were two exactly balanced six-verse descriptions, each beginning **I hear that**... (**κλύω μὲν**..., **κλύω δὲ**...). Vv. 1–2 do not mean 'I hear Cybele's women...' as Kannicht 331 and Allan 131 suggest; these women are not in Thebes and were not the play's chorus.

cymbals . . . *(celebrate their goddess)* . . . the gods' wise songstress and healer. I hear, too, that Lydian and Bactrian maidens dwelling by the river Halys worship the Tmolian goddess, Artemis, in her laurel-shaded grove, sounding the *magadis* with pluckings of *trigônoi (and)* responsive strummings of *pêktides*, while with a Persian melody the welcomed *aulos* accompanies the dancing.

1–5. Asian Cybele...wealthy Phrygians: in historic times Cybele was especially associated with Phrygia (a gold-rich kingdom: cf. the legend of its king Midas) and with her cult centre at Pessinus, 130 km. SW of Ankara in modern Turkey. Her cult spread into the Greek settlements in Asia Minor, and thence into mainland Greece, in the archaic period. In Greek contexts she was sometimes identified with the Cretan Rhea, mother of Zeus and the senior Olympian gods: »» *LIMC* VIII, 'Kybele'. **mitra-wearing:** the women's exotic headbands (esp. Lydian, e.g. Alcman fr. 1.67, Sappho fr. 98a.10f., 98b.1–3) may be ritually significant (cf. Eur. *Bacch.* 833 with Dodds's note). **drums... rhomboi...cymbals**: typifying the loud ecstatic music made for Cybele and similar deities. Images of Cybele usually show her holding a *phialê* (libation-bowl) and *tympanum* (a large flat **drum** or tambourine). A **rhombos** ('bull-roarer') was a strip of wood attached to a handle and swung like a rattle to make a loud whirring noise (cf. Eur. *Helen* 1362f. with Kannicht's note; Levaniouk 2007, 177–79). **hand-clashed...cymbals:** ἀντίχερσι here is lit. 'counter-handed' (though ἀντίχειρ normally means 'thumb'). **the gods' wise songstress and healer:** Cybele's 'songs' are presumably incantations, linked with the healing powers which she has as a mother goddess.

6–8. The **Artemis** worshipped by **Lydian and Bactrian maidens** is the Mother Goddess in her west Asian form, now best known as the Artemis of Ephesus (»» *LIMC* II, 'Artemis Ephesia'), but pre-Greek and long-established in Lydia. **Tmolian** refers to Mt. Tmolos, the range east of Smyrna (Izmir) between the Cayster (Little Maeander) and Hermos (Gediz) valleys with the Lydian capital Sardis (Sart) on its northern flank. The **river Halys** was the border between the Lydian and Persian empires until king Croesus disastrously invaded the latter in 547 (Hdt. 1.72, 1.75). **Bactrian maidens** (i.e. from Afghanistan) and

a Persian melody (11) are exotic elaborations with no specific reference. **her laurel-shaded grove:** laurel was sacred to both Artemis and Apollo, mythically created (with the palm-tree) to aid Leto when she gave them birth on the island of Delos (e.g. Eur. *Hec.* 458–61).

9–11. sounding the *magadis etc.*: *trigônon* and *pêktis* were names for types of small finger-plucked harp, strongly associated with Lydian music (»» Maas–Snyder 1989, 40, 147–55; West 1992b, 70–72; on the *pêktis*, West 1997). They play together in Sophocles' *Mysians*, F 412 (hence Casaubon's **⟨τ'⟩**, otherwise we have 'worship the goddess with responsive pluckings of triangular *pêktides*'). Athenaeus's speakers (and hence most modern scholars) assume that the *magadis* was another type of harp, or another name for one, but most if not all of the early poetic references seem to be to a musical effect, specifically a 'descant' played an octave higher than the basic melody (»» Barker 1988, esp. 102, cf. 2014, 82–84; West 1992b, 72f.). Here the 'descant' is played on the higher-pitched *pêktis*, and the meaning is probably 'sounding a descant as they play their *trigôna* and *pêktides* in concert'. **responsive strummings: ἀντιζύγοις ὁλκοῖς** are probably 'counterbalanced drawings' of fingers across strings, cf. Pindar fr. 125 ψαλμὸν ἀντίφθογγον 'antiphonal plucking', Soph. F 412 ἀντί-σπαστα 'responding (sounds of the *pêktis*)', Phrynichus **F 11** ἀντίσπαστα μέλη 'responding songs', all cited a little earlier by Athenaeus (see above on Phrynichus **F 11**). Or **ἀντιζύγοις** might mean 'counter-strung', referring to pairs of strings an octave apart on the *pêktis* itself (West 1997, 49). **the welcomed (ξενωθείς) *aulos*:** the aulos-player is welcomed as a guest into the group of harp-playing women.

ABBREVIATIONS AND REFERENCES

1. ABBREVIATIONS

For standard abbreviations of classical authors and works see LSJ or *OCD*. Tragic fragments are cited from *TrGF*. Editions of classical texts are usually cited by editor's name (e.g. 'Ion F 108 Leurini', 'Fraenkel on A. *Ag.* 218') or abbreviated title (e.g. *FGrH*, *PCG*).

AC	*L'Antiquité Classique*
AJPh	*American Journal of Philology*
APF	*Archiv für Papyrusforschung*
ASNP	*Annali della Scuola Normale Superiore di Pisa*
BICS	*Bulletin of the Institute of Classical Studies*
C&M	*Classica et Mediaevalia*
CQ	*Classical Quarterly*
CR	*Classical Review*
DGE	F. R. Adrados *et al. Diccionario Griego-Español.* Numerous volumes. Madrid. 1980– . Available in part on line.
DK	H. Diels, W. Kranz. *Die Fragmente der Vorsokratiker.* Two volumes. Sixth edition. Berlin. 1951–52.
FGrH	F. Jacoby *at al. Die Fragmente der griechischen Historiker*. Numerous volumes. Berlin. 1923–99. Now available on line.
GEF	M. L. West. *Greek Epic Fragments*. Cambridge, MA. 2003.
GRBS	*Greek, Roman and Byzantine Studies.*
GrSat	R. Krumeich, N. Pechstein, B. Seidensticker. *Das griechische Satyrspiel.* Darmstadt. 1999.
HSCPh	*Harvard Studies in Classical Philology*
IEG	M. L. West. *Iambi et Elegi Graeci.* Two volumes. Second edition. Oxford. 1989, 1992.
IG	*Inscriptiones Graecae.* Numerous volumes. Berlin.
JHS	*Journal of Hellenic Studies*
KG	R. Kühner, B. Gerth. *Ausführliche Grammatik der griechischen Sprache.* Teil II. Two volumes. Third edition. Hannover. 1898.
LGPN	P. M. Fraser, E. Matthews *et al. Lexicon of Greek Personal Names.* Numerous volumes. 1987– . Also available on line.
LIMC	*Lexicon Iconographicum Mythologiae Classicae.* Nine volumes, each in two parts. Zurich. 1981–98.
LSJ	H. G. Liddell, R. Scott. *A Greek-English Lexicon.* Ninth edition, revised by H. Stuart Jones and R. McKenzie. Oxford. 1940.

MusTr	B. Gauly *et al. Musa tragica: die griechische Tragödie von Thespis bis Ezechiel.* Göttingen. 1991.
M–W	R. Merkelbach, M. L. West. *Fragmenta Hesiodea*. Oxford. 1967.
New Pauly	*Brill's New Pauly: Encyclopaedia of the Ancient World.* Numerous volumes. Leiden. 2002– . Also available on line.
OCD	*The Oxford Classical Dictionary*. Fourth edition. Oxford. 2012.
PCG	R. Kassel, C. Austin. *Poetae Comici Graeci*. Eight volumes in ten. Berlin. 1983— .
PCPhS	*Proceedings of the Cambridge Philological Society*
PMG	D. L. Page. *Poetae Melici Graeci*. Oxford. 1962.
PMGF	M. Davies. *Poetarum Melicorum Graecorum Fragmenta.* Oxford. 1991.
P. Oxy.	*The Oxyrhynchus Papyri.* Numerous volumes. London.
RE	*Paulys Realencyclopädie der classischen Altertumswissenschaft: neue Bearbeitung.* Numerous volumes. Stuttgart. 1894–1980.
RFIC	*Rivista di Filologia e di Istruzione Classica.*
Rhet. Gr.	L. von Spengel, *Rhetores Graeci.* Three volumes. Leipzig. 1853–56.
TAPhA	*Transactions of the American Philological Association*
TrGF	B. Snell, R. Kannicht, S. Radt. *Tragicorum Graecorum Fragmenta.* Five volumes in six. Göttingen, 1971–2004.
ZPE	*Zeitschrift für Papyrologie und Epigraphik.*

2. REFERENCES

Allan, W. 2004. Religious Syncretism: The New Gods of Greek Tragedy. *Harvard Studies in Classical Philology* 102: 113–55.

Allan, W. 2008. *Euripides. Helen.* Cambridge.

Alvoni, G. 2006. Nur Theseus oder auch Peirithoos? Zur Hypothesis des Pseudo-Euripideischen 'Peirithoos'. *Hermes* 134: 290–300.

Alvoni, G. 2008. Eracle ed Eaco alle Porte dell'Ade (Critias fr. 1 Sn.–K.). *Philologus* 152: 40–48.

Alvoni, G. 2011. Ist Critias Fr. 1 Sn.–K. Teil des 'Peirthoos'-Prologs? Zu Wilamowitzens Memorandum über die 'Peirithoosfrage'. *Hermes* 139: 120–30.

Alvoni, G. 2012. Autogenerazione della divinità: Da Crizia (fr. 3 e 4 Sn.–K) al dio cristiano. *Zeitschrift für Antike und Christentum* 16: 477–86.

Angiò, F. 1989. Etica aristocratica ed azione politica in Crizia. *Quaderni di Storia* 15: 141–48.

Arnim, H. von. 1913. *Supplementum Euripideum.* Bonn.

Arnott, W. G. 1996. *Alexis: the fragments. A commentary.* Cambridge.

Arnott, W. G. 2007. *Birds in the Ancient World from A to Z.* London.

Assaël, J. 2008. Étude de deux fragments de poésie euripidéenne sur l'Éther. In Auger–Peigney 2008: 465–79.

Auger, D. and Peigney (eds) 2008. *Φιλευριπίδης. Mélanges offerts à François Jouan* (Paris–Nanterre):

Austin, C. 1968. *Nova Fragmenta Euripidea in Papyris Reperta.* Berlin.

Austin, C. and Olson, S. D. 2004. *Aristophanes: Thesmophoriazusae*. Oxford.

Ax, W. 2001. Dikaiarchs *Bios Hellados* und Varros *De vita populi Romani*. In Fortenbaugh–Schütrumpf 2001: 279–310.

Badian, E. 1996. Phrynichus and Athens οἰκήια κακά. *Scripta Classica Israelica* 15: 55–60.

Baltzly, D. 2014. Stoicism. *The Stanford Encyclopedia of Philosophy* (Spring 2014 edition). https://plato.stanford.edu/archives/ spr2014/entries/stoicism/.

Barker, A. D. 1984. *Greek Musical Writings, I: The musician and his art*. Cambridge.

Barker, A. D. 1988. Che cos'era la 'mágadis'?. In B. Gentili and R. Pretagostino (eds), *La Musica in Grecia. Atti del convegno internazionale sulla musica greca, Urbino, 18–20 Ott. 1985* (Rome, 1988): 96–107.

Barker, A. D. 2014. *Ancient Greek Writers on their Musical Past: studies in Greek musical historiography*. Pisa.

Barone, C. 1978. Neofrone e la Medea di Euripide. *RFIC* 106: 129–36.

Barrett, W. S. 1964. *Euripides: Hippolytos.* Oxford.

Bartsch, H. 1843. *De Chaeremone Poeta Tragico.* Mainz.

Battegazzore, A. 1962. Crizia: drammi. In A. Battegazzore and M. Untersteiner, *Sofisti. Testimonianze e Frammenti, IV*: *Antifonte, Crizia*. Florence: 274–317.

Battegazzore, A. 1970. Il termine καθέδρα nella hypothesis del Piritoo di Crizia. In *Mythos. Scripta in honorem Marii Untersteiner* (Gena, 1970): 75–80.

Battegazzore, A. and Carlini, A. 1989. Critias. In *Corpus dei papiri filosofici greci e latini (CPF)* I.1* (Academici – Cyrenaici): 442–66. Florence.

Battezzato, L. 2013. Dithyramb and Greek Tragedy. In Kowalzig and Wilson 2013: 93–110.

Beazley, J. D. Attic Red-figure Vase-painters. Revised ed., 3 volumes. Oxford.

Bélis, A. 1986. L'aulos phrygien. *Revue Archéologique*, 1986.1: 21–40.

Bentley, R. 1691. *Epistola ad Cl. V. Joannem Millium.* Appendix to E. Chilmead (ed.), *Joannis Antiocheni cognomento Malalae Historia Chronica.* Oxford.

Bentley, R. 1699. *A Dissertation upon the Epistles of Phalaris, with an answer to the objections of the Hon. Charles Boyle Esq.* London.

Biles, Z. P. 2006–7. Aeschylus' afterlife: reperformance by decree in 5th C. Athens? *Illinois Classical Studies* 31–32: 206–42.

Biles, Z. P. and Olson, S. D. 2015. *Aristophanes: Wasps*. Oxford.

Blumenthal, A. von. 1939. *Ion von Chios. Die Reste seiner Werke.* Stuttgart.

Bolling, G. M. 1925. *The External Evidence for Interpolation in Homer*. Oxford.

Bond, G. W. 1981. *Euripides: Heracles*. Oxford.

Bosher, K. 2012. Hieron's Aeschylus. In K. Bosher (ed.), *Theater Outside Athens* (Cambridge, 2012): 97–111.

Braund, D. and Hall, E. 2014. Gender, role and performer in Athenian iconography: a masked tragic chorus with *kalos* and *kale* captions from Olbia. *JHS* 134: 1–11.

Bremer, J. M. and Calder, W. M. 1994. Prussia and Holland. Wilamowitz and Two Kuipers. *Mnemosyne* 47: 177–216.

Bremmer, J. N. 1998. Aëtius, Arius Didymus and the Transmission of Doxography. *Mnemosyne* 51: 154–60.

Broggiato, M. 2000. Athenaeus, Crates and Attic glosses: a problem of attribution. In D. Braund, J. Wilkins (eds), *Athenaeus and his World: Reading Greek Culture in the Roman Empire* (Exeter, 2000): 364–70.

Broggiato, M. 2014a. Eratosthenes, Icaria and the origins of tragedy. *Mnemosyne* ser. 4, 67: 885–99.

Broggiato, M. 2014b. Aristophanes and Aeschylus' *Persians*: Hellenistic discussions on Ar. *Ran,* 1028f. *Rheinisches Museum* 157: 1–15.

Brown, M. K. 2002. *The* Narratives *of Konon*. Munich.

Bühler, W. 1999. *Zenobii Athoi Proverbia: 5, Libri secundi proverbia 41–108 complexum etc.* Göttingen.

Bultrighini, U. 1999. *'Maledetta democrazia': Studi su Crizia*. Alessandria.

Burkert, W. 1985. *Greek Religion.* Transl. J. Raffan. Cambridge, MA.

Caire, E. 1998 *Critias d'Athènes: sophiste et tyran.* Diss. Université de Provence Aix–Marseille I.

Caire, E. 2016. *Penser l'oligarchie à Athènes aux v*^{e} *et iv*^{e} *siècles*. Paris.

Calame, C. 2001. *Choruses of Young Women in Ancient Greece*. Transl. D. Collins, J. Orion. Revised edition (orig. French, 1977). Lanham MD.

Campbell, D. A. 1988. *Greek Lyric III.* Loeb Classical Library 144. Cambridge, MA and London.

Campbell, D. A. 1993. *Greek Lyric V.* Loeb Classical Library 476. Cambridge, MA and London.

Capps, E. 1943. A New Fragment of the List of Victors at the City Dionysia. *Hesperia* 12: 1–11.

Carlini, A. 1968. Un nouvo frammento di tragedia Greca. *ASNP* 37: 163–71.

Carlini, A. 2012. Due frammenti di tragedia (*Piritoo*?) di uno stesso *volumen*: P. Köln 2 e PSI inv. 3021. In G. Bastianini *et al.* (eds), *Harmonia: scritti di filologia classica in onore di Angelo Casanova* (Florence, 2012): 183–94.

Caroli, M. 2012. Caroli, Menico. Erodoto VI 21, 2: una censura teatrale e 'libraria'? *Atene e Roma* n.s. 6: 157–79.

Carpenter, T. H. *et al.* 1989. *Beazley Addenda: additional references to ABV, ARV*^{2} *and Paralipomena*. Oxford.

Cataudella, Q. 1932. Sulla 'Teogonia' di Antifane e sui frammenti del 'Piritoo' di Euripide. *Athenaeum* n.s. 10: 259–68.

Ceccarelli, P. 1997. La Pirrica di Frinico e le Pyrrhichai attribuite a Frinico figlio di Melanthas. In S. Alessandri (ed.), *Ἱστορίη: studi offerti...a Giuseppe Nenci.* Galatina: 77–93.

Ceccarelli, P. 2013 Circular choruses and the dithyramb in the Classical and Hellenistic period: a problem of definition. In Kowalzig and Wilson 2013, 153–70.

Centanni, M. 1997. *Atene assoluta: Crizia dalla tragedia alla storia.* Padova.

Cerri, G. 1977. La Ktisis di Ione di Chio: prosa o versi? *Quaderni Urbinati di Cultura Classica* n.s. 26: 127–31.

Chantry, M. 1999. *Scholia vetera in Aristophanis Ranas*. Scholia in Aristophanem 3.1a. Groningen.

Cipolla, P. 2003. *Poeti minori del dramma satiresco.* Amsterdam.

Cipolla, P. 2006. Le citazioni dei tragici in Ateneo. In P. Cipolla (ed.), *Studi sul teatro greco* (Amsterdam, 2006): 79–136.

Cipolla, P. 2011. Sugli anapesti di Trag. Adesp. F 646a Sn.–K. *Lexis* 29: 131–72.

Cockle, W. 1970. P. Oxy. xvii. 2078: Euripides(?) or Critias(?), *Pirithous*. *CR* n.s. 20: 136–37.

Collard, C. 2005. Euripidean fragmentary plays. The nature of their sources and their effect on reconstruction. In F. McHardy, J. Robson, D. Harvey (eds), *Lost Dramas of Classical Athens* (Exeter, 2005): 49–62.

Collard, C. 2007. *Tragedy, Euripides and Euripideans. Selected Papers.* Bristol.

Collard, C. 2009. Atreids in fragments (and elsewhere). In Cousland–Hume 2009: 309–20.

Collard, C. and Cropp, M. J. 2008a. *Euripides: Fragments. Aegeus–Meleager.* Cambridge, MA.

Collard, C. and Cropp, M. J. 2008b. *Euripides: Fragments. Oedipus–Chrysippus, Other fragments.* Cambridge, MA.

Collard, C., Cropp, M. J., Gibert, J. 2004. *Euripides: Selected Fragmentary Plays, 2. Philoctetes etc.* Warminster.

Collard, C., Cropp, M. J, Lee, K. H. 2009. *Euripides: Selected Fragmentary Plays, 1. Telephus etc.* Reprinted with corrections and addenda. Oxford.

Colomo, D. 2011. 5093. Rhetorical Epideixeis. In D. Colomo and J. Chapa (eds), *The Oxyrhynchus Papyri, Volume LXXVI* (London, 2011), 84–171.

Conacher, D. J. 1988. *Euripides: Alcestis*. Warminster.

Connor, W. R. 1989. City Dionysia and Athenian democracy. *C&M* 40: 7–32.

Corbato, C. 1948. L'Anteo di Agatone. *Dioniso* 11: 163–72.

Cousland, J. R. C. and Hume, J. R. (eds). 2009. *The Play of Texts and Fragments: Essays in honour of Martin Cropp*. Leiden.

Cropp, M. J. 2005. Lost tragedies: a survey. In Gregory (ed.) 2005: 271–92.

Cropp, M. J. 2013. *Euripides: Electra*. Second edition. Oxford.

Cropp, M. J. and Fick, G. H. 1985. *Resolutions and Chronology in Euripides. The fragmentary tragedies*. London.

Csapo, E. 2004. The politics of the New Music. In P. Murray and P. Wilson (eds), *Music and the Muses: the culture of mousikē in the classical Athenian city* (Oxford, 2004): 207–48.

Csapo, E. 2008. Star Choruses. Eleusis, Orphism, and New Musical Imagery and Dance. In Revermann–Wilson 2008: 262–90.

Csapo, E. 2010. *Actors and Icons of the Ancient Theater*. Chichester.

Csapo, E. 2012. 'Parade abuse', 'From the wagons'. In C. W. Marshall and G. A. Kovacs (eds), *No Laughing Matter. Studies in Athenian Comedy* (London, 2012): 19–34.

Csapo, E. 2015. The earliest phase of 'comic' choral entertainments in Athens. The Dionysian Pompe and the 'birth' of comedy. In S. Chronopoulos and C. Orth (eds), *Fragmente einer Geschichte der griechischen Komödie* (Heidelberg, 2015): 66–108.

Csapo, E. and Miller, M. (eds) 2007a. *The Origins of Theater in Ancient Greece and Beyond: From Ritual to Drama*. Cambridge.

Csapo, E. and Miller, M. 2007b. General Introduction. In Csapo–Miller 2007a: 1–39.

Csapo, E. and Slater, W. 1995. *The Context of Ancient Drama*. Ann Arbor.

Csapo, E. et al. (eds). 2014. *Greek Theatre in the Fourth Century B.C.* Berlin.

Csapo, E. and Wilson, P. 2015. Drama Outside Athens in the Fifth and Fourth Centuries BC. In Lamari (ed.) 2015: 316–95.

Csapo, E. and Wilson, P. 2020. *A Social and Economic History of the Theatre to 300 BC, II: Theatre Beyond Athens*. Cambridge.

Dale, A. M. 1954. *Euripides: Alcestis*. Oxford.

Dale, A. M. 1968. *The Lyric Metres of Greek Drama.* Second edition. Oxford.

D'Alessio, G. 2013. 'The Name of the Dithyramb': diachronic and diatopic variations. In Kowalzig and Wilson (eds) 2013: 113–32.

Davidson, J. F. 1999. Rhadamanthys and the family of Herakles. *AC* 68: 247–52.

Davies, J. K. 1971. *Athenian Propertied Families, 600–300 B.C.* Oxford.

Davies, M. 1989. Sisyphus and the invention of religion ('Critias' *TrGF* 1 (43) F 19 = B 25 DK). *BICS* 36: 16–32.

Davies, M. and Finglass, P. J. 2014. *Stesichorus: The Poems. Edited with Introduction, Translation and Commentary.* Cambridge.

Defradas, J. 1967 Une image présocratique du temps. *Revue des Études Grecques* 80: 152–9.

Del Rincón Sánchez, F. 2007. *Trágicos menores del siglo V a.C. (de Tespis a Neofrón): estudio filológico y literario.* Madrid.

Delattre, D. 2007. *Philodéme de Gadara,* Sur La Musique, *Livre IV.* Two volumes. Paris.

Denniston, J. D. 1954. *The Greek Particles.* Second edition. Oxford.

Depew, D. 2007. From hymns to tragedy: Aristotle's genealogy of poetic kinds. In Csapo–Miller 2007a: 126–49.

Dickey, E. 2007. *Ancient Greek Scholarship A guide to finding, reading, and understanding scholia, commentaries, lexica and grammatical treatises from their beginnings to the Byzantine period.* Oxford.

Diels, H. 1879. *Doxographi Graeci*. Berlin.

Diggle, J. 1994. *Euripidea. Collected Essays*. Oxford.

Diggle, J. 1998. *Tragicorum Graecorum Fragmenta Selecta.* Oxford.

Diggle, J. 2008. Did Euripides plagiarise the *Medea* of Neophron? In Auger–Peigney 2008: 405–13..

Dihle, A. 1977. Das Satyrspiel 'Sisyphos'. *Hermes* 105: 28–42.

Dobrov, G. 2001. *Figures of Play. Greek Drama and Metafictional Poetics.* Oxford and New York.

Dodds, E. R. 1960 *Euripides. Bacchae.* Second edition. Oxford.

Dover, K. J. 1974. *Greek Popular Morality in the time of Plato and Aristotle.* Berkeley.

Dover, K. J. 1980. *Plato: Symposium.* Cambridge.

Dover, K. J. 1986. Ion of Chios: his place in the history of Greek literature. In J. Boardman and C. E. Vaphopoulou-Richardson (eds), *Chios. A conference at the Homereion in Chios, 1984* (Oxford, 1986): 27–37.

Dover, K. J. 1993. *Aristophanes: Frogs.* Oxford.

Dunbar, N. 1995. *Aristophanes: Birds.* Oxford.

Egli, F. 2003. *Euripides im Kontext zeitgenössischer intellektueller Strömungen.* Munich.

Eidinow, E. 2007. *Oracles Curses, and Risk among the Ancient Greeks*. Oxford.

Erbse, H. 1977. *Scholia Graeca in Homeri Iliadem (Scholia Vetera)*. Volume 5. Berlin.

Fantuzzi, M. 2007. Epigram and theater. In P. Bing, J. S. Bruss (eds), *Brill's Companion to Hellenistic Epigram* (Leiden): 475–95.

Farmer, M. 2017. *Tragedy on the Comic Stage.* New York.

Federico, E. 2015. *Ione di Chio: Testimonianze e frammenti.*. Tivoli.

Finglass, P. J. 2015a. Stesichorus, master of narrative. In Finglass and A. Kelly (eds), *Stesichorus in Context*, 83–97.

Finglass, P. J. 2015b. Ancient Reperformances of Sophocles. In Lamari (ed.) 2015: 207–23.

Finglass, P. J. P. 2016. A new fragment of Sophocles' *Tereus*. *ZPE* 200: 61–85.

Forrest, W. G. 1956. The First Sacred War. *Bulletin de Correspondance Hellénique* 80: 33–52.

Fortenbaugh, W. W., Schütrumpf, E. eds 2001. *Dicaearchus of Messana. Text, translation, and discussion.* New Brunswick, NJ.

Fowler, R. L. 2013. *Early Greek mythography, II. Commentary.* Oxford.

Francis, E. D. 1975. Menandrian maids and Mithraic lions. *Glotta* 53: 43–66.

Frazer, J. G. 1921. *Apollodorus: The Library.* Two volumes. London and Cambridge, MA.

Fritzsche, F. V. 1845. *Aristophanis Ranae.* Zürich.

Gagné R. 2013. Dancing letters: the "Alphabetic tragedy" of Kallias', in R. Gagné and M. Govers Hopman (eds), *Choral Mediations in Greek Tragedy* (Cambridge, 2013): 297–316.

Gallavotti, C. 1933. Nuove hypotheseis di drammi Euripidei. *RFIC* 11: 177–88.

Gantz, T. N. 1993. *Early Greek Myth.* Baltimore and London.

Garvie, A. F. 1994. *Homer: Odyssey Books VI–VIII.* Cambridge.

Garvie, A. F. 2009. *Aeschylus: Persae*. Oxford.

Garzya, A. 1952. Osservazioni sulla lingua di Crizia. *Emerita* 20: 401–12.

Garzya, A. 1988. Temistio e I primordi della tragedia. In M. Wissemann (ed.), *Roma renascens. Beiträge zur Spätantike und Rezeptionsgeschichte* (Bern, 1988): 65–77.

Ghiron-Bistagne, P. 1976. *Recherches sur les acteurs dans la Grèce antique.* Paris.

Gildersleeve, B. L. 1980. *Syntax of Classical Greek. From Homer to Demosthenes.* Groningen. Reprint of 1900 edition.

Gill, C. J. 1995. *Personality in Greek Epic, Tragedy, and Philosophy. The self in dialogue.* Oxford.

Giordano, D. 1961. Neofrone di Sicione, poeta tragico del IV sec. a. C. *Dioniso* 35: 73–88.

Goodwin W. W. 1889. *Syntax of the Moods and Tenses of the Greek Verb.* London and New York.

Gow, A. S. F. and Page, D. L. 1965. *The Greek Anthology. Hellenistic Epigrams.* Two volumes. Cambridge.

Grand-Clément, A. 2009. Sophocle, le maître d'école et les 'langages de la couleur': à propos du fragment 6 de Ion de Chios. In M. Carastro (ed.), *L'Antiquité en couleurs: catégories, pratiques, représentations* (Grenoble, 2009), 63–81.

Gregory, J. (ed.) 2005. *A Companion to Greek Tragedy.* Malden, MA and Oxford.

Grossardt, P. 2001. *Die Erzählung von Meleagros. Zur literarischen Entwicklung der kalydonischen Kultlegende*. Leiden.

Hagel, S. 2010. *Ancient Greek Music. A New Technical History.* Cambridge.

Halliday, W. R. 1927. Tenes. *CQ* 21: 37–44.

Halliwell, F. S. 1980. *Personal Jokes in Aristophanes.* Diss. Oxford (internet-accessible).

Halliwell, F. S. 1984. Ancient Interpretations of ὀνομαστὶ κωμῳδεῖν in Aristophanes. *CQ* n.s. 34: 83–88.

Harsh, P. W. 1937. Repetition of lines in Euripides. *Hermes* 72: 435–49.

Harvey, D. 2000. Phrynichos and his Muses. In D. Harvey and J. Wilkins (eds), *The Rivals of Aristophanes: Studies in Athenian Old Comedy* (London, 2000): 91–134.

Haviaras, N. 2007. The Poet and the Place: a modern Chian persepective on Ion of Chios and his home island. In Jennings and Katsaros 2007, 64–72.

Heath, M. 2013. Aristotle *On Poets.* A critical evaluation of Richard Janko's edition of the fragments. *Studia Humaniora Tartuensia* 14: 1–27.

Hedreen, G. M. 2007. Myths of ritual in Athenian vase-paintings of silens. In Csapo–Miller 2007a: 150–95.

Henderson, J. G. W. 2007. The hocus of a hedgehog: Ion's versatility. In Jennings and Katsaros 2007: 17–44.

Henrichs, A. 1975. Philodems De pietate als mythographische Quelle. *Cronache Ercolanesi* 5: 5–38.

Herington, C. J. 1985. *Poetry into Drama. Early tragedy and the Greek poetic tradition.* Berkeley.

Herter, H. 1973. Theseus. *RE* Suppl. 13: 1045–1238.

Hiller, E. 1874. Über einige Personenbezeichnungen griechischer Dramen. *Hermes* 8: 442–56.

Hoffmann, H. 1951. *Chronologie der attischen Tragödie.* Diss. Hamburg.

Holwerda, D. 1997. Ein verkanntes Bacchisches Dichterfragment. *Mnemosyne* ser. 4, 50: 321–23.

Hose, M. 1994. Zur Elision des –αι im Tragödienvers. *Hermes* 122: 32–43.

Housman, A. E. 1928. Oxyrhynchus Papyri XVII. 2078. *CR* 42: 9.

Hunger, H. 1967. Palimpsest-fragmente aus Herodians ΚΑΘΟΛΙΚΗ ΠΡΟΣΩΙΔΙΑ, Buch 5–7 (Cod. Vindob. Hist. gr. 10). *Byzantinische Jahrbuch* 16: 1–33.

Hutchinson, G. O. 1985. *Aeschylus: Septem contra Thebas.* Oxford.

Huxley, G. L. 1965. Ion of Chios. *GRBS* 6: 29-46.

Huxley, G. L. 1986. Aetolian Hyantes in Phrynichus. *GRBS* 27: 235–37.

Huys, M. 2005. Some Notes on a Kellis Ostracon with the Legend of Tennes and Hemithea. *ZPE* 152: 203–8.

Iakov, D. 2012. *Η Άλκηστη του Ευριπίδη. Ερμηνευτική έκδοση.* Two volumes. Athens.

Ieranò, G. 2013. 'One who is fought over by all the tribes': the dithyrambic poet and the city of Athens. In Kowalzig and Wilson 2013: 368–86.

Irmici, V. 2016. Crizia, F 1,14 e la prosodia di ἀνύω. *Glotta* 92: 135–38.

Jacoby, F. 1904. *Das Marmor Parium.* Berlin.

Janko, R. 2000. *Philodemus:* On Poems, *Book 1.* Oxford.

Janko, R. 2011. *Philodemus:* On Poems, *Books 3–4, with the fragments of Aristotle,* On Poets. Oxford.

Jennings, V. and Katsaros, A. (eds). 2007. *The World of Ion of Chios.* Leiden.

Jocelyn, H. D. 1967. *The Tragedies of Ennius.* Cambridge.

Jouan, F. 1966. *Euripide et les légendes des chants Cypriens.* Paris.

Jouan, F. and H. Van Looy. 2003. *Euripide, Tragédies, Tome VIII.4. Fragments de drames non identifiés.* Paris.

Kaibel, G. 1899. *Comicorum Graecorum Fragmenta, I.* Berlin.

Kannicht, R. 1969. *Euripides. Helena.* Two volumes. Heidelberg.

Kannicht, R. 1996. Zum Corpus Euripideum. In C. Mueller-Goldingen and K. Sier (eds), *AHNAIKA: Festschrift für Carl Werner Müller*: 21–31. Stuttgart.

Karamanou, I. 2003. The myth of Alope in Greek tragedy. *AC* 72: 25–40.

Karamanou, I. 2010, Aristotle's *Poetics* as a source for lost tragedies. In *Actas del XII Congreso Español de Estudios Clásicos,* II.505–13 (Madrid). Revised in Karamanou, *Refiguring Tragedy. Studies in plays preserved in fragments and their reception* (Berlin, 2019): 61–72.

Kassel, R. 1958. *Untersuchungen zur griechischen und römischen Konsolations-literatur.* Munich

Kaster, R. A. 1997. *Guardians of Language. The grammarian and society in late antiquity.* Berkeley.

Kearns, E. 1989. *The Heroes of Attica.* London.

Kerkhecker, A. 1999. *Callimachus' Book of Iambi*. Oxford.

Körte, A. 1932. Literarische Texte mit Ausschluss der christlichen. *APF* 10: 19–70.

Koster, W. J. W. 1973. De Phrynichi Trag. fr. IX,1 et X; denuo de Pindari fr. 189 Sn. *Mnemosyne* 26: 393–95.

Kovacs, D. 1986. On Medea's great monologue. *CQ* 36: 343–52.

Kovacs, J. L. 1997. Concealment and Gnostic Exegesis: Clement of Alexandria's Interpretation of the Tabernacle. *Studia Patristica* 31: 414–37.

Kowalzig, B. 2007. 'And now all the world shall dance!' (Eur. *Bacch.* 114): Dionysus' choroi between drama and ritual. In Csapo–Miller 2007a: 221–53.

Kowalzig, B. 2008. Nothing to do with Demeter? Something to do with Sicily! Theater and society in the early fifth-century west. In Revermann–Wilson 2008: 128–57.

Kowalzig, B. and Wilson, P. (eds) 2013. *Dithyramb in Context*. Oxford.

Kron, U. 1976. *Die zehn attischen Phylenheroen. Geschichte, Mythos, Kult und Darstellungen.* Berlin.

Krumeich, R. 2002. 'Euain ist schön'. Zur Rühmung eines zeitgenössischen Schauspielers auf attischen Symposiongefässen. In S. Moraw, E. Nölle (eds), *Die Geburt des Theaters in der griechischen Antike*. Mainz.

Kuiper, K. 1888. *Wijsbegeerte en Godsdienst in het Drama van Euripides.* Haarlem.

Kuiper, K. 1907. De Pirithoo fabula Euripidea. *Mnemosyne* 35: 354–85.

Kuiper, K. 1908a. De Euripideae fabulae Pirithoi fragmento nuper reperto. *Mnemosyne* 36: 335–41.

Kuiper, K. 1908b. De vocabuli ΤΡΟΠΟΣ vi atque usu per saecula VI et V. *Mnemosyne* 36: 419–34.

Lamari, A. 2015. Aeschylus and the Beginning of Tragic Reperformances. In Lamari (ed.) 2015: 189–206.

Lamari, A. 2017. *Reperforming Greek Tragedy. Theater, Politics and Cultural Mobility in the Fifth and Fourth Centuries BC*. Berlin.

Lamari, A. (ed.). 2015. *Reperformances of Drama in the Fifth and Fourth Centuries BC: authors and contexts.* Trends in Classics 7.2. Berlin.

Larson, J. 1995. *Greek Heroine Cults.* Madison WI.

Latte, K. 1968. *Kleine Schriften zu Religion, Recht, Literatur und Sprache der Griechen und Römer.* Munich.

Lefkowitz, M. R. 2012. *The Lives of the Greek Poets.* Second edition. Baltimore.

Lesky, A. 1925. *Alkestis, der Mythus und das Drama.* Sitzungsberichte der Akademie der Wissenschaften in Wien, Philosophisch-Historische Klasse, 203, 2. Vienna.

Lesky, A. 1972. *Die tragische Dichtung der Hellenen.* Third edition. Göttingen. Translated by M. Dillon as *Greek Tragic Poetry* (New Haven, 1983)

Leurini, L. 1973–4. Hesychiana. *Museum Criticum* 8–9: 239–45.

Leurini, L. 1984. Nuovi frammenti di Ione di Chio dal Lessico di Fozio. *Studi Italiani di Filologia Classica* ser. 3, 2: 156–73.

Leurini, L. 1985. La Suda, Callimaco e la ΠΟΛΥΕΙΔΕΙΑ di Ione di Chio. *Annali della Facoltà di Lettere e Filosofia dell'Università di Cagliari* n.s. 6: 5–13.

Leurini, L. 1990. Appunti sulla produzione scenica di Ione di Chio. *Annali della Facoltà di Lettere e Filosofia dell' Università di Cagliari* n.s. 11: 5–31.

Leurini, L. 2000. *Ionis Chii Testimonia et Fragmenta.* Second edition. Amsterdam.

Leurini, L. 2006. Ione di Chio 1960–2005. *Lustrum* 48: 7–44.

Levaniouk, O. 2007. The toys of Dionysus. *HSCPh* 103: 165–202.

Lévêque P. 1955. *Agathon.* Paris.

Librán Moreno, M. 2011. Neofrón 15 T 1–3 Sn.-K. y la *Medea* de Eurípides. *Lexis* 29: 113–29.

Lightfoot, J. L. 1999. *Parthenius of Nicaea. The poetic fragments and the Ἐρωτικὰ Παθήματα.* Oxford.

Lissarague, F. 1999. Publicity and performance: kalos inscriptions in Attic vase-painting. In S. Goldhill, R. Osborne (eds), *Performance Culture and Athenian Democracy* (Cambridge, 1999): 359–73.

Lloyd-Jones, H. 1966. Problems of early Greek tragedy: Pratinas and Phrynichus. In *Estudios sobra la tragedia griega* (Madrid, 1966): 11–33. Reprinted in Lloyd-Jones 1990: 225–37.

Lloyd-Jones, H. 1967. Heracles at Eleusis. *Maia* n.s. 19: 206–29. Reprinted in Lloyd-Jones 1990: 167–87.

Lloyd-Jones, H. 1990. *Greek Epic, Lyric and Tragedy. The Academic Papers of Sir Hugh Lloyd-Jones.* Oxford.

Lloyd-Jones, H. 2005. *Supplementum Supplementi Hellenistici.* Berlin.

Lucarini, C. M. 2013. Il monologo di Medea (Eurip. *Med.*, 1056–1080) e le altre *Medee* dell'antichità (con *Appendice* su Carcino). *ASNP* ser. 5, 5: 164–96.

Luppe, W. 1969. Zu einen Choregeninschrift aus Aixone (IG II/III^2 3091). *APF* 19: 147–51.

Luppe, W. 1974. Nochmals zur Choregeninschrift IG II/III^2 3091. *APF* 22/23: 211–12.

Luppe, W. 1980. Die Papyri aus der Herakles-Tragödie P. Colon. inv. 263 und PSI inv. 3021. In R. Pintaudi (ed.), *Miscellanea Papyrologica in memoria di H. C. Youtie* (Florence, 1980): 141–46.

Luppe, W. 1984. Zum Tennes-Mythos im 'Mythographus Homericus' P. Hamb. 199. *ZPE* 56: 31–32.

Luppe, W. 1989. Die 'Tennes'-Hypothesis. *APF* 35: 7–10.

Luppe, W. 1993. Eine neue Lesung in der Tennes-Hypothesis. *APF* 39: 15–16.

Maas, M., Snyder, J. 1989. *Stringed instruments of ancient Greece*. New Haven.

MacDowell, D. M. 1971. *Aristophanes: Wasps*. Oxford.

Machìna, I. 1955. Le tragedie di Agatone. *Dioniso* 18: 19–41.

Maltomini, F. 2001. Nove epigrammi ellenistici rivisitati (PPetrie II 49 b). *ZPE* 134: 55–66.

Mansfeld, J. 2016. Theodoret of Cyrrhus's *Therapy of Greek Diseases* as a source for the Aëtian *Placita*. *Studia Philonica Annual* 28: 151–68.

Manuwald, B. 1983. Der Mord an den Kindern. Bemerkungen zu den Medea-Tragödien des Euripides und des Neophron. *Wiener Studien* 17: 27–61.

Markantonatos, A. 2013. *Euripides'* Alcestis*: narrative, myth & religion*. Berlin.

Martano, A., Matelli, E., Mirhady, D. (eds), 2012. *Praxiphanes of Mytilene and Chamaeleon of Heraclea*. Piscataway, NJ.

Mastromarco, G. 2012. Erodoto e la *Presa di Mileto* di Frinico. In G. Bastianini *et al.* (eds), *Harmonia. Scritti in onore di Angelo Casanova* (Florence, 2012): 483–94.

Mastronarde, D. J. 2002. *Euripides: Medea*. Cambridge.

Mastronarde, D. 2010. *The Art of Euripides. Dramatic Technique and Social Context*. Cambridge.

Matthaios, S. 2015. Greek Scholarship in the Imperial Era and Late Antiquity. In Montanari *et al.* 2015: 184–296.

Mazzarino, S. 1957. Sui Δίκαιοι ἢ Πέρσαι ἢ Σύνθωκοι di Frinico. *Rheinisches Museum* 100: 200.

Meccariello, C. 2014. *Le Hypotheseis Narrative dei Drammi Euripidei. Testo, contesto, fortuna*. Rome.

Melero, A. 2012/ Critias, *Pirítoo* fgs. 2.1–4–5 Snell. In A. Melero *et al.* (eds), *Textos fragmentarios del teatro griego antiguo: problemas, estudios y nuevas perspectivas* (Lecce, 2012): 119–40.

Merkelbach, R. 1985. Weisse [κναξζβι]-Milch (Zu Thespis 1 F 4 Snell). *ZPE* 61: 293–96.

Mette, H. J. 1959. *Die Fragmente der Tragödien des Aischylos*. Berlin.

Mette, H. J. 1983. Perithoos–Theseus–Herakles bei Euripides. *ZPE* 50: 13–19.

Michelini, A. N. 1989. Neophron and Euripides' Medeia 1056–80. *TAPhA* 119: 115–35.

Michelini, A. N. 2009. The 'packed-full' drama in late Euripides: *Phoenissae*. In Cousland–Hume 2009: 169–81.

Millis, B. W. 2014. Inscriptional public records of the dramatic contests at Athens: IG II^2 2318–2323a and IG II^2 2325. In Csapo et al. 2014: 425–45.

Millis, B. W. and Olson, S. D. 2012. *Inscriptional Records for the Dramatic Festivals in Athens : IG II^2 2318–2325 and related texts.* Leiden.

Mirhady, D. C. 2012. Something to do with Dionysus: Chamaeleon on the origins of tragedy. In Martano *et al.* 2012: 387–409.

Montanari, F., Matthiaos, St., Rengakos, A. 2015. *Brill's Companion to Ancient Greek Scholarship.* Two volumes. Leiden.

Moorhouse, A. C. 1946. 'AN with the future. *Classical Quarterly* 40: 1–10.

Mossman, J. M. 2011. *Euripides: Medea.* Oxford.

Muecke, F. 1982. A Portrait of the Artist as a Young Woman. *CQ* 32: 41–55.

Mülke, M. 2000. Phrynichos und Athen: der Beschluss über die *Miletu Halosis* (Herodot 6, 21, 2). In S. Gödde, Th. Heinze (eds), *Skenika: Beiträge zum antiken Theater und seiner Rezeption* (Darmstadt, 2000): 233–46.

Musa, G. 2005. Una Θησέως ἐπιγραφή nel *Telefo* di Agatone (fr. 4 Sn.–K.). *Eikasmos* 16: 125–34.

Nails, D. 2002. *The People of Plato. A prosopography of Plato and the other Socratics.* Indianapolis.

Nervegna, S. 2014. Performing classics: the tragic canon in the fourth century and beyond. In E. Csapo et al. (eds), *Greek Theatre in the Fourth Century B.C.* (Berlin): 157–88.

Nestle, W. 1903. Kritias: eine Studie. *Neue Jahrbücher für das Klassische Altertum etc.* 6: 81–107, 178–99. Reprinted in Nestle, *Griechische Studien* (Stuttgart, 1948): 253–320.

Nicole, J. 1907. *L'Apologie d'Antiphon, d'après des fragments inédits sur papyrus d'Égypte.* Geneva.

Nielsen, T. H., Roy, J. 1998. The Azanians of Northern Arcadia. *Classica et Mediaevalia* 49: 5–44.

Obbink, D. 2006. A new Archilochus poem. *ZPE* 156: 1–9.

Obbink, D. 1996, *Philodemus* On Piety, *Part 1. Critical Text etc.* Oxford.

Olding, G. 2007a. Shot from the canon: sources, selections, survivals. In Jennings–Katsaros 2007: 45–63.

Olding, G. 2007b. Ion the wineman: the manipulation of myth. In Jennings–Katsaros 2007: 139–54.

Olson S. D. 1998. *Aristophanes: Peace.* Oxford.

Olson S. D. 2006. *Athenaeus. The Learned Banqueters: Books I–III.106e.* Cambridge, MA.

O'Sullivan, P., Collard, C. 2013. *Euripides,* Cyclops *and Major Fragments of Greek Satyric Drama.* Oxford.

Page, D. L. 1938. *Euripides: Medea.* Oxford.

Page, D. L. 1941. *Select Papyri, III: Literary Papyri, Poetry*. Cambridge, MA and London.

Pančenko, D. V. 1980. Euripides or Critias? [Russian with English summary] *Vestnik Drevnei Istorii* 151: 144–62.

Papastamati-von Moock, C. 2014. The Theatre of Dionysus Eleuthereus in Athens. New data and observations on its 'Lycurgan' phase. In Csapo et al. 2014: 15–76.

Parker, L. P. E. 2007. *Euripides: Alcestis*. Oxford

Parker, R. C. T. 2005. *Polytheism and society at Athens*. Oxford.

Pearson, A. C. 1909. Phrixus and Demodice. A note on Pindar, *Pyth*. iv.162f. *CR* 23: 255–57.

Pechstein, N. 1998. *Euripides Satyrographos: ein Kommentar zu den euripideischen Satyrspielfragmenten*. Stuttgart, Leipzig.

Pfeiffer, R. 1949. *Callimachus, I. Fragmenta*. Oxford.

Pickard-Cambridge, A. W. 1933. Tragedy. In J. U. Powell (ed.), *New Chapters in the History of Greek Literature: Third Series* (Oxford, 1933): 68–155.

Pickard-Cambridge, A. W. 1962. *Dithyramb, Tragedy and Comedy*. Second edition, revised by T. B. L. Webster. Oxford. First edition 1927.

Pickard-Cambridge, A. W. 1988. *The Dramatic Festivals of Athens*. Second edition revised by J. Gould and D. M. Lewis (1968), with supplement and corrections. Oxford.

Pitcher S. M. 1939. The Anthus of Agathon. *AJPh* 60: 145–69.

Polito, M. 2005. I racconti di fondazione su Tenedo: il τενέδιος πέλεκυς e la Αἰολέων στρατιά. In A. Mele et al. (eds), *Eoli ed Eolide: tra madrepatria e colonie* (Naples, 2005): 187–99.

Pontani, F. 2015. Scholarship in the Byzantine Empire (529–1453). In Montanari *et al.* 2015: 297–455.

Power, T. 2010. *The Culture of Kitharôidia*. Cambridge MA.

Pritchard, J. B. 1969. *Ancient Near Eastern Texts Relating to the Old Testament*. Third edition. Princeton.

Rabe, H. 1908. Aus Rhetoren-Handschriften. *Rheinisches Museum* 63: 127–51.

Radt, S. L. 1971. Aristoteles und die Tragödie. *Mnemosyne* ser. 4, 24: 189–205.

Rau, P. 1967. *Paratragodia. Untersuchung einer komischen Form des Aristophanes*. Munich.

Regtuit, R. 2007. *Scholia in Aristophanis Thesmophoriazusas et Ecclesiazusas*. Scholia in Aristophanem 3.2/3: Groningen.

Reitzenstein, R. 1897. *Geschichte der griechischen Etymologika*. Leipzig.

Reitzenstein, R. 1907. *Der Anfang des Lexikon des Photios*. Leipzig and Berlin.

Revermann. M. 2006. *Comic Business. Theatricality, Dramatic Technique, and Performance Contexts of Aristophanic Comedy*. Oxford.

Revermann. M. and Wilson, P. (eds). 2008. *Performance, Iconography, Reception. Studies in honour of Oliver Taplin*. Oxford.

Richardson, N. J. 1974. *The Homeric Hymn to Demeter.* Oxford.

Roisman, J. 1988. On Phrynichos' *Sack of Miletos* and *Phoinissai*. *Eranos* 1988: 15–23.

Roos, E. 1951. *Die tragische Orchestik im Zerrbild der altattischen Komödie.* Stockholm.

Rosenbloom, D. S. 1993. Shouting 'fire' in a crowded theater: Phrynichos's *Capture of Miletos* and the politics of fear in early Attic tragedy. *Philologus* 137: 159–96.

Rosenbloom, D. 2006. *Aeschylus: Persians*. London.

Rossum-Steenbeek, M. van. 1998. *Greek Readers' Digests? Studies on a selection of subliterary papyri.* Leiden.

Rostagni, A. 1927. Un più completo frammento del 'Fenice o Ceneo' di Jone di Chio. *RFIC* 55: 378–81.

Rotstein, A. 2016. *Literary History in the Parian Marble*. Washington, DC.

Runia, D. 1996. Atheists in Aëtius: Text, Translation and Comments on *De Placitis* 1.7.1–10. *Mnemosyne* 49: 542–76.

Rutishauser, B. 2001. Island strategies: the case of Tenedos. *Revue des Études Anciennes* 103: 197–204.

Sansone, D. 1985. Orpheus and Eurydice in the fifth century. *C&M* 36: 53–64.

Saunders, T. J. 2001. Dicaearchus' historical anthropology. In Fortenbaugh–Schütrumpf 2001: 237–54

Schierl, P. 2006. *Die Tragödien des Pacuvius*. Berlin.

Schmid, W. 1940. *Geschichte der griechischen Literatur*, I.3.1. Munich.

Schorn, S. 2004. *Satyros auf Kallatis. Sammlung der Fragmente mit Kommentar.* Basel.

Schütrumpf, E. 2001. Dikaiarchs Βίος Ἑλλάδος und die philosphie des vierten Jahrhunderts. In Fortenbaugh–Schütrumpf 2001: 255–77.

Scullion, S. 2002a. Tragic dates. *CQ* n.s. 52: 81–101.

Scullion, S. 2002b. 'Nothing to do with Dionysus': tragedy misconceived as ritual. *CQ* n.s. 52: 102–37.

Scullion, S. 2003. Euripides and Macedon, or the Silence of the *Frogs*. *CQ* n.s. 53: 389–400.

Scullion, S. 2005. Tragedy and religion: the problem of origins. In Gregory (ed.) 2005: 23–37.

Seaford, R. A. S. 1984. *Euripides: Cyclops*. Oxford.

Seaford, R. A. S. 2007. From ritual to drama: a concluding statement. In Csapo–Miller (eds) 2007a: 379–401.

Selden, J. 1629. *Marmora Arundelliana.* London.

Sickinger, J. P. 1999. *Public Records and Archives in Classical Athens.* Chapel Hill and London.

Simon, E. 1955. Ixion und die Schlangen. *Jahreshefte des Osterreichischen Archäologisches Institutes in Wien* 42: 5–26.

Simon, E. 1995. Laertes und Sisyphos. In D. Rössler, V. Stürmer (eds), *Gedenkschrift für Wolfgang Schindler* (Berlin, 1995): 55–59.

Slattery, S. 2016. 5292, Sophocles, *Tereus*. In *The Oxyrhynchus Papyri* 82: 8–14.

Smyth, H. W. 1920. *Greek Grammar.* Cambridge MA.

Snell, B. 1971. *Szenen aus Griechischen Dramen.* Berlin.

Sommerstein, A. H. 1983. *Aristophanes: Wasps.* Warminster.

Sommerstein, A. H. 1994. *Aristophanes: Thesmophoriazusae.* Warminster.

Sommerstein, A. H. 2005. *Aristophanes: Peace.* Second edition. Oxford.

Sommerstein, A. H. 2008. *Aeschylus: Fragments.* Cambridge MA.

Sommerstein, A. H., Fitzpatrick, D., Talboy, T. 2006. *Sophocles: Selected Fragmentary Plays, I.* Oxford.

Specht, E. 2001. Tenedos und Tennes: zur frühen Geschichte der Insel. *Hyperboreus* 7: 25–36.

Stackmann, K. 1950. Senecas Agamemnon. Untersuchung zur Geschichte des Agamemnonstoffes nach Aischylos. *C&M* 11: 180–221.

Steffen, V. 1954. Ad *Rhadamanthi* fabulae Euripideae argumentum papyraceum observationes. In B. Bilinski *et al.*, *Trágica II* (Wroclaw, 1954): 73–78.

Steffen, V. 1979. *De Graecorum Fabulis Satyricis.* Wrocłav.

Stephanopoulos, Th. 1980. *Umgestaltung des Mythos durch Euripides*. Athens.

Stephanopoulos, Th. 1988. Tragica I. *ZPE* 73: 202–47

Stephanopoulos, Th. 2014. Marginalia tragica II. *Logeion* 4: 193–200.

Stevens, A. 2007. Ion of Chios: tragedy as commodity at the Athenian exchange. In Jennings–Katsaros 2007: 243–65.

Stevens, P. T. 1971. *Euripides: Andromache.* Oxford.

Stewart, E. 2016. An Ancient Theatre Dynasty: The Elder Carcinus, the Young Xenocles and the Sons of Carcinus in Aristophanes. *Philologus* 160: 1–18.

Stewart, E. 2017. *Greek Tragedy on the Move: The Birth of a Panhellenic Art Form c. 500–300 BC.* Oxford.

Sutton, D. F. 1980. *The Greek Satyr Play.* Meisenheim am Glan.

Sutton, D. F. 1987a. The theatrical families of Athens. *AJPh* 108: 9–26.

Sutton, D. F. 1987b. *Two Lost Plays of Euripides*. New York, Bern etc.

Swift, L. A. 2012. Archilochus the 'anti-hero'?: heroism, flight and values in Homer and the new Archilochus fragment (P.Oxy LXIX 4708). *JHS* 132: 139–55.

Swift, L. A. 2014. Telephus on Paros: genealogy and myth in the 'new Archilochus' poem (*P. Oxy*. 4708). *CQ* n.s. 64: 433–47.

Taplin, O. P. 2007. *Pots and plays: interactions between tragedy and Greek vase-painting of the fourth century B.C.* Malibu.

Taplin, O. P. 2012. How was Athenian tragedy played in the Greek West? In K. Bosher (ed.), *Theater Outside Athens* (Cambridge, 2012): 226–50.

Tarán, L. Gutas, D. 2012. *Aristotle: Poetics.* Leiden.

Tarrant, R. J. 1976. *Seneca: Agamemnon*. Cambridge.

Tracy, S. V. 2015. The dramatic festival inscriptions of Athens: the inscribers and phases of inscribing. *Hesperia* 84: 553–81.

Vahtikari, V. 2014. *Tragedy Performances outside Athens in the Late Fifth and the Fourth Centuries BC*. Helsinki.

Valerio, F. 2010. Il mondo di Ione di Chio. Riflessione a margine di una recente publicazzione. *Quaderni Urbinati di Cultura Classica* n.s. 94: 159–78.

Waern I. 1956. Zum Tragiker Agathon. *Eranos* 54: 87–100.

Walker, A. 1992. Eros and the eye in the Love-letters of Philostratus. *PCPhS* 38: 132–48.

Webster, T. B. L. 1970. *The Greek Chorus*. London.

Welcker, F. G. 1841. *Die griechischen Tragödien, mit Rücksicht auf den epischen Cyclus. Dritte Abtheilung*. Bonn.

West, M. L. 1966. *Hesiod: Theogony*.

West, M. L. 1968. Notes on newly-discovered fragments of Greek authors. *Maia* 20: 195–205.

West, M. L. 1971. *Greek Philosophy and the Orient*. Oxford.

West, M. L. 1977. Notes on papyri. *ZPE* 26: 37–43.

West, M. L. 1979. The Prometheus trilogy. *JHS* 99: 130–48 (reprinted with postscript, 2013a: 250–86).

West, M. L. 1983. *The Orphic Poems*. Oxford.

West, M. L. 1985a. *The Hesiodic Catalogue of Women: Its Nature, Structure and Origins*. Oxford.

West, M. L. 1985b. Ion of Chios. *BICS* 32: 71–8 (repr. 2013a: 424–36).

West, M. L. 1989. The chronology of early Attic tragedy. *CQ* 39: 251–54 (reprinted, 2013d: 151–56).

West, M. L. 1990. *Studies in Aeschylus*. Stuttgart.

West, M. L. 1992a. Analecta musica. *ZPE* 92: 1–54.

West, M. L. 1992b. *Ancient Greek Music*. Oxford.

West, M. L. 1997. When is a Harp a Panpipe? The meanings of πηκτίς. *CQ* 47: 48–55 (reprinted, 2013a: 208–19).

West, M. L. 2000. Iliad and Aethiopis on the stage. *CQ* 50: 338–52 (reprinted, 2013d: 226–49).

West, M. L. 2001. *Studies in the Text and Transmission of the Iliad*. Munich, Leipzig.

West, M. L. 2006. Archilochus and Telephos. *ZPE* 156: 11–17 (reprinted, 2013d: 6–16).

West, M. L. 2013a. *Hellenica, III: Philosophy, Music etc*. Oxford.

West, M. L. 2013b. *The Epic Cycle: a Commentary on the Lost Troy Epics*. Oxford.

West, M. L. 2013c. λυκάβας, λυκηγενής, ἀμφιλύκη. *Glotta* 89: 253–64.

West, M. L. 2013d. *Hellenica II: Lyric and Drama*. Oxford.

Whitmarsh, T. 2014. Atheistic aesthetics. The Sisyphus fragment, poetics and the creativity of drama. *Cambridge Classical Journal* 60: 109–26.

Wilamowitz-Moellendorff, U. von. 1875. *Analecta Euripidea.* Berlin.

Wilamowitz-Moellendorff, U. von. 1880. Excurse zu Euripides Medeia. *Hermes* 15: 481–523 (reprinted, 1935: 17–59).

Wilamowitz-Moellendorff, U. von. 1907a. Zum Lexikon des Photios. *Sitzungsberichte der Preussischen Akademie der Wissenschaften*, 1907: 2–14 (reprinted, 1962: 528–41).

Wilamowitz-Moellendorff, U. von. 1907b. Response to Kuiper 1907. In Bremer–Calder 1994: 211–16.

Wilamowitz-Moellendorff, U. von. 1920. *Platon. Leben und Werke.* Two volumes. Berlin.

Wilamowitz-Moellendorff, U. von. 1921. *Griechische Verskunst.* Berlin.

Wilamowitz-Moellendorff, U. von. 1927. Lesefrüchte 218–230. *Hermes* 62: 276–98 (reprinted, 1962: 431–53).

Wilamowitz-Moellendorff, U. von. 1929. Lesefrüchte 249–266. *Hermes* 64: 458–90 (reprinted, 1962: 476–508).

Wilamowitz-Moellendorff, U. von. 1935. *Kleine Schriften, I.* Berlin.

Wilamowitz-Moellendorff, U. von. 1962. *Kleine Schriften, IV.* Berlin.

Wildberg, C. 2002. *Hyperesie und Epiphanie: ein Versuch über die Bedeutung der Götter in den Dramen des Euripides.* Munich.

Wilson, P. J. 1999–2000. Euripides' tragic muse. *Illinois Classical Studies* 24–25: 427–29.

Wilson, P. J. 2000. *The Athenian Institution of the Khoregia: the chorus, the city and the stage.* Cambridge.

Wilson, P. J. 2003. The Sound of Cultural Conflict: Kritias and the culture of *mousikê* in Athens. In C. Dougherty, L. Kurke (eds), *The Cultures within Ancient Greek Culture* (Cambridge, 2003): 181–206.

Wilson, P. J. 2007. Sicilian choruses. In P. Wilson (ed.), *The Greek Theatre and Festivals* (Oxford, 2007): 351–77.

Wright, M. E. 2013a. Comedy versus tragedy in *Wasps*. In E. Bakola, L. Prauscello, M. Telò (eds), *Greek Comedy and the Discourse of Genres* (Cambridge, 2013): 205–25.

Wright, M. E. 2013b. Poets and poetry in later Greek comedy. *CQ* 63: 603–22.

Wright, M. E. 2016. *The Lost Plays of Greek Tragedy, I: Neglected Authors.* London.

Zardini, F. 2009. *The Myth of Herakles and Kyknos. A Study in Greek Vase-Painting and Literature*. Verona.

Zeitlin, F. 1996. *Playing the Other. Essays on Gender and Society in Classical Greek Literature*. Chicago.

Zogg, F. 2014, *Lust am Lesen. Literarische Anspielungen in* Frieden *des Aristophanes.* Munich.

INDEXES

(a) Tragic poets *(* means 'see also (c) Sources')*

(b) Titles *(S and S? denote attested and likely satyr-plays)*

Eitheoi (Youths) [Thespis]
Erginus Achaeus$^{S?}$
Erigone Philocles, Iophon? (p. 124)
Eurytidae (Sons of Eurytus) Ion

Hephaestus Achaeus^{S}
Hermione? Philocles (F 2)
Hesione? Demetrius
Hiereis (Priests) [Thespis]

Iliou Persis (Sack of Troy) Iophon
Iris Achaeus^{S}
Ixion Callistratus

Katapeira (The Test) Achaeus
Kêres (Death-spirits) Aristias$^{S?}$

Laertes Ion
Leucippus Iophon? (p. 124)
Libyes (Libyans) see *Antaeus*
Licymnius Xenocles
Linus Achaeus^{S}
Lycaon Xenocles
Lycurgeia, tetralogy Polyphrasmon

Medea Neophron, Euripides II, Melanthius
Mega Drama Ion
Milêtou Halôsis (Capture of Miletus) Phrynichus
Moirai (Fates) Achaeus^{S}
Mômos (Blame) Achaeus$^{S?}$
Mysians Agathon

Nauplius Philocles

Oedipodea, tetralogy Meletus I/II (p. xv n.)
Oedipus Achaeus, Xenocles, Nicomachus
Oeneus Philocles
Omphale Ion^{S}, Achaeus^{S}
Orestes Euripides II
Orpheus Aristias$^{S?}$

Palaistai (Wrestlers) Pratinas^{S}
Pandionis, tetralogy Philocles
Penelope Philocles
Pentheus [Thespis], Iophon
Persai (Persians) see *Dikaioi*
Perseus Aristias(?) (p. 52)
Philoctetes Achaeus, Philocles
Phoenissae (Phoenician Women) Phrynichus
Phoenix/Caeneus Ion (p. 86)
Phoenix B Ion (p. 86)
Phorbas see *Athla Peliou*
Phrixus Achaeus
Phrouroi (Guards) Ion
Pirithous Achaeus, Critias?
Pleuroniai (Women of Pleuron) Phrynichus
Polyxena Euripides II
Priam Philocles

Rhadamanthys Critias?

Semele Diogenes
Sisyphus(?) Critias?
Synthôkoi see *Dikaioi*

Tantalus Phrynichus, Aristias(?) (p. 52), Aristarchus
Telephus Iophon, Agathon
Tennes Critias?
Tereus Philocles
Teucer Ion
Theseus Achaeus
Thyestes Iophon? (p. 124), Agathon

(c) Sources *(^{b} denotes brief fragments)*

(d) General

www.ingramcontent.com/pod-product-compliance
Lightning Source LLC
Chambersburg PA
CBHW071542110726
47908CB00007B/1970

* 9 7 8 1 7 8 6 9 4 2 0 3 6 *